Klaus Solberg Söilen

Digital Marketing

Tools, Techniques and Best Practices for Graduate Students and Managers

Springer

Klaus Solberg Söilen
Halmstad University
Halmstad, Sweden

ISSN 2192-4333 ISSN 2192-4341 (electronic)
Springer Texts in Business and Economics
ISBN 978-3-031-69517-9 ISBN 978-3-031-69518-6 (eBook)
https://doi.org/10.1007/978-3-031-69518-6

This Springer imprint is published by the registered company Springer Nature Switzerland AG
The registered company address is: Gewerbestrasse 11, 6330 Cham, Switzerland

With deep affection, gratitude and admiration

to Oksana Mont

Preface

This book on digital marketing addresses graduate students and practitioners in particular but can also be used at the undergraduate level. While theory is crucial for understanding, few other business functions emphasize the importance of early practice as much as digital marketing. It is practically impossible to learn digital marketing without hands-on exercises or experience. For this reason, there is a gap in the literature between theory in digital marketing and practice. This book tries to close this gap.

Realizing the importance of practice, I started an outsourcing marketing services firm at the dawn of the digital age, helping companies not only with webpages but also with SEO and programming. Although the company thrived for a few years, my primary goal was to gain practical knowledge rather than generate profit, and I continued my role as a university teacher throughout this journey. I'd like to think that this experience was useful in writing this book.

Throughout my academic career, I have basically been interested in two areas: intelligence studies and marketing. In the last decade, these two areas have really come together, centering around larger questions of digitalization. In the late 1990s, general marketing books would discuss competitive and business intelligence. By the turn of the millennium, they began incorporating all aspects of environmental scanning, analyzing both micro and macro factors influencing a company. Today, this approach often forms the centerpiece of many general marketing textbooks, like that of Sven Hollensen on *Global Marketing*.

As an undergraduate business student specializing in marketing, I had the valuable opportunity to learn from several experts across various fields. I gained insights into advertising through my work with Dodge & Mansfield in Simi Valley. My understanding of marketing was further developed by working for Marketing & Financial Management in Woodland Hills under Burnet D. Brown. I picked up my PR skills with the Ventura Police Department and explored international marketing through my experience at Twentieth Century Fox in Beverly Hills, doing mostly market research in movie theaters. These all became valuable experiences when I later started to teach marketing.

This book has taken about four years to complete. Two years ago, when I thought I had a manuscript ready, OpenAI was introduced, necessitating a complete revision of large parts of the manuscript. The last version of the book, which had been used as a wiki and to which students contributed over the years, was over 750 pages in

2022. My goal was to reduce it to half, so many illustrations and examples had to go, unfortunately, but I also needed to add diagrams and useful, practical tables, so the number of pages quickly grew again. AI has been used with care in this book, basically for grammar, syntax, some examples, and fact-checking. A footnote has been added to sections and chapters wherever ChatGPT 4o has been used to create new content.

I have been using a version of this book as a compendium for my marketing lectures for over two decades now. Each course has provided valuable student input, making some of the parts in this book a product of co-creation. Naming every student who contributed over the years would fill many pages, so I will acknowledge their collective contribution here. Seeing how students embrace this topic is truly inspiring and brings much hope for the next generation. That has especially been my experience when teaching digital marketing in China. You could literally see how students went directly from the lectures out to start their own companies, often in the evening, while studying at the university during the day. Their eagerness to learn is unparalleled in my experience and has borne fruit for all to see today.

Only a small part in this book is built on my own research, so most of what is written is owed to the authors in the sources cited at the end in the reference list. The final reference list was too large to even consider here, so at the end I even had to make a selection. I have chosen not to cite each author in the text when I could avoid it as this is meant to be an easy book to read. Note also that much useful knowledge in digital marketing comes not from academics, but from practitioners, at the end often from webpages. I think this is one of the liberating aspects of digital marketing; it does not fall prey to academic snobbery but is all about what works. Most useful and valuable contributions come from practitioners, with academics often working with great delays when it comes to understanding new features and software. A major reason for this is that the field moves so quickly.

I have been significantly influenced by many authors with whom I have had sporadic contact over the years, but I would first like to mention Dave Chaffey and Sven Hollensen. I would like to thank them both for their inspiration and friendly help: Chaffey for providing me with material for my lectures, often on short notice, and Hollensen for his excellent understanding of marketing. Another person who, like me, has taught both marketing and intelligence and who has served as a mentor since I started teaching at Copenhagen Business School some 25 years ago is Per Jenster. His pedagogical approach and engagement with students have been a great inspiration.

I would also like to thank the community of marketing academics in Sweden at our different universities and colleges across the country, with whom I have had the great pleasure of working for more than two decades. First, the marketing department at Halmstad University, including Svante Andersson, Navid Ghannad, Ulf Aagerup (now in Jönköping), and Venilton Reinert (soon to retire). I would also like to honor the memory of two marketing teachers in our department who have passed away during this time, Gabriel Awuah and Thomas Helgesson, whose memories are very dear to us all. Special thanks to my PhD student in B2B digital marketing, Maryam Lashgari, for her contributions to the B2B chapter.

Special thanks to Jonas Kågström in Gävle for being a fellow judge and a central part of the organizing committee of the Swedish Championship in Business and Economics ("SM i Ekonomi") for more than 10 years. His efforts have been instrumental in spreading interest in digital marketing to students for a generation.

Another organization that has played a crucial role in uniting teachers in business and economics in Sweden is the Swedish Academy of Business and Management (FEKIS), which I have had the opportunity to attend over many years. I would like to thank Anders Pehrsson at Växjö University and Ulf Johansson at Lund University for their significant contributions to the field of marketing in Sweden. Evert Gummesson in Stockholm has been instrumental in promoting the relational perspective in marketing internationally. Göran Svensson at Kristiania University College, Norway, was my co-teacher in scientific methods at Halmstad University for many years and has greatly helped advance the marketing discipline in Scandinavia, especially in eastern Norway. I also appreciate Bjørn-Tore Flåten and his staff at Agder University in Norway for their efforts to develop advanced courses in marketing education. Finally, Kwaku Atuahene-Gima from Ghana, who was at CEIBS in Shanghai during my short time as a visiting scholar there. We had contact later when he returned to develop new marketing programs in Africa and came to visit us in Halmstad.

Thanks also to Bart H. M. Gerritsen at TU Delft (now retired) for showing me what brilliance is, and to the staff at the School of Industrial Engineering and Management (ITM) at KTH in Stockholm for being so welcoming. To Prof. Scott Erickson at Ithaca, New York, for friendly support over many years, to Alessandro Comai at the International University of Japan also for friendship outside of work, to Christine Vallaster at the University of Salzburg for trying to initiate cooperation with Halmstad, and to Gerson Tontini at FURB—Regional University of Blumenau, Brazil, for contributions to research on the KANO model.

Finally, I would like to thank my editor, Prashanth Mahagaonkar at Springer, not only for his patience in waiting for this book to be completed but also for his profound interest and understanding of the subjects on which Springer publishes.

Halmstad, Sweden Klaus Solberg Söilen

2nd of July, 2024

Introductory Case: Marketing Campaign for a Sports Shoe Company

Digital marketing is essentially the process of getting your message out to people online. It starts with the message you want to communicate.

Throughout this book, we are going to use a case of a sports shoe company, and we will denote the place in the text with a logo[1]:

For a company in the shoe business, that message could be: "Our latest sports shoes provide unparalleled comfort and performance, designed to help you achieve your best in any sport." We then define our segments, in this case, athletes, casual wearers, and fitness enthusiasts. We identify the most effective channels to reach each audience based on the segment, for example, short video clips for TikTok to engage younger, tech-savvy users.

Once the channels are identified, we tailor the content accordingly. This content could include text, images, audio, or video, and is a crucial part of content marketing. The next step is to distribute this content online. This can be done for free through search engine optimization (SEO), which involves using various techniques to ensure our content appears in search results, or through paid advertising, where we pay to have our content displayed in specific places.

It's important to note that we don't start with creating content. We begin with the process of segmentation. We can proceed to the actual content creation only when we know what channels to use.

One of the greatest advantages of digital marketing is the ability to measure viewer reactions. In traditional marketing, often referred to as "brick-and-mortar marketing," this was mostly guesswork. Companies like Nielsen did a decent job of rating customer behavior, but there was always a significant margin of error, and it was difficult to pinpoint which aspects of a campaign were effective. Was it the billboard on Sunset Boulevard or the TV commercial during *The Dynasty* show

[1] <Footnote ID="Fn1"><Para ID="Par17">Logo created by author.</Para></Footnote>

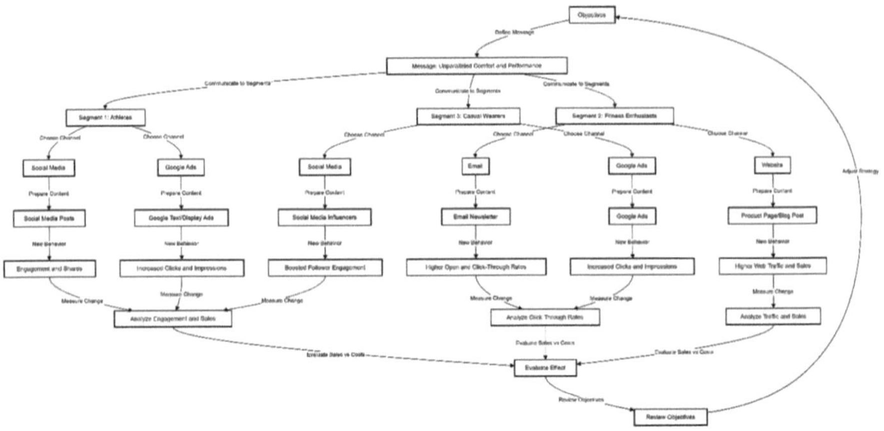

Fig 1 The digital marketing process

(1980s)? Well, it was hard to know. Much like can be seen in the TV series *Mad Men*, companies decided to throw large advertising money at products because they thought it was working. Those days are now mostly over.

With digital marketing, we can measure changes in behavior from our potential customers. We can track how they interact with our content, what questions they have, how many become leads, and, most importantly, who actually makes a purchase. This is measurable change in behavior. We can then compare the revenue generated from the marketing effort to the costs incurred. If we made a profit, we have a reason to try another round, often with adjustments based on what we learned.

Digital marketing requires a much larger reach to achieve the same number of respondents, leads, and sales compared to physical stores. In digital marketing, the steps from reach to sales are more extensive due to the broader audience and the necessity to filter through a larger pool of potential customers to achieve actual outcomes. In contrast, physical stores have a more direct path from reach to sales, with a smaller and more targeted customer base.

At the end, we want to know if we achieved our objective. Do customers believe "Our latest sports shoes provide unparalleled comfort and performance, designed to help you achieve your best in any sport," or are they buying for another reason? This feedback loop helps refine our strategy and improve future campaigns, as seen in Fig 1:

We can describe this in detail in a table that provides a structured overview of how different forms of content can be tailored for various channels, ensuring that the marketing message is effectively communicated to each target audience segment, as seen in Table 3:

The objective of the marketing campaign is to increase sales of the new sports shoes and to create brand awareness and customer engagement. The initial message communicated to the target audience is that the latest sports shoes provide unparalleled comfort and performance, designed to help individuals achieve their best in any sport.

After launching the campaign, the company measures changes in behavior among potential customers and those who bought the products. On social media, they observe increased engagement, including likes, shares, and comments on posts, as well as a rise in the number of followers. The click-through rates on ads and posts are also monitored to assess interest and engagement levels.

For Google Ads, the click-through rates and conversion rates are measured to determine how many people clicked on the ads and made a purchase. The email campaign's effectiveness is gauged by tracking open rates, click-through rates, and conversion rates from the emails to the website.

On the website, the company monitors traffic to the product page, the duration of visits, and the number of purchases made. They also track interactions with the blog post to see if it generates interest and drives traffic to the product page.

Finally, the overall impact on sales is analyzed by comparing the revenue generated from the campaign to the costs incurred. The company evaluates whether the campaign achieved the objective of increasing sales and if customers believe the message about unparalleled comfort and performance. If the objectives are not fully reached, the company analyzes the reasons and makes adjustments for future marketing efforts.

What we aim to do in the rest of the book is to delve deeper into each step of this process, exploring various tools, techniques, and best practices on topics that are crucial for digital marketing. The selected topics follow a logical progression, starting with broad technical fundamentals and gradually becoming more specific and focused.

Contents

List of Figures

List of Tables

About this Book

Detailed Synopsis of the Book

This comprehensive book on digital marketing addresses both theoretical and practical aspects of the field, making it an essential resource for graduate students, practitioners, and undergraduate students. It begins with an introductory case study on a marketing campaign for a sports shoe company, setting the stage for understanding the digital environment. The book delves into key concepts such as the micro- and macro-environment, the role of digital technology in marketing, and various online marketing tools. It contrasts old media with new media and explains the importance of a balanced marketing strategy and mixed mode buying.

The subsequent chapters explore the significance of big data and data mining in real-time performance measurement, predictive marketing, and personalized digital experiences. A dedicated chapter on data quality emphasizes its importance, detailing methods of data collection and the challenges and benefits associated with maintaining high data quality. Customer analytics are thoroughly covered, including profiles, personas, and personalization, highlighting the role of technology and practical applications.

The book also covers monitoring performance through KPIs, emphasizing data-based decision-making and the implementation of business intelligence. A detailed chapter on search engine optimization (SEO) provides insights into enhancing online visibility through meta tags and other criteria. Click analytics, online buying processes, and checkout and payment options are explored, offering practical guidance and examples.

The text addresses building an attractive site structure, optimizing for mobile interfaces, and the role of influencers, celebrity endorsements, and opinion leaders in marketing. It includes a chapter on storytelling in marketing, emphasizing the power of narratives and social media strategies. Stealth marketing and the impact of video-first strategies in a digital world are also discussed.

The chapters on the use of music in digital marketing, drafting storylines, embedding content, and real-time video editing highlight the creative aspects of digital marketing. Social CRM, personal branding, building brands online, and online partnerships are examined, illustrating the intersection of digital marketing with various business functions.

The book concludes with advanced topics such as omnichannel marketing, gamification strategies, cross-selling and upselling, AI and marketing automation, geolocation of visitors, dropshipping, browsing and purchasing online, and B2B digital marketing. It addresses the impact on employment, the evolution of PR and communications, the art and science of copywriting, and ethics in digital marketing. The final chapters cover banner and native advertising, digital cultures, business models, cookies and privacy concerns, Google Ads, e-governance, social networks and e-learning, and digital healthcare, providing a holistic view of the digital marketing landscape.

I have tried not to allow too many overlaps in this book, but some chapters are more related, as can be seen in Table 1.

There are some digital marketing topics not covered in this book, though they are few. For instance, I could have included a special chapter on payment systems like blockchain and blockchain technology, especially since it has been one of my research interests. However, I felt it would be more appropriate to leave this for the finance discipline. Instead, I have added some on cryptocurrencies and digital currencies as an alternative way of payment.

Table 1 Topics covered in this book

Common denominator	Selection of chapters	Chapter numbers
Introduction to Digital Marketing	Understanding the Digital Environment, Big Data and Data Mining	1, 2
Data Quality and Customer Analytics	Data Quality, Customer Analytics	3, 4
Performance and Optimization	Monitoring Performance and Crushing the Numbers, SEO, Click Analytics	5, 6, 7
Online Transactions	The Online Buying Process, Checkout and Payment Options	8, 9
E-commerce and Site Structure	The e-commerce website and mobile app, Building an Attractive Site Structure, Information Architecture	10, 11, 12
Mobile Marketing	Mobile Interface	13
Influencers and Storytelling	The Role of Influencers, Celebrity Endorsements, and Identifying Opinion Leaders, Storytelling in Marketing	14, 15
Stealth and Video Marketing	Stealth Marketing on Social Media, The Video-First World	16, 17
Music and Storyline	Why Music Matters in Digital Marketing, Drafting the Storyline	18, 19
Embedding and Real-Time Editing	Embedding, Real-Time Video Editing	20, 21
CRM and Branding	Social CRM, Personal Branding, Building Brands Online	22, 23, 24
Online Partnerships	Online Partnerships	25
Omnichannel and Gamification	Omnichannel Marketing, Gamification Strategies	26, 27
Selling Strategies	Cross-Selling and Upselling	28
AI and Automation	AI and Marketing Automation	29

(continued)

Table 1 (continued)

Geolocation and Dropshipping	Geolocation of Visitors, Dropshipping	30, 31
Online Consumer Behavior	Browsing and Purchasing Online	32
B2B Marketing	B2B Digital Marketing	33
Employment and PR	Impact on Employment, The Evolution of PR and Communications	34, 35
Copywriting and Ethics	The Art and Science of Copywriting, Ethics in Digital Marketing	36, 37
Advertising	Banner and Native Advertising, Display Campaigns	38
Digital Cultures	Digital Cultures	39
Strategies and Models	Strategies and Business Models in Digital Marketing	40
Privacy and Ads	Cookies and Privacy Concerns, Using Google Ads in Digital Marketing	41, 42
E-governance	E-governance	43
Social Networks and E-learning	Social Networks and E-learning	44
Digital Healthcare	Digital Healthcare	45

Some General Definition

While most definitions are provided within each chapter and listed accordingly, I thought it would be helpful to start with some general definitions here. This is particularly useful since many terms in digital marketing overlap and can be confusing. By providing these foundational definitions at the outset, readers can have a clearer understanding of the key concepts that will be discussed throughout the book, as seen in Table 2:

This book includes numerous examples, which come with both advantages and disadvantages. Omitting examples could make the book relevant for a longer period, as companies cease to exist, and new ones enter the market. However, I find it very useful to provide a clear understanding of what this discipline entails, so I have mostly decided to keep them.

Furthermore, I have developed a special case from the start to provide an example used in the majority of the chapters. The case is a fictitious—but quite realistic—example of a sports shoes company, which later in the chapters becomes known as HeritageStride. This approach is intended to help readers, especially students and managers, understand the more technical parts of the book by providing a consistent reference. Whenever there is a larger section about HeritageStride, I have used a logo created by ChatGPT to indicate the spot. The logo looks like this:

Table 3 presents a structured content strategy across multiple channels for promoting a new line of sports shoes. The table outlines specific content types for each channel, such as social media visual posts and influencer partnerships, which aim to showcase the shoes' performance and appeal through high-quality images, videos, and testimonials.

Table 2 Terms used, focus, and differences

Term	Definition	Scope	Examples	Focus
E-Marketing	Marketing using electronic media and applications	All electronic channels	Email marketing, SMS marketing, digital billboards	Broad electronic channels
E-Commerce	Buying and selling goods/services over the Internet	Online transactions	Online retail (Amazon), online banking, PayPal	Transactional activities
Digital marketing	All marketing efforts using digital channels	All digital devices and platforms	SEO, social media marketing, mobile advertising	Digital devices and platforms
Internet marketing	Marketing activities conducted over the Internet	Internet-specific	SEM, affiliate marketing, online ads, influencer marketing	Online channels
Online marketing	Synonymous with Internet marketing	Internet-specific	Same as Internet marketing	Online channels
Mobile marketing	Marketing through mobile devices and apps	Mobile devices	SMS marketing, mobile apps, in-app advertising	Mobile device-specific
Social media marketing	Marketing on social media platforms	Social media platforms	Facebook ads, Instagram posts, X (former Twitter) campaigns	Social media platforms
Content marketing	Creating and distributing valuable content to attract customers	Various digital platforms	Blog posts, videos, infographics, podcasts	Content creation and distribution
Email marketing	Sending promotional messages via email	Email platforms	Newsletters, promotional emails, drip campaigns	Email-specific
Affiliate marketing	Earning commissions by promoting other products/services	Internet-specific	Blog affiliate links, website banners, influencer codes	Referral and commission-based
SEO (search engine optimization)	Optimizing content to rank higher in search engine results	Search engines	Keyword optimization, backlink building, meta tags	Improving search engine rankings
SEM (search engine marketing)	Paid marketing efforts to increase search engine visibility	Search engines	Google AdWords/Ads, Bing Ads, pay-per-click (PPC)	Paid search visibility
Viral marketing	Encouraging users to share marketing messages	Internet and social media	Viral videos, memes, trending hashtags	Rapid sharing and engagement
Influencer marketing	Partnering with influencers to promote products/services	Social media and blogs	Sponsored posts, brand ambassadorships, product reviews	Leveraging influencer audience

Table 3 Descriptions for a sports shoe campaign across different digital channels

Channel	Content type	Description	Example
Social media	Visual post	A high-quality image or video of athletes wearing the new sports shoes during training or competition, with a caption emphasizing comfort and performance	Caption example: "Elevate your game with our newest sports shoes. Experience unmatched comfort and peak performance in every step. #SportShoes #UnleashYourPotential"
	Stories/reels	Short, engaging clips showing the shoes in action, highlighting key features like cushioning, support, and grip	Content example: Clips of athletes showcasing shoe performance in various sports activities
	Influencer partnerships	Collaborate with athletes or fitness influencers to showcase the shoes in their posts and stories, with personal testimonials about their experience	Content example: Posts and stories by influencers discussing their experience with the shoes, using tags and hashtags related to the product
Google Ads	Text ad	A concise, compelling ad focusing on key benefits and a call to action	Example: "Discover the ultimate in comfort and performance with our latest sports shoes. Shop now and elevate your game!"
	Display ad	Eye-catching banner ads with images of the shoes and a tagline	Example: "Unmatched Comfort. Peak Performance. Shop Now!"
Email campaign	Newsletter	An email featuring a detailed description of the new sports shoes, customer testimonials, and a special discount code for subscribers	Subject line: "Unlock Your Best Performance with Our New Sports Shoes!" Body: High-quality images, a brief introduction to the features, and a prominent call-to-action button directing to the product page
Website	Product page	Detailed descriptions, high-resolution images, and videos of the shoes, highlighting their unique features. Include customer reviews and a call-to-action to buy	Content example: An interactive product page with a carousel of images, feature highlights, and customer testimonials
	Blog post	An article about the development of the new shoes, their benefits, and how they compare to previous models or competitors	Example title: "Why Our New Sports Shoes Are a Game Changer for Athletes"

This pedagogical assistance aims to facilitate comprehension and application of the concepts discussed throughout the book. Let's see if it is useful.

The Structure of Each Chapter

Each chapter begins with a definition and a general introduction, sometimes referred to as a background. The focus then shifts to practical applications, emphasizing how to execute each part rather than extensively discussing research findings. The aim is to prioritize action over discussion.

Although I generally avoid bullet points, recognizing their value for managers, I have included them where necessary. Each chapter concludes with a list of key takeaways specifically for managers. This is not a comprehensive list but a curated selection, typically limited to a maximum of ten points to avoid being overwhelming.

The length of the chapters varies, with some, like B2B, being quite extensive due to my own research and work with PhD students in this area. Other chapters are much shorter. My intention was to ensure that no chapter is longer than necessary.

About the Author

Klaus Solberg Söilen is Professor of Management at Halmstad University, Sweden. He has taught management-related courses for more than 25 years and has been a consultant for even longer. Before entering academia, he worked at several multinational companies, including KPMG Oslo. He has more than a hundred publications to his name and was the editor-in-chief of the *Journal of Intelligence Studies in Business* (JISIB) for 12 years, until 2024. He has also published scholarly and practice-based books, including *Exhibit Marketing and Trade Show Intelligence* (Springer, 2013).

Professor Klaus Solberg Söilen (Source: Göte Karlsson Foto/Magnus Karlsson)

Understanding the Digital Environment 1

1.1 A Broad Introduction to Digital Marketing

Digital marketing is not just a simple continuation of the discipline of marketing but a whole new ball game with its own logic, skills, and specialties. It integrates the advancements of information technology with business practices and research. As such, it is a result of the digital age or information age that began in the mid-twentieth century, just two generations ago. It is no exaggeration to say that digital marketing is a disruptive force that is transforming the entire business world. Few people understood this as well as Jeff Bezos, the founder of Amazon. He also understood that it was all about the speed of growth, foregoing profit in the short run, and investing the money back into the company until it was no longer threatened by new entrants.

Let us have a look at some of the key features that separate the old from the new marketing, the "brick" from the "click," as shown in Table 1.1.

For the discipline of marketing, this transformation means that customer data are not only more readily available but also more reliable, as business transactions occur on devices practically anywhere in the world 24/7. For managers, it means they now have more accurate tools for making decisions.

The flip side of this coin is that we have entered a surveillance world unparalleled in history, where customers risk becoming victims of fraud (for example, dark patterns that trick customers) or deception (for example, deepfakes that alter a person's face in an image or video).

The transformation of marketing and business into what today has become e-commerce, or e-com, started just a generation ago, with the first website created in 1991 by scientists at The European Organization for Nuclear Research (CERN) and in Silicon Valley. During the past three decades, we have witnessed dramatic developments that continue to amaze us daily as new products and services are introduced, enabling people to find products, seek entertainment, and make friends online. This online landscape has become fiercely competitive over the last decade. Take online streaming services as an example: for a while, it looked like there was

K. Solberg Söilen, *Digital Marketing*, Springer Texts in Business and Economics, https://doi.org/10.1007/978-3-031-69518-6_1

Table 1.1 Differences and similarities between brick-and-click marketing

Aspect	Traditional marketing	Digital marketing	Common features
Mediums	TV, radio, print ads, billboards	Social media, websites, email, search engines, mobile apps	Both aim to reach and engage potential customers
Interactivity	Mostly one-way communication (from company to consumer)	Highly interactive, allows for two-way communication	Both require content creation to engage audiences
Reach	Limited to geographical boundaries	Global reach with the internet	Both can target specific demographics and markets
Cost	Generally high cost for production and distribution	Can be low-cost or scalable based on budget	Both involve budget planning and allocation
Analytics	Difficult to measure, often relies on surveys and estimates	Real-time analytics, detailed metrics available	Both use data to inform strategies and measure success
Speed	Slow to execute and adjust campaigns	Quick to implement and modify campaigns	Both require strategic planning
Customization	Limited customization, more generalized messaging	High degree of customization, personalized content	Both aim to create compelling messages
Examples	Newspaper ads, TV commercials, flyers	Social media ads, SEO, content marketing, PPC	Both use storytelling to convey brand messages
Features	Tangible, physical ads, static content	Dynamic, multimedia content, interactive ads	Both require creative and strategic thinking
Customer feedback	Indirect, through market research and focus groups	Direct, instant feedback via comments, reviews, and shares	Both value customer feedback for improvement
Accessibility	Requires physical presence or tangible distribution	Accessible anytime, anywhere with internet access	Both strive to be accessible to their target audiences
Engagement	Limited engagement opportunities	High engagement through social media, email, etc.	Both seek to build customer relationships

going to be room for many large players, but now, we basically only have two, Netflix and YouTube. How it will be in a few years, we do not know.

When the first applications of digital marketing emerged, many thought they were "quick, cheap, and easy" to use. In today's technological landscape, business solutions demand special training. The very existence of these technologies—platforms, software, servers, and their multiple functions—has become a competitive instrument, causing old businesses to go bankrupt on a massive scale. Social media platforms like TikTok, Facebook, and Instagram undergo constant changes in features to try to capture and keep their customers clued to the screen for as long as possible, what we understand by engagement optimization, achieved through different retention strategies. Companies can connect user data with geographical locations with powerful mobile devices such as smartphones and tablets. By combining the customer's location and time, we can send out more targeted advertising.

Those companies that cannot harvest this information will be at a disadvantage and will often be outcompeted, and then, it can go very quickly. The entry barrier to becoming a major e-com actor has become much higher. Previously, one could set up a simple web page for a few hundred dollars. Today, to build any trust directly with customers on a broad scale, you need a sophisticated web page often costing in the hundreds of thousands, often having to do with long washup procedures. "Washup" in web development refers to a thorough review process after significant project milestones, involving issue identification, resolution, and planning for the next steps. This process is labor-intensive and involves multiple stakeholders, detailed reviews, and potential rework, all of which contribute to the high costs of professional web development projects. Ensuring high quality through rigorous testing and client involvement further adds to the complexity and expense.

Larger e-com actors like Alibaba and Amazon invest massively in data capacity. Cloud service companies like Amazon Web Services (AWS), Microsoft Azure, and Google Cloud require even more storage capacity. In a short time, most major companies will have sophisticated, human-like AI-driven support services that will make the old chatbots look like they were invented in the Stone Age.

Data storage is offered by data center facilities, real estate-like companies that run Internet and cloud data centers. The largest ones are located in China and the USA, with relatively unknown names like Range International in Langfang and Switch SuperNAP in Nevada. As the amount of data increases and the technology in these centers typically has a life expectancy of less than 10 years, new ones are being built at a rapid pace. This is the major reason that Nvidia has become such a hot stock lately. Data centers are often constructed in remote locations in stable countries for security reasons, near cheap energy sources to reduce costs, and in cold climates to reduce the need for cooling energy.

But before we get lost in all the data, let us consider how many digital customers are there and what do they buy? This will again give us an idea of what sectors dominate today and their market shares.

According to Statista, eMarketer, and Nielsen, the numbers for 2023 are as follows, as seen in Table 1.2.

Digital customers buy a wide range of products online, including electronics, apparel, groceries, beauty products, and media. These purchases are often driven by the convenience, variety, and ease of access that online shopping offers. For example, people buy computers, smartphones, clothing, shoes, groceries, cosmetics, e-books, and airline tickets through digital platforms.

In contrast, offline customers often buy items that fulfill immediate needs and daily necessities, such as fresh produce, health services, and household goods. They value the traditional retail experience and the ability to physically interact with products before buying them.

E-com companies also need good and affordable infrastructure to be competitive. Here, Alibaba has an advantage over Amazon, as it can easily access China's global superhighway, known as the "Belt and Road Initiative" (BRI), and it has

Table 1.2 Digital customers across product categories

Product category	Online purchase (%)	Common online purchases	Common offline purchases
Travel	80%	Airline tickets, hotel bookings	Travel agency bookings
Media	70%	E-books, music, streaming subscriptions	Physical books, CDs/DVDs
Electronics	60%	Computers, smartphones, accessories	Televisions, home appliances
Apparel	55%	Clothing, shoes, accessories	High-end fashion, tailored clothing
Beauty products	45%	Cosmetics, skincare products	Perfumes, specialty skincare
Household goods	35%	Furniture, decor, cleaning supplies	Large furniture, hardware store items
Groceries	25%	Packaged foods, beverages, non-perishables	Fresh produce, meats, dairy
Health services	20%	Health supplements, online consultations	Prescription medications, doctor visits

close cooperation with the largest postal network in the world with almost 1 million employees, China Post. For customers, this means faster and cheaper shipping. All of this constitutes what we can call the digital environment.

The ability for anyone with a computer to start a digital marketing company without significant investments is advantageous for individuals and presents a major opportunity for developing countries. Traditionally, people in these regions were too distant from potential customers to be considered for jobs. Since Elance launched in 1999, the number of freelance marketing platforms has grown considerably. Upwork, for instance, is a merger between two earlier platforms, Elance and oDesk. This expansion has opened new revenue streams and job opportunities for individuals worldwide, as seen in Table 1.3.

1.2 Key Concepts of the Digital Environment

The digital environment is the technological, political, and social context that e-commerce and, therefore, digital marketing operate within. It includes all actors that have an influence on our business, both those actors and organizations that we have an influence on (micro-environment) and those we do not have an influence on (macro-environment). The larger the company, the more we need to understand our digital environment as it affects our value chain, and changes can have abrupt consequences.

When digital photography technology advanced, Kodak, despite inventing the digital camera, struggled to transition from film, leading to a significant loss in market share as customers rapidly shifted to digital cameras and smartphones. Competitors like Canon and Sony quickly adapted to the digital trend, capturing

Table 1.3 Online freelancer services

Company/ platform	Major differences	HQ location	Approx. number of users	How they define themselves
Upwork	Broad range of services; project-based and hourly work; robust freelancer vetting	Santa Clara, USA	18 million+	"The world's work marketplace connecting millions of businesses with independent talent around the globe"
Fiverr	Services start at $5; focuses on gigs with predefined prices; wide variety of categories	Tel Aviv, Israel	3 million+	"A global online marketplace for freelance services, starting at $5"
Toptal	High-quality freelancers; rigorous screening process; focus on top 3% of talent	San Francisco, USA	100,000+	"An exclusive network of the top freelance software developers, designers, finance experts, and project managers"
Guru	Wide range of categories; offers WorkRooms for project management; flexible payment terms	Pittsburgh, USA	3 million+	"A platform to find and hire expert freelancers for any job"
PeoplePerHour	Strong UK presence; offers per-hour and project-based work; freelancer profiles and ratings	London, UK	2.5 million+	"A marketplace connecting businesses with an international community of freelancers available to work hourly or per project"
99designs	Specializes in design services; design contests and 1-to-1 projects; community voting for designs	Melbourne, Australia	1.4 million+	"A global creative platform that makes it easy for designers and clients to work together to create designs they love"
Freelancer	Large and diverse marketplace; wide range of categories; offers contests and projects	Sydney, Australia	50 million+	"The world's largest freelancing and crowdsourcing marketplace by number of users and projects"

(continued)

Table 1.3 (continued)

Company/ platform	Major differences	HQ location	Approx. number of users	How they define themselves
Gigster	Focuses on high-quality software development; on-demand teams; project management support	San Francisco, USA	Not publicly available	"A smart software development service that combines top engineering talent with a scientific approach to project management"
SimplyHired	Job search engine; lists freelance, part-time, and full-time jobs across multiple industries	Sunnyvale, USA	Not publicly available	"A job search engine that connects job seekers and employers through job listings and career resources"
TaskRabbit	Local freelance services; focuses on physical tasks like home improvement, delivery, personal assistance	San Francisco, USA	1.5 million+	"A task-based service platform where you can hire local professionals to help with various tasks and errands"
Outsourcely	Focus on long-term remote work; ideal for startups; various categories including IT, customer service	San Francisco, USA	400,000+	"A platform connecting startups and businesses with remote workers from around the world"
Workana	Popular in Latin America; wide range of services; focus on IT, design, writing, and marketing	Buenos Aires, Argentina	2 million+	"A freelance platform that connects professionals and companies to collaborate on remote work projects"
FlexJobs	Focuses on remote, part-time, and freelance job opportunities; subscription-based service	Boulder, USA	Not publicly available	"A job service specializing in remote, part-time, freelance, and flexible jobs"
CloudPeeps	Connects businesses with freelance marketers, content creators, community managers; quality-focused	San Francisco, USA	20,000+	"A marketplace that connects businesses with the best freelance talent for marketing, content creation, and more"
Hubstaff talent	Free resource for finding remote talent; includes time tracking and team management tools	Indianapolis, USA	90,000+	"A free resource for companies looking to find remote talent across the globe"

market share that Kodak lost. The digital environment's technological and social shifts drastically impacted Kodak's value chain and overall business strategy.

1.3 Micro- and Macro-Environment and the Four Main Objectives in Marketing

All companies that want to succeed must understand their customers and the market. This is the main objective of the study of marketing (Objective number 1). Marketing is the job of bringing the company's products and services to the market. This is the minimum expectation for marketing employees. Others in the company, often the founders, come up with ideas of what to produce. Now, it is our job to bring that product to the market. To get this done, we need to have knowledge about the market (industry experience) and be able to continuously gather information or insights about the market, which is studied under market intelligence.

Our second objective is to understand our competitors (O2). In many companies, there is enough work simply focusing on the market and the customers. It may also be that other people in the company, like those in production, keep an eye on competitors. However, in most cases, competitors are seen as part of the market forces and are thus placed under the marketing function. This has again given rise to the specialty of competitor analysis and competitor intelligence.

We are also expected to know all about media and possible channels, both in theory and in practice, as that is how we can be visible in the market (O3). While it is advantageous to understand other actors, like our suppliers, employees, and stakeholders, there will probably be other people in the company who keep a closer eye on these, but in many types of analysis, we need to have at least an overview. From a marketing perspective, we shall group them together in a fourth objective (O4).

So, while keeping with the example of the sports shoes business in the introductory chapter we get, in Table 1.4.

Having an influence on all of these actors means we can communicate with them in a way that influences their behavior. For example, we may persuade a customer to buy our products, a supplier to reduce their prices, or a neighbor to allow for an expansion of our factory on their land (against a payment).

The macro factors are forces that influence the market but upon which we as a company have little or no influence, basically because we are too small. We cannot define these factors as objectives on our part but shall call them "forces" instead.

Economic forces (F1) set the primary conditions for the market. We have no reason to be there if no one can afford our products in this market. There is probably little we can do to change these conditions. A market may be a country, a region, or

Table 1.4 The main objective of marketing

Objective	Description	Example
O1	Understanding customers and the market. This involves gathering market intelligence to know customer needs and market dynamics	Conduct surveys to understand what features customers look for in sports shoes, such as durability, comfort, and style. Analyze market trends to identify the most popular types of sports shoes
O2	Understanding competitors. This includes competitor analysis and intelligence to stay aware of market competition	Study competitors like Nike and Adidas to understand their product offerings, pricing strategies, and marketing campaigns. Monitor their new releases and customer feedback
O3	Knowledge of media and channels. This ensures visibility in the market through various media and distribution channels	Develop a strong online presence through social media advertising, collaborations with influencers, and an e-commerce website. Use targeted ads on platforms like Instagram and Facebook
O4	Overview of other actors (suppliers, employees, stakeholders). This objective groups together to understand other relevant actors	Maintain good relationships with suppliers for quality materials. Ensure employee satisfaction and engagement. Communicate effectively with stakeholders about business strategies and performance

a smaller area like a city or town. Other conditions are set by a country's political and legal institutions and represent what we shall call political and legal forces (F2). These may change, like when a new government is elected or new laws are passed, but there is usually nothing we as a company can do to control it. Indirectly, multinational companies try to influence politicians through public relations (altering the public's mind) and lobbying (altering the politicians' minds), but this is costly and time-consuming work and can be ethically problematic. Technological forces like a country's infrastructure take much money and time to change (F3). Sociocultural forces are even more difficult to influence. Together with ecological issues and physical and geographical boundaries, they belong to a group of factors we have little influence on. We shall clump them together as "other forces" (F4), as seen in Fig. 1.1.

The study of marketing can be seen as a branch of economics. Economics is the study of how we use scarce resources to gain a competitive advantage. It can be for us an individual, an organization, a company, a state, or a country (competitive unit).

It can mean focusing only on units operating today, for example, for the sports shoes company this year or this quarter, as done in much neoclassical economics, or it can include the interests of the next generation of shoes company owners, as encouraged in a more evolutionary approach to economics.

For the study of digital marketing, the unit in this book shall be the company, unless otherwise stated. The time perspective for company decisions varies. Most

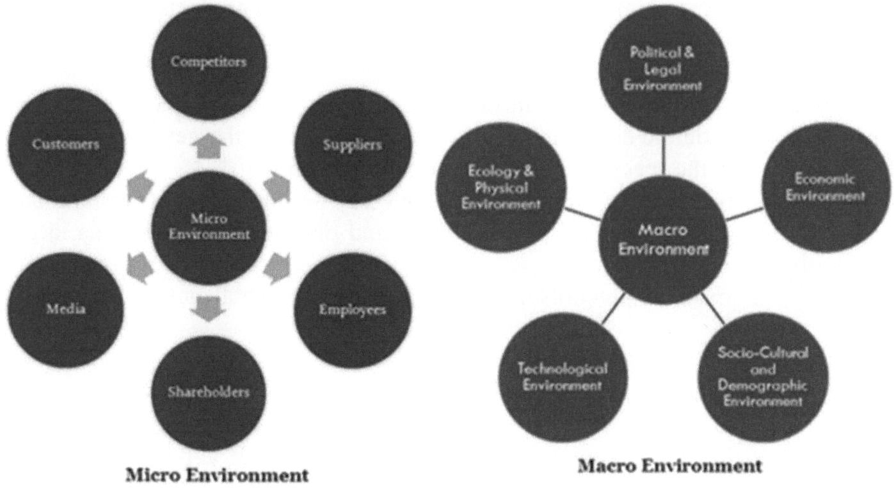

Fig. 1.1 Micro and macro factors

companies focus on this year's results, divided into four quarterly reports. Larger companies or companies with better financial positions can afford to think further ahead. Some will argue that thinking further ahead helps avoid short-term problems. Whatever our unit of analysis or time horizon, all companies must engage in the activity of environmental scanning to have a chance to compete.

1.4 How Digital Technology Supports Marketing

Once we have a good understanding of our digital environment, the next step is to determine how best to leverage it for marketing purposes. Our goals are not only to sell online but also to serve our clients, communicate with them, explore cost-saving opportunities, and identify prospects for upselling (selling more expensive products) and cross-selling (selling other product categories).

We operate in a process of identifying, anticipating, and satisfying what customers want, anticipating how they prefer to make their purchases, and ensuring they are satisfied. A version of this process tailored for digital marketing includes the "5Ss": selling, serving, speaking, saving, and sizzling:

1. Selling: Not only do we aim to sell products online, but we also strive to create a seamless and efficient purchasing experience.
2. Serving: We address our customers' needs through online dialog and feedback mechanisms, ensuring they feel supported and valued.
3. Speaking: Maintaining ongoing communication with clients post-purchase is crucial in encouraging repeat business and building loyalty.
4. Saving: Digital platforms offer opportunities to save money across various business areas, including marketing, real estate, and distribution.

5. Sizzling: We spread information about our company and products to new online venues, discovering new customer groups and product offers.[1]

Whether it is the 5Ss or 7Ss in other frameworks, these divisions are clever reminders of the online environment's vast possibilities. In the next step, we will delve deeper into the specific digital marketing applications.

By embracing the digital marketing framework, we can better understand and meet the needs of our customers, drive sales, and optimize our operations in the ever-evolving digital landscape. Let us explore how these principles are practically applied to maximize the potential of our digital marketing strategies.

1.5 How We Apply Digital Marketing

The world of digital marketing encompasses a multitude of applications. Social media management, content marketing, automation, and community building are some of the most utilized groups of applications and software. While some companies choose to engage in all these areas, others focus only on what works best for them based on their size and specific needs.

To effectively use digital marketing, companies should consider its various applications: as an advertising medium, a direct-response medium, a platform for sales transactions, a lead-generation method, a distribution channel, a customer service mechanism, and a relationship-building medium. We shall look at each one in more detail:

1.5.1 An Advertising Medium

Advertising mediums include print, outdoor, broadcast, and digital advertising, each serving to deliver messages to target groups. The goal is to draw attention to a brand, product, or service, increase awareness, and drive sales. Three important factors to consider are the target audience, the budget, and the message. Table 1.5 shows the advantages and disadvantages of different advertising media:

1.5.2 A Direct-Response Medium

Effective direct-response marketing channels include digital marketing, email marketing, direct mail, and direct sales. Examples include publishing a Facebook post, creating podcasts, and hosting X (former Twitter) chats.

A direct-response medium consists of three main elements: an offer (1), supporting information (2), and a response mechanism (3). Success requires all three elements. This medium aims to trigger a customer's immediate response, where sales

[1] Chaffey and Smith (2013).

Table 1.5 Selecting the advertising medium

Advertising medium	Description	Advantages	Disadvantages
Print advertising	Includes journals, newspaper advertisements, flyers, and magazine ads. Oldest and most widely used form, considered trustworthy	Helps gain loyal customers	Limited reach compared to the internet
Outdoor advertising	High reach, includes banners, billboards, telephone booths, bus stops, subways, taxis, and point-of-sale displays	High reach Low-cost Flexible Quickly captures attention	Can be disruptive in traffic May cause accidents
Broadcast advertising	Includes radio and television. Expensive but efficient and flexible with strong reach and reliability	High reach Strong reliability Flexible	High cost No guarantee of ad views
Digital advertising	Most widely used today, allows for easy segmentation to reach broad or specific audiences. Includes internet, social media, mobile phones, videos, and podcasts	– High reach capacity – Cost-effective – Easy to find target audience – Ability to track interactions	– Less credible due to spam, scams, and fake promotion

copy should prompt the buying decision. After presenting the right offer, we deliver relevant information to help consumers make informed decisions. Lastly, the response mechanism should be simple and automated to encourage positive responses.

1.5.3 A Platform for Sales Transactions

A point of sale (POS) is where customers make payments for products or services. While many companies still use manual methods and cash registers, digital POS systems simplify sales transactions and reduce costs. A digital POS can handle payment processing, inventory management, customer relationship management (CRM), and financial data management (FDM).

1.5.4 A Lead-Generation Method

Lead generation is a marketing process that stimulates consumer interest to increase sales. It can be separated into inbound and outbound marketing, as seen in Table 1.6.

Table 1.6 Inbound and outbound marketing

Marketing type	Description	Methods	Advantages	Disadvantages
Inbound marketing	Helps potential customers find a company before they are ready to purchase, turning early awareness into brand preference and leads	Content marketing SEO Websites Blogs Social media	Builds long-term relationships Cost-effective Attracts targeted audience Enhances brand credibility	Takes time to see results Needs consistent effort and quality content Can be competitive
Outbound marketing	Companies reach out to audiences through various channels to attract attention among those unaware of their products or services	Email marketing Display ads Pay-per-click ads Direct mail Events	Immediate results Wide reach Can target specific demographics Good for short-term campaigns	Often seen as intrusive Can be expensive Lower engagement rates Higher risk of being ignored
Combining inbound and outbound	Enhances marketing efforts by integrating both strategies, leading to more views, shares, and customer feedback	Integrating inbound and outbound methods	Maximizes reach and engagement Balances short-term and long-term goals More comprehensive strategy	Needs careful coordination Can be resource-intensive Needs clear measurement and ana

The purpose of lead generation is to identify potential customers. If we have a strong lead, let us say in B2B, it also means that we are willing to invest some money in obtaining this person or company as our customer.

1.5.5 A Distribution Channel

Distribution involves how goods reach consumers, passing through a chain of businesses until arriving at the end-consumer. Channels can be short with few intermediaries or long with many stops. There are two types: direct (consumer buys from the producer) and indirect (consumer buys from a retailer or wholesaler). Direct channels are often cheaper than indirect ones, as can be read out in Table 1.7.

By using both direct and indirect channels, Apple can balance the benefits of higher control and profitability with the advantages of wider market reach and customer convenience. This dual approach helps Apple maintain its strong market presence and customer loyalty.

Table 1.7 An example of this is the distribution of Apple products

Distribution channel	Description	Process	Advantages	Disadvantages
Direct channel	Apple sells products directly to consumers through its own retail stores and online stores	Apple designs and manufactures products Products are shipped directly to apple retail stores or sold through the online store	Full control over branding, pricing, and customer service Collects valuable customer data Higher profit margins	Limited market reach Higher operational costs for managing retail stores
Indirect channel	Apple partners with retailers and wholesalers such as best buy, Amazon, and mobile carriers (e.g., Verizon, AT&T)	Apple ships products to wholesalers and large retailers Intermediaries sell products to end consumers	Broader market access Additional services provided by retailers and carriers (e.g., financing, technical support)	Reduced control over pricing and customer service Higher cost due to intermediary markups Potential inconsistencies in customer experience

1.5.6 A Customer Service Mechanism

Customer service is crucial for ensuring buyer satisfaction and encouraging repeat business. Companies are increasingly adopting automated customer service to reduce costs and increase efficiency.

Amazon, for example, offers 24/7 customer service via phone, email, and chat. However, balancing automation with human interaction is important as many customers prefer direct contact. FAQs can save money but may not suit less tech-savvy customers. Automated follow-up systems, such as surveys, can improve service without sacrificing quality. With new AI-enhanced service functions all of these relics will soon be passed over to the history books.

1.5.7 A Relationship-Building Medium

Networking is essential for developing business relationships, both physically and digitally. It involves exchanging ideas and information that can be collected, analyzed, and stored for future use. Leadership and influencing are key methods for relationship building, altering people's attitudes, strategies, and decisions. Public relations (PR) is another method, often used in times of crisis to alter consumer perceptions. PR professionals work as storytellers for the company, using unpaid or earned media to reach as many people as possible.

Companies often communicate frequently to achieve increased value, enhance the brand, beat competitors, offer customer rewards, and improve customer service. Engaging with a mix of entertaining and exciting messages helps reach potential customers frequently without being annoying. Rewarding customers for their purchases encourages loyalty and repeat business. Excellent customer service is essential, especially in e-commerce, where free shipping and quick delivery times are competitive factors. This leads to positive word-of-mouth and new customers.

1.6 Online Marketing Tools

Social media marketing means that we use social media platforms like Facebook or TikTok to communicate with current and potential customers. It is an effective, though increasingly expensive, way to drive website traffic and build a brand by publishing content, listening to followers, and commenting on postings. If done well, we seem engaged, concerned, and up to date. As such, it is important for a ubiquitous and seamless marketing effort where we show that we can move in the same environment as our customers.

Marketers use various online communication tools when developing communication strategies or executing online marketing campaigns. As suggested by Chaffey and Smith, these tools can be categorized into six primary groups. Below in Table 1.8 is a brief but expanded explanation of each:

The table provides a structured overview of different online communication tools used in digital marketing, highlighting their methods, advantages, and disadvantages.

1.7 Old Media vs. New Media

The Internet has significantly impacted how consumers behave and make decisions in the buying process. It has made it possible for customers to find and purchase a desired product or service in a matter of seconds, a process that could take hours before. However, we cannot forget traditional media, which still constitutes a big part of our lives. A balance of both "brick" and "click" therefore is the best way for a marketer to approach his profession.

Traditional media, also called old media, is what most of us have grown up with, and we still spend a significant amount of time away from our screens, especially during the day. Table 1.9 shows us what age groups can be reached when and where online:

Children and teenagers (6–17 years) predominantly use screens for educational purposes, social media, and entertainment, with boys spending more time on gaming and online videos, while girls favor social media and communication platforms. Young adults (18–34 years) balance screen time between work/study, social media, and entertainment, with males more focused on gaming and online videos and females on social media, online shopping, and streaming services. Adults (35–54 years) use screens mainly for work-related tasks, news, and social media, with men spending more time on news and sports and women on social media and online shopping. Seniors (55+ years) primarily engage with news, social media, and

Table 1.8 Online communication tools

Tool	Description	Methods	Advantages	Disadvantages
Search marketing	Making a website easily accessible through online searches	– Paid placements (sponsored links) – Natural placement (SEO)	– Quick visibility with paid placements – Long-term visibility with SEO	– Paid placements can be costly – SEO requires time and resources
Online PR	Managing a company's image through online channels	– Websites – Blogs – Social media	– Enhances brand perception – Aligns communication with company goals	– Needs constant monitoring – Potential for negative feedback online
Online partnership	Collaborating with third parties to promote a website	– Online sponsorship – Co-branding – Affiliate marketing – Aggregators – Link building	– Expands reach through partnerships – Shares resources and audiences	– Depends on partner reliability – May dilute brand identity
Interactive ads	Engaging potential customers actively through interactive content	– E-quizzes – Surveys – Interactive TV programs – Video games	– Creates memorable interactions – Enhances user engagement	– Can be costly to develop – Needs creative content
Opt-in email	Obtaining permission to send communications to potential customers	– Registration – Content exchange	– Builds a willing audience – Higher engagement rates	– Can be seen as spam if overused – Needs maintenance of the email list
Social media marketing	Using social media platforms to engage with customers	– Posting content – Responding to comments – Sharing updates	– Drives website traffic – Builds brand awareness – Engages with a large audience	– Needs constant activity – Risk of negative public feed

entertainment, with men focusing on news and informational websites and women on social media and communication with family and friends.

And yes, studies and surveys typically indicate that approximately 20–30% of men's screen time includes consuming pornographic content. For women, this percentage is significantly lower, often ranging between 3 and 10% of their total screen time.[2]

Traditional media includes radio, television, magazine ads, billboard ads, and newspapers. As long as we watch regular programs on TV (linear TV, as opposed to

[2] Friedman (2023, September 5).

Table 1.9 Screen time across age groups and sex[a]

Age group	Time of day	General screen time activities	Sex differences
6–17 years	Morning	Educational purposes, quick entertainment before school	Boys: More time on gaming and online videos Girls: More time on social media and communication platforms
	Afternoon	Homework, social media, gaming	Boys: More time on gaming and online videos Girls: More time on social media and communication platforms
	Evening	Entertainment, social media, online communication	Boys: More time on gaming and online videos Girls: More time on social media and communication platforms
18–34 years	Morning	Checking social media, news, emails	Males: More time on gaming and online videos Females: Higher usage of social media, online shopping, and streaming services
	Afternoon	Work/study, social media breaks	Males: More time on gaming and online videos Females: Higher usage of social media, online shopping, and streaming services
	Evening	Entertainment, social media, online shopping	Males: More time on gaming and online videos Females: Higher usage of social media, online shopping, and streaming services
35–54 years	Morning	News, emails, social media	Males: More time on news, sports, and online videos Females: Higher engagement with social media and online shopping
	Afternoon	Work-related screen time, social media breaks	Males: More time on news, sports, and online videos Females: Higher engagement with social media and online shopping
	Evening	Entertainment, social media, family activities	Males: More time on news, sports, and online videos Females: Higher engagement with social media and online shopping
55+ years	Morning	News, emails, social media	Males: More time on news and informational websites Females: Higher engagement with social media and online communication with family and friends

(continued)

Table 1.9 (continued)

Age group	Time of day	General screen time activities	Sex differences
	Afternoon	Leisure activities (watching videos, reading, social media)	Males: More time on news and informational websites Females: Higher engagement with social media and online communication with family and friends
	Evening	Entertainment (TV, streaming services)	Males: More time on news and informational websites Females: Higher engagement with social media and online communication with family and friends

[a]Verified using ChatGPT 4 (June 2024)

on-demand TV that we can stream on YouTube and other places), old media will remain relevant. Large billboard ads still look impressive. As marketers, we do not have a predisposition to replace bricks with clicks. Instead, We are interested in where the customer is moving during the day (customer journey), whether it is taking the car or train to work or shopping in a nearby mall. We simply want to be visible where our customers are, that is all. If they spent all of their time in zoos, we would have something called "Marketing at zoos"; we simply do not have a preference.

What makes clicks more attractive are two things: segmentation and target marketing. It is easier to find our customers online, and it is easier to track their behavior. That does not mean that it is necessarily easier to communicate with them. It may be that setting up a stand at the entrance of a zoo will give us more and better communication. As more marketing moves online, offline marketing becomes less competitive and thus more attractive. However, at the end of the day, we want to find a good combination. For example, sending a physical postcard these days is much more valuable than getting another (spam) email. Table 1.10 shows examples of old and new media:

1.7.1 The Balanced Marketing Strategy

Finding the right balance—or mix—between online and offline marketing involves leveraging the strengths of each medium to create a cohesive and effective strategy. Let us consider a local coffee shop aiming to increase foot traffic and boost online sales of coffee beans and merchandise.

The coffee shop can use social media advertising on platforms like Facebook and Instagram to reach local coffee enthusiasts. By creating visually appealing posts showcasing the shop's ambiance and specialty drinks, they can attract attention and drive engagement. Additionally, running targeted ads with special discounts

Table 1.10 Old vs. new media

Type of media	Characteristics and examples	Pros	Cons
Traditional media	Radio, television, magazine ads, billboard ads, newspapers, postcards, coupons, direct mail (catalogs, flyers), yellow pages, brochures, in-store displays, transit advertising (ads on buses, subways, taxis), cinema advertising, telephone directories, sponsorships (sports events, concerts), product placements, trade shows and exhibitions, posters, door hangers, vehicle wraps, public relations events, telemarketing, event marketing (expos, fairs), community sponsorships (local events, charities), guerrilla marketing (flash mobs, street teams)	Familiar to most people, still relevant for certain audiences, can be impressive (e.g., large billboards)	Limited segmentation and targeting, harder to track consumer behavior, often more expensive than online
Online media	Display ads such as banners and pop-ups, search engine marketing through platforms like Google ads and Bing ads, affiliate marketing, email marketing, native advertising, retargeting ads, and sponsored content. Social media, influencer marketing, sponsored posts, social media contests and e-giveaways, hashtag campaigns, and using stories and live videos for promotion. Mobile phone advertising includes SMS marketing, mobile app ads, in-app advertising, push notifications, location-based marketing, QR codes, and mobile game advertising. Video advertising includes ads on YouTube and other video platforms, video content marketing, live streaming, webinars, video collaborations, and vlogging. Podcast advertising includes sponsorships, host-read ads, pre-recorded ads, branded podcasts, product placements, and interview sponsorships	Easier segmentation and targeting, cost-effective, high reach, trackable customer interactions	Less credible due to spam and fake promotions, not necessarily easier to communicate effectively
Example	Setting up a stand in front of a grocery store to directly engage with customers	Direct interaction, better communication, builds personal connection	Time-consuming, limited reach compared to online, requires physical presence

available both in-store and online helps bridge the gap between digital and physical sales.

Email marketing is another powerful tool. By building an email list of in-store visitors and online purchasers, the shop can send out weekly newsletters featuring new products, upcoming events, and exclusive offers. These emails can include discount codes redeemable both in-store and online, encouraging customers to interact with the brand across multiple channels.

SEO and content marketing are also essential. By optimizing the website for local search terms like "best coffee shop in [City]" and regularly updating the blog with content about coffee brewing tips, bean origins, and customer testimonials, the shop can drive organic traffic to its website and promote its online store.

On the offline front, the coffee shop can place ads in local newspapers, magazines, and community bulletin boards to reach potential customers who may not be as active online. Outdoor advertising, such as banners, flyers, and billboards near high-traffic areas, can effectively grab attention and direct people to the shop. Sponsoring local events like farmers' markets and festivals allows the shop to offer free samples and distribute discount codes, enhancing its presence in the community.

To integrate these efforts, the coffee shop should ensure consistent branding and messaging across all channels, whether customers see an ad online or in a local newspaper. By using online platforms to promote offline events and vice versa, they create a seamless marketing experience.

Regularly reviewing the performance data from both online and offline efforts helps in making data-driven decisions. If online ads drive more foot traffic, the shop can increase investment in those ads. Conversely, if print ads are effective, expanding that campaign would be beneficial.

By combining these tactics, the coffee shop can create a balanced marketing strategy that maximizes its reach and effectiveness, continually analyzing and adjusting the mix of online and offline efforts based on what drives the best results, according to the model in Fig. 1.2.

Besides, our customers are not going to be all for click or brick; they are going to use a combination of online and offline touchpoints, even for the same purchasing process, which we call mixed-mode buying. In our sports shoes example, it is not uncommon to try a pair of shoes in a store and then buy them at the cheapest outlet online.

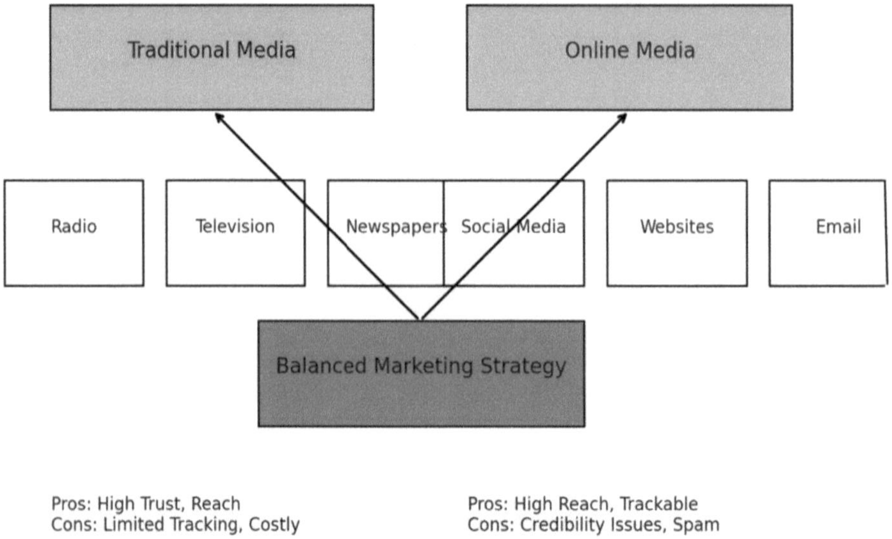

Fig. 1.2 Finding the balance between online brick-and-click marketing

1.8 Mixed-Mode Buying in Digital Marketing

Mixed-mode buying refers to a purchasing behavior where consumers use multiple channels and methods to complete a transaction. This approach combines both online and offline elements, offering a seamless shopping experience that leverages the strengths of each mode.

Key aspects and examples of mixed-mode buying are

1. Research online, purchase offline (ROPO): Consumers might research products online, compare prices, read reviews, and check availability but then go to a physical store to make the purchase. This method is common for items that customers prefer to see or try before buying, such as clothing or electronics.
2. Online purchase with in-store pickup: Customers buy products online and choose to pick them up at a nearby store. This method, also known as "click and collect," combines the convenience of online shopping with the immediacy of getting the product from a local store.
3. In-store browsing, online purchase: Shoppers might visit a physical store to browse products, get a feel for the quality, or try them on and then make the purchase online. This can be due to better online prices, the availability of different sizes or colors, or the convenience of home delivery.

4. Mobile integration: Shoppers use their mobile devices to scan barcodes or QR codes in-store to get more information about products, compare prices, and read reviews. They might then choose to buy the product either online or in-store, depending on the best deal or convenience.
5. Hybrid retail models: Businesses that combine their physical and digital operations to provide a unified shopping experience. For example, a retailer might offer digital kiosks in their stores where customers can order items not available in the physical location and have them shipped to their home.

We can make a diagram that shows these two processes, as in Fig. 1.3.

The diagram illustrates a mixed-mode buying process, where customers switch between online and offline shopping at various stages. Initially, customers research products, either online by visiting an e-commerce website or offline by visiting a physical store. They can add products to an online cart and proceed to checkout or browse and purchase directly in-store. Switching points are included, allowing customers to transition from online to offline shopping and vice versa. Finally, customers receive their products through home delivery, in-store pickup, or direct in-store purchase, ending the buying process.

Example: A customer might see a new smartphone in a physical electronics store and try it out to understand its features. After confirming it meets their needs, they go home and compare prices on various e-commerce websites. Finding a better deal online, they order it for home delivery. Alternatively, they might order it online but choose to pick it up at the store to avoid shipping delays.

Mixed-mode buying offers customers the best of both worlds, providing flexibility and convenience. By integrating online and offline experiences, businesses can meet diverse customer preferences, leading to higher satisfaction. Additionally, businesses can leverage mixed-mode buying to drive traffic both to their online platforms and physical stores, creating more sales opportunities. This approach also allows businesses to collect comprehensive data across channels, enabling more personalized marketing strategies and improved inventory management. Overall, mixed-mode buying enhances retail strategies and increases customer satisfaction by catering to various shopping preferences.

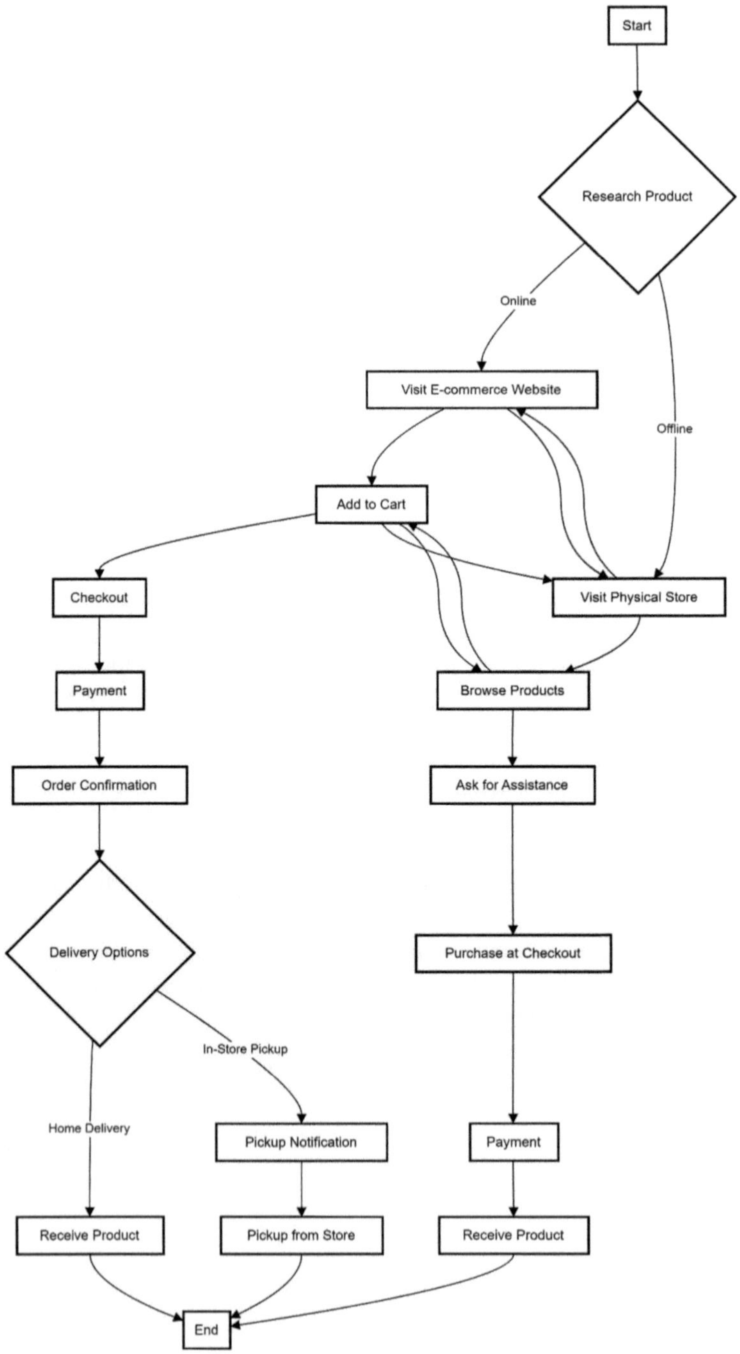

Fig. 1.3 Mixed-mode buying process

References

Chaffey, D., & Smith, P. R. (2013). *eMarketing eXcellence: Planning and optimizing your digital marketing*. Routledge.

Friedman, J. (2023, September 5). How much porn do Americans really watch? *Psychology Today*. Retrieved from https://www.psychologytoday.com/us/blog/everyone-on-top/202309/how-much-porn-do-americans-really-watch

Big Data and Data Mining 2

Big data and data mining have revolutionized the marketing landscape, transforming how businesses understand and engage with their customers. In today's digital age, every interaction with technology generates data, creating vast amounts of information that require sophisticated techniques to analyze and derive meaningful insights. Data mining is the process of extracting valuable patterns from large datasets, enabling companies to make informed decisions. This chapter outlines the key steps in data mining, including data collection, cleaning, integration, storage, analysis, pattern recognition, interpretation, and decision-making. These steps harness the power of big data to provide actionable insights, making businesses more competitive and innovative.

Companies like Google, Facebook, and Amazon are data-driven, collecting user data to enhance their marketing strategies. The use of cookies and other tracking technologies allows these companies to gather detailed information about users' online behaviors, facilitating targeted advertising and personalized experiences. However, this data collection also raises privacy concerns, contributing to what is known as the surveillance society. Despite these concerns, the value of big data in predicting customer behavior and improving business outcomes is undeniable.

In summary, big data and data mining are powerful tools that enable businesses to understand their customers better, predict behaviors, and optimize marketing strategies. By effectively managing and analyzing large datasets, companies can create personalized experiences, improve customer loyalty, and drive business success.

2.1 Background

This chapter is about big data and data mining, describing how to understand and use these new digital tools from a marketing perspective.

Whenever we engage with technical devices today, be it an ATM, a phone call to a government office, or a request over the Internet, data is created. As soon as we

K. Solberg Söilen, *Digital Marketing*, Springer Texts in Business and Economics, https://doi.org/10.1007/978-3-031-69518-6_2

gather more data than what we can possibly oversee, there is a demand to make sense of it all, perform analysis, and draw conclusions from the data. This sense-making is done through the process called data mining, as depicted in Fig. 2.1.

The process of data mining using big data involves several critical steps:[1]

1. Big data collection: The first step is gathering vast amounts of raw data from various sources. These sources can include social media platforms, sensors, and

Fig. 2.1 The data mining process using big data

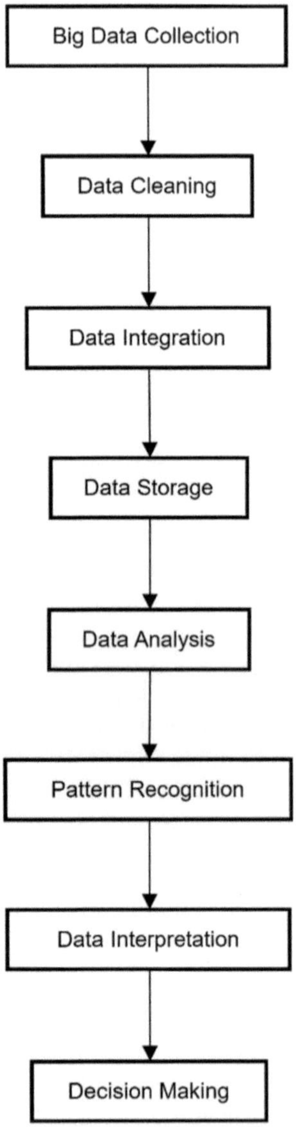

[1] Verified using ChatGPT 4 (June 2024).

transactional data from e-commerce sites. The goal is to collect as much relevant data as possible to have a comprehensive dataset for analysis.
2. Data cleaning: Once the data is collected, it needs to be cleaned. This involves removing inaccuracies, inconsistencies, and irrelevant information that could skew the results. Data cleaning ensures that the dataset is accurate and of high quality.
3. Data integration: After cleaning, the data from different sources must be integrated to provide a unified view. This step involves combining data that might be stored in different formats and locations into a cohesive dataset that can be analyzed as a whole.
4. Data storage: The cleaned and integrated data is then stored in databases or data warehouses. This storage is essential for efficient access and processing. Modern data storage solutions are designed to handle large volumes of data and provide quick retrieval times.
5. Data analysis: With the data stored and ready, the next step is to analyze it. This involves applying statistical and computational techniques to identify patterns, trends, and correlations within the data. Data analysis can be performed using various tools and software designed for big data.
6. Pattern recognition: During the analysis, advanced algorithms, including machine learning techniques, are used to recognize patterns within the data. These patterns can reveal valuable insights about customer behavior, market trends, and other critical business metrics.
7. Data interpretation: Once patterns are recognized, they need to be interpreted. This step involves making sense of the identified patterns and deriving meaningful insights that can inform decision-making processes.
8. Decision-making: Finally, the insights gained from data interpretation are used to make informed decisions. These decisions can help improve business processes, predict future trends, enhance customer satisfaction, and achieve various other business goals.

This entire process leverages the vast amounts of data available in the digital age to provide businesses with actionable insights, helping them stay competitive and innovative.

Every time we press a button on a keyboard, that "interaction" is or can be registered. The data comes from various sources, including social media, e-commerce, bank transactions, government records, and mass media. Companies like Google, Facebook, and Amazon use data to stay innovative and competitive. We say that these companies are data-driven. What they do is collect data from online users and use that data for marketing. Not only that, the biggest asset of many of these companies is exactly that, all the data they have gathered. This data is valuable because it is targeted; we know who entered it and how to reach that person with targeted ads. Users essentially provide this data for free in exchange for using the services these companies provide "for free." This does not mean that everything on these platforms is free, normally just the access to them. By clicking the accept button to the "cookie policy" upon landing on their sites, we consent to this exchange.

A cookie is a small file that websites send to monitor our activity on their website and store that information so that it is easy and quick to use the next time we visit. For example, if you visit an online store and look at a pair of shoes, the website will store this information. The next time you visit, it might show you a discount offer for those shoes, making your shopping experience more personalized and engaging.

The data is often accessed by multiple businesses, and to top it all, those businesses may even be required to give national security organizations access to the same data. Thus, for all the data we enter, there will be multiple copies, located in different countries worldwide, all depending on where the servers are located. This gives an idea of what we call the surveillance society, where our digital marks and behavior on the computer are registered by multiple parties, some to monetize on it, others to register our actions and beliefs, according to the process depicted in Fig. 2.2.

Note that there is no "I don't accept" button on web pages. On some web pages, you can scroll down and read the content without accepting it. But regardless of whether we press the OK button, companies see our IP (Internet Protocol) number and can gather our data once we have landed on their site. The actual button is a result of the General Data Protection Regulation (GDPR) enacted in the European Union in May 2018 and the ePrivacy Directive (the "cookie law"), first passed in 2002 and updated in 2009. Most companies use this function just to be on the safe side, in case they get sued.

For older users, these messages might remind them of the disturbing pop-up ads of the 1990s that were eventually blocked by browsers after 2004. Pop-up ads were particularly annoying because they disrupted the user experience by suddenly appearing and obscuring the content being viewed, often requiring manual closure and sometimes appearing in rapid succession. Both cookies and pop-up ads are poor solutions for visitors to web pages because they disrupt the user experience by either tracking personal data without explicit consent (cookies) or interrupting content consumption with intrusive messages (pop-up ads). On the other hand, if individuals were allowed to keep all of their personal data and online prints private, that would make digital marketing much less predictable.

To give you an idea of how powerful these listening techniques have become, large vendors will often know what a company is about to buy before they say so themselves. How? Well, as a supplier, you can buy the surfing data from data providers and data brokers based on the company IP number. You cannot see which person is surfing for what, but you can see what a collected group of employees at the company is surfing for. So, if you see that many employees are searching for a specific software type in a specific company, you may assume that they are in the market for one. This makes sales so much easier.

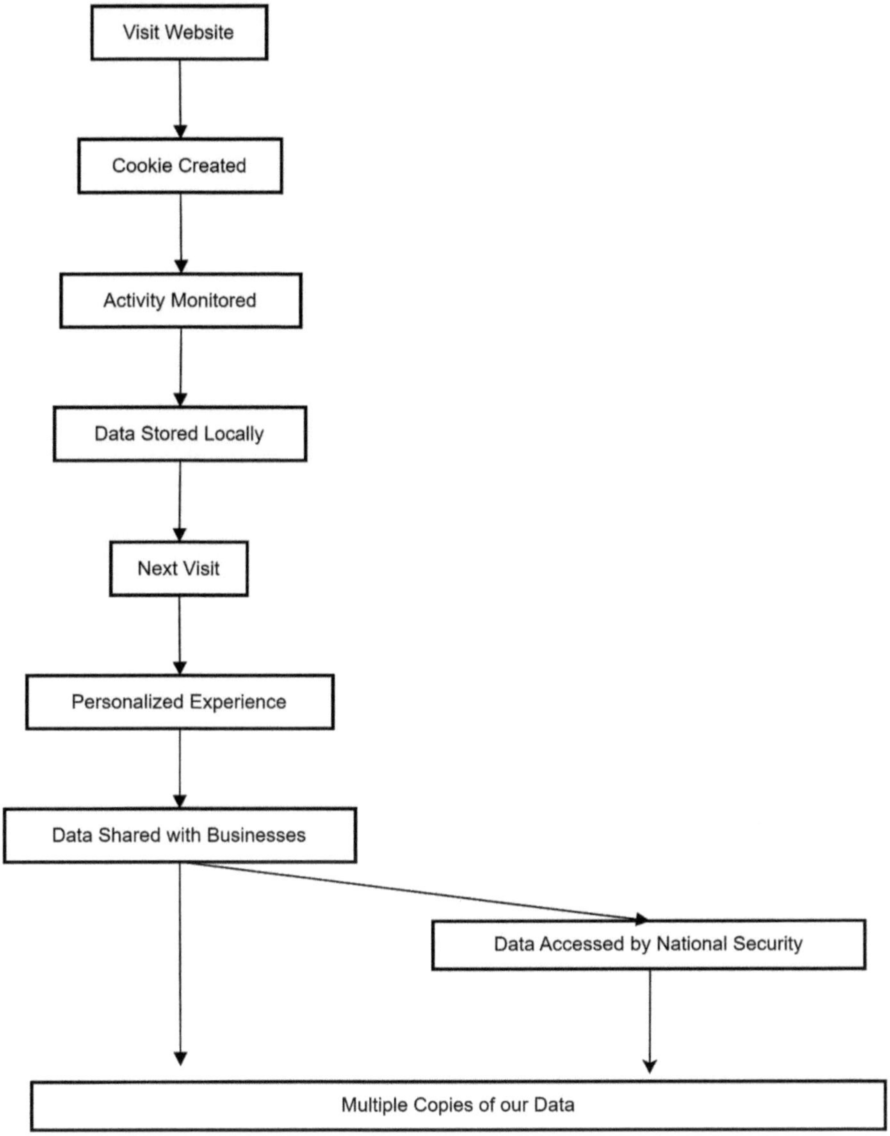

Fig. 2.2 Process from visiting a web page to having several copies of our online behavior

An IP address is a unique string of numbers separated by periods that identifies each computer using the Internet Protocol to communicate over a network. These addresses can be traced back to the company or individual that is using them.

Here are some key points regarding traceable IP numbers for companies:[2]

[2] Verified using ChatGPT 4 (June 2024).

1. Static IP addresses: Many companies use static IP addresses, which do not change over time. These are often easier to trace back to a specific company or organization because they are assigned by Internet service providers (ISPs) to a particular entity and remain constant.
2. Dynamic IP addresses: While some companies might use dynamic IP addresses that change periodically, the ISP can still trace these addresses back to the company using their records.
3. Geolocation: IP addresses can often be geolocated to determine the geographic location of the company. This is done by mapping IP addresses to physical locations, although the precision can vary.
4. Privacy concerns: Companies often use various methods to protect their IP addresses from being easily traceable, such as using Virtual Private Networks (VPNs) or proxy servers. However, the original IP address can often still be traced by legal authorities or ISPs if necessary.
5. Usage in marketing: In marketing, companies may use IP addresses to gather data on visitors to their websites. This can include information on the visitor's geographic location, ISP, and sometimes even their browsing behavior.

Overall, while there are methods to obscure or protect IP addresses, they are inherently traceable due to the nature of how the Internet Protocol functions.

The names of the data providers are not household names like those services accessed directly by customers. This is exactly because they are much like back-office functions, as seen in Table 2.1.

With the collection of user data, companies can adapt and adjust to evolving customer expectations and predict future online behavior to provide a positive and relevant customer experience.

Big data and data mining are tools that are of great use for marketers. The data opens up possibilities for both digital marketers and online customers. For instance, a person interested in fishing might go online and search for nearby fishing lakes. As they type in their search words, Google will present information not only about nearby lakes but also advertisements for various related items, such as fishing gear. This type of strategic marketing would not be possible without data mining and

Table 2.1 Data providers and brokers

Company	Headquarters	Number of employees	Yearly sales (approx.)
Oracle Data Cloud	Redwood Shores, California, USA	137,000	$40 billion
Experian	Dublin, Ireland	17,000	$5.2 billion
Equifax	Atlanta, Georgia, USA	11,000	$3.5 billion
TransUnion	Chicago, Illinois, USA	8000	$2.7 billion
Epsilon	Irving, Texas, USA	8000	$2.3 billion
CoreLogic	Irvine, California, USA	5200	$1.8 billion
Acxiom	Conway, Arkansas, USA	3000	$900 million
Neustar	Sterling, Virginia, USA	1800	$500 million

cookies. It can also be a bit scary. If you send an email in Gmail to a golf club wanting to participate in one of their courses for beginners, you may get a YouTube video for golf beginners in your timeline as you watch your favorite news subscriptions, especially because YouTube is owned by Google. We are used to giving up a part of our privacy for free access to information on the web.

To summarize, big data and data mining work by collecting and analyzing vast amounts of data to extract valuable insights. These insights help businesses to target their marketing efforts more effectively, ultimately enhancing the customer experience and driving sales. Different data sources have different uses, as exemplified in Table 2.2.

By understanding and utilizing these data sources, marketers can create more effective campaigns, better meet customer needs, and stay competitive in the ever-evolving digital landscape.

2.1.1 Key Concepts of Big Data and Data Mining

Big data is a large amount of data that marketers collect, store, and analyze to be able to make better business decisions that again can lead to better company profit and growth. Data is as many now know measured in bits and bytes.

One bit contains a value of 0 or 1. Eight bits make a byte. We have kilobytes (1.000 bytes), megabytes (1000^2 bytes), gigabytes (1000^3 bytes), terabytes (1000^4 bytes), petabytes (1000^5 bytes), exabytes (1000^6 bytes), and zettabytes (1000^7 bytes). This manuscript is for example about 4.83 MB or 5,065,920 bytes.

There are three characteristics of big data: huge volumes of data, an extremely high velocity of data, and a wide variety of data. But how big is big? In 1999, it was 1 GB. Today it is more like 1 TB. 1 TB is what many private individuals have on their external hard drive today, and the unit comes at around 100 USD. A 5 TB hard drive costs about double. The largest drives today have a capacity of more than 50 TB, and all of this will soon change.

Now, data mining is a digital process that extracts valuable data from an extensive data set. We use software or an algorithm to discover an unknown pattern. We may for example want to know what products customers buy together when they visit our e-com store.

Table 2.2 Examples of data sources and their uses

Data source	Example use case
Social media	Targeted ads based on user interests and interactions
E-commerce	Personalized product recommendations
Bank transactions	Fraud detection and financial product offers
Government records	Tailored citizen services and information
Mass media	Audience analysis for better content creation

Basically, three forms of machine learning are involved: classification, association, and numeric estimation. In classification learning, we want to classify different products in our store into categories.

We feed the software with specific data of customers arranged in "attributes" or "input attributes" (sex, age, profession, credit rating, what products they have bought before) called training data and try to predict whether or not a new customer will buy a specific product, like a toaster (output attribute). Our dataset is going to consist of both numeric (ex. age) and nominal (ex. product type) attributes. Each person is described as an example or instance. The more examples we have the better the algorithm is going to get at making predictions. In classification exercises, the output must be nominal. If we want to know the probability of a consumer buying a product like a toaster, we need to go from classification to numeric estimation, but input attributes may be a combination of nominal and numeric values. It is common that we hire a data scientist to do this kind of work, as it is quite specialized. It is even more common to buy off-the-shelf software or subscribe to some web service that does it for us.

Companies that work with digital marketing use different web analytics packages which enable them to track the performance of their websites and customer behavior continually. These services make it possible for companies to get insights into customer's behavior during online interactions. In web analytics, user data collected measures the websites' performance and customer behavior. Marketers can then focus on what to prioritize and improve with reports and analyses of online data.

2.2 Real-Time Performance Measurements

The digital world is always active, and it is safe to say that the Internet never sleeps. The online activities that occur are too valuable to businesses trying to gain a profit. The Internet can provide useful data from different online activities, such as visits to a website or a picture liked on Facebook. The use of big data and data mining is a way for digital businesses to actively manage customer relationships and gain a much deeper understanding of their customers. For instance, Amazon uses data analytics to recommend products to users based on their browsing history and past purchases.

Big data refers to extremely large data sets, which were previously used mainly by institutions and governments due to their high cost. The term has been in use since the 1990s, popularized by John Mashey. With the correct customer data, businesses can plan and measure efforts to build long-term customer relationships. The goal of working with big data and data mining should not be to collect the most data possible by buying expensive technology or hiring additional people to analyze the data. Instead, the key is to make better use of the data collected and work toward the company's goals. Not all user information is valuable, and the wrong data or incorrect assumptions from collected data can lead us to fall into data traps, which means missing opportunities or facing expensive failures while focusing on the wrong data. For example, if a company focuses solely on the number of website visits without considering user engagement, it might miss out on understanding customer preferences and behavior.

Online businesses use big data and data mining to turn data into valuable insights and add business value. Real-time performance measurements will lead to wiser decisions. For example, Netflix uses real-time data to suggest movies and shows to users, improving customer satisfaction and retention. Thus, they know what new productions to start and when to stop another season from being produced of a show with little interest. That is why NCIS has more than 20 seasons. Big data and data mining allow marketers to create prediction models and apply predictive marketing based on observations of customers' online behavior. This way, they can have information about a prospect long before an actual salesperson is in contact with them. In the physical world, body language and physical expressions describe customers' behavior, giving hints to the seller. In the digital world, marketers work with information collected from visitors and online users, store and analyze the information to predict how a customer will act online, and use that information to expose the customer to relevant content.

When a customer is exposed to relevant content, it raises the chances of them making a purchase and having an excellent customer experience, thus increasing customer value and business profit. For example, when a user searches for hiking boots, an online store might show personalized ads for hiking gear, leading to higher conversion rates and customer satisfaction.

When trying to determine which qualities in a product are necessary for customer satisfaction and which are less important, the KANO model is very useful, as described in Table 2.3.

The table summarizes the Kano model categories with descriptions and examples specific to a sports shoes company to help understand different customer preferences in product development and satisfaction. For anyone interested in getting into further details, there is a series of studies which make finer nuances to this framework.[3] As AI can handle more complex models, we can also expect future versions of the KANO model to be more nuanced.

By utilizing big data, companies can adapt and adjust to evolving customer expectations and predict future online behavior to provide a positive and relevant

[3] Tontini et al. (2017) show that the dimension "friendliness" has a direct impact on loyalty if the company has a below market average performance, which may lead customers to switch service providers. "Flexibility on collection and delivery" has a direct impact if the company has a higher performance, contributing to customers' intention to continue using the service. Another finding is that, if the company delivers good service recovery after the customer found faults in the service and if customers trust the company service, they say they intend to continue to work with the company. Tontini et al. (2013) show that the impact of a superior level of "attractive" and "one-dimensional" attributes, on customer satisfaction decreases about 60% to 70% if "Basic" attributes are unfulfilled.

Table 2.3 The KANO model

Category	Description	Examples for sports shoes company
Must-be quality	These are the basic requirements that customers expect and take for granted. When done well, customers are neutral; when done poorly, customers are very dissatisfied	Car: functioning brakes Hotel: clean room Call center: greeting customers Sports shoes company: durable sole, comfortable fit
One-dimensional quality	These attributes result in satisfaction when fulfilled and dissatisfaction when not fulfilled. They are spoken and often areas of competition	Car: acceleration Hotel: waiting service Call center: time taken to resolve an issue Sports shoes company: lightweight design, stylish appearance
Attractive quality	These attributes provide satisfaction when achieved but do not cause dissatisfaction when not fulfilled. They are often unexpected and delight customers	Car: advanced parking sensor, four-wheel steering Hotel: free food Call center: special offers, proactive issue escalation, and resolution Sports shoes company: customizable color options, built-in fitness tracker
Indifferent quality	These attributes do not result in either customer satisfaction or dissatisfaction. They might be key to design and manufacturing but go unnoticed by customers	Call center: highly polite speaking, very prompt responses Hotel: similar indifferent attributes Sports shoes company: type of shoelaces, packaging material
Reverse quality	These attributes result in dissatisfaction when highly achieved. Not all customers are alike, and preferences vary	Call center: excessive jargon, pleasantries, or scripts Hotel: elaborate photographs that set high expectations not met upon visiting Sports shoes company: overly complex design, too many color options that confuse the customer

customer experience. This strategic use of data helps businesses stay competitive and innovative, ensuring they meet customer needs effectively.

2.3 Living in an Online Society: Harnessing Big Data for Customer Value

We are all living in an online society, meaning that we are online and available for communication most of the time when we are not asleep, and some even then. Whether through our tablets, computers, phones, wristwatches, or televisions, people have access to media all the time. It does not matter if a person is standing in the shower or at a shopping mall; we are almost always connected. Marketers are responding to the customers of this new online era and transforming our digital marketing to focus on how to take advantage of all of this data to create customer value. For example, a shopper receiving a personalized coupon on their phone while browsing a store is a direct application of big data in action.

The importance of using customer data has always been crucial for maintaining customer relationships and gaining customer loyalty. The main issue has been how to make practical and effective use of the massive amount of data available. Through continuous modernization, technology has allowed the complex nature of analytics to become more disciplined, thereby increasing its impact. Marketers have now become more skilled at sourcing data from diverse customer touchpoints. For instance, online retailer Amazon built an entire empire by observing and analyzing customer behavior. By noting what customers were purchasing and searching for and then exposing them to relevant content, Amazon thrived in enhancing the customer experience.

Due to customers evolving and becoming more fragmented every day, companies must now enhance their marketing strategies to make better connections with their customer base and gain a competitive advantage. The role of business intelligence (BI) and business analytics is significant in creating relevant marketing that improves customer relationships. Business intelligence involves fact-based and data-driven decision-making with analytic technologies that use knowledge derived from big data.

A business can integrate big data and connect it with previously held data, enhancing the different approaches used to process Internet data, such as business intelligence. Big data can complement existing implementations and improve data processing. Big data has evolved as a combination of data management technologies that have progressed over time. Companies use large amounts of data to discover concealed patterns that indicate significant changes for marketers. For instance, changes in the customer buying process are critical for marketers to address before it is too late. We know someone has been surfing the web for a new vacuum cleaner for the last 2 days. If we do not act quickly, he will buy one from another vendor, and the opportunity is gone. So we decide to buy and add and place in that person's Facebook timeline as part of a narrow group we are segmenting.

The data in big data comes from everywhere: posts on social media, transaction records, GPS signals, and climate information are just a few examples. Big data is not only used by marketers but also in a wide range of areas and professions such as space administrations and pharmaceutical facilities, where extreme amounts of data are gathered and valuable insights are extracted. For example, NASA uses big data to analyze space missions and improve future explorations. Big data is also used by businesses to store data for legal reasons in case of possible court cases.

Customer touchpoints are more specific than channels; they include the different steps in which the customer interacts with a brand. In the digital world, there are customer touchpoints without physical interaction, such as online reviews and online chat. For example, a customer reading reviews about a product on a website and then chatting with customer service for more information is interacting with multiple touchpoints.

Here is an example from a project we did many years ago about how data is collected through the customer journey of people going to a shopping mall, as shown in Fig. 2.3. The idea behind this project was to try to make shopping malls more attractive again through the use of digital marketing.

Customer touchpoints are critical for collecting data in the context of big data and data mining. Each interaction between a customer and a business, whether online or offline, generates valuable data. This data can be analyzed to gain insights into customer behaviors, preferences, and trends. By understanding these patterns, businesses can tailor their marketing strategies and improve customer experiences. Data mining helps in identifying these patterns from large datasets, enabling businesses to make informed decisions. Therefore, effectively managing and analyzing customer touchpoints is essential for leveraging big data to enhance marketing efforts and overall business strategies.

To coordinate data mining across a large number of technical equipment and customer relationship management (CRM) systems, several integrated technologies are necessary. First, tracking and identifying customers need locating technologies that work both online and offline, utilizing GPS-based mobile technology and IP-based information. Data mining and inference technologies then monitor customer behaviors and preferences by analyzing their online orientations and profile changes. Cross-channel communication technology is crucial for reaching customers, appraising them, and submitting incentives to encourage visits to stores. Additionally, gamification and immersive technologies engage customers through enhancing experiences.

Finally, the transaction process involves various enterprise information systems such as the enterprise resource planning (ERP) system, CRM system, customer experience management (CEM) system, and content management system (CMS), all working together to handle transaction processing, customer data integration, and personalized marketing strategies, as can be seen in Fig. 2.4.

Coordinating data mining across various technical systems, such as CRM and ERP, requires handling large volumes of diverse data types generated at high speed and ensuring their accuracy. The vast and varied data from tracking customer activities, both online and offline, must be processed quickly and reliably to provide

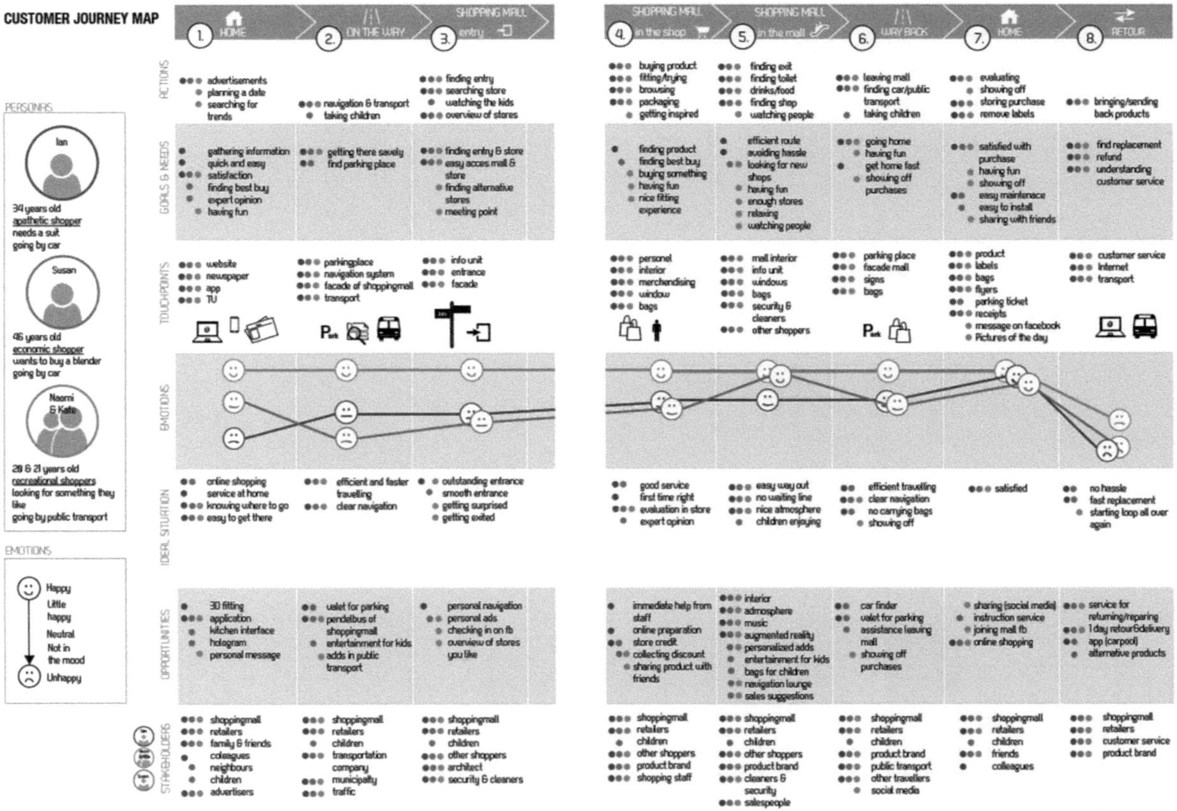

Fig. 2.3 Customer Journey Map, for each of the three given personas (left) (From Gerritsen et al. (2014)). Source: Gerritsen, B. H., Soilen, K. S., de Visser, P. B., Hoogreef, P. J., Hulst, K., Janssen, M. L., ... & Consenheim, E. (2014). Social media coming to the mall: A cross-channel response. In: Schaefer, D. (Ed.). *Product development in the socio-sphere: Game changing paradigms for 21st century breakthrough product development and innovation* (pp. 169–235). Springer

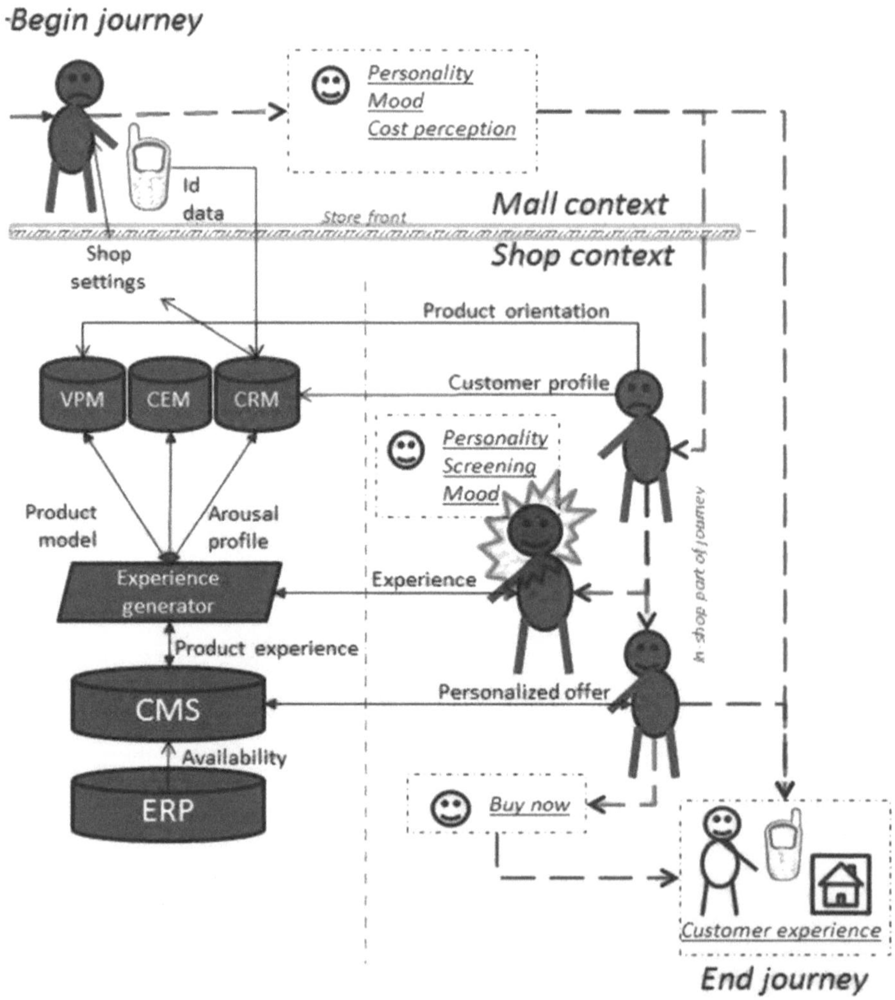

Fig. 2.4 Information flows in the shopping mall to build up the customer experience. Source: Gerritsen, B. H., Soilen, K. S., de Visser, P. B., Hoogreef, P. J., Hulst, K., Janssen, M. L., ... & Consenheim, E. (2014). Social media coming to the mall: A cross-channel response. In: Schaefer, D. (Ed.). *Product development in the socio-sphere: Game changing paradigms for 21st century breakthrough product development and innovation* (pp. 169–235). Springer

valuable insights. This integration is essential for effective customer engagement and targeted marketing strategies. Advanced analytics and technologies help manage this complex data ecosystem, enhancing business operations and customer experiences.

In this jungle of e-complexity, we need some tools and models to help us navigate. One such framework is called the four Vs.

2.4 The Four Vs of Big Data

The 4Vs (volume, variety, velocity, and veracity) are used to describe the characteristics and challenges of managing big data. They help organizations understand the complexity of big data and guide strategies for effective data processing and analysis.

2.4.1 Volume

The volume stands for the extreme amount of data that online users generate. Not all of it is valuable and can be described as white noise before it has been processed and stored. The size of big data can extend beyond petabytes of information, and it includes data from all varieties such as clickstreams, videos, and searches. For instance, a single social media platform like Facebook generates vast amounts of data daily from user interactions, posts, and multimedia uploads.

2.4.2 Variety

Variety represents the different types of online data. Data can be categorized as structured, unstructured, and semi-structured, as shown in Table 2.4.

It is good to be aware that the number of dimensions in big data and data mining can easily lead to issues when the features inputted to describe the problem are inadequate. These can be problematic because they can result in unintelligible models, which extend processing time and provide no real value.

2.4.3 Velocity

Velocity refers to the flow of data derived from continuous online activity. Internet activity never stops; it could be commercial activities, social interactions, e-commerce, and many more. A business must be able to match the speed of the data flows and process it in real time (IRT), which is defined as the time frame aligned with the user's short online interactions. For instance, during an online shopping event like Black Friday, e-commerce sites need to process vast amounts of transactions and customer data quickly to manage inventory and personalize offers.

Table 2.4 Types of data

Type of data	Description	Examples	Characteristics	Challenges
Structured data	Exists in traditional databases and is organized into charts based on specific rules	Company sales records stored in a relational database	Organized, defined, easy to access, and relatively easy to work with	Limited to predefined formats and structures, may not capture all data nuances
Unstructured data	Not organized and taken from various sources like text documents.	Emails, claim forms, web pages, social media comments	Not organized, comes from diverse sources, requires substantial preprocessing	Difficult to analyze, requires advanced processing and cleaning before analysis
Semi-structured data	Falls between structured and unstructured data; elements are separated with tags that help define the data	HTML or XML files with a consistent structure but not a rigid table format	Partially organized, elements tagged, more flexible than structured data but more organized than unstructured data	Needs special parsing techniques to interpret tags, balancing structure and flexibility

The velocity of big data matters in digital marketing because a business needs to meet its customers' expectations regarding the content it provides to be successful due to the high competitiveness of the digital world. For example, Netflix uses real-time data to recommend shows and movies to its users based on their viewing habits.

2.4.4 Value

Value is the worth derived from using the data. Not all data is valuable, and it can be an unnecessary cost for a business to store and process. Value can come from both structured and unstructured data; it is viewed as a way to gain information to make better business decisions and have the right insights before taking action· For instance, Amazon uses customer purchase history data to recommend products, which significantly enhances the shopping experience and increases sales.

2.5 Common Data Mining Tasks

As mentioned, businesses can collect an unusual amount of data through customers' digital interactions. The size and breadth of this data make it challenging to manage and extract valuable insights from it. Fortunately, there are programs available to help acquire this information. However, human oversight remains crucial in the data mining process to ensure the software provides accurate analyses and avoids costly errors.

Data mining is an interdisciplinary process that involves multiple technological fields. It includes the preparation and exploration of data, and various technological companies offer products that visualize this exploration, making data more accessible and easier to understand. Examples of visualization methods include statistical graphs and charts, which help uncover relationships and patterns in the data, aiding in effective business decision-making.

Once the data is understood and prepared, modeling techniques can be applied. Successful modeling requires well-defined variables and data encoding. Data mining aims to solve existing or potential future problems by making clear predictions and actionable insights. For instance, an online retailer may use data mining to identify which products are frequently bought together, helping optimize inventory and marketing strategies.

There are several common tasks in digital marketing that data mining can accomplish:[4]

- Description of hidden trends: Identifying patterns in big data that can reveal shifts in customer behavior. For example, a sudden increase in searches for eco-friendly products could indicate a growing consumer preference for sustainability.
- Approximation of variables: Estimating and predicting the value of a numeric variable based on other information. For instance, marketers might estimate future sales of a new product by analyzing historical data on similar product launches.
- Categorization of variables: Classifying variables into categories rather than numeric values. An example is categorizing customer feedback into positive, negative, or neutral sentiments.
- Association of different attributes: Finding correlations between attributes. A digital marketer might use this to recommend complementary products to customers, such as pairing a camera with a memory card.
- Prediction: Predicting future outcomes based on existing data. For example, predicting customer churn by analyzing engagement and purchase history.
- Clustering: Segmenting similar data into groups without a target variable. This can be used to identify distinct customer segments for targeted marketing campaigns.

When starting a data mining project, aligning the objectives with business goals is crucial. If the goal is to enhance customer experience, it may be necessary to gather new data on customer satisfaction through surveys or polls. Incomplete data can complicate the process, as machine learning algorithms require comprehensive datasets to function effectively.

Data mining is particularly useful in areas like social media marketing. For example, Facebook can analyze users' past behaviors, such as clicks, likes, and posts, to create personalized content marketing strategies. Social media interactions

[4] Verified using ChatGPT 4 (June 2024).

Table 2.5 Common data mining tasks

Task	Description	Example
Description of hidden trends	Identifying patterns in big data to reveal shifts in customer behavior	Detecting an increase in searches for eco-friendly products
Approximation of variables	Estimating and predicting numeric values based on other information	Predicting future sales of a new product based on historical data of similar product launches
Categorization of variables	Classifying variables into categories	Sorting customer feedback into positive, negative, or neutral sentiments
Association of different attributes	Finding correlations between different attributes	Recommending complementary products, such as pairing a camera with a memory card
Prediction	Predicting future outcomes based on existing data	Predicting customer churn by analyzing engagement and purchase history
Clustering	Segmenting similar data into groups without a target variable	Identifying distinct customer segments for targeted marketing campaigns

provide valuable data, but the large and often unstructured nature of this data necessitates data mining techniques to extract meaningful insights, as shown in Table 2.5.

Consider our company producing sports shoes. By analyzing purchasing habits and customer preferences, the company can recommend specific shoe models tailored to individual users. This involves using structured data (such as purchase history) and unstructured data (such as customer reviews). The company clusters customers with similar buying habits through data mining and predicts which products they might prefer, enhancing customer satisfaction and engagement.

2.6 Predictive Marketing

Big data technologies enable predictive marketing, often synonymous with data mining. Predictive marketing involves building customer profiles and integrating online and offline data, which is then accessible to employees interacting with customers. This approach significantly enhances customer service. Predictive analytics—a set of tools and algorithms—encompasses a broad range of statistical and mathematical techniques to identify patterns in data and predict future customer actions·

When working with big data and predictive marketing, it is crucial not to oversimplify big data into its three primary characteristics (the four Vs). Managing big data involves various types of data, which could range from processing large amounts of simple data to handling small amounts of very complex data, both structured and unstructured. Data management must ensure veracity, which can be considered the fifth V. This is vital in predictive marketing to ensure the prediction's accuracy and value.

Predictive marketing models can assess how a customer interacts with a website or the frequency of clicks on an email. These models, called "likelihood to buy" models, predict if a person is ready to make a purchase. By considering demographics and data such as age, gender, and job title, the model compares the behavior and attributes of previous purchasers to prospects with similar attributes. This helps marketers know how to communicate with potential customers to increase revenue. For example, an online clothing retailer might use predictive models to identify which customers are likely to buy a new product based on their past purchases and browsing history.

Predictive modeling, also known as data mining, requires intelligent resources to deliver real value. Therefore, businesses often outsource this service to specialized firms. For instance, a small e-commerce business might hire an external firm to handle its predictive analytics, allowing it to compete with larger companies.

The key to managing individual customer lifetime value and customer equity is to offer experiences tailored to each person's needs. The more personalized the customer experience, the more likely the customer will become loyal. The mindset of "one size fits all" does not work if a company aims to provide a personalized experience.

Despite widespread application, many customers still desire a more personalized experience. They often view marketing efforts as unwanted spam and are tired of it. Different demographics, psychographics, geographics, and other factors determine customer expectations regarding a customized experience. Marketers must understand their customers on a deeper level to build brand loyalty. Therefore, applying big data strategies and predictive analytics early on is beneficial.[5] An example of this process is shown in Table 2.6.

This process ensures that businesses can effectively leverage big data and predictive analytics to enhance customer experience and drive growth.

Click analytics is a predictive marketing approach used to anticipate which ads customers are likely to click on. Companies like Facebook and Google generate revenue by providing a platform for advertisements. By collecting data and predicting online behavior, these companies display ads that are more likely to be clicked, improving ad relevance and timing. The more clicks an ad receives, the more revenue it generates. For example, a digital marketer at Google might analyze click patterns to optimize ad placements, ensuring that the most relevant ads are shown to the right audience.

For example, a streaming service like Netflix customizes its recommendations based on individual viewing habits, increasing customer satisfaction and retention. It is because these companies are so good at giving customers what they want through digital marketing that they have become so popular. Box office revenues are still bigger than income from streaming services, but this is likely to change in the

[5] Idem.

Table 2.6 Predictive marketing process from data collection to actionable insights

Step	Description	Example
1. Data collection	Gathering data from various online and offline sources	E-commerce website collects data on customer purchases and browsing history
2. Data integration	Combining online and offline data to create comprehensive customer profiles	Retailer integrates in-store purchase data with online shopping behavior
3. Data analysis	Using predictive analytics tools and algorithms to identify patterns and predict future actions	Streaming service analyzes viewing habits to recommend shows
4. Modeling	Developing predictive models to assess customer behavior and likelihood to buy	Clothing retailer creates a model to predict which customers are likely to buy a new collection
5. Implementation	Applying insights to tailor marketing strategies and improve customer interactions	Online bookstore uses predictive insights to recommend books
6. Continuous improvement	Regularly updating models and strategies based on new data and insights	Digital marketer at Google optimizes ad placements based on click analytics

Table 2.7 Major streamingservices

Company	HQ	Annual sales (billion $)	Employees	Type
Disney	Burbank, CA, USA	67.4	223,000	Both
Amazon Prime Video	Seattle, WA, USA	31.8	160,000	Streaming service
Netflix	Los Gatos, CA, USA	29.7	9400	Streaming service
Warner Bros.	Burbank, CA, USA	13.4	8000	Hollywood studio
Universal Pictures	Universal City, CA, USA	11.9	11,000	Hollywood studio
Sony Pictures	Culver City, CA, USA	8.9	9800	Hollywood studio
Apple TV+	Cupertino, CA, USA	8.0	2000	Streaming service
HBO Max	Burbank, CA, USA	7.0	3000	Streaming service
Paramount Pictures	Hollywood, CA, USA	6.8	5000	Hollywood studio
Hulu	Santa Monica, CA, USA	4.4	3000	Streaming service

future. The major players in the movie entertainment business divided by streaming and box office companies, or both, are as seen in Table 2.7.

These figures are based on various market analyses and reports, reflecting the latest data available in 2024. Netflix continues to dominate the market, while Disney+ and Amazon Prime Video also hold significant shares. Other platforms like

HBO Max and Hulu have smaller but notable portions of the market, showing the diverse landscape of streaming services today.

2.7 The CRM Strategy

Businesses often use data mining when developing a customer relationship management (CRM) strategy. Customer profiles can be created based on characteristics such as age and gender in business-to-customer (B2C) scenarios or industry type in business-to-business (B2B) scenarios.

When a company aims to enhance its marketing campaign to provide a more relevant customer experience, it should focus on specifying each targeted campaign instead of using batch and blast campaigns. Batch and blast campaigns distribute the same marketing message to a large group of customers without considering the different interests and segments of the customers. Table 2.8 shows three key dimensions to consider for personalized and relevant customer experiences.

Amazon, for example, excels in these three dimensions by skillfully managing its big data. By storing customer searches and previous purchases along with other information, Amazon creates accurate representations of what products a customer might buy at different points in their customer journey. Their data-driven strategies allow them to achieve measurable results.

A company selling technological products might use big data and analytics to make geographical segmentations but can go further by utilizing data to add new target segments based on purchase behaviors and technological life cycles. This can improve the timing and rhythm of marketing communications.

Table 2.8 Key dimensions to consider for personalized and relevant customer experiences

Factor	Description	Example
Target audience	Knowing the audience and the segment is crucial. The company should understand why they are targeting them. Is it a new customer they want to build a relationship with or an old customer they wish to reconnect with?	A fitness brand might target new customers with introductory offers and loyal customers with exclusive discounts
Communication rhythm	The frequency of communication matters. Sending too many emails can be annoying, causing customers to unsubscribe. The communication should be neither too frequent nor too infrequent but should have the right rhythm	A beauty subscription box service might send a welcome email upon sign-up, follow up with a weekly newsletter, and offer personalized product recommendations monthly
Relevant content and offers	What content should be available and at what time is it best to expose the customer to it? Consider the customer's stage in their journey	If a customer has previously looked at a product without buying it, a reminder to complete the purchase can be relevant

Segmentation and predictive modeling are vital when using user data for marketing purposes. When data is segmented, it is important to

1. Understand the underlying purpose behind the segmentation.
2. Know how the treatment of customers in different segments will differ.
3. Determine how customers in different segments should react to offers.
4. Identify specific characteristics that will allocate customers to segments.

Knowledge-based systems use data mining tools to retrieve information about customers and transactions, resulting in better communication with customers. The key to knowledge-based marketing is understanding customers and their online behavior patterns. Measures such as size, frequency, and recency of purchases, known as recency-frequency-monetary value analysis (RFM), help recognize customer categories and make purchase predictions. This approach targets groups most likely to purchase a product or service, exposing customers to more relevant offers. For example, a travel agency might use RFM analysis to identify frequent travelers and target them with exclusive travel deals and packages.

In the example with our sports shoes company, an RFM analysis working procedure may look something like this, as in Fig. 2.5.

This workflow illustrates the RFM analysis process for a sports shoes company, including specific examples of customer segments based on their recency, frequency, and monetary values.

For the actual calculation of RFM, let us consider:[6]

1. Recency (R): Calculate the number of days since the customer's last purchase.
2. Frequency (F): Count the total number of purchases the customer made in the last year.
3. Monetary (M): Sum the total amount of money the customer spent in the last year.

Let us consider an example for the sports shoes company:

Variables:

- last_purchase: Days since the customer's last purchase,
- total_purchases: Number of purchases in the last year,
- total_spend: Amount of money spent in the last year.

Mathematical expressions:

[6] Verified using ChatGPT 4 (June 2024).

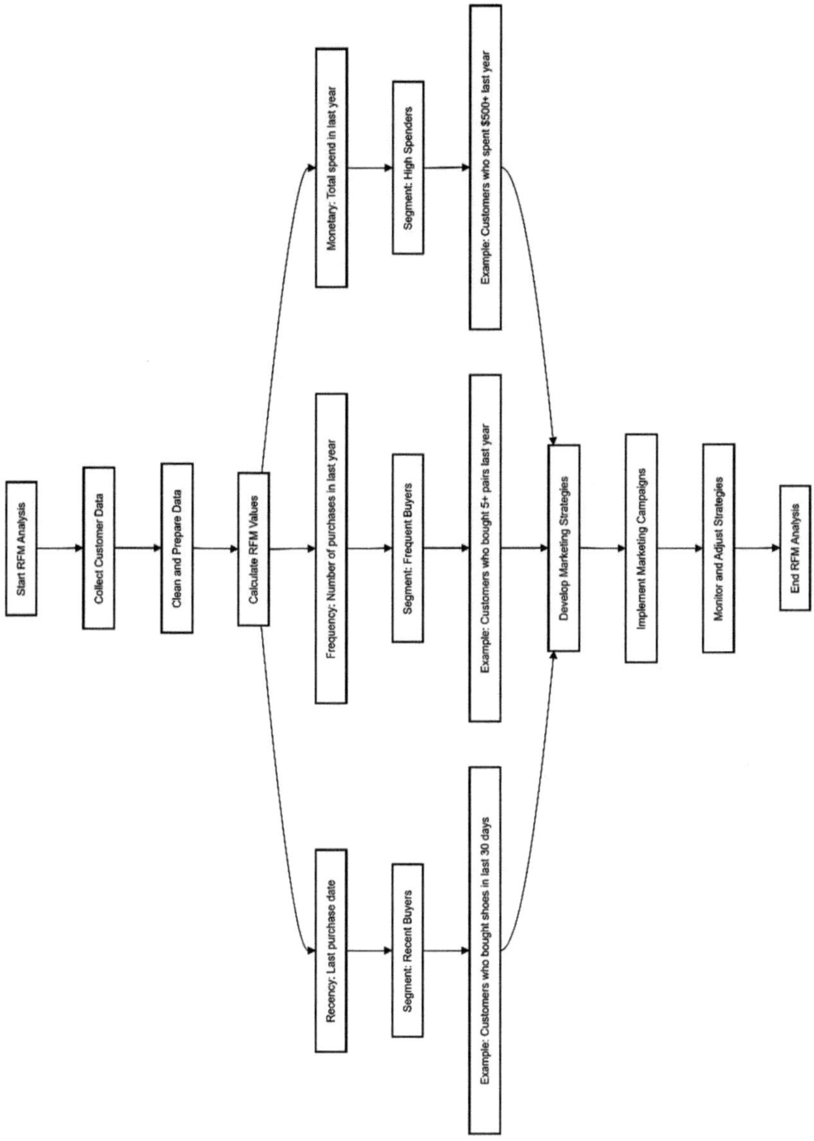

Fig. 2.5 The RFM analysis from a workflow perspective

1. Recency (R):
   R = current_date − last_purchase_date
   Example: R = 30 days
2. Frequency (F):
   F = total_purchases
   Example: F = 5 purchases
3. Monetary (M):
   M = total_spend
   Example: M = 500 dollars

   Example calculation:
   Given:

- R = 30 days (Score 5)
- F = 5 purchases (Score 3)
- M = 500 dollars (Score 3)

The RFM score is.

$$\text{RFM\_score} = 5 \cdot 100 + 3 \cdot 10 + 3 = \underline{533.}$$

This combined score helps categorize customers into segments for targeted marketing strategies.

2.8 Geolocation and Personalized Marketing Using Big Data

Big data and data mining also enables marketers to locate customers through GPS settings and IP addresses, allowing for targeted geographical segmentation to enhance customer experiences. For instance, a person using the Amazon app in northern Canada is more likely to receive a recommendation for warm shoes, which is relevant to the climate of that area, rather than a suggestion for surfboards. This approach ensures that the content and offers are tailored to the customer's specific needs and context, making them more valuable and effective.

When utilizing big data, it is crucial to consider privacy regulations, which can vary significantly depending on geographic locations. For example, the European Union's General Data Protection Regulation (GDPR) imposes strict guidelines on data usage, requiring explicit consent from users before their data can be collected and used for marketing purposes. In contrast, regulations in other regions may be less stringent. Marketers must be aware of and comply with these varying regulations to ensure that their data usage is appropriate and legal.

Here are some examples in practice:

1. Retail example: A clothing retailer can use big data to analyze the purchasing patterns of customers in different regions. If data shows that customers in coastal

areas tend to buy more swimwear during the summer months, the retailer can send targeted promotions for swimwear to customers in those areas as summer approaches.
2. Food delivery service: A food delivery app can use geolocation data to offer personalized deals. For instance, during a snowstorm, the app can send push notifications promoting hot meals and drinks to customers in affected areas, enhancing the relevance of the offer and increasing the likelihood of conversions.
3. Travel industry: Travel companies can use big data to tailor their marketing efforts based on the customer's location and travel history. For example, if a customer frequently travels to tropical destinations, the company can offer personalized deals on beach resorts and related travel packages, making the offers more appealing and timely.

By leveraging big data and respecting privacy regulations, businesses can create more personalized and relevant customer experiences, ultimately driving higher engagement and satisfaction.

2.9 Customizing Digital Experiences Through Drop Shipping

Drop shipping is a separate chapter in the book, but for now, another way to enhance digital online experiences is by integrating drop shipping into a marketing strategy. This approach serves as the middleman that connects products from outside sources directly to consumers. Drop shipping is a retail fulfillment method where a store does not keep the products it sells in stock. Instead, when a store sells a product, it purchases the item from a third party—usually a wholesaler or manufacturer—and has it shipped directly to the customer. As a result, the seller does not have to handle the product directly. It adds value to customer experience by helping businesses meet a broader range of customer needs. By reducing locational limits, businesses can reach more customers as third-party sellers ship products directly to them.

For example, a small online boutique might not have the capacity to stock a wide variety of products. By using drop shipping, the boutique can offer an extensive range of items without needing to invest in inventory. When a customer orders a product, the third-party supplier ships it directly to the customer. This method expands the boutique's product offerings and meets more customer demands. The problem here is often that it takes too long to get the product. The seller promises a quick delivery but does not foresee the longer delivery times, sometimes shipping all the way from China. The problem is often that there is no shared responsibility toward the customer.

However, when it does work, customer data is analyzed, information about a customer's shopping behavior is known, and drop shipping provides an easy way to offer more products beyond the business's original inventory. This can expose the customer to even more relevant products, further satisfying their needs. For instance, an online retailer can use predictive data to market a specific product to a potential customer. When the customer places an order on the retailer's site, the supplier then ships the product directly to the customer.

Here are some examples in practice:

1. Niche market expansion: A fitness equipment retailer may primarily stock gym equipment but, through drop shipping, can offer a wide range of related products like yoga mats, protein supplements, and sportswear without holding inventory. This allows the retailer to cater to a broader customer base interested in various fitness-related products.
2. Seasonal products: A retailer specializing in winter clothing can use drop shipping to offer summer apparel during the off-season. This strategy helps maintain customer engagement year-round without the risk of unsold seasonal inventory.
3. Personalized recommendations: An online electronics store can analyze customer data to understand preferences and behaviors. If data shows that a customer frequently purchases smart home devices, the store can use drop shipping to offer related products like smart thermostats or security cameras, even if these items are not part of the store's regular inventory.

By incorporating drop shipping and leveraging customer data, businesses can offer a more personalized and extensive range of products, ultimately enhancing the customer experience and increasing satisfaction. This does not mean that drop shipping is an area without its problems.

2.9.1 The Last-Milage Problem

One aspect of drop shipping, as well as freight shipping and transportation of goods to customers in general, is what is known as the last-milage problem. Although largely solved today, this was not the case just 2 years ago. The challenge was figuring out how to get the package from the store or post office to the customer's doorstep. Initially, some proposed solutions included deliveries by local retirees or special companies in each municipality. Eventually, prices decreased significantly, and products are now delivered directly to our door by smaller specialized delivery companies or dropped off in special metal boxes centrally located. Some customers still prefer to save money and pick up their packages from the local store, which can result in occasional rush hour queues. The ultimate solution was to offer a range of delivery options, effectively eliminating the last-mile problem as a major obstacle to e-commerce.

The research on this topic highlights that respondents prefer home delivery over other last-mile delivery methods. However, inconvenient delivery times during the day on working days are perceived as problematic. Customers are not willing to pay for the current level of home delivery services but are willing to spend on fast and same-day delivery. The study suggests that logistics management should improve delivery times, speed, and timing to charge more since customers are willing to pay extra for improved services. Additionally, customers are inclined to purchase more products to avoid shipping fees, allowing firms to adjust their business models accordingly. The need for home delivery after working hours is emphasized, and hiring part-time or informal workers could meet this demand. Legal barriers related to identification when picking up packages were identified, requiring integration with logistical management systems. Adapting delivery services to customer behavior can bridge the last-mile delivery gap, improve customer satisfaction, and be financially rewarding. These findings are applicable globally, with logistics management needing to align with societal infrastructure and customer routines.[7]

References

Gerritsen, B. H., Soilen, K. S., de Visser, P. B., Hoogreef, P. J., Hulst, K., Janssen, M. L., Horselenberg, L., Van Dijk, R. R., & Consenheim, E. (2014). Social media coming to the mall: A cross-channel response. In *Product development in the socio-sphere: Game changing paradigms for 21st century breakthrough product development and innovation* (pp. 169–235). Springer.

Patowary, M. M. I., Peulers, D., Richter, T., Melovic, A., Nilsson, D., & Söilen, K. S. (2023). Improving last-mile delivery for e-commerce: The case of Sweden. *International Journal of Retail & Distribution Management.*

Tontini, G., Söilen, K. S., & Zanchett, R. (2017). Nonlinear antecedents of customer satisfaction and loyalty in thirdparty logistics services (3PL). *Asia Pacific Journal of Marketing and Logistics, 29*(5), 1116–1135

Tontini, G., Solberg Søilen, K., & Silveira, A. (2013). How interactions of service attributes affect customer satisfaction: A study of the Kano model's attributes. *Total Quality Management & Business Excellence, 24*(11–12), 1253–1271

Further Reading

Chen, H., Chiang, R. H., & Storey, V. C. (2012). Business intelligence and analytics: From big data to big impact. *MIS Quarterly, 36*(4), 1165–1188.

Davenport, T. H., & Patil, D. J. (2012). Data scientist: The sexiest job of the 21st century. *Harvard Business Review, 90*(10), 70–76.

Dean, J., & Ghemawat, S. (2008). MapReduce: Simplified data processing on large clusters. *Communications of the ACM, 51*(1), 107–113.

Demirkan, H., & Delen, D. (2013). Leveraging the capabilities of service-oriented decision support systems: Putting analytics and big data in cloud. *Decision Support Systems, 55*(1), 412–421.

Dumbill, E. (2013). Making sense of big data. *Big Data, 1*(1), 1–2.

Gandomi, A., & Haider, M. (2015). Beyond the hype: Big data concepts, methods, and analytics. *International Journal of Information Management, 35*(2), 137–144.

Hashem, I. A. T., Yaqoob, I., Anuar, N. B., Mokhtar, S., Gani, A., & Khan, S. U. (2015). The rise of "big data" on cloud computing: Review and open research issues. *Information Systems, 47*, 98–115.

Hilbert, M., & López, P. (2011). The world's technological capacity to store, communicate, and compute information. *Science, 332*(6025), 60–65.

[7] Patowary et al. (2023).

Jagadish, H. V., Gehrke, J., Labrinidis, A., Papakonstantinou, Y., Patel, J. M., Ramakrishnan, R., & Shahabi, C. (2014). Big data and its technical challenges. *Communications of the ACM, 57*(7), 86–94.

Kaisler, S., Armour, F., Espinosa, J. A., & Money, W. (2013). Big data: Issues and challenges moving forward. In *2013 46th Hawaii International Conference on System Sciences* (pp. 995–1004). IEEE.

Kitchin, R. (2014). Big data, new epistemologies and paradigm shifts. *Big Data & Society, 1*(1), 1–12.

Laney, D. (2001). 3D data management: Controlling data volume, velocity, and variety. *META Group Research Note, 6*(70), 1.

Manyika, J., Chui, M., Brown, B., Bughin, J., Dobbs, R., Roxburgh, C., & Hung Byers, A. (2011). *Big data: The next frontier for innovation, competition, and productivity*. McKinsey Global Institute.

Mashey, J. R. (1999). Big data and the next wave of InfraStress problems, solutions, opportunities. In *1999 USENIX annual technical conference (USENIX ATC 99)*.

McAfee, A., & Brynjolfsson, E. (2012). Big data: The management revolution. *Harvard Business Review, 90*(10), 60–68.

Russom, P. (2011). Big data analytics. *TDWI Best Practices Report, Fourth Quarter, 19*, 1–34.

Sagiroglu, S., & Sinanc, D. (2013). Big data: A review. In *2013 International Conference on Collaboration Technologies and Systems (CTS)* (pp. 42–47). IEEE.

Schmidt, E., & Cohen, J. (2013). *The new digital age: Reshaping the future of people, nations and business*. Vintage.

Villars, R. L., Olofson, C. W., & Eastwood, M. (2011). Big data: What it is and why you should care. *IDC White Paper, 14*, 1–14.

White, T. (2012). *Hadoop: The definitive guide*. O'Reilly Media.

Data Quality

3

3.1 Introduction to Data Quality

In recent years, the rapid growth of digital innovation has enabled businesses to store increasingly larger databases. However, with this growth comes the challenge of maintaining data quality. Larger quantities of data often lead to inconsistencies, making it crucial for marketers to trust the data they work with. High-quality data is essential for organizational strategy, decision-making, and IT issues, yet many companies overlook its importance.

For instance, a sports shoes company that wants to expand its online presence must ensure that the customer data it collects is accurate and up-to-date to effectively target and engage potential customers.

To ensure the quality of data, academicians and practitioners have been trying to develop ways to improve data handling techniques professionally and safely. In today's digital age, it is common for organizations to store their data in data warehouses, as listed in Table 3.1, both for current use and future business decisions:

These figures reflect the competitive landscape of the data warehouse market, where companies like AWS, Google, and Microsoft dominate with significant market shares and large user bases. Each of these companies offers different features and benefits tailored to various organizational needs, ranging from large enterprises to smaller businesses.

To ensure data quality, academicians and practitioners have developed professional and safe data handling techniques. In today's digital age, organizations commonly store their data in data warehouses for current use and future business decisions. Companies like Amazon Web Services (AWS), Google BigQuery, and

K. Solberg Söilen, *Digital Marketing*, Springer Texts in Business and Economics, https://doi.org/10.1007/978-3-031-69518-6_3

Table 3.1 Major data warehouses and their market share

Company	Headquarters	Market share	Number of users
Amazon Web Services (AWS)	Seattle, USA	36%	Millions
Google (BigQuery)	Mountain View, USA	20%	Millions
Microsoft (Azure Synapse)	Redmond, USA	19%	Millions
Oracle (Autonomous Data Warehouse)	Redwood City, USA	11%	Millions
IBM (Db2 Warehouse)	Armonk, USA	5%	Hundreds of Thousands
SAP (Datasphere)	Walldorf, Germany	4%	Hundreds of Thousands
Snowflake	Bozeman, USA	3%	Hundreds of Thousands
Teradata	San Diego, USA	2%	Hundreds of Thousands
Cloudera	Palo Alto, USA	1%	Hundreds of Thousands
Yellowbrick	Palo Alto, USA	<1%	Tens of Thousands

Source: https://www.marketsandmarkets.com/Market-Reports/data-warehouse-as-a-service-market-191544663.html

Microsoft Azure Synapse dominate the data warehouse market, offering robust solutions that help businesses manage vast amounts of data efficiently.

3.2 Understanding Data Quality

Data quality is vital for organizational functionality and decision-making. As companies become more digital, relying on data quality and information systems is imperative. Poor data quality can lead to higher costs and poor decisions, which can devastate an organization. Although definitions of data quality vary, many describe it as "fitness for use," meaning data is considered high quality when it suits its intended purpose.

For example, in the context of our sports shoes company, high-quality data would include accurate customer demographics, purchase histories, and preferences. This information allows the company to create targeted marketing campaigns, design products that meet customer needs, and improve overall customer satisfaction.

High-quality data is crucial for marketers to make effective decisions and provide value through services. Poor data quality can lead to increased operational costs and customer loss. In our sports shoes company example, inaccurate data might lead to ineffective marketing efforts, wasted resources, and missed sales opportunities.

3.3 Key Concepts in Data Quality

We may say that there are two major concepts in data quality:

- Data quality dimensions: Accuracy, reliability, timeliness, currency, relevance, completeness, and consistency are key dimensions that define data quality.
- Customer data quality: Marketers collect customer data to understand behavior and satisfaction. High-quality data provides trustworthy information for personalized interactions.

3.4 Importance of Data Quality

Data is the most valuable asset for many companies, but it must have quality to be valuable. Ensuring high-quality data can lead to improved decision-making, reduced operational costs, and increased customer satisfaction.

For instance, our sports shoes company can use high-quality data to identify market trends, optimize inventory management, and enhance customer loyalty programs. Or when Netflix decides to spend another 100 million USD on a new season of a series, they are going to make sure they know exactly what people thought about the first one.

When insufficient effort is placed into ensuring high-quality data, companies may make wrong decisions based on poor information, leading to operational and time-consuming costs. High-quality data is essential for reducing financial costs and easing decision-making. For example, if the sports shoes company relies on outdated or incorrect sales data, it might overproduce certain styles that do not meet current customer demands, resulting in excess inventory and lost revenue.

3.5 Data Collection Methods

The most important data collection tools include

- Customer relationship management (CRM): CRM helps businesses maximize customer experience and follow up on consumer behavior. For CRM to work

effectively, it relies on a trustworthy, quality database. Successful CRM processes require excellent cooperation and information-sharing across departments. In the case of our sports shoes company, a CRM system can track customer interactions, purchase history, and preferences, enabling personalized marketing and improved customer service.
- Cookies: Cookies facilitate the collection of customer data by placing small files on the user's computer.

3.6 Data Quality Dimensions in Detail

The way we check for the quality dimension in data includes variables such as:[1]

- Accuracy: Ensures that data is reliable, accurate, and free from errors. Old or incorrect data can lead marketers to target the wrong group of consumers. For the sports shoes company, accurate data means knowing which products are popular among different demographic groups and ensuring marketing efforts are correctly targeted.
- Reliability: Describes how dependable and capable the data is. Knowing the data's source is crucial for determining its reliability. The sports shoes company must ensure that its data sources, whether first-party customer data or third-party market research, are trustworthy and reliable.
- Timeliness: Refers to the age of the collected data and its relevance to current reality. Continuous data collection is essential for timeliness and applicability. The sports shoes company needs up-to-date sales data to make informed decisions about inventory and marketing strategies.
- Currency: Measures how up-to-date the information is and its relevance to the present situation. For the sports shoes company, current data on customer preferences and market trends is essential for staying competitive.
- Relevance: Assesses how valuable the data is for the specific task it is intended for. Ensuring that the data is adapted to the task from the beginning saves time and money. For example, data on customer feedback is relevant for improving product designs and customer service.
- Completeness: Determines how well the database aligns with reality. Data is considered complete when all mandatory values are included. In the sports shoes company, completeness means having comprehensive data on all customer transactions and interactions.
- Consistency: Refers to how comparable the data is across various systems and processes. Equivalent data stored consistently makes it easier to manage and use. For the sports shoes company, consistent data across all sales channels (online and offline) is crucial for accurate reporting and analysis.

[1] Verified using ChatGPT 4 (June 2024).

3.7 The Benefits and Challenges of Data Quality

Ensuring high-quality data can lead to numerous benefits, including improved decision-making, reduced operational costs, and increased customer satisfaction. High-quality data helps reduce financial costs and ease decision-making.

For instance, if the sports shoes company consistently maintains high-quality data, it can streamline operations, reduce errors, and enhance customer experiences.

Conversely, poor data quality can have significant disadvantages. It can lead to misleading or incomplete information, resulting in marketers making incorrect decisions based on untrustworthy data. For example, if the sports shoes company uses outdated customer data, it might launch an ineffective marketing campaign targeting the wrong audience. Companies then spend significant time and money cleaning their databases instead of implementing high-quality data management practices from the start.

3.8 Key Takeaways

In summary, data quality is a critical aspect of modern business operations. Ensuring high-quality data can lead to improved decision-making, reduced operational costs, and increased customer satisfaction. Organizations must prioritize data management and invest in systems and processes that maintain data accuracy, reliability, timeliness, currency, relevance, completeness, and consistency. By doing so, businesses can harness the full potential of their data, gaining a competitive edge in the market and driving long-term success.

For the sports shoes company, maintaining high-quality data is essential for understanding customer preferences, optimizing marketing strategies, and improving overall business performance. By investing in data quality, the company can ensure that it meets customer expectations, stays ahead of competitors, and drives sustainable growth.

3.9 Conclusion

Digital marketing is not just about getting the hardware and people with new skills but making sure that all the data that goes into the system is valuable.

More organizations are recognizing the importance of high-quality data in the digital age. Large databases are standard tools used across different departments to access valuable information for decision-making and analysis. Data mining is the technique that allows organizations to analyze and divide large quantities of data into understandable information they can act on. Another benefit of high-quality data is that it allows us to trace the data's origin, making it easier to trust the information.

Overall, ensuring data quality is essential for any business looking to succeed in today's competitive environment. High-quality data helps reduce costs, improve decision-making, and enhance customer satisfaction, ultimately leading to better business outcomes. For our sports shoes company, this means being able to provide customers with the best products and services, informed by accurate and reliable data.

This reflects the competitive landscape of the data warehouse market, where companies like AWS, Google, and Microsoft dominate with significant market shares and large user bases. Each of these companies offers different features and benefits tailored to various organizational needs, ranging from large enterprises to smaller businesses.

Further Reading

Chen, H., Chiang, R. H., & Storey, V. C. (2012). Business intelligence and analytics: From big data to big impact. *MIS Quarterly, 36*(4), 1165–1188.

Davenport, T. H., & Patil, D. J. (2012). Data scientist: The sexiest job of the 21st century. *Harvard Business Review, 90*(10), 70–76.

Dean, J., & Ghemawat, S. (2008). MapReduce: Simplified data processing on large clusters. *Communications of the ACM, 51*(1), 107–113.

Demirkan, H., & Delen, D. (2013). Leveraging the capabilities of service-oriented decision support systems: Putting analytics and big data in cloud. *Decision Support Systems, 55*(1), 412–421.

Dumbill, E. (2013). Making sense of big data. *Big Data, 1*(1), 1–2.

Gandomi, A., & Haider, M. (2015). Beyond the hype: Big data concepts, methods, and analytics. *International Journal of Information Management, 35*(2), 137–144.

Hashem, I. A. T., Yaqoob, I., Anuar, N. B., Mokhtar, S., Gani, A., & Khan, S. U. (2015). The rise of "big data" on cloud computing: Review and open research issues. *Information Systems, 47*, 98–115.

Hilbert, M., & López, P. (2011). The world's technological capacity to store, communicate, and compute information. *Science, 332*(6025), 60–65.

Jagadish, H. V., Gehrke, J., Labrinidis, A., Papakonstantinou, Y., Patel, J. M., Ramakrishnan, R., & Shahabi, C. (2014). Big data and its technical challenges. *Communications of the ACM, 57*(7), 86–94.

Kaisler, S., Armour, F., Espinosa, J. A., & Money, W. (2013). Big data: Issues and challenges moving forward. In *2013 46th Hawaii international conference on system sciences* (pp. 995–1004). IEEE.

Kitchin, R. (2014). Big data, new epistemologies and paradigm shifts. *Big Data & Society, 1*(1), 1–12.

Laney, D. (2001). 3D data management: Controlling data volume, velocity, and variety. *META Group Research Note, 6*(70), 1.

Manyika, J., Chui, M., Brown, B., Bughin, J., Dobbs, R., Roxburgh, C., & Hung Byers, A. (2011). *Big data: The next frontier for innovation, competition, and productivity*. McKinsey Global Institute.

McAfee, A., & Brynjolfsson, E. (2012). Big data: The management revolution. *Harvard Business Review, 90*(10), 60–68.

Patowary, M. M. I., Peulers, D., Richter, T., Melovic, A., Nilsson, D., & Söilen, K. S. (2023). Improving last-mile delivery for e-commerce: The case of Sweden. *International Journal of Retail & Distribution Management.*

Russom, P. (2011). Big data analytics. TDWI best practices report. *Fourth Quarter, 19*, 1–34.

Sagiroglu, S., & Sinanc, D. (2013). Big data: A review. In *2013 international conference on collaboration technologies and systems (CTS)* (pp. 42–47). IEEE.

Schmidt, E., & Cohen, J. (2013). *The new digital age: Reshaping the future of people, nations and business*. Vintage.

Villars, R. L., Olofson, C. W., & Eastwood, M. (2011). Big data: What it is and why you should care. *IDC White Paper, 14*, 1–14.

White, T. (2012). *Hadoop: The definitive guide*. O'Reilly Media.

4 Customer Analytics; Profiles, Personas, Personalization

For a sports shoes company, understanding customer preferences, purchasing behavior, and brand engagement is crucial. This knowledge helps tailor marketing messages and product offerings to match customer needs and enhance satisfaction.

Before the Internet, brands communicated primarily through one-way channels like press, radio, and television, exerting considerable control over consumers. However, the digital era has transformed marketing into an interactive dialog between consumers and brands, focusing on providing personalized experiences. Customers now expect companies to understand and respond to their desires, posing significant challenges for businesses. To succeed, companies must move beyond segmentation to deliver personalized messages that resonate with individual customers. For example, two customers of the same age, gender, and socioeconomic status may have completely different interests and purchasing behaviors, highlighting the limitations of relying solely on demographic data.

Customer analytics forms the foundation and leads to the creation of customer profiles and personas, ultimately resulting in personalization. Customer profiles are built using behavioral and demographic data, while personas involve segmentation to understand various customer types. This process leads to personalized marketing strategies, enhancing customer engagement and increasing sales.

For instance, the sports shoes company can use behavioral data to understand customer interactions and demographic data for targeted offers.

In today's connected world, customer analytics is more critical than ever. Customers have constant access to information about products, prices, and shopping locations, making it essential for companies to understand and predict their behavior. The sports shoes company, for example, needs to gather and analyze data

K. Solberg Söilen, *Digital Marketing*, Springer Texts in Business and Economics, https://doi.org/10.1007/978-3-031-69518-6_4

to anticipate customer needs and deliver relevant offers. Personalized marketing strategies, though resource-intensive, are essential for engaging customers and driving sales. Creating accurate customer profiles and buyer personas allows the company to tailor its marketing efforts, resulting in higher customer engagement and satisfaction.

4.1 Background

Customer analytics is the foundation of success in the digital age, significantly impacting sales and marketing strategies. The shift from brand-centric to customer-centric marketing demands that companies deliver relevant content based on behavioral data, not just demographic data. This approach requires tools like customer profiles, personas, and personalization to understand customers deeply.

For a sports shoes company, understanding customer preferences, purchasing behavior, and engagement with the brand is crucial. This knowledge helps tailor marketing messages and product offerings to match customer needs and enhance satisfaction.

Before the Internet, brands had considerable control over consumers, communicating primarily through one-way channels like press, radio, and television. However, the digital era has transformed marketing into an interactive dialog between consumers and brands, with a focus on providing personalized experiences. Customers now expect companies to understand and respond to their desires, posing a significant challenge for businesses. To succeed, companies must move beyond segmentation to deliver personalized messages that resonate with individual customers, as highlighted in Fig. 4.1. For instance, two customers of the same age, gender, and socioeconomic status may have completely different interests and purchasing behaviors, highlighting the limitations of relying solely on demographic data.

Explanation of the figure:

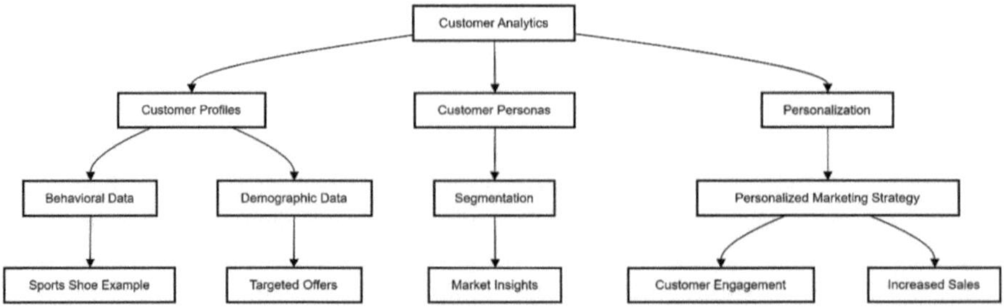

Fig. 4.1 The relationship between customer analytics, profiles, personas, and personalization

- Customer analytics forms the foundation and leads to the creation of customer profiles and customer personas and ultimately personalization.
- Customer profiles are built using behavioral data and demographic data.
- Customer personas involve segmentation to understand various customer types.
- Personalization leverages these profiles and personas to create a personalized marketing strategy.
- This strategy leads to customer engagement and increased sales.
- Examples include using behavioral data to understand customer interactions (like the sports shoe example) and demographic data for targeted offers.
- Segmentation provides market insights which are crucial for developing effective strategies.

The figure shows how Customer Analytics drives the process of understanding and segmenting customers, which is then used to create personalized marketing strategies to enhance customer engagement and sales.

4.2 Key Takeaways

In today's connected world, customer analytics is more critical than ever. Customers have constant access to information about products, prices, and shopping locations, making it essential for companies to understand and predict their behavior.

The sports shoes company, for example, needs to gather and analyze data to anticipate customer needs and deliver relevant offers. Personalized marketing strategies, though resource-intensive, are essential for engaging customers and driving sales. Creating accurate customer profiles and buyer personas allows the company to tailor its marketing efforts, resulting in higher customer engagement and satisfaction.

4.3 Customer Analytics

Customer analytics platforms answer key questions about customer behavior and interactions. To get meaningful insights, companies must ask open and specific questions. Building relationships with individual customers, rather than large groups, is crucial for effective marketing. For instance, the sports shoes company can use customer analytics to track purchase history, browsing behavior, and preferences, allowing for personalized recommendations and targeted marketing campaigns.

Customer analytics involves using mathematical models and algorithms to classify, describe, and predict customer behavior. By analyzing historical data and applying it to current information, companies can anticipate future needs and preferences. This process helps create more effective marketing campaigns, reducing costs by targeting likely buyers and increasing sales and customer loyalty. It also helps identify dissatisfied customers, enabling the company to address issues before they harm the brand's reputation.

The sports shoes company can leverage customer analytics to enhance its marketing strategies. By understanding each customer's behavior, the company can offer personalized experiences that build loyalty and drive sales. For example, analyzing purchase patterns and feedback can help the company design new products that meet customer preferences, improving overall satisfaction and engagement.

4.4 The Role of Technology

Technology plays a vital role in customer analytics, enabling companies to gather and analyze vast amounts of data. The competition between brands intensifies the need for customer-centric strategies and personal experiences. Customers expect seamless interactions across various channels, from traditional to digital. Every purchase, whether in-store or online, generates data that companies can analyze to identify buying patterns, improve satisfaction, and predict future needs.

For the sports shoes company, utilizing big data and advanced analytics tools can provide a deeper understanding of customer behavior. However, the effectiveness of these tools depends on the company's ability to interpret and act on the data. The data must be relevant, updated, and substantial enough to draw meaningful conclusions. By accurately analyzing collected data, the company can create a detailed and credible picture of each customer, enabling personalized marketing strategies that enhance the customer experience. The first step is to know what each type of software can do, as exemplified in Table 4.1.

An explanation of the content in the table:[1]

[1] Verified using ChatGPT 4 (June 2024).

Table 4.1 Types of technology and software commonly used in companies for customer analytics

Technology/software	Primary function	Examples
Customer relationship management (CRM) systems	Manage customer data, track interactions, sales automation	Salesforce, HubSpot CRM, Microsoft dynamics
Data management platforms (DMP)	Collect, manage, and analyze data from various sources	Adobe Audience Manager, Oracle BlueKai
Marketing automation tools	Automate marketing processes, personalized email campaigns	Marketo, Pardot, Mailchimp
Web analytics tools	Track and analyze website traffic and user behavior	Google analytics, Adobe analytics
Data analytics platforms	Analyze large datasets to gain insights	Tableau, Looker, IBM Watson Analytics
Personalization engines	Deliver personalized content and experiences	Dynamic Yield, Evergage, Optimizely
Customer data platforms (CDP)	Unify customer data from multiple sources into a single view	Segment, Tealium, mParticle
Social media analytics tools	Analyze social media interactions and engagement	Hootsuite, Sprout Social, Brandwatch
A/B testing tools	Test different marketing strategies and website elements	Optimizely, VWO, Unbounce
Predictive analytics software	Predict future customer behavior based on historical data	SAS Predictive Analytics, RapidMiner
Data visualization tools	Visualize data to identify trends and insights	Tableau, Power BI, Domo
Big data platforms	Process and analyze large volumes of data	Hadoop, Apache Spark, Cloudera
Machine learning algorithms	Develop predictive models and segment customers	TensorFlow, scikit-learn, Amazon SageMaker
Business intelligence (BI) tools	Provide reporting and dashboards for data analysis	SAP BusinessObjects, QlikView, IBM Cognos
Customer feedback tools	Collect and analyze customer feedback and surveys	SurveyMonkey, Qualtrics, Medallia

- Customer relationship management (CRM) systems: Used to manage customer relationships and track interactions. Examples include Salesforce, HubSpot CRM, and Microsoft Dynamics.
- Data management platforms (DMP): These platforms collect, manage, and analyze data from various sources to create targeted marketing campaigns. Examples are Adobe Audience Manager and Oracle BlueKai.
- Marketing automation tools: These tools automate marketing processes such as email campaigns, social media posting, and lead management. Examples include Marketo, Pardot, and Mailchimp.
- Web analytics tools: Used to track and analyze website traffic and user behavior. Google Analytics and Adobe Analytics are common examples.
- Data analytics platforms: These platforms help analyze large datasets to gain insights. Examples include Tableau, Looker, and IBM Watson Analytics.

- Personalization engines: These engines deliver personalized content and user experiences based on customer data. Examples are Dynamic Yield, Evergage, and Optimizely.
- Customer data platform (CDP): CDPs unify customer data from multiple sources into a single view for better customer understanding and targeting. Examples include Segment, Tealium, and mParticle.
- Social media analytics tools: These tools analyze social media interactions and engagement to inform marketing strategies. Examples are Hootsuite, Sprout Social, and Brandwatch.
- A/B testing tools: These tools test different marketing strategies and website elements to determine the most effective approach. Examples include Optimizely, VWO, and Unbounce.
- Predictive analytics software: These software solutions predict future customer behavior based on historical data. Examples include SAS Predictive Analytics and RapidMiner.
- Data visualization tools: These tools help visualize data to identify trends and insights easily. Examples include Tableau, Power BI, and Domo.
- Big data platforms: These platforms process and analyze large volumes of data. Common examples are Hadoop, Apache Spark, and Cloudera.
- Machine learning algorithms: These algorithms are used to develop predictive models and segment customers. Examples include TensorFlow, scikit-learn, and Amazon SageMaker.
- Business intelligence (BI) tools: BI tools provide reporting and dashboards for data analysis. Examples are SAP BusinessObjects, QlikView, and IBM Cognos.
- Customer feedback tools: These tools collect and analyze customer feedback and surveys to improve products and services. Examples include SurveyMonkey, Qualtrics, and Medallia.

The table provides an overview of the technologies and software used in the industry to implement customer analytics and personalization effectively.

4.5 Practical Applications and Benefits

So, what does all of this mean, what is it for? Well, customer analytics helps companies create more effective marketing campaigns based on a deep understanding of customer demographics, decision processes, browsing behavior, and purchase history.

For example, the sports shoes company can use this data to design targeted promotions and personalized offers, increasing the likelihood of customer engagement and purchases. The company can also identify trends and preferences, allowing it to stay ahead of competitors by meeting customer demands more effectively.

By investing in customer analytics, the sports shoes company can improve customer satisfaction, loyalty, and overall business performance. Understanding customer behavior enables the company to develop products and services that align with customer needs, ultimately driving growth and profitability.

4.6 Conclusion

Customer analytics is a critical component of modern marketing, providing valuable insights that drive personalized experiences and customer-centric strategies.

For the sports shoes company, leveraging customer analytics can enhance marketing efforts, improve customer satisfaction, and increase sales. By understanding and predicting customer behavior, the company can deliver relevant offers and build lasting relationships with its customers. Investing in customer analytics is essential for staying competitive in the digital age and achieving long-term success.

Further Reading

Adam, M., Wessel, M., & Benlian, A. (2020). AI-based chatbots in customer service and their effects on user compliance. *Electronic Markets, 30*(3), 427–445. https://doi.org/10.1007/s12525-019-00353-7

Baker, T. (2016). Data privacy in the digital age. *Journal of Business Ethics, 134*(2), 255–269. https://doi.org/10.1007/s10551-014-2418-8

Bhat, S., Pande, N., & Awasthi, A. (2018). Artificial intelligence: Transforming the future of marketing. *Journal of Business Research, 94*, 120–137. https://doi.org/10.1016/j.jbusres.2018.02.017

Breur, T. (2011). Data quality essentials for customer relationship management. *Journal of Database Marketing & Customer Strategy Management, 18*(1), 15–24. https://doi.org/10.1057/dbm.2011.3

Brown, B., Chui, M., & Manyika, J. (2011). Are you ready for the era of 'big data'? *McKinsey Quarterly, 4*(1), 24–35. Retrieved from https://www.mckinsey.com/business-functions/mckinsey-digital/our-insights/are-you-ready-for-the-era-of-big-data

Chen, H., Chiang, R. H. L., & Storey, V. C. (2012). Business intelligence and analytics: From big data to big impact. *MIS Quarterly, 36*(4), 1165–1188. https://doi.org/10.2307/41703503

Davenport, T. H., & Harris, J. G. (2017). *Competing on analytics: Updated, with a new introduction: The new science of winning*. Harvard Business Review Press.

Godse, M., & Garg, S. (2012). Cloud computing and its application to big data. *International Journal of Computer Applications, 38*(3), 17–20. https://doi.org/10.5120/4645-6734

Gupta, S., Hanssens, D. M., Hardie, B. G., Kahn, W., Kumar, V., Lin, N., & Sriram, S. (2006). Modeling customer lifetime value. *Journal of Service Research, 9*(2), 139–155. https://doi.org/10.1177/1094670506293810

Hennig-Thurau, T., Gwinner, K. P., Walsh, G., & Gremler, D. D. (2004). Electronic word-of-mouth via consumer-opinion platforms: What motivates consumers to articulate themselves on the Internet? *Journal of Interactive Marketing, 18*(1), 38–52. https://doi.org/10.1002/dir.10073

Hoberg, P., Krcmar, H., & Welz, B. (2017). Skills for digital transformation. *IT Professional, 19*(6), 14–19. https://doi.org/10.1109/MITP.2017.4241459

Järvinen, J., & Karjaluoto, H. (2015). The use of Web analytics for digital marketing performance measurement. *Industrial Marketing Management, 50*, 117–127. https://doi.org/10.1016/j.indmarman.2015.04.009

Kietzmann, J., Paschen, J., & Treen, E. (2018). Artificial intelligence in advertising. *Journal of Advertising Research, 58*(3), 263–267. https://doi.org/10.2501/JAR-2018-037

Lim, W. M. (2021). Data analytics and the role of emotion in the digital marketing age. *Journal of Business Research, 125*, 920–927. https://doi.org/10.1016/j.jbusres.2019.08.036

Luo, X., & Sun, J. (2015). Strategic value of big data: A research agenda. *Journal of Management Information Systems, 32*(2), 171–199. https://doi.org/10.1080/07421222.2015.1063292

Manyika, J., Chui, M., Brown, B., Bughin, J., Dobbs, R., Roxburgh, C., & Hung Byers, A. (2011). *Big data: The next frontier for innovation, competition, and productivity*. McKinsey Global Institute. Retrieved from https://www.mckinsey.com/business-functions/mckinsey-digital/our-insights/big-data-the-next-frontier-for-innovation

Marr, B. (2016). *Big data in practice: How 45 successful companies used big data analytics to deliver extraordinary results*. Wiley.

McAfee, A., & Brynjolfsson, E. (2012). Big data: The management revolution. *Harvard Business Review, 90*(10), 60–68. Retrieved from https://hbr.org/2012/10/big-data-the-management-revolution

Patowary, M. M. I., Peulers, D., Richter, T., Melovic, A., Nilsson, D., & Söilen, K. S. (2023). Improving last-mile delivery for e-commerce: The case of Sweden. *International Journal of Logistics Research and Applications, 26*, 872. https://doi.org/10.1080/13675567.2022.2034479

Provost, F., & Fawcett, T. (2013). *Data science for business: What you need to know about data mining and data-analytic thinking*. O'Reilly Media.

Rust, R. T., & Huang, M. H. (2014). The service revolution and the transformation of marketing science. *Marketing Science, 33*(2), 206–221. https://doi.org/10.1287/mksc.2013.0836

Shankar, V., & Yadav, M. S. (2011). Innovations in shopper marketing: Current insights and future research issues. *Journal of Retailing, 87*, S29–S42. https://doi.org/10.1016/j.jretai.2011.04.007

Stone, M., & Woodcock, N. (2014). Interactive, direct and digital marketing: A future that depends on better use of business intelligence. *Journal of Research in Interactive Marketing, 8*(1), 4–17. https://doi.org/10.1108/JRIM-07-2013-0046

Wedel, M., & Kannan, P. K. (2016). Marketing analytics for data-rich environments. *Journal of Marketing, 80*(6), 97–121. https://doi.org/10.1509/jm.15.0413

Monitoring Performance and Crushing the Numbers, KPIs

5

5.1 Background

In today's information society, managers and organizations are flooded with data. To make the best decisions, it is essential to transform data into structured information presented in an easy-to-read format that supports analysis. Various software vendors have developed solutions called dashboards. Efficient distribution of dashboards can reduce the need for financial and operational reports and contribute to better decision-making and improved performance.

Organizations often rely on metrics for monitoring and decision-making, expecting professionals to think quantitatively and make data-driven decisions. Key performance indicators (KPIs) are essential to understanding performance and decision-making. KPIs are quantitative or qualitative measures that enable organizations to measure their effectiveness in achieving strategic and operational goals. KPIs vary and can be based on industry-specific standards. They can be referred to in a digital or non-digital context and usually relate to all business areas, such as financial structures, productivity, or consumer behavior.

5.2 Key Takeaways

Data-based decision-making involves using data and various metrics to make strategic business decisions to achieve set goals in an organization. Including the entire organization in the process creates engagement, essential for regularly analyzing information. Decision support systems are used to collect and sort data, making it easier to find critical information. Setting performance targets and indicators helps the company achieve its strategic goals. The KPI is a metric that allows companies to show their success. Using KPIs, businesses can see in which direction they are heading and if course corrections are necessary. Clear and simple KPIs focused on relevant metrics, regularly reviewed and reported, with long-term and sustainable goals, are essential.

K. Solberg Söilen, *Digital Marketing*, Springer Texts in Business and Economics, https://doi.org/10.1007/978-3-031-69518-6_5

5.3 Data-Based Decision-Making

Organizations make decisions based on data, a valuable asset to support decision-making. Data-driven decision-making is defined as "the practice of basing decisions on the analysis of data rather than solely on intuition." This approach ensures faster and more informed decisions, leading to a stronger bottom line, greater creativity, commercial success, and more commitment and collaboration from employees.

A culture that encourages critical thinking and curiosity becomes the norm, requiring people to have access to the information they need and the knowledge and authority to act on it. Creating these features encourages data-driven decision-making at multiple levels, allowing companies to examine and review information regularly to discover essential insights that lead to action.

5.3.1 Measures to Make Data-Driven Decisions

To make data-driven decisions, companies should

- Identify business goals: Understand the organization's goals, such as increased sales or brand awareness.
- Investigate business groups for essential data sources: Ensure people throughout the organization understand the goals to guide analytical distribution.
- Collect and prepare the information needed: Build an effective dashboard with reliable and efficient data sources.
- View and explore data: Use visual elements like charts and graphs to convey insights and influence decisions.
- Develop insights: Communicate ideas engagingly, discovering opportunities and risks that affect success.
- Act on and share your insights: Take action based on discoveries, collaborating through dashboards or informative text and visualizations.

5.4 Business Intelligence (BI)

Business intelligence (BI) is a set of concepts and methods that, with fact-based support systems, can improve business decisions. BI focuses on the processes, tools, and methods that enable data-based decision-making, allowing for effective and objective decisions. BI software and methods enable a systematic, integrated strategy combining business strategy with core processes and activities.

Dashboards that are methodical and well designed can effectively display important performance-related charts and indicators, helping people in an organization focus on the most important activities and drivers. Most dashboards are graphic, dynamic, and easy to use, empowering more people to monitor and analyze relevant information for informed decisions.

Dashboards are applications presenting data from a BI system, facilitating the analysis and monitoring of business processes. Data is translated into tables and charts, making it easier to understand and act upon.

5.5 Key Performance Indicators (KPIs)

KPIs are metrics that show, over a limited period, how effective a company is at achieving goals. By implementing and analyzing KPIs, businesses can see if development is moving in the desired direction. KPIs are often the most valuable content in dashboards, providing insights into various areas of the business.

Monitoring KPIs helps organizations spend more time on important activities that drive performance and less time on less relevant activities. KPIs can also be tools for internal and external communication, creating a consistent message and driving behaviors that align with the organization's goals and strategies.

5.5.1 Leading and Lagging KPIs

Leading KPIs predict the future and measure metrics leading to the goal, while lagging KPIs are historical metrics that measure success in achieving set goals. Combining both types of KPIs is advantageous for organizations.

5.5.2 Implementation, Feedback, and Control of KPIs

Goal structure, follow-up, and feedback are crucial for successful goal management and strategy. Implementing KPIs involves identifying essential metrics, setting relevant goals, and monitoring progress to make necessary adjustments.

5.5.3 Traffic Signal

Using a "traffic light" system with green, orange, and red color schemes to show status is a popular method for presenting KPIs.

5.5.4 Different Objectives with Different Aims

KPIs should be designed based on the organization's set goals. Clear goals ensure that measures are taken when necessary. Some KPIs should be channel-specific, while others relate to overall business goals.

5.5.5 Smart KPI

The SMART criteria evaluate the relevance of performance indicators, ensuring they are specific, measurable, attainable, relevant, and time-specific.

5.6 The Digital Marketing Environment with KPIs and Web Analytics

Digital marketing uses digital technology to promote products or services. Measuring success for business initiatives and resources is crucial, particularly in digital marketing. KPIs can measure the effectiveness of digital marketing efforts, informing strategy adjustments to achieve goals.

5.6.1 Examples of KPIs Used in Digital Marketing

Here is a list of the more common KPIs:

- Unique visitors to the site: Indicates the effectiveness of other marketing efforts
- Bounce rate: Shows how long visitors stay on the site and their next actions
- Conversion rate: Measures how often visitors follow the call to action
- Geography: Provides insights into where visitors are coming from
- Comments and social: Measures engagement with content
- Sales revenue: Tracks revenue generated by digital marketing efforts

By effectively monitoring and analyzing these KPIs, organizations can make data-driven decisions that enhance their marketing strategies and improve overall business performance.

5.7 Key Takeaways

Monitoring performance and utilizing KPIs are critical for modern organizations to achieve strategic and operational goals. Transforming data into structured, actionable insights allows businesses to make informed decisions that drive success. The integration of business intelligence tools, effective dashboards, and well-designed KPIs enables companies to track progress, identify areas for improvement, and adapt strategies as needed. In digital marketing, KPIs and web analytics are crucial for assessing campaign effectiveness and optimizing customer engagement. A strong focus on data-driven decision-making and continuous evaluation of KPIs leads to better performance, increased customer satisfaction, and sustained business growth.

5.7.1 Example of the Sports Shoes Company

Consider our sports shoes company that uses customer analytics to tailor its marketing strategies. The company sets KPIs such as the number of unique visitors to its website, the bounce rate, and the conversion rate for online purchases. By analyzing these KPIs, the company identifies that a high bounce rate on a specific product page indicates a need for better product descriptions and images. The company also tracks sales revenue generated by different marketing campaigns to determine which strategies are most effective. By regularly reviewing and adjusting its KPIs, the sports shoes company can optimize its marketing efforts, improve customer engagement, and increase sales.

By implementing these practices, the sports shoes company can stay competitive in the market, continuously improving its strategies based on data-driven insights and achieving long-term success. To start to get an idea of how to use KPIs, see Fig. 5.1.

This figure outlines the key processes for monitoring performance and using KPIs in a sports shoes company. The process begins with identifying business goals, such as increasing sales and brand awareness, and setting specific goals for each department. Data is then collected and prepared from various sources, including sales data, customer feedback, and CRM systems. This data is visualized and analyzed using dashboards to identify trends, top-selling products, and customer preferences. Insights are developed to understand factors driving sales, identify underperforming areas, and comprehend customer behavior. These insights are acted upon by adjusting marketing strategies, optimizing inventory, and enhancing customer experiences, with the entire cycle being continuously monitored and refined using KPIs such as sales revenue, conversion rates, and customer satisfaction. To lead these processes is what will be expected of you if you have a graduate education in marketing.

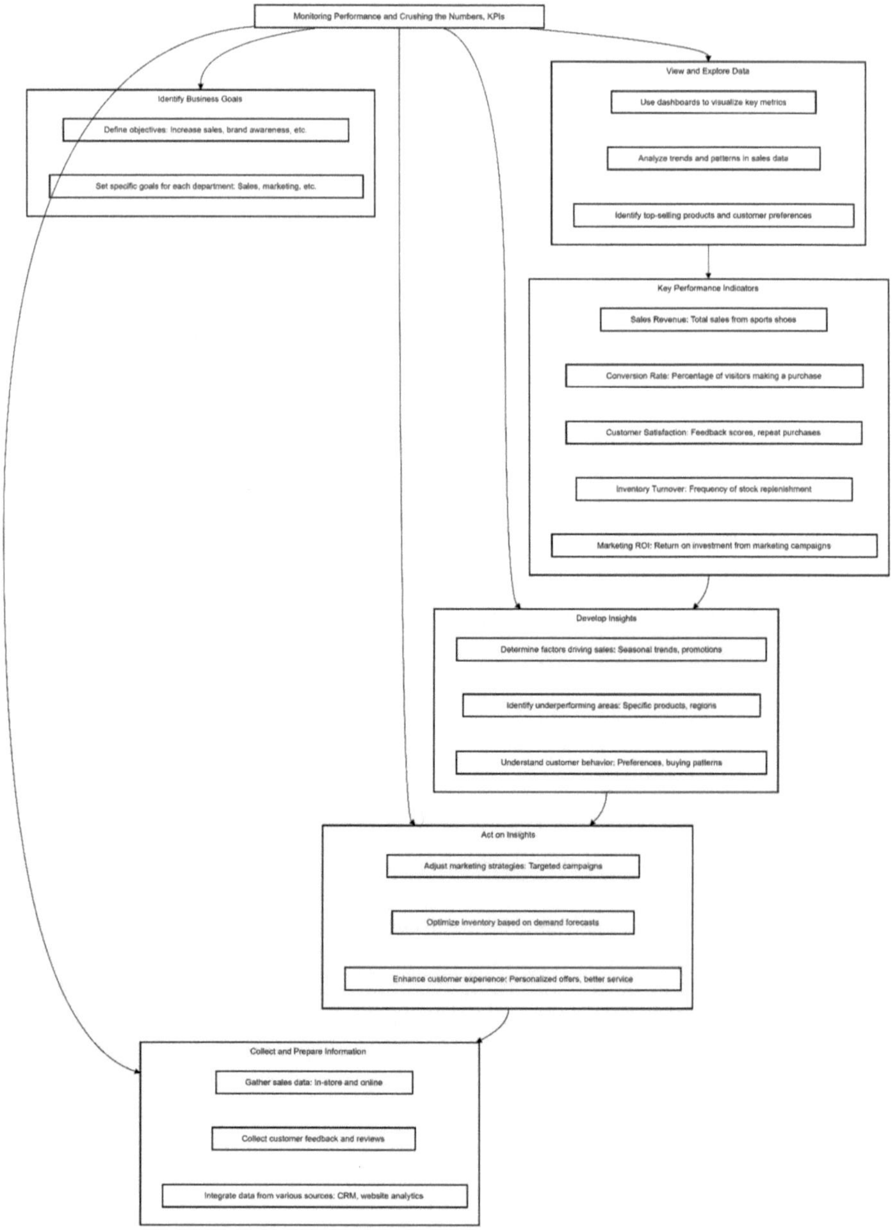

Fig. 5.1 Key processes for monitoring performance and using KPIs

Further Reading

Brynjolfsson, E., & Hitt, L. M. (1998). Beyond the productivity paradox. *Communications of the ACM, 41*(8), 49–55.

Chaffey, D., & Patron, M. (2012). From web analytics to digital marketing optimization: Increasing the commercial value of digital analytics. *Journal of Direct, Data and Digital Marketing Practice, 14*(1), 30–45.

Eckerson, W. W. (2006). *Performance dashboards: Measuring, monitoring, and managing your business*. Wiley.

Few, S. (2006). *Information dashboard design: The effective visual communication of data*. O'Reilly Media.

Friedman, T. L. (2007). *The world is flat: A brief history of the twenty-first century*. Picador.

Goes, P. B. (2014). Big data and IS research. *MIS Quarterly, 38*(3), iii–viii.

Kaplan, R. S., & Norton, D. P. (2004). Measuring the strategic readiness of intangible assets. *Harvard Business Review, 82*(2), 52–63.

Ko, H., & Abdul-Muhmin, A. G. (2010). Predicting online-purchase intentions: A two-factor theory perspective. *Journal of Business Research, 63*(9–10), 979–985.

Lashgari, M., Sutton-Brady, C., Solberg Söilen, K., & Ulfvengren, P. (2018). Adoption strategies of social media in B2B firms: A multiple case study approach. *Journal of Business & Industrial Marketing, 33*(5), 730–743.

Marr, B. (2015). *Big data: Using smart big data, analytics and metrics to make better decisions and improve performance*. Wiley.

McAfee, A., & Brynjolfsson, E. (2012). Big data: The management revolution. *Harvard Business Review, 90*(10), 60–68.

Morrison, A., & Wensley, R. (1991). Boxing up or boxed in?: A short history of the Boston Consulting Group share/growth matrix. *Journal of Marketing Management, 7*(2), 105–129.

Patowary, M. M. I., Peulers, D., Richter, T., Melovic, A., Nilsson, D., & Söilen, K. S. (2023). Improving last-mile delivery for e-commerce: The case of Sweden. *International Journal of Logistics Management., 26*, 872.

Rayport, J. F., & Jaworski, B. J. (2004). *Introduction to e-commerce*. McGraw-Hill/Irwin.

Ross, J. W., & Beath, C. M. (2006). Sustainable IT outsourcing success: Let enterprise architecture be your guide. *MIS Quarterly Executive, 5*(4).

Sheth, J. N., & Sisodia, R. S. (2002). Marketing productivity: Issues and analysis. *Journal of Business Research, 55*(5), 349–362.

Söilen, K. S., Kovacevic, M. A., & Jallouli, R. (2012). Key success factors for Ericsson mobile platforms using the value grid model. *Journal of Business Research, 65*(9), 1335–1345.

Wixom, B. H., & Watson, H. J. (2010). The BI-based organization. *International Journal of Business Intelligence Research, 1*(1), 13–28.

Yoo, Y., Boland, R. J., Jr., Lyytinen, K., & Majchrzak, A. (2012). Organizing for innovation in the digitized world. *Organization Science, 23*(5), 1398–1408.

Search Engine Optimization (SEO) 6

6.1 Background: Enhancing Online Visibility

Today, hardly a major decision is made without somewhere along the line someone using search engines. Thus, it is not surprising that companies want to be visible on page one of a search. The section on Google's first page where websites compete for relevance to appear first is called the "Search Engine Results Page" (SERP). The goal of SEO is to optimize a website so it appears as high as possible in the organic (non-paid) listings on the SERP. The topmost section of the SERP often features paid advertisements, also known as Google Ads or sponsored links, while the lower sections contain organic search results.

Search engine optimization (SEO) is the process of improving the ranking of websites based on specific search terms by managing incoming links and the characteristics of websites. Search engines return the most relevant documents based on complex algorithms that consider a plethora of constantly changing criteria or ranking factors. While the exact ranking algorithms of search engines like Google, Bing, and Yahoo are not published, these search engines provide guidelines for web content developers. These guidelines include producing qualitative content, targeted use of keywords, integrating social media components, and maintaining proper link architecture. Different SEO techniques are exemplified in Table 6.1.

The table outlines key SEO techniques and provides examples of how our sports shoes company can implement them to improve their search engine rankings and attract more customers.

Some website administrators have attempted to manipulate these algorithms using a technique known as black hat SEO. This involves tactics like posting duplicate content, buying links to increase backlink volumes, and keyword spamming.

K. Solberg Söilen, *Digital Marketing*, Springer Texts in Business and Economics, https://doi.org/10.1007/978-3-031-69518-6_6

Table 6.1 SEO techniques

SEO technique	Description	Example for sports shoes company
Keyword research	Identifying and targeting relevant keywords that potential customers use	Using tools like Google keyword planner to find keywords like "best running shoes," "affordable sports shoes," and "comfortable basketball sneakers." creating content around these terms
On-page SEO	Optimizing individual web pages to rank higher and earn more relevant traffic	Optimizing product descriptions, title tags, meta descriptions, and headers on product pages. Ensuring each shoe product page includes relevant keywords naturally
Content creation	Developing high-quality, valuable content that engages and informs the audience	Writing blog posts about "top 10 running shoes for Marathon training" or "how to choose the perfect basketball shoes." creating guides on shoe care and maintenance
Technical SEO	Ensuring a website meets technical requirements to improve organic search ranking	Improving site speed, mobile-friendliness, secure connections (HTTPS), and fixing crawl errors. Ensuring fast-loading product pages and easy navigation on mobile devices
Link building	Acquiring high-quality backlinks from other websites to improve domain authority	Partnering with fitness bloggers or sports websites to write guest posts that link back to the company's website. Getting featured in online sports magazines
User experience (UX)	Enhancing the overall experience users have on the website	Ensuring a seamless and intuitive shopping experience with easy navigation, quick load times, and clear call-to-action. Providing detailed product information and reviews
Local SEO	Optimizing for local search queries	Listing the sports shoes company on Google my business and local directories. Creating location-specific content, like "best sports shoes in New York"
Social media integration	Using social media platforms to drive traffic and engagement	Sharing user-generated content featuring customers wearing the sports shoes. Running social media campaigns and contests that link back to the website
Analytics and reporting	Monitoring SEO performance and making data-driven decisions	Using Google analytics and search console to track keyword rankings, traffic sources, and user behavior. Adjusting strategies based on performance metrics
Mobile optimization	Ensuring the website is mobile-friendly and provides a good user experience on mobile devices	Ensuring the website is responsive and easy to navigate on smartphones and tablets. Implementing mobile-specific SEO practices to enhance visibility

However, such practices are usually detected by search engines, resulting in penalties such as delisting or lower quality scores.

6.1.1 Decision Models in SEO

Recent findings on SEO have been supplemented to establish decision models for search engine ranking, helping website administrators improve performance and achieve better Internet marketing results. One such technique is the DEMATEL method, which addresses interdependencies and feedback among criteria to form an influential network relation map.

Traditional methods like the analytic hierarchy process (AHP) and analytic network process (ANP) assume that dimensions and criteria are independent, which is often not the case in the real world. The DEMATEL method overcomes the issues of dependence and feedback among criteria, enabling search engines to rank data effectively and provide valuable decision models for improving website performance.

This process is organized as follows:

1. Identification of SEO criteria: Based on a literature review, the criteria for SEO are identified.
2. Hybrid models: Establishing a division model of search engine ranking and performance improvements using hybrid models.
3. Empirical strategy model: Demonstrating the usefulness of a high search engine ranking strategy.

6.1.2 Search Engine Optimization Criteria

SEO involves procedures to improve the ranking of websites for specific search terms on search engines by managing incoming links and website characteristics. This section, based on past literature, identifies the main dimensions of SEO: internal and external website optimization, as seen in Table 6.2.

Research has shown that meta tags are crucial for internal website optimization, while site guides are significant for external website optimization. Meta tags have been proven to significantly improve search effectiveness by associating results from multiple search engines in the form of a metasearch engine. Keywords also enhance visibility by increasing their frequency in titles and content.[1]

Using the DEMATEL method, studies have found that experts are more concerned with meta tags and keywords and less with linkages and social media. Meta tags emerged as the most important criterion for internal website optimization, while site guides were the most significant for external optimization.

---

[1] Dye (2008).

Table 6.2 Internal and external website optimization

Optimization type	Components	Examples
Internal website optimization		
Website design	Ensuring the design is user-friendly and accessible	A travel blog optimizing its website by including keywords like "best travel destinations" in its titles and content, using meta tags to describe each page, and offering articles in English and Spanish
Meta tags	Using appropriate meta tags to describe the content of the website	
Keywords	Including relevant keywords in titles, text, and other elements	
Content	Providing high-quality, relevant content	
Photo links	Optimizing images with proper tags and descriptions	
Multilingual text	Offering content in multiple languages if applicable	
External website optimization		
Site guide	Submitting the website to site guides and directories	An e-commerce site submitting its URL to a site guide, sharing products on social media platforms, and collaborating with influencers to get backlinks
Social media	Utilizing social media platforms to drive traffic	
Backlinks	Obtaining links from other reputable, optimized websites	

By integrating these strategies, businesses can effectively improve their search engine rankings and enhance their online presence, ensuring they reach their target audience and achieve their marketing goals.

6.2 Meta Tags in Digital Marketing

The use of meta keyword tags in SEO has significantly declined and is now considered somewhat obsolete. Google, the dominant search engine, no longer uses meta keywords for indexing and ranking purposes. This change occurred because the meta keyword tag was frequently abused through practices like keyword stuffing, leading to low-quality content appearing in search results. As a result, Google decided to disregard this tag to maintain the integrity of its search results.

However, the meta keyword tag is not entirely useless. Some smaller search engines, such as Baidu and Yandex, may still use them to some extent. Additionally, meta keywords can be useful for internal purposes, such as creating an internal

Table 6.3 Meta tags and examples

Meta tag	Description	Example	Importance
Meta keywords attribute	A series of keywords relevant to the page in question	Meta name="keywords" content="travel, best destinations, holiday tips"	Very low to obsolete
Title tag	The text that appears at the top of the browser, also known as the "title" of your page for search engines	<title>Best Travel Destinations for 2024</title>	Very high
Meta description attribute	A short overview of the content on the page	Meta name="description" content="Discover the best travel destinations for 2024. Plan your perfect holiday with our comprehensive guides and tips."	High
Meta robots attribute	Instructions for search engine robots on what to do with the page	Meta name="robots" content="index, follow"	High
Meta content type	Declares the character set for the page	Meta http-equiv="Content-Type" content="text/html; charset=utf-8"	High (for correct page rendering)
Viewport	Used for mobile devices	Meta name="viewport" content="width=device-width, initial-scale=1"	High (for mobile SEO)

tagging system within a website's CMS, which can help prevent keyword cannibalization and streamline content management.

There are a few major types of meta tags that are worth knowing about, as illustrated in Table 6.3, even though there are more than these six. Some are less common, not relevant in web marketing, or out of use. The ones worth using regularly can increase your traffic by letting Google know who you are and what you provide.[2]

6.2.1 Meta Keywords Attribute

The meta keyword tag was beneficial years ago but is no longer as effective today. Google has devalued this tool due to "keyword stuffing," where marketers inserted unrelated keywords to pirate traffic from popular pages. This practice led to Google devaluing the importance of meta keywords in its ranking algorithm.[3]

---

[2] Morris (2019).

[3] Morris (2019).

6.2.2 Title Tag

The most important of all meta tags is the title tag, visible to the average user and significantly impacting search rankings. This tag appears at the top of the browser and helps clarify information for SEO purposes. For instance, a recipe blog might use a title tag like "Easy Chocolate Cake Recipe" to attract searchers looking for that specific recipe.

6.2.3 Meta Description Attribute

This meta tag provides key takeaways from the page's content, useful for search engines and searchers. While Google often picks a snippet of text from the page itself, a well-crafted meta description can entice searchers to click through from the search engine results page (SERP). For example, an online bookstore might use a meta description like "Discover a wide range of books from various genres with fast delivery" to attract potential buyers.

6.2.4 Meta Robots Attribute

This tag tells search engines what to do with your page. It includes two parts: Index or Noindex, to show whether your page should appear in search results, and Follow or NoFollow, indicating whether the search engine should follow the links on your page.

6.2.5 Meta Content Type

This meta tag declares the character set of the page and should be on every presented page. Omitting this tag can affect how the page renders in the browser. It specifies the character encoding for the HTML document. Ensuring the correct rendering of the page is essential, although it does not directly influence SEO rankings.

6.2.6 Viewport

The viewport controls the layout on mobile browsers. With the increase in mobile traffic, ensuring a good mobile user experience is crucial for SEO. Without it, the mobile experience of the website may suffer, resulting in lost views.

We can illustrate these tags with a description of each one and examples, as in Fig. 6.1.

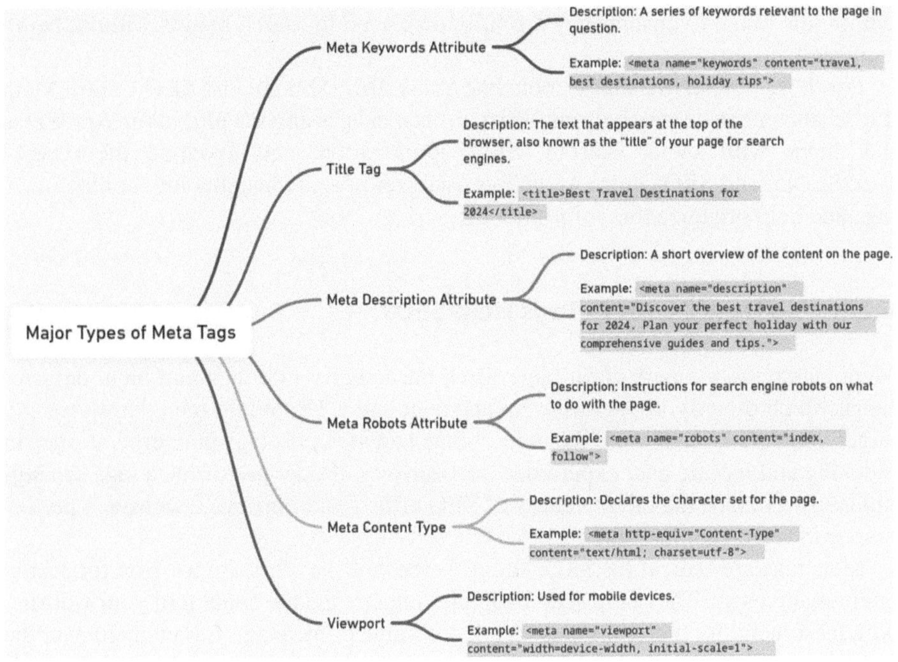

Fig. 6.1 Major types of meta tags

6.2.7 How Meta Tags Affect Digital Marketing

The old saying about not judging a book by its cover is contrary to what covers are designed for in marketing, as they create the first impression. The title and description tags are the cover for your web page, influencing most visitors' initial impressions. This is not just about search engines but also about how users perceive the Internet.[4] For example, on Amazon, the picture, title, and price are the primary elements that attract customers.

To succeed with brand tags, companies should treat them like an elevator pitch, using them to sell something effectively within a limited space. The tags also determine the appearance of automated social media posts and can facilitate email marketing efforts. In 2017, Google search results' character limit for title tags was 78 on mobile devices and 70 on desktops, with 60 characters being the recommended limit.[5] The latest guidelines indicate that Google does not have a strict character limit for title tags, but it typically displays the first 50–60 characters of a title on desktop devices and up to 78 characters on mobile devices. This means that while there is no enforced character limit, it is generally recommended to keep title tags

[4] Patel (2020).

[5] Idem.

within this range to ensure they are fully displayed in search results without being truncated.

For those new to meta tags, tools like Yoast, BuzzStream, and SEO Centro Meta Tag Analyzer can be very helpful. Yoast, for instance, is an SEO plugin for WordPress that helps with social sharing, SEO optimization, and updating meta tags.[6] BuzzStream and SEOCentro Meta Tag Analyzer provide insights into competitors' tags and help organize this information.[7]

6.2.8 So How Do Meta Tags Help SEO?

Meta tags remain a part of on-page SEO, particularly title tags and meta descriptions, which directly impact user engagement and CTR. While meta keywords are largely outdated, other tags like meta robots and viewport tags play crucial roles in indexing and mobile user experience, respectively. Proper use of meta tags can significantly enhance the effectiveness of SEO efforts and improve a website's performance in search engine rankings.

Meta tags are critical for SEO, acting as the website's first impression for search engines and users. They help search engines understand the content of your website, which is crucial for high rankings. While the value of meta tags has evolved over the past decade, they remain useful to SEO.

For example, an e-commerce site might use meta tags to ensure its products appear in relevant search results, improving visibility and driving organic traffic. Without the right meta tags, achieving high search engine rankings organically is challenging. According to Patel (2020), 93% of all online experiences begin with a search engine, and 75% of users never scroll past the first page, emphasizing the importance of effective SEO.

Meta tags are also a part of HTML. While their role in signaling search engines has changed over the years due to the evolution of the Internet, they remain crucial for creating the first impression. Some examples are as follows:

- The title tag significantly impacts search engine rankings.
- Descriptive tags can encourage users to visit your website.
- Meta keywords are largely disregarded by most search engines.

Despite some negative perceptions about meta tags, when used correctly, they can be effective. For high search rankings, meta tags should accompany high-quality content focused on user satisfaction. Sticking to the core essentials makes it easier for browsers to understand the content.[8]

This overview highlights the significance of meta tags in digital marketing, with examples to illustrate their practical applications.

[6] Yoast (2020).

[7] BuzzStream (2020), SEO toolcentre (2020).

[8] Patel (2020).

Some related terms at the end: HTML (Hypertext Markup Language) is the standard language used to create and design web pages by structuring content with elements like headings, paragraphs, and images. ASP (Active Server Pages) is a server-side scripting language developed by Microsoft, used to create dynamic, interactive web pages by embedding scripts within HTML code. When a web page containing ASP code is requested, the server processes the ASP code to generate HTML content dynamically, which is then sent to the client's browser for display. HTML handles the presentation and structure of the content, while ASP manages the logic and dynamic aspects, such as database interactions and form handling. Together, HTML and ASP enable the creation of interactive, data-driven web applications by combining static content with dynamic server-side processing.

6.3 Managerial Takeaways

Here are ten key takeaways for managers from this Chapter:

1. Importance of SEO: Enhancing online visibility through SEO is crucial for appearing high on search engine results pages (SERP), which drives organic traffic and improves marketing outcomes.
2. Keyword Research: Identifying and targeting relevant keywords that potential customers use is essential. Tools like Google Keyword Planner help find the right keywords to optimize content.
3. On-page SEO: Optimizing individual web pages, including title tags, meta descriptions, headers, and product descriptions, ensures higher ranking and more relevant traffic.
4. Content creation: High-quality, valuable content that engages and informs the audience is a critical component of SEO. This includes blog posts, guides, and articles related to the business's products or services.
5. Technical SEO: Ensuring that the website meets technical requirements, such as site speed, mobile-friendliness, and secure connections, is necessary to improve organic search ranking.
6. Link building: Acquiring high-quality backlinks from reputable websites boosts domain authority and improves search engine rankings. Collaborations and guest posts are effective strategies for this.
7. User Experience (UX): Enhancing the overall user experience on the website, including easy navigation, fast loading times, and clear calls-to-action, is vital for retaining visitors and improving SEO.
8. Local SEO: Optimizing for local search queries by listing the business on Google My Business and creating location-specific content helps attract local customers.
9. Analytics and reporting: Monitoring SEO performance through tools like Google Analytics and Search Console allows managers to make data-driven decisions and adjust strategies based on performance metrics.

10. Meta tags: Proper use of meta tags, including title tags, meta descriptions, and viewport tags, remains essential for on-page SEO. Although meta keywords are less significant now, other meta tags still play crucial roles in search engine indexing and user engagement.

By integrating these strategies, businesses can effectively improve their search engine rankings, enhance their online presence, and achieve their marketing goals.

References

BuzzStream. (2020). *Extract title and meta description from URLs*. Retrieved June 4, 2020, from http://tools.buzzstream.com/meta-tag-extractor

Dye, K. (2008). Website abuse for search engine optimization. *Network Security, 2008*(3), 4–6.

Morris, K. (2019, July 24). *The ultimate guide to SEO meta tags*. [Blog post]. Retrieved from https://moz.com/blog/the-ultimate-guide-to-seo-meta-tags

Patel, N. (2020). *Why meta tags are so important for your online marketing efforts*. Retrieved June 4, 2020, from https://neilpatel.com/blog/why-meta-tags-are-so-important/

SEO Tool Centre. (2020). *SEO Centro meta tag analyzer*. Retrieved June 1, 2020, from https://seotoolscentre.com/keyword-position-checker

Yoast. (2020). *WordPress SEO plugin*. Retrieved June 4, 2020, from https://yoast.com/wordpress/plugins/seo/

Further Reading

Agarwal, V., & Lavy, S. (2007). Meta tags: Evaluating the impact of metadata and keyword placement on search engine ranking. *Journal of Digital Marketing, 5*(2), 85–101.

Chen, Y., & Dominguez, C. (2015). The role of meta tags in search engine optimization: An empirical study. *Journal of Web Marketing, 9*(3), 112–128.

Cutts, M. (2011). SEO for Google. *Journal of Online Marketing, 8*(2), 98–105.

Hinton, G., & Salakhutdinov, R. (2006). Reducing the dimensionality of data with neural networks. *Science, 313*(5786), 504–507.

Jiang, J., & Zhang, Y. (2008). SEO techniques for better ranking: A practical approach. *Online Journal of Web Marketing, 11*(4), 145–160.

Kent, M. L., & Taylor, M. (2002). Toward a dialogic theory of public relations. *Public Relations Review, 28*(1), 21–37.

Kilgarriff, A., & Grefenstette, G. (2003). Introduction to the special issue on the web as corpus. *Computational Linguistics, 29*(3), 333–347.

Liu, B. (2012). *Web data mining: Exploring hyperlinks, contents, and usage data*. Springer.

MacDonald, M. P. (2008). *Search engine optimization: An hour a day*. Wiley.

Mohammad, S., & Hirst, G. (2012). Distributional measures as proxies for semantic relatedness. *Computational Linguistics, 38*(4), 673–725.

Moz. (2018). *The beginner's guide to SEO*. Retrieved from https://moz.com/beginners-guide-to-seo

Page, L., Brin, S., Motwani, R., & Winograd, T. (1998). *The PageRank citation ranking: Bringing order to the web*. Stanford InfoLab.

Patel, N., & Sharma, A. (2013). Advanced SEO: Tactics and strategies. *Journal of Digital Marketing, 6*(3), 135–149.

Richards, K. (2010). *Best practices in search engine optimization: A guide for marketers*. Marketing Science Institute.

Sahu, K. K., & Choudhary, R. (2017). Impact of meta tags on SEO: An analytical study. *International Journal of Web and SEO Studies, 12*(1), 45–59.
Sullivan, D. (2016). *Search engine land's guide to SEO*. Retrieved from https://searchengineland.com/guide/what-is-seo
Wu, C., & Wang, Z. (2014). Technical SEO: An in-depth look at website performance and search visibility. *Web Development Journal, 10*(2), 89–105.
Zhang, M., & Dong, Y. (2019). The role of meta tags in improving search engine ranking. *International Journal of Digital Marketing, 15*(1), 67–82.

Click Analytics

7

7.1 Introduction

Many of us sit and "click" all day in front of a screen at work, often without considering that these choices—what we choose to click on, how often, if we return to the same web page—are the single most important information on the web. This is because it is an expression of our most clear choices and needs. We do not lie when we sit in front of a computer. What we click on is what we are truly interested in, 100% for sure. Put differently, we do not sit in front of the computer and pretend to click on something we are not interested in to impress others or because it is fun. Clicking is for real. So it is no wonder that click analytics have become the core of digital marketing.

Click analytics is a subset of web analytics that focuses specifically on tracking and analyzing user clicks on a website, as illustrated in Table 7.1. It helps understand user behavior by monitoring which elements users click on, how often they click, and the sequence of their clicks. This data provides insights into how users interact with the website's interface, what elements are most engaging, and where potential issues in the user experience might lie.

Click analytics focuses on tracking and analyzing the specific actions users take on a web page, such as where they click, how often they click, and the sequence of their clicks. This type of analytics provides insights into user behavior and preferences by showing exactly what users are interested in based on their clicking patterns. Unlike web analytics, which looks at overall website performance and user engagement, click analytics drills down into the granular details of user interactions. This helps businesses optimize their website layout, improve user experience, and tailor content to better meet user needs. By understanding click patterns, companies can make more informed decisions to enhance their digital marketing strategies.

By analyzing how consumers click and navigate on websites, companies can gauge the popularity of their products or services and use this information to improve their marketing strategies.

K. Solberg Söilen, *Digital Marketing*, Springer Texts in Business and Economics, https://doi.org/10.1007/978-3-031-69518-6_7

Table 7.1 Click analytics and web analytics compared

Aspect	Click analytics	Web analytics
Focus	Tracking individual user clicks on specific elements	Analyzing various aspects of website performance and user behavior
Purpose	Optimize UI/UX by understanding interactions	Provide a comprehensive view of website effectiveness and performance
Tools	Heatmaps, click maps, session recordings	Google analytics, adobe analytics, Matomo
Scope	Element-level insights	Overall site metrics including traffic, user behavior, and performance
Granularity	Detailed analysis of user clicks	High-level overview of user behavior trends and site performance
Example (sports shoes company)	Identify which shoe models and call-to-action buttons get the most clicks	Analyze site traffic sources, page views, bounce rates, and conversion rates

7.1.1 Definitions

When working on click analytics, there are a number of related terms used which we need to understand[1]:

1. Conversion funnel: This term describes the three steps of a consumer's journey from a marketing campaign to a purchase. The steps include clicking on an advertisement, navigating the website, and deciding whether to make a purchase. It is called a funnel because consumers are guided through increasingly fewer navigation options at each step.
2. Web analytics: This involves measuring, collecting, analyzing, and reporting web data to understand and improve web usage. It is also used in business and market research to measure web traffic and campaign effectiveness.
3. Hypermedia: Refers to clicking on text links or other media (images, movies, graphics) on a web browser to navigate to new websites.
4. Log file: A file stored on a web server that records every time someone downloads a piece of information (a page or image). Log files are less commonly used by companies today.
5. Inbound sources (Top Referrals): Links on other websites that lead users to the website when clicked.
6. Outbound destinations: Links that navigate users away from the website when clicked.

[1] Verified using ChatGPT 4 (June 2024).

To illustrate these terms with an example from our sports shoes company's digital marketing, consider the following scenario:

The sports shoes company runs a digital marketing campaign featuring ads for their latest running shoes. When a potential customer sees an ad and clicks on it, they enter the first step of the conversion funnel. The customer is then taken to the company's website, where they browse through various product pages and eventually decide to purchase a pair of running shoes. The funnel narrows at each step, guiding the customer from initial interest to final purchase.

The sports shoes company uses web analytics to measure the effectiveness of their digital marketing campaign. They track metrics such as the number of visitors to their website, the bounce rate, and the average time spent on product pages. By analyzing this data, they can determine which aspects of their campaign are successful and which need improvement. For example, if web analytics reveal a high bounce rate on certain product pages, the company may need to optimize those pages to better engage visitors.

On the company's website, visitors can click on various forms of hypermedia to navigate through the site. For example, clicking on an image of a pair of shoes takes the user to a detailed product page. Similarly, clicking on a video showcasing the shoes' features might lead to a page with customer reviews and additional product information. This interactive use of text links, images, and videos helps create a seamless browsing experience.

Although less commonly used today, the sports shoes company's web server still maintains log files that record each time a piece of information is downloaded. These log files capture data such as when a visitor views a product image or downloads a sizing chart. While modern analytics tools have largely replaced log files, they can still provide valuable historical data for the company.

The company monitors inbound sources to see which external websites are driving traffic to their site. For instance, they might find that a popular running blog frequently refers readers to the company's website through product reviews and recommendations. Recognizing these top referrals allows the company to strengthen relationships with influential sites and optimize their marketing efforts.

On the company's website, there are outbound links that navigate users to other sites. For example, clicking on a link to the company's Instagram page or YouTube channel takes users away from the main website. The company tracks these outbound destinations to understand where their visitors go after leaving the site, which helps them refine their digital marketing strategy and improve cross-platform engagement.

By effectively utilizing these digital marketing terms and techniques, the sports shoes company can enhance their online presence, engage customers more effectively, and ultimately drive higher sales.

7.2 Click Analytics in Digital Marketing

Click analytics represents the first step in the conversion funnel and focuses on analyzing clicks (point-and-click) on websites. This method tracks user clicks to determine website performance, identify high- and low-usage areas, and improve content. Click analytics is an ongoing process requiring frequent updates to the website based on the collected data.

Click analytics provides several benefits, including identifying texts or pictures that attract clicks, determining which links receive the most clicks, detecting high- and low-usage areas on the website, viewing the website from both technical and user perspectives, analyzing desktop vs. mobile user behavior, and assessing user responses to website changes and updates.

Various click analytic tools are available, such as Google Analytics In-Page Analytics, ClickHeat, and Crazy Egg, which format collected data into reports and charts for easy interpretation:

> Google Analytics In-Page Analytics visually displays click data by overlaying it on the current website. It segments data into specific groups (e.g., device type) and provides an overview report with useful statistics.
>
> ClickHeat is a heat mapping tool that visually displays clicks using colors. Warmer colors indicate more clicks, while cooler colors indicate fewer or no clicks. This tool is user-friendly for those with less experience in click analytics.
>
> Crazy Egg is a more advanced click analytic tool that converts click data into three types of reports: heatmap, site overlay, and confetti view. It requires a monthly subscription with different packages available.

Various types of clicks serve different functions on a computer:

- Single-click: Selecting an object by pressing the mouse button once.
- Point-and-click: Moving the input device to a specific location and clicking.
- Double-click: Selecting an object by clicking twice without moving the mouse.

Creating effective online ads requires understanding consumer behavior and preferences. Ads must be relevant and credible to attract clicks. Factors like ad size, color, and placement influence click rates. Search advertising is particularly effective due to precise targeting.

> Clickbait uses intriguing headlines or teasers to attract clicks by arousing curiosity. Unlike traditional headlines, clickbait provides minimal information to encourage clicks.

A growing trend is consumers ordering products online and then picking them up at a physical location or store, known as "click and collect." This concept is derived from "research online, buy offline," combining online customer experience with offline retail, enhancing customer relationships with sustainable value.

Various methods exist for companies to attract clicks to their websites, including ads, pop-ups, and banners on search engines. These methods incur costs based on their pricing models. Pay-per-click (PPC) is a performance-based pricing model where companies pay a fee for each click that leads a user from the referring site to the destination site. Another model, cost-per-action (CPA), involves paying the publisher only when a specific action (like a sale or registration) is completed. Cost-per-click (CPC) measures the actual cost per click on an advertisement.

Clickstreams record a user's path through a website, summarizing their activities. This data helps understand how the site is used, user responses to promotions, and navigation patterns. Detailed web server logs are used to collect clickstream data.

Click-through rate (CTR) measures the effectiveness of email campaigns by calculating the percentage of recipients who click through an email. It helps analyze campaign performance, including content and link placement.

To measure CTR, divide the number of clicks an email received by the number of times the email was opened, and then, multiply by 100. Tracking unique link clicks (one click per user) and all link clicks (counting multiple clicks by the same user) provides insights into the effectiveness of email content and engagement.

Companies collect data from user clicks through various methods, often using more than one technique. When a click occurs, it is logged by the website using user patterns. Click tracking systems use a unique click code for each link to log the click information on a tracking server before redirecting the user to the destination link. This process requires adding appropriate tracking elements to each file manually.

7.3 Key Takeaways

Here are some key takeaways for managers for this chapter:

1. In the digital age, the choices users make when clicking on web elements provide crucial insights into their preferences and needs, making click analytics a core component of digital marketing.
2. Click analytics involves tracking specific user interactions on a web page, such as where users click, how often, and in what sequence, to optimize user interface and user experience.
3. Unlike web analytics, which provides a broad overview of website performance, click analytics focuses on detailed user behavior, helping businesses understand which elements are most engaging and where potential issues lie.
4. By analyzing click data, companies can identify popular products or services and refine their marketing strategies to better meet customer demands.
5. Conversion funnels illustrate the consumer journey from clicking an advertisement to making a purchase, guiding businesses in creating effective marketing campaigns.
6. Web analytics measures and analyzes overall website performance and user engagement, including metrics like site traffic, bounce rates, and conversion rates.
7. Hypermedia involves using various media types, such as text links, images, and videos, to navigate the web, enhancing the interactive experience for users.

8. Log files, although less common today, record every download of information from a web server, providing valuable historical data for companies.
9. Monitoring inbound sources helps companies identify external websites that drive traffic to their site, allowing them to strengthen relationships with influential sites.
10. Tracking outbound destinations reveals where visitors go after leaving the company's website, aiding in the refinement of digital marketing strategies and cross-platform engagement.

By effectively utilizing these insights and techniques, companies like the sports shoes company can enhance their online presence, engage customers more effectively, and ultimately drive higher sales.

Click analytics focuses on understanding user behavior by tracking and analyzing specific clicks on a website, providing detailed insights into which elements are most engaging. This method helps businesses optimize their website layout and improve user experience by identifying high and low-usage areas and understanding user interactions.

Conversion funnels illustrate the customer's journey from clicking on an advertisement to making a purchase, guiding them through fewer options at each step. Various tools like Google Analytics In-Page Analytics, ClickHeat, and Crazy Egg help visualize and interpret click data. Effective online ads must be relevant and credible, with factors like size, color, and placement influencing click rates. Additionally, methods such as pay-per-click, cost-per-action, and click-through rates measure the effectiveness of digital marketing campaigns, helping companies refine their strategies based on detailed user interaction data.

Further Reading

Anderson, P., & Tushman, M. L. (1990). Technological discontinuities and dominant designs: A cyclical model of technological change. *Administrative Science Quarterly, 35*(4), 604–633.

Barney, J. B. (1991). Firm resources and sustained competitive advantage. *Journal of Management, 17*(1), 99–120.

Christensen, C. M. (1997). *The innovator's dilemma: When new technologies cause great firms to fail*. Harvard Business Review Press.

Day, G. S. (1994). The capabilities of market-driven organizations. *Journal of Marketing, 58*(4), 37–52.

Hamel, G., & Prahalad, C. K. (1994). *Competing for the future*. Harvard Business Review Press.

March, J. G. (1991). Exploration and exploitation in organizational learning. *Organization Science, 2*(1), 71–87.

Porter, M. E. (1980). *Competitive strategy: Techniques for analyzing industries and competitors*. Free Press.

Teece, D. J., Pisano, G., & Shuen, A. (1997). Dynamic capabilities and strategic management. *Strategic Management Journal, 18*(7), 509–533.

Tushman, M. L., & O'Reilly, C. A. (1996). Ambidextrous organizations: Managing evolutionary and revolutionary change. *California Management Review, 38*(4), 8–30.

The Online Buying Process

8

8.1 Online Buying

The online buying process involves customers searching for, comparing, and purchasing products or services through the Internet, typically using various electronic devices. It includes stages such as awareness, consideration, decision-making, and post-purchase engagement to build long-term satisfaction and loyalty. By finding alternative suppliers, customers can compare prices, delivery options, and payment methods to help them make purchase decisions. Common online purchases include tickets, books, travel, hotels, and music.

Customers can make purchases online through a wide range of electronic devices such as computers (both desktop and laptops), smartphones, tablet computers, smartwatches, and smart speakers. Online stores simulate the physical experience of walking into a store by allowing customers to look at pictures of products and read descriptions that detail functions and prices. Online stores make it easy for customers to search for different models, articles, and brands. They require access to the Internet and a valid payment method (e.g., credit card or PayPal) to perform transactions. For physical products (e.g., clothes, food, furniture), the e-tailer ships the product to the customer. For digital products (e.g., music, software, and other digital files), the e-tailer often sends these directly over the Internet. What they all have in common is an often rather lengthy buying process, as depicted in Fig. 8.1.

Ledger in the form of bullet points:

- A (customer awareness): Customers become aware of products through digital marketing campaigns.
  - A1 (digital marketing campaigns): Advertising efforts to increase awareness.
- B (identify needs): Customers identify their basic and social needs.
  - B1 (basic and social needs): Fundamental and socially influenced desires.
- C (research and consideration): Customers research and compare different products and brands.
  - C1 (price comparison tools): Tools to compare prices from different retailers.

K. Solberg Söilen, *Digital Marketing*, Springer Texts in Business and Economics, https://doi.org/10.1007/978-3-031-69518-6_8

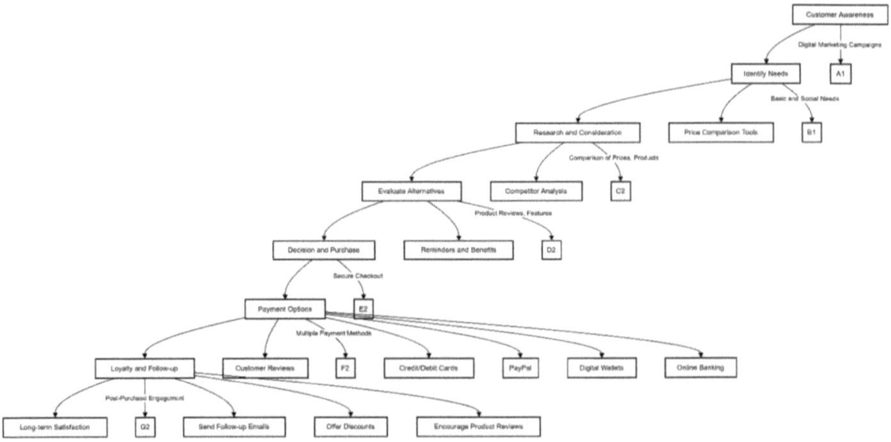

Fig. 8.1 The online buying process

  - C2 (comparison of prices and products): Evaluating different products and their prices.
- D (evaluate alternatives): Customers evaluate alternative products based on reviews and features.
  - D1 (competitor analysis): Considering alternative products from competitors.
  - D2 (product reviews and features): Evaluating products based on reviews and features.
- E (decision and purchase): Customers make a purchase decision and proceed to checkout.
  - E1 (reminders and benefits): Sending reminders and highlighting product benefits.
  - E2 (secure checkout): Ensuring a secure checkout process.
- F (payment options): Providing multiple payment methods.
  - F1 (multiple payment methods): Offering various payment options.

    P1 (credit/debit cards): Traditional payment methods.

    P2 (PayPal): Online payment system.

    P3 (digital wallets): Electronic devices or services for transactions.

    P4 (online banking): Internet banking services.
- G (loyalty and follow-up): Engaging with customers post-purchase to build loyalty.
  - G1 (post-purchase engagement): Activities to engage customers after purchase.

    L1 (sending follow-up emails): Follow-up on the purchase.

    L2 (offering discounts): Encouraging repeat purchases.

    L3 (encouraging product reviews): Asking for reviews about the product and experience.

- H (long-term satisfaction): Achieving long-term customer satisfaction through continuous engagement and quality service.

This diagram outlines the online buying process for a sports shoes company. It starts with customer awareness, often driven by digital marketing campaigns. Customers then identify their needs, both basic and social, and proceed to the research and consideration stage, where they use tools like price comparison websites to evaluate different products. After considering alternatives, customers decide and purchase, ideally through a secure checkout process. Various payment options, such as credit/debit cards, PayPal, and digital wallets, are available. Post-purchase, the company focuses on building customers with follow-up emails, offering discounts, and encouraging product reviews, leading to long-term satisfaction.

8.1.1 Terminology

Several abbreviations and alternative terms are commonly used within online buying. "Electronic retail" is often referred to as "e-tailing." Terms such as virtual store, online storefront, e-shop, e-store, web-shop, web-store, internet-shop, and online-store all share the same meaning. A software application (often referred to as an "app") is developed to enable customers to browse products from their smartphones or tablet computers. A smartphone is a multi-purpose mobile computing device, and a tablet computer (or "tablet") is a mobile device with a touch screen, typically larger than a smartphone.

Note that there is a difference between online buying and online shopping: Online shopping generally refers to the entire process of searching for, comparing, and selecting products or services over the Internet, typically used in a B2C (business-to-consumer) context. It emphasizes the consumer's experience, browsing, and decision-making process.

Online buying, on the other hand, often implies a more straightforward, transactional approach focused on the purchase itself. It is frequently used in a B2B (business-to-business) context, where the emphasis is on efficiency, bulk purchases, and meeting specific business needs rather than the broader shopping experience.

8.2 How Online Buying Once Started

Online buying began to evolve with the creation of Arpanet, the precursor to the modern Internet. However, it was not until the early 1990s that online shopping gained momentum and reached a wider audience. The launch of the World Wide

Web (WWW) in 1992, combined with the introduction of the web browser Netscape Navigator in 1994, made this possible. This development enabled the creation of virtual stores where people from around the world could begin shopping. The World Wide Web, commonly known as the Web, is a system of interlinked hypertext documents and multimedia content accessible via the Internet. It enables users to navigate between pages using web browsers, providing a vast network of information and services.

Ordering by phone is an older form of distance shopping but is not considered online shopping; it is more akin to mail order since both the presentation of the product and the order are handled manually. An early example is Amazon.com, which opened in 1995. Amazon's revenue grew from $1.6 million in 1996 to $1.6 billion in 1999. The period from 1995–1999 is considered the "golden years" for online shopping when significant investments were made, modern warehouses were built, and the Internet became the fastest-growing technology in history. However, the IT bubble burst at the turn of the millennium, causing many IT companies worldwide to go bankrupt. The crisis began in 2000 and continued into 2001. After the crisis, the IT market recovered and has continued to grow ever since. What it means is that we may expect new periods of decline when investors again become optimistic about future market opportunities. These cycles seem to be part of the free market economy.

8.2.1 Growth in Online Buying

The growth in online buying is consistently rising for now at least. It is estimated that e-business will increase by over 500% from 2014 to 2023. The Internet will represent 53% of all sales to consumers in the next decade, compared to 20% today. This is due to the younger generation, which has grown up with the Internet, representing more than half of the adult population in many Western countries.

8.3 Advantages of Online Buying[1]

Let us consider some of the advantages of online buying:

1. Opening hours: Online shops are open 24/7, offering customers the convenience to shop at any time.
2. Prices: Online shops often have more competitive prices since they do not incur the high costs of maintaining multiple physical stores (Kao, 2006).
3. Comfort: Customers can shop from home and get products delivered directly to their doorsteps, often with multiple payment options.
4. Overview: Customers can easily compare prices and products across multiple online shops (Alreck et al., 2009).

[1] Verified using ChatGPT 4 (June 2024).

5. Range of supply: Online shops can offer a wider range of products, including rare and low-frequency items.
6. Interactivity: Customers can leave reviews and interact with the shop's helpdesk.
7. Offers: Customers often receive discounts on future purchases (Sarkar, 2011).

8.4 Disadvantages of Online Buying

1. Phishing scam: The risk of fraudulent sellers and stolen credit card information.
2. Freight: Additional shipping costs can negate the savings from lower product prices.
3. Delivery times: Waiting for delivery, which can be delayed for various reasons.
4. Place of delivery: Difficulty receiving packages during work hours or needing to pick them up from a local point.
5. Damaged or missing goods: Risk of receiving damaged or incomplete orders.
6. Lack of customer service: Limited personal assistance for advice or problem resolution.
7. Product deviance: Products may not meet expectations, and return policies can be complex and costly.

8.5 Customers

Online customers need access to the Internet and a valid payment method like a credit card or PayPal account to make transactions. There is a correlation between attitudes toward online shopping and people's education level and personal income. Those with higher education and income are more inclined to purchase online. Increased exposure to technology also fosters a more positive attitude toward new digital channels and online shopping sites.

8.5.1 Customer Behavior Online

Marketing in the digital environment does not guarantee the anticipated effect on customers' buying behavior. Customers consider various information sources, such as recommendations, online reviews, and search engine results, which influence their decisions. This makes it harder for sellers to control and influence buyers through online marketing.

In an online shopping environment, interactive decisions can affect customers' buying behavior. Online reviews can influence buying decisions, and customers tend to be more interactive online. Factors essential for customer behavior in digital environments include risk and trust. Offline shoppers tend to be more loyal, whereas online customers are less loyal and more likely to switch between different shops.

There are three important things to consider that might affect customers' buying behavior:

Firstly, the customer does not have the possibility to examine the product prior to the purchase to see if it meets their wants and needs.
Secondly, customers can be concerned regarding after-sales service.
And, thirdly, customers can have concerns that they do not fully understand the language used on the web page of the online shop. So there is a risk that the perception that the customers have regarding the three factors can affect their online buying behavior.

Online sellers focus a lot on the customer trust aspect since it is a factor that affects customers' behavior in a digital environment. The product design or company ideas hardly ever meet the expectations of all customers. The customer's buying behavior is based on rational expectations influenced by emotional trust, product information, and reviews from other customers.

8.6 The Online Buying Process: An Overview Step-by-Step

The buyer's decision journey in digital marketing is often divided into distinct stages: awareness, consideration, intent, purchase, and loyalty. Each stage involves specific marketing strategies to influence the buyer effectively.

8.6.1 Awareness

Creating awareness involves recognizing the audience's problems and presenting a solution through the company's products or services. This stage focuses on making potential customers aware of their needs and how the company can address them. We could also divide the process into the following elements:

8.6.2 Needs

This stage addresses the basic necessities such as food, clothing, and shelter. It involves understanding the fundamental requirements of the customers and ensuring the products meet these needs.

8.6.3 Wants

Wants are socially influenced desires, such as branded clothing or gourmet food. This stage goes beyond basic needs to cater to the aspirational aspects of consumer behavior.

8.6.4 Customer Insights

Gathering customer insights involves collecting information to deliver products or services that meet customers' needs and wants. This process helps create valuable content and offerings tailored to specific customer segments.

8.6.5 Consideration

In the consideration stage, customers research and compare companies to find the best solution to their problem. They use tools like price comparison websites to evaluate different options and narrow down their choices.

8.6.6 Price Comparison Tools

These tools help customers evaluate and compare products from different retailers to find the best prices. They play a crucial role in the consideration stage by providing detailed comparisons and influencing purchasing decisions.

8.6.7 Intent

Understanding the customer's intent during the buying process is crucial. Initially, the buyer has a clear goal and knows their main problem, making it easy to find a suitable product. As they gather more information, factors like price and guarantees become more relevant. This guiding decision-making process eventually leads to the purchase.

8.6.8 Purchase

In the purchase stage, the customer has evaluated and compared several alternatives and is ready to make the buying decision. Ideally, this process is quick and straightforward, but there is a risk of abandonment. Marketers need to remind customers of the benefits of their product or service through follow-up emails and other reminders to ensure the purchase is completed.

8.6.9 Payments and Checkout

When purchasing online, customers have multiple payment options beyond credit or debit cards. Common payment methods include the following:

- Apple/Google Pay
- Bitcoin
- Cash on delivery (C.O.D)
- Check
- Digital wallets
- Electronic money
- Gift cards
- Online banking
- PayPal
- Postal money order
- Cryptocurrencies

More on these in detail in the next chapter.

8.6.10 Loyalty

After making a purchase, customers evaluate the product and decide whether it meets their expectations. Encouraging customers to write reviews or send follow-up messages with special offers can create a positive relationship and enhance brand loyalty. Understanding the entire purchasing process and implementing a strategic follow-up can lead to increased customer loyalty and long-term satisfaction.

8.7 The Example with Our Sports Shoes Company

Our sports shoes company wants to start planning how to succeed with the online buying process. What should they do, how long will it take, what kind of competencies will they need, and how much will it cost? We need to start with the basics and try to define a working process and then see how long time it may take and what it may cost, like in Table 8.1. These are only approximations.

Market research is essential to understand the market dynamics, competitors, and customer preferences. It helps in defining targeted strategies for our sports shoes company. Defining goals and KPIs is crucial as clear objectives and measurable KPIs help in tracking progress and ensuring alignment with business goals. Website development is a critical step to creating an online presence, ensuring a seamless and secure shopping experience for customers.

Table 8.1 Starting the e-commerce project

Step	Description	Duration	Approximate cost	Competences required
1. Market research	Conduct research to understand market needs, competition, and customer behavior	4 weeks	$5000	Market research analyst, data analyst
2. Define goals and KPIs	Establish clear business objectives and key performance indicators (KPIs)	1 week	$1000	Business strategist, data analyst
3. Website development	Develop an e-commerce website with a user-friendly interface and secure payment options	8 weeks	$15,000	Web developer, UX/UI designer, IT specialist
4. Product catalog setup	Organize and upload product images, descriptions, and prices to the website	2 weeks	$2000	Content manager, product manager
5. Payment gateway integration	Integrate multiple payment options like PayPal, credit cards, and digital wallets	1 week	$2000	IT specialist, financial analyst
6. Logistics and inventory management	Establish a system for inventory tracking and logistics coordination	3 weeks	$3000	Supply chain manager, IT specialist
7. SEO and SEM implementation	Optimize website for search engines and set up search engine marketing campaigns	4 weeks	$5000	SEO specialist, SEM specialist
8. Social media and content marketing	Develop a content marketing strategy and promote it on social media platforms	4 weeks	$4000	Content creator, social media manager
9. Customer support setup	Implement a customer support system including live chat and email support	2 weeks	$3000	Customer support manager, IT specialist
10. Launch and promotion	Officially launch the website and start promotional campaigns	1 week	$5000	Marketing manager, PR specialist
11. Monitoring and analytics	Set up monitoring tools to track performance and make data-driven decisions	Ongoing	$2000/month	Data analyst, business strategist
12. Customer feedback and improvement	Collect customer feedback and continuously improve the online buying process	Ongoing	$1000/month	Customer support, UX/UI designer

The next step is setting up the product catalog. Organizing products effectively on the website is vital to attract and retain customers. Payment gateway integration is another important step, as providing various payment options increases convenience and trust among customers. Efficient logistics and inventory management ensure timely delivery and customer satisfaction.

Implementing SEO and SEM increases website visibility and attracts more traffic through search engines. Social media and content marketing engage customers and drive traffic through compelling content and a strong social media presence. Setting up customer support ensures that customers can get help easily, improving their overall experience.

A well-coordinated launch and promotional campaign can significantly boost initial traffic and sales. Continuous monitoring and analytics help in making informed decisions and optimizing strategies. Regular customer feedback and improvement enhance customer satisfaction and loyalty. This structured approach helps the sports shoes company effectively plan and execute its online buying process, ensuring a comprehensive and successful digital marketing strategy.

References

Alreck, P. L., DiBartolo, G. R., Diriker, M., Dover, H. F., Passyn, K. A., & Settle, R. B. (2009). Time pressure, time saving, and online shopping: Exploring a contradiction. *Journal of Applied Business Research (JABR), 25*(5), 85–101.

Kao, C. (2006). Interval efficiency measures in data envelopment analysis with imprecise data. *European journal of operational research, 174*(2), 1087–1099.

Sarkar, A. (2011). Impact of utilitarian and hedonic shopping values on individual's perceived benefits and risks in online shopping. *International Management Review, 7*(1), 58–65.

Further Reading

Amit, R., & Zott, C. (2001). Value creation in e-business. *Strategic Management Journal, 22*(6–7), 493–520.

Brynjolfsson, E., & Hitt, L. M. (2000). Beyond computation: Information technology, organizational transformation and business performance. *Journal of Economic Perspectives, 14*(4), 23–48.

Chesbrough, H. W. (2003). *Open innovation: The new imperative for creating and profiting from technology*. Harvard Business Review Press.

CoinMarketCap. (n.d.). *Cryptocurrency charts*. Retrieved June 28, 2024, from https://coinmarketcap.com/charts/

Hagel, J., & Singer, M. (1999). *Net worth: Shaping markets when customers make the rules*. Harvard Business Review Press.

Kaplan, R. S., & Norton, D. P. (2001). *The strategy-focused organization: How balanced scorecard companies thrive in the new business environment*. Harvard Business Review Press.

Laudon, K. C., & Laudon, J. P. (2012). *Management information systems: Managing the digital firm*. Pearson.

Osterwalder, A., & Pigneur, Y. (2010). *Business model generation: A handbook for visionaries, game changers, and challengers*. Wiley.

Porter, M. E. (2001). Strategy and the internet. *Harvard Business Review, 79*(3), 62–78.

Söilen, K. S., & Benhayoun, L. (2021). Household acceptance of central bank digital currency: The role of institutional trust. *International Journal of Bank Marketing, 40*(1), 172–196.

Tapscott, D. (1996). *The digital economy: Promise and peril in the age of networked intelligence*. McGraw-Hill.

Checkout and Payment Options 9

9.1 Background

Digital payments began with the advent of the Internet in 1969, but they truly took off in 1989 when Tim Berners-Lee developed a new way to publish content online. A significant shift occurred in the 1990s with the emergence of e-commerce. Stanford Federal Credit Union was a pioneer in mobile payment methods, but it was not until 1996 that micro-payments became mainstream. Amazon, founded in 1994, and PayPal, launched in 1998, were major catalysts in the development of digital payments, emphasizing security and ease of use.

The modern era has seen a vast array of payment options tailored to consumer preferences and enhanced checkout processes. Security and convenience are paramount, with services like PayPal, credit cards, and digital wallets leading the way. However, future trends indicate a shift toward even more flexible payment methods. Security and decryption are closely related as decryption is the process of converting encoded or encrypted data back into its original form, making it readable and accessible, which is crucial for maintaining data security and confidentiality. Effective security mechanisms ensure that only authorized parties can decrypt and access sensitive information, thereby protecting it from unauthorized access or breaches.

A checkout refers to the customer's decision-making process from interest in a product to the final payment. There are two main types of checkout pages: single-page and multi-page. Payment options include micro-payments, which are small transactions conducted online, often used for digital goods and services.

Due to multiple fraud cases, customers have become more critical and may not trust a site enough to enter their credit or debit card information online. Instead, they often prefer to use a third-party payment system, like PayPal. If a company's website does not offer such a payment solution, it risks losing the customer, even though the product and price are good. Therefore, there are specific rules for setting up a well-functioning checkout function, as presented in Table 9.1.

K. Solberg Söilen, *Digital Marketing*, Springer Texts in Business and Economics, https://doi.org/10.1007/978-3-031-69518-6_9

Table 9.1 Succeeding with the checkout function[a]

Rule	Description
Simple and intuitive design	Ensure the checkout process is straightforward and easy to navigate with a clear layout
Guest checkout option	Allow customers to checkout without creating an account to reduce friction and increase conversions
Progress indicators	Use progress bars or steps to show customers where they are in the checkout process
Multiple payment options	Offer various payment methods like credit/debit cards, PayPal, and digital wallets for convenience
Security features	Display security badges and use SSL encryption to assure customers their data is protected
Clear call-to-action buttons	Use prominent and clearly labeled buttons for actions like "proceed to payment" and "place order"
Auto-fill and address lookup	Implement auto-fill for forms and address lookup to speed up the checkout process
Review order summary	Provide a detailed order summary before the final purchase for customers to review
Mobile-friendly checkout	Optimize the checkout process for mobile users to ensure a seamless experience on all devices
Save cart feature	Allow customers to save their cart for later, which can help reduce cart abandonment
Easy editing	Enable customers to easily modify their cart items, quantities, and shipping options
Transparent shipping costs	Clearly display shipping options and costs early in the checkout process to avoid surprises
Customer support access	Provide easy access to customer support in case customers encounter issues during checkout
Confirmation and follow-up emails	Send order confirmation and follow-up emails to keep customers informed about their purchase status
Return and refund policy	Clearly state the return and refund policies to build trust and confidence in the purchase process

[a]Verified using ChatGPT 4 (June 2024)

These rules help ensure a smooth and efficient checkout process, which can enhance customer satisfaction and reduce cart abandonment rates.

9.2 Definitions: A Selection of Online Payment Methods

Here is a list of some terms often used with the checkout process:

1. Credit and debit cards
   - Debit card: Linked to a checking account, money is deducted directly with no interest.
   - Credit card: Allows borrowing from the bank with a bill at the end of the month and may have an interest if the limit is exceeded. Fraud protection and insurance are common features.

2. Online banking
   - A secure method where transactions are processed through the customer's online banking site. No need to enter card details repeatedly.
3. Digital wallets
   - Secure software that stores customer information for easy transactions. Popular since the mid-1990s, digital wallets are now a major payment method.
4. Apple/Google Pay
   - Contactless payment solutions integrated into smartphones. Apple Pay launched with the iPhone 6; Google Pay uses NFC technology in Android devices.
5. PayPal
   - The most widely used online payment service with over 431 million users in 2023. Allows payments via balance or linked bank cards, emphasizing security through VeriSign and fraud monitoring. PayPal's biggest competitors include Stripe, Square, and Apple Pay, which also offer robust digital payment solutions for both consumers and businesses.
6. Cash on delivery (C.O.D.)
   - Payment is made at the time of delivery. Common in sectors where trust is a significant factor, like clothing.
7. Bitcoin
   - A virtual or digital currency allowing anonymous transactions without government regulation. Uses cryptography for security and is stored in a digital wallet. Bitcoin's biggest competitors include Ethereum, which offers smart contract functionality; Ripple (XRP), known for its fast cross-border payments; Litecoin, valued for its quicker transaction times; and Bitcoin Cash, which aims to provide a more scalable solution with faster transaction processing.

Cryptocurrencies are digital or virtual currencies that use cryptography for security and operate on decentralized networks based on blockchain technology. These currencies are designed to be secure, transparent, and immutable, allowing for peer-to-peer transactions without the need for intermediaries such as banks.[1] A list of examples is provided in Table 9.2.

Bitcoin (BTC) has the advantage of being the most recognized and widely accepted cryptocurrency, often referred to as digital gold due to its limited supply and extensive adoption. Its large, secure blockchain network provides confidence to investors. However, Bitcoin's high transaction fees and slow processing times can be significant drawbacks, making it less suitable for everyday transactions.

Ethereum (ETH) stands out for its support of smart contracts and decentralized applications (dApps), offering a versatile platform for more than just transactions. It holds the second-largest market cap, ensuring high liquidity. On the downside, Ethereum suffers from high gas fees and network congestion, although the Ethereum 2.0 upgrade aims to address these issues.

[1] Oubrich et al., (2021).

Table 9.2 List of some popular cryptocurrencies

Cryptocurrency	Headquarters/owners	Value in USD	Total market capitalization (USD)
Bitcoin (BTC)	Decentralized	$61,210.45	$1.21 trillion
Ethereum (ETH)	Ethereum Foundation, Switzerland	$3334.02	$398.24 billion
Tether (USDT)	Tether Limited, Hong Kong	$1.00	$83.11 billion
Binance Coin (BNB)	Binance, Cayman Islands	$261.34	$41.47 billion
USD Coin (USDC)	Circle, USA	$1.00	$32.61 billion
XRP (XRP)	Ripple Labs, USA	$0.4797	$26.71 billion
Dogecoin (DOGE)	Decentralized	$0.1273	$18.44 billion
Cardano (ADA)	IOHK, Switzerland	$0.3908	$13.97 billion
Avalanche (AVAX)	Ava Labs, USA	$28.74	$11.32 billion
TRON (TRX)	TRON Foundation, Singapore	$0.1225	$10.68 billion

Tether (USDT) offers the stability of being a stablecoin pegged to the US dollar, making it a popular choice for trading and storing value in volatile markets. This stability provides a safe haven for investors during market fluctuations. However, concerns about Tether's reserves and transparency have been ongoing issues, raising questions about its long-term reliability.

Binance Coin (BNB) benefits from its association with Binance, one of the largest cryptocurrency exchanges. It offers lower transaction fees on the Binance platform and can be used for various applications within the Binance ecosystem. Nonetheless, its value is heavily tied to the success and regulatory status of Binance, which can be a risk factor.

USD Coin (USDC) is another stablecoin, providing the stability of the US dollar with transparency and regular audits that boost investor confidence. It is widely accepted and used in various financial applications. However, like all stablecoins, it faces regulatory scrutiny and the inherent risks associated with fiat currency backing.

XRP, created by Ripple Labs, is designed for fast and low-cost international payments, making it an efficient alternative to traditional banking systems. Its partnerships with financial institutions enhance its utility. However, XRP has faced legal challenges, particularly with the SEC, which have affected its adoption and market performance.

Dogecoin (DOGE) started as a meme but has gained popularity for its low transaction fees and strong community support. It is often used for tipping and charitable donations. The downside is its inflationary supply model and reliance on social media hype, which can lead to significant volatility.

Cardano (ADA) offers a research-driven approach to blockchain development, aiming for scalability, security, and sustainability. Its proof-of-stake consensus algorithm is more energy-efficient than Bitcoin's proof-of-work. However, Cardano is still in the development phase for many of its features, and its actual utility in the market is yet to be fully realized.

Avalanche (AVAX) provides high throughput and near-instant finality, making it a strong competitor for DeFi applications. Its unique consensus mechanism ensures robustness and security. Nevertheless, it faces competition from other smart contract platforms, and its long-term adoption is uncertain.

TRON (TRX) focuses on decentralizing the Internet, offering high throughput and low transaction costs, which are beneficial for content creators. However, TRON has been criticized for centralization issues and concerns about its governance model, which might hinder its growth.[2]

Cryptocurrencies are used less often in e-commerce primarily due to volatility, regulatory uncertainty, and low consumer adoption. The fluctuating value of cryptocurrencies makes pricing unstable and poses risks for both consumers and merchants. Additionally, the regulatory environment surrounding digital currencies is still evolving, creating uncertainty and compliance challenges for businesses. Lastly, despite growing awareness, the adoption rate among consumers remains low, with many preferring traditional payment methods due to familiarity and perceived security.

Retailers often partner with e-payment providers like PayPal to ensure secure transactions. Building customer trust involves explaining security measures (SSL/SET) and providing alternative ordering methods such as phone or chat. For security, we have the following systems:

- Secure electronic transactions, a certification developed by Visa and Mastercard, aims to increase user confidence and efficiency in e-commerce.
- Secure socket layer creates a secure passage between server and browser, protecting user data from hackers. Essential for building customer trust.

Selecting the appropriate payment method depends on geographical and demographic factors. Options should cater to different currencies and provide a smooth customer experience.

9.3 The Checkout Process

A well-designed checkout process minimizes cart abandonment. Steps include product page, shopping cart page, review items, billing and shipping information, payment info, and order confirmation, as seen in Fig. 9.1.

A multi-step checkout is a smaller checkout function of a page that guides the customer through the process, building trust but potentially causing fatigue. The opposite would be the one-step checkout where all information is on one page, faster and easier for customers but may require more data capacity.

[2] https://coinmarketcap.com

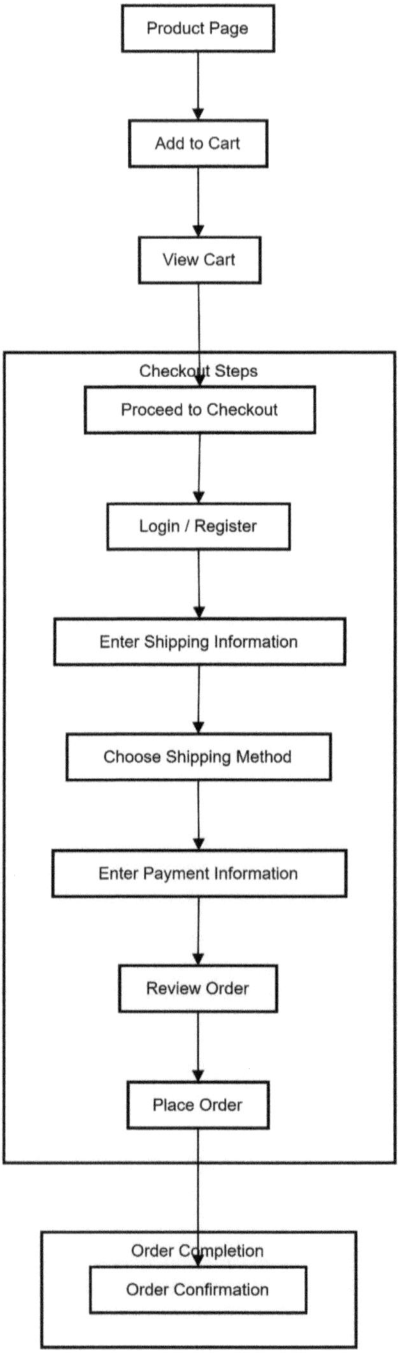

Fig. 9.1 A standard checkout function

9.4 Cart Abandonment

Cart abandonment is influenced by unexpected costs, complicated processes, and security concerns. Quite often, it happens simply because the customer did not intend to buy at all but was merely window shopping, just looking around and trying different possibilities. Sometimes, customers add items to their cart to see if the shipping cost changes with additional products. High shipping costs, particularly from the USA to Europe, can make purchases prohibitive. Similarly, since the UK left the EU, purchases from England to other European countries often take longer and are subject to various tariffs, making the purchasing experience less attractive. Many customers have learned which countries to avoid for e-commerce and what works and what does not.

Table 9.3 shows some of the most common reasons for cart abandonment and how these problems can be solved.

The travel industry has the highest cart abandonment rate, followed by finance, retail, and fashion. This may be due to the initial excitement of planning a trip and

Table 9.3 Common reasons for cart abandonment and potential fixes

Reason for cart abandonment	Description	Potential fixes
Unexpected costs	Additional charges such as shipping, taxes, and fees surprise customers at checkout	Display all costs upfront, including shipping and taxes, before customers reach the checkout page
Complex checkout process	A lengthy or complicated checkout process with too many steps or forms	Simplify the checkout process by minimizing the number of steps and forms. Use a progress indicator
Mandatory account creation	Forcing customers to create an account before they can complete a purchase	Offer a guest checkout option. Allow customers to create an account after the purchase if they wish
Security concerns	Lack of trust in the website's security measures or the safety of their payment information	Display security badges and SSL certificates. Offer trusted payment options
High shipping costs	Expensive shipping costs can discourage customers from completing their purchase	Offer free shipping over a certain purchase amount or flat-rate shipping
Long delivery times	Customers may abandon their cart if the estimated delivery time is too long	Provide various shipping options, including expedited shipping. Clearly state delivery times
Lack of payment options	Not offering a preferred payment method can result in cart abandonment	Offer multiple payment options such as credit/debit cards, PayPal, and digital wallets
Comparison shopping	Customers might add items to their cart for comparison purposes and then leave	Implement wish lists or save-for-later options. Send cart reminder emails
Website performance	Slow loading times, crashes, or errors during the checkout process	Optimize website speed and ensure reliable performance during checkout
Not ready to purchase	Customers are just browsing or saving items for later	Send cart abandonment emails. Offer limited-time discounts or promotions

then suddenly realizing the costs involved, leading to a change of mind. While it is always allowed to dream and dreams are as real as purchases, potential customers often face different kinds of obstacles along the way. These obstacles, such as high prices, unexpected costs, or complicated booking processes, can lead to cart abandonment despite genuine interest in the web pages they visit. When we see this behavior, what we want to do is to try to engage with the visitor, to learn more about how he or she thinks.

9.5 Key Takeaways

Here are some of the key takeaways from this chapter:

- Offering multiple and secure payment options such as PayPal, credit/debit cards, and digital wallets is crucial to gaining customer trust and preventing cart abandonment.
- A well-designed checkout process should be simple and intuitive, featuring elements like guest checkout options, progress indicators, and clear call-to-action buttons to enhance the user experience.
- Unexpected costs, especially high shipping fees, are a primary reason for cart abandonment. Displaying all costs upfront and offering solutions like free shipping can mitigate this issue.
- Providing a variety of payment methods and optimizing the checkout process for mobile users are key strategies to improve conversion rates and reduce cart abandonment.
- Security concerns are significant barriers to completing online transactions. Displaying security badges, using SSL encryption, and offering trusted payment options can address these concerns.
- Long delivery times and high shipping costs can deter customers from completing purchases. Offering expedited shipping options and clearly stating delivery times can help.
- Monitoring and analyzing customer behavior through tools like Google Analytics and Crazy Egg can provide insights into the checkout process and identify areas for improvement.
- Engaging with customers who abandon their carts through reminder emails or limited-time promotions can recover potential lost sales.

Continuous improvement and adaptation to customer feedback are essential for maintaining a smooth and efficient checkout process, thereby enhancing overall customer satisfaction and loyalty.

Reference

Oubrich, M., Hakmaoui, A., Benhayoun, L., Söilen, K. S., & Abdulkader, B. (2021). Impacts of leadership style, organizational design and HRM practices on knowledge hiding: The indirect roles of organizational justice and competitive work environment. *Journal of Business Research, 137*, 488–499.

Further Reading

Chiu, C. M., Wang, E. T., Fang, Y. H., & Huang, H. Y. (2014). Understanding customers' repeat purchase intentions in B2C e-commerce: The roles of utilitarian value, hedonic value and perceived risk. *Information Systems Journal, 24*(1), 85–114.

Collier, J. E., & Sherrell, D. L. (2010). Examining the influence of control and convenience in a self-service setting. *Journal of the Academy of Marketing Science, 38*(4), 490–509.

Dahlberg, T., Mallat, N., Ondrus, J., & Zmijewska, A. (2008). Past, present and future of mobile payments research: A literature review. *Electronic Commerce Research and Applications, 7*(2), 165–181.

de Kervenoael, R., Soopramanien, D., Elms, J., & Hallsworth, A. (2014). Perceived risk, risk reduction strategies (RRS) and satisfaction: The case of the online retailing in experience products. *Journal of Retailing and Consumer Services, 21*(4), 619–629.

Featherman, M. S., & Pavlou, P. A. (2003). Predicting e-services adoption: A perceived risk facets perspective. *International Journal of Human-Computer Studies, 59*(4), 451–474.

Mallat, N. (2007). Exploring consumer adoption of mobile payments—A qualitative study. *The Journal of Strategic Information Systems, 16*(4), 413–432.

Marzocchi, G. L., & Zammit, A. (2006). Self-scanning technologies in retail: Determinants of adoption. *The Service Industries Journal, 26*(6), 651–669.

Özkan, S., & Kanat, I. E. (2011). E-government adoption model based on theory of planned behavior: Empirical validation. *Government Information Quarterly, 28*(4), 503–513.

Yang, S., Lu, Y., Gupta, S., Cao, Y., & Zhang, R. (2012). Mobile payment services adoption across time: An empirical study of the effects of behavioral beliefs, social influences, and personal traits. *Computers in Human Behavior, 28*(1), 129–142.

Zhou, T. (2013). An empirical examination of continuance intention of mobile payment services. *Decision Support Systems, 54*(2), 1085–1091.

The E-Commerce Website and Mobile App 10

10.1 Introduction

This chapter focuses on the critical elements of e-commerce websites and mobile apps, emphasizing the importance of an effective landing page. It explains the history and significance of the Internet, highlighting that every website's entry point is the landing page, which sets the stage for user interaction. The chapter details various types of landing pages, such as homepages, splash pages, and squeeze pages, and their roles in converting visitors into customers. Key optimizations for landing pages, like using the F-layout, addressing banner blindness, and employing A/B and multivariate testing, are discussed to improve user engagement and conversion rates. Additionally, the chapter covers bounce rates, their calculation, and the importance of understanding the reasons behind high bounce rates to enhance site performance and user experience.

It may be of help, to get a larger perspective of what we are studying here, to start with an image of how an e-commerce process is designed at length. As can be seen in Fig. 10.1 the checkout function as we discussed in the last chapter is a substantial part.

The e-commerce process involves several key steps that guide a customer from initial interest to final purchase and beyond. First, the customer arrives on the landing page, which is designed to capture their attention and guide them further into the website. This is followed by the consideration phase, where the customer explores different products and compares options. Next, in the intent phase, the customer decides to make a purchase and proceeds to add items to the cart. The checkout process is then initiated, where the customer provides payment and shipping information, ensuring a seamless and secure transaction. Finally, the post-purchase phase focuses on customer retention and loyalty through follow-up communications and customer support. This comprehensive process ensures that the customer has a smooth and engaging shopping experience from start to finish.

K. Solberg Söilen, *Digital Marketing*, Springer Texts in Business and Economics, https://doi.org/10.1007/978-3-031-69518-6_10

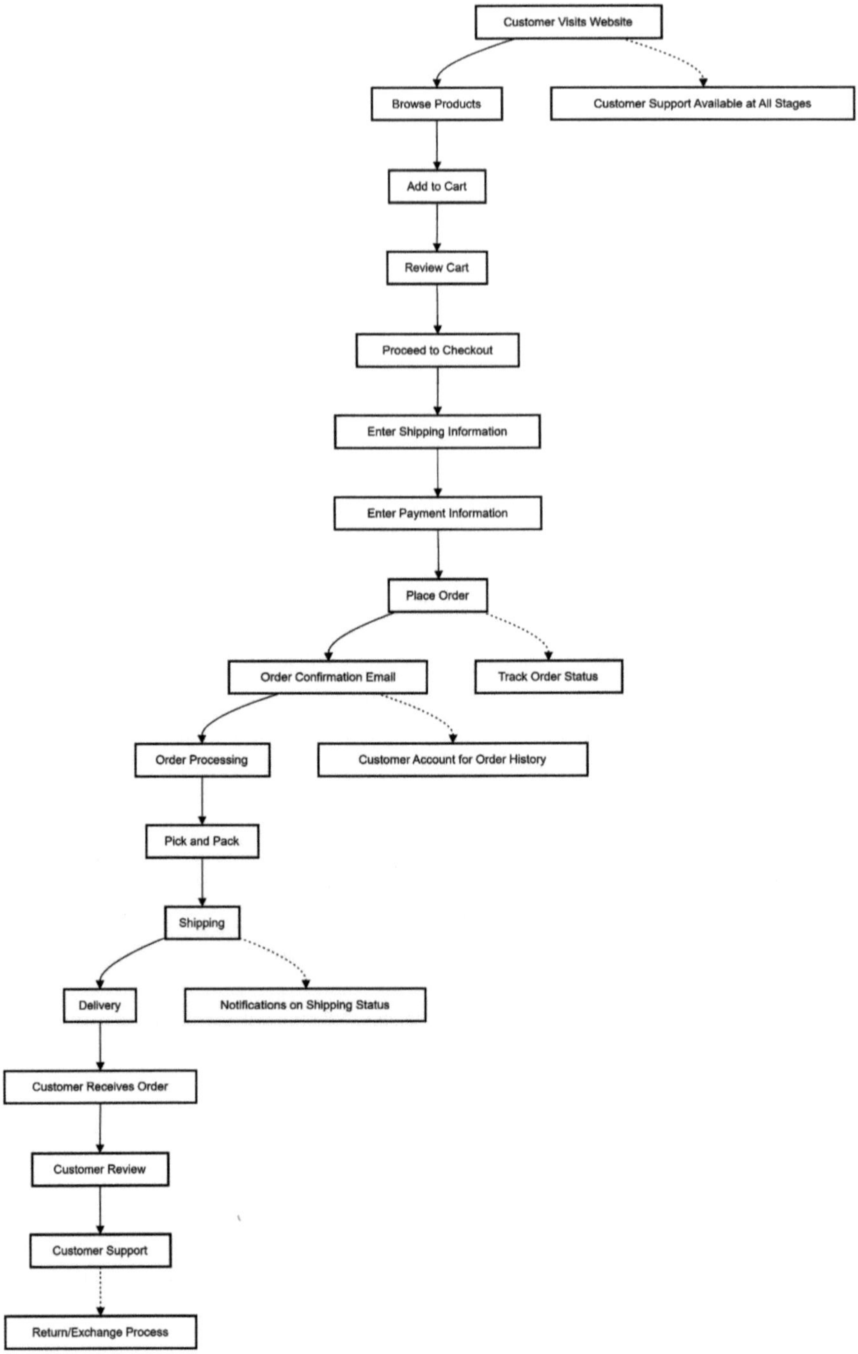

Fig. 10.1 The e-commerce process

10.2 Landing Page (Phase One)

Creating a good landing site involves several critical considerations. Firstly, ensure the landing page has a clear and compelling headline that immediately communicates the value proposition to capture visitors' attention. Secondly, the design should be clean and visually appealing, with a strong focus on usability, including easy navigation and mobile optimization. Thirdly, include a prominent and persuasive call-to-action (CTA) that guides visitors toward the desired action, whether it is making a purchase, signing up for a newsletter, or downloading a resource. Additionally, use high-quality images and relevant multimedia to enhance engagement and provide a clear context for the product or service offered. Finally, optimize the landing page for speed, as slow loading times can significantly increase bounce rates and decrease user satisfaction.

10.3 The Consideration Phase

During the consideration phase, customers are actively researching and comparing different options to find the best solution for their needs. This phase requires providing detailed and relevant information about the products or services offered, including specifications, benefits, and unique selling points. Customer reviews and testimonials play a crucial role, as potential buyers seek social proof and experiences from other users to inform their decisions. Interactive tools such as product comparison charts, calculators, and FAQs can help customers evaluate different options more effectively. It is also important to ensure that the content is easily accessible and understandable, helping customers feel confident in their research and ultimately guiding them toward the next stage of the buying process.

10.4 The Intent Phase

To succeed in the intent phase, it is crucial to understand and align with the customer's goal during their buying process. This phase often involves ensuring the product or service meets the customer's specific needs and providing clear, persuasive information that addresses their concerns and motivations. Interactive and personalized content, such as personalized recommendations and targeted offers, can significantly influence the customer's decision. Detailed product descriptions, high-quality images, and videos help to reinforce the product's value and suitability. Additionally, addressing any potential barriers, such as shipping costs or return policies, and offering reassurance through guarantees or customer service availability can help convert intent into a purchase decision.

We have already discussed the checkout function, so we shall go straight to the last phase.

10.5 The Post-Purchase Phase

To succeed in the post-purchase phase, it is essential to maintain and enhance customer satisfaction and loyalty. Start by providing clear and timely communication, such as order confirmation and tracking information, to keep customers informed about their purchase status. Offering excellent customer support, including easy return and exchange policies, helps resolve any issues quickly and builds trust. Engaging with customers through follow-up emails that request feedback or offer discounts on future purchases can encourage repeat business. Additionally, creating loyalty programs or offering exclusive deals can foster a sense of community and reward loyal customers. Finally, utilizing customer reviews and testimonials to improve products and services ensures that the feedback loop remains active and customer-centric.

10.6 Optimizing Landing Pages for Better Conversion

Several types of landing pages are frequently used, including homepages, search transfer pages, and category browse pages. Homepages are often used by smaller companies due to their simplicity and cost-effectiveness, while larger companies use homepages to promote merchandise. Other types of landing pages include splash pages, squeeze pages, referral pages, and unsubscribe pages, each serving different marketing purposes. The Pareto principle, or the 80/20 rule, suggests that 80% of effects come from 20% of causes, meaning that 20% of the pages often generate 80% of the traffic. Optimizing the landing page is critical as it significantly impacts the purchase process.

The concept of a 100% conversion rate is theoretical. Visitors to a site fall into three categories: "Yesses," who will take the desired action; "Noes," who will never take the desired action; and "Maybes," who might be convinced to take the desired action. Focusing on "maybes" can improve conversion rates by adjusting the landing page to turn "maybe-maybes" into "yes-maybes," thereby increasing the conversion rate.

Studies show users read websites in an F-pattern, starting from the top left and moving right, then down. Designing landing pages with this pattern in mind ensures key content is seen. Banner blindness occurs when visitors consciously or unconsciously ignore ads, wasting approximately 44% of ad spending. Changing banner placement can increase visibility and improve engagement.

10.7 A/B Testing

A/B testing, or bucket testing, compares two versions of a web page to see which performs better and is an essential tool in digital marketing. For example, a marketer might test two headlines to see which generates higher conversion rates. The process is illustrated in Fig. 10.2.

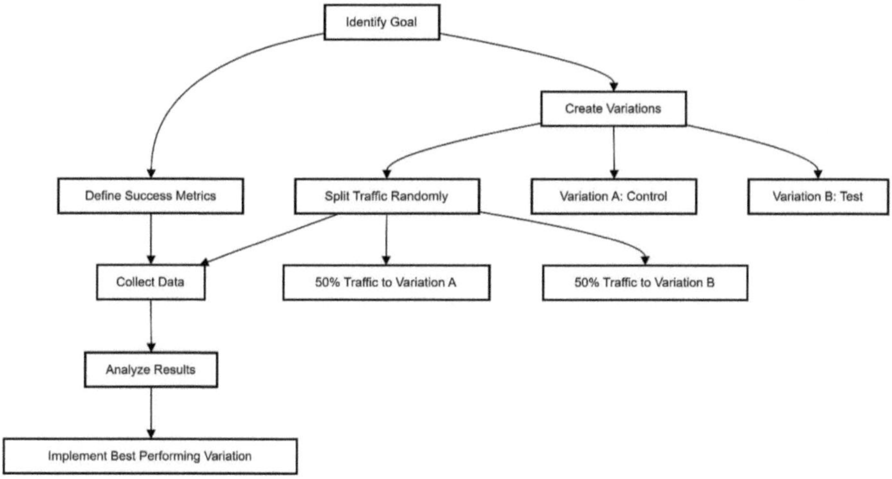

Fig. 10.2 A/B testing

The steps in the process are as follows:[1]

1. Identify goal: Determine the objective of the test, such as increasing click-through rates or conversion rates.
2. Define success metrics: Set clear metrics for what constitutes success, such as the number of clicks or purchases.
3. Create variations: Develop different versions of the web page or element to be tested (e.g., variation A: control, variation B: test).
4. Split traffic randomly: Use a tool to randomly direct a portion of traffic to each variation, ensuring a fair comparison.
5. Collect data: Monitor user interactions with each variation, gathering data on the defined metrics.
6. Analyze results: Compare the performance of each variation using statistical methods to determine which version is more effective.
7. Implement best-performing variation: Apply the winning variation across the entire user base to optimize performance.

The reason we do A/B testing is to determine which version of a web page or element performs better in achieving a specified goal, such as increasing click-through rates or conversions. By splitting traffic between two variations, it helps identify the more effective design or content based on user interactions. This method provides data-driven insights, reducing reliance on assumptions and enhancing decision-making accuracy. Ultimately, A/B testing helps optimize user experience and improves overall website performance by implementing the best-performing variations.

[1] Verified using ChatGPT 4 (June 2024).

Our sports shoes company has decided to improve the click-through rate on their product page by conducting an A/B test on the "Buy Now" button. In the A version, they use a green button with the text "Buy Now," while in the B version, they use a blue button with the text "Shop Now." They split their website traffic equally between the two versions to see which one attracts more clicks. After running the test for a week, they found that the green "Buy Now" button has a 15% higher click-through rate than the blue "Shop Now" button. Based on these results, the company decided to implement the green "Buy Now" button across their site to boost conversions.

10.8 Multivariate Testing

Multivariate testing is a method used to evaluate multiple variables simultaneously to determine which combination produces the best outcome. Unlike A/B testing, which tests only one variable at a time, multivariate testing allows companies to experiment with several elements, such as headlines, images, and call-to-action buttons, on a single page. This method is particularly useful when the goal is to optimize various aspects of a web page to improve user engagement and conversions.

For our sports shoes company, they might use multivariate testing on their product page by testing different combinations of images (showing shoes from different angles), headlines (emphasizing different features like comfort or style), and call-to-action buttons (varying the text and color). By running this test, the company can identify the most effective combination that leads to higher click-through rates and sales.

However, one weakness of multivariate testing is its complexity; it requires a larger sample size to achieve statistically significant results due to the multiple variables being tested. Additionally, the process can be time-consuming and resource-intensive, making it less suitable for small websites with limited traffic. Despite these challenges, multivariate testing can provide comprehensive insights, allowing businesses to fine-tune their web pages for maximum impact.

10.8.1 Multivariate Testing Explanation and Calculation Example[2]

Multivariate testing involves measuring the performance of multiple combinations of variables. The basic formulas and three steps used are as follows:

1. Combination Calculation:

$$\text{Total Combinations} = \prod_{i=1}^{n} v_i$$

where v_i is the number of variations for each element.

2. Conversion Rate (CR):

$$\text{Conversion Rate} = \frac{\text{Number of Conversions}}{\text{Total Visitors}} \times 100$$

3. Statistical Significance:

   To determine if the results are statistically significant, we often use a z-test:

$$z = \frac{p_1 - p_2}{\sqrt{p(1-p)\left(\frac{1}{n_1} + \frac{1}{n_2}\right)}}$$

where p_1 and p_2 are the conversion rates of the two variations, p is the pooled probability of conversions, and n_1 and n_2 are the sample sizes.

Let us take an example. Our sports shoes company wants to test three variables on their product page:

1. Headline: variation A (emphasizing comfort), variation B (emphasizing style)
2. Images: variation 1 (single image), variation 2 (image gallery)
3. Call-to-action (CTA) button: variation X (green button), variation Y (red button)

This results in

$$\text{Total Combinations} = 2(\text{Headlines}) \times 2(\text{Images}) \times 2(\text{CTAs}) = 8\text{combinations}$$

Assume we run the test and collect the following data shown in Table 10.1.

[2] Verified using ChatGPT 4 (June 2024).

Table 10.1 Multivariate testing explanation

Combination	Visitors	Conversions	Conversion Rate (CR)
A1X	1000	50	5%
A1Y	1000	55	5.5%
A2X	1000	60	6%
A2Y	1000	65	6.5%
B1X	1000	45	4.5%
B1Y	1000	50	5%
B2X	1000	55	5.5%
B2Y	1000	60	6%

Analysis of results:

a. Best-performing combination: A2Y (headline A, image gallery, red button) with a 6.5% conversion rate.
b. Compare against other combinations to check for statistical significance. For example, comparing A2Y and B1X:

$$p_1 = 0.065, \quad n_1 = 1000$$
$$p_2 = 0.045, \quad n_2 = 1000$$

$$p = \frac{50+65}{2000} = 0.055$$

$$z = \frac{0.065 - 0.045}{\sqrt{0.055 \times 0.945\left(\frac{1}{1000} + \frac{1}{1000}\right)}} \approx 2.33$$

- A z-value of 2.33 indicates that the difference is statistically significant at the 5% significance level.

Conclusion:

By conducting multivariate testing, our sports shoes company determined that the best combination for their product page is using a headline emphasizing comfort, an image gallery, and a red CTA button. This combination resulted in the highest conversion rate of 6.5%. This method provides valuable insights for optimizing web page elements, though it requires a larger sample size and more complex analysis compared to simpler A/B testing.

10.9 Mobile Landing Pages

Effective mobile landing pages must be concise and quick to load. Given the increasing use of mobile devices for browsing and shopping, it is essential to optimize landing pages for mobile users. This includes ensuring that the page layout is responsive and adapts to different screen sizes, minimizing load times by compressing images and reducing heavy scripts, and simplifying navigation to make it easy for users to find what they need quickly. Additionally, touch-friendly elements like buttons and links should be appropriately sized and spaced to avoid accidental clicks.

10.9.1 Common Mistakes

Common mistakes on landing pages can significantly hinder their effectiveness. One of the primary issues is the lack of a clear unique selling proposition (USP), which can confuse visitors about the page's purpose and value. Poor call-to-action (CTA) design is another frequent problem; CTAs should be prominent, compelling, and easy to find. Headlines that fail to capture interest can result in visitors leaving the page without engaging further. Non-mobile-friendly layouts can alienate a significant portion of users who browse on their smartphones or tablets. Low traffic due to poor search engine optimization (SEO) means that even a well-designed landing page might not get the visibility it needs. Finally, not understanding the target audience can lead to irrelevant content that does not resonate with visitors, further reducing the page's effectiveness. Addressing these issues involves clear messaging, strong CTAs, mobile optimization, good SEO practices, and audience research to ensure relevance.

10.10 Bounce Rates

Bounce rate is a crucial metric representing the percentage of visitors who leave a website after viewing only one page. A high bounce rate can indicate various issues with a website's performance or user experience. It is essential for understanding customer behavior and improving site engagement. By analyzing bounce rates, businesses can identify problems that may be causing visitors to leave prematurely and take steps to address these issues.

10.10.1 Definitions

The most important terms used to understand this chapter include the following:

- Bounce rate: The percentage of single-page visits, where visitors leave the site from the landing page without interacting with other pages

- Exit rate: The percentage of exits from a page, regardless of prior activity on the site
- Conversion rate: The percentage of visitors who complete a desired action, such as making a purchase or filling out a form
- CTR (click-through rate): The ratio of users who click on an ad to those who see it

Bounce rates happen for several reasons. Visitors might find that the page does not meet their expectations or needs, leading them to leave immediately. Slow loading times can frustrate users, causing them to exit before the page fully loads. Poor design, confusing navigation, and intrusive pop-ups can also drive visitors away. Inaccurate SEO strategies can lead to irrelevant traffic, resulting in high bounce rates because the visitors did not find what they were looking for.

10.10.2 Addressing High Bounce Rates

To address high bounce rates, it is important to ensure that the landing page meets user expectations. This involves optimizing the page for relevant keywords so that it attracts the right audience. Improving page load times through efficient coding and optimized images can keep visitors from leaving out of frustration. A clean, intuitive design with straightforward navigation helps users find what they need quickly, encouraging them to explore further. Reducing the use of disruptive elements like pop-ups and ensuring that the page content is engaging and relevant can also help retain visitors.

10.10.3 Detailed Example

For example, a sports shoes company noticing a high bounce rate might start by analyzing their landing page speed. If it is slow, they can compress images and streamline code to improve load times. They might also review their SEO strategy to ensure that their keywords are attracting the right audience interested in sports shoes. Simplifying the design of the landing page, ensuring that it is easy to navigate, and providing clear, compelling content about their products can help keep visitors engaged. By offering interactive elements like videos of the shoes in use or customer reviews, they can further reduce bounce rates and increase user interaction.

10.11 Key Takeaways

Here are some strategic takeaways for managers from this chapter:

- Landing page optimization: Ensure landing pages are optimized for clarity, engagement, and conversion. A clear and compelling headline, intuitive design, prominent call-to-action (CTA), and quick loading times are essential to capture and retain visitor interest.
- Customer journey mapping: Strategically design the customer journey from the landing page through consideration and intent phases to post-purchase engagement. Use detailed product information, customer reviews, and interactive tools to guide customers smoothly toward making a purchase.
- Use of A/B and multivariate testing: Implement A/B and multivariate testing to continuously optimize landing pages and other key website elements. Testing different headlines, images, and CTAs can provide data-driven insights to improve user engagement and conversion rates.
- Reducing bounce rates: High bounce rates can indicate issues with website performance or user experience. Focus on improving page load times, simplifying navigation, and ensuring content relevance to retain visitors and encourage deeper site engagement.
- Mobile optimization: Given the increasing use of mobile devices for shopping, ensure that landing pages and the overall site are optimized for mobile users. Responsive design, fast loading times, and simplified navigation are crucial for a seamless mobile experience.
- Strategic SEO and traffic management: Optimize search engine strategies to attract the right audience and reduce bounce rates. Ensure that SEO efforts align with the content and user expectations to drive relevant traffic to the site.
- Customer feedback integration: Use customer feedback to continuously improve the user experience. Implement feedback mechanisms such as reviews and surveys to understand customer needs and address any pain points.
- Post-purchase engagement: Develop strategies for post-purchase engagement to enhance customer loyalty. Follow-up communications, excellent customer support, and loyalty programs can encourage repeat business and positive word-of-mouth.
- Addressing security concerns: Ensure that the website is perceived as secure by prominently displaying security badges and offering trusted payment options. This can alleviate customer concerns about data security and enhance trust.
- Data-driven decision-making: Use analytics tools to monitor key performance metrics such as conversion rates, bounce rates, and customer engagement. Make data-driven decisions to optimize the e-commerce site continually and adapt to changing customer behaviors and market trends.

Your landing site is much like the entrance of a shop; it is the first impression of the visitor. If we do not like what we see in the windows we will not enter the store. It is much the same online.

Further Reading

Cyr, D., Head, M., & Ivanov, A. (2006). Design aesthetics leading to m-loyalty in mobile commerce. *Information & Management, 43*(8), 950–963.

Fang, X., Chan, S., Brzezinski, J., & Xu, S. (2005). Moderating effects of task type on wireless technology acceptance. *Journal of Management Information Systems, 22*(3), 123–157.

Kim, J., & Lee, K. H. (2002). Critical design factors for successful e-commerce systems. *Behaviour & Information Technology, 21*(3), 185–199.

Lee, Y. C., & Koubek, R. J. (2010). Understanding user preferences based on usability and aesthetics before and after actual use. *Interacting with Computers, 22*(6), 530–543.

Liao, C., Palvia, P., & Lin, H. N. (2006). The roles of habit and website quality in e-commerce. *International Journal of Information Management, 26*(6), 469–483.

Loiacono, E. T., Watson, R. T., & Goodhue, D. L. (2007). WebQual: An instrument for consumer evaluation of websites. *International Journal of Electronic Commerce, 11*(3), 51–87.

Tarafdar, M., & Zhang, J. (2005). Analyzing the influence of website design parameters on website usability. *Information Resources Management Journal, 18*(4), 62–80.

Venkatesh, V., & Davis, F. D. (2000). A theoretical extension of the technology acceptance model: Four longitudinal field studies. *Management Science, 46*(2), 186–204.

Wells, J. D., Valacich, J. S., & Hess, T. J. (2011). What signal are you sending? How website quality influences perceptions of product quality and purchase intentions. *MIS Quarterly, 35*(2), 373–396.

Zhang, P., & von Dran, G. M. (2000). Satisfiers and dissatisfiers: A two-factor model for website design and evaluation. *Journal of the American Society for Information Science, 51*(14), 1253–1268.

Information Architecture 11

11.1 Definition

Information architecture (IA) is about helping people understand their surroundings and find what they are looking for, both in the real world and online. A comparison between a traditional architect and an information architect is that while a traditional architect designs and plans buildings, an information architect designs and plans websites and organizes their content.

IA is the practice of organizing and structuring content in websites, applications, and other digital spaces to facilitate easy navigation and understanding. It involves creating a blueprint for the design, which includes the hierarchy, navigation, and categorization of information. The main components of IA are as follows:[1]

1. Organization systems: These define how information is categorized and structured, including the taxonomy and metadata used.
2. Labeling systems: These are the names and terminology used to represent different pieces of content and navigation options.
3. Navigation systems: These help users move through the content, such as menus, links, and breadcrumbs.
4. Search systems: These enable users to find specific information through search bars and filters.
5. Interaction design: This involves designing the way users interact with the content and navigation elements to ensure a seamless experience.

Together, these components help create an intuitive and user-friendly digital environment.

The work of information architects draws on deep roots in cognitive psychology, semiotics, cybernetics, discrete mathematics, and architecture. The term "information architecture" originates from the 1970s. From that point, IA has become

[1] Verified using ChatGPT 4 (June 2024).

K. Solberg Söilen, *Digital Marketing*, Springer Texts in Business and Economics, https://doi.org/10.1007/978-3-031-69518-6_11

something everyone looks into, even if they do not have a specific IA employee, but it is also an area associated with some hype, which can sometimes overshadow practical challenges.

According to the Information Architecture Institute, "a good IA helps people to understand their surroundings and find what they're looking for—in the real world as well as online." Now, the IA of anything can always become better, so it is also important to know when to draw the line, that is, when to say that it is good enough. To address the issue of knowing when to stop refining the information architecture (IA), set clear objectives and success criteria from the beginning. Regularly review user feedback and analytics to ensure the IA meets the defined goals and user needs. Once the IA effectively facilitates navigation and achieves the desired user experience and business outcomes, consider it sufficient, and focus on other areas for improvement.

Peter Morville (2006) defines information architecture as follows:

1. The structural design of shared information environments.
2. The combination of organization, labeling, search, and navigation systems within websites and intranets.
3. The art and science of shaping information products and experiences to support usability and findability.
4. An emerging community of practice that focuses on bringing the principles of architecture into the design and model of digital landscapes.

To clearly divide this chapter from the next on "**Building an Attractive Site Structure,**" we are going to focus on the conceptual and strategic aspects here and the practical, implementation-oriented aspects in Chap. 12.

11.2 Components of Information Architecture

11.2.1 Organization Systems: Taxonomy, Categorization, and Metadata

Organization systems, including taxonomy, categorization, and metadata, are fundamental to effective information architecture. Taxonomy refers to the hierarchical classification of information, enabling users to navigate through categories and subcategories logically. Categorization involves grouping similar items together, which helps in creating intuitive and user-friendly structures that enhance discoverability. Metadata is the data about data, providing context and additional information such as author, date, and keywords, which improve searchability and content management.

To create an effective taxonomy, start by conducting a thorough content inventory and understanding the relationships between different types of content. Use card sorting exercises to see how users naturally group information, which can inform your categorization approach. Develop clear and consistent naming conventions for categories and subcategories to ensure users can easily find what they are looking for.

When defining metadata, focus on the most relevant attributes that will aid in search and retrieval. Implement standardized metadata schemas to maintain consistency and enhance interoperability across different systems. Regularly review and update your taxonomy, categorization, and metadata to adapt to changing user needs and content evolution.

By organizing information systematically through taxonomy, categorization, and metadata, you can create a more navigable and efficient information architecture, ultimately enhancing user experience and engagement.

11.2.2 Labeling Systems: Naming Conventions and Terminology

Labeling systems, which encompass naming conventions and terminology, are crucial for the clarity and usability of information architectures. Naming conventions involve creating consistent and meaningful names for categories, pages, and elements within a website or application. These conventions help users quickly understand and navigate the content. Terminology refers to the specific words and phrases used within the labeling system, ensuring that they are clear, relevant, and familiar to the target audience.

To develop effective naming conventions, begin by understanding your users' language and preferences through user research and testing. Use terms that are simple, descriptive, and intuitive, avoiding jargon unless it is well understood by your audience. Ensure consistency in naming by adhering to predefined rules and guidelines, such as always using nouns or verbs for certain types of labels, which aids in predictability and user confidence.

When defining terminology, consider the context in which terms will be used. Employ user-centered design principles by involving users in the process through methods like card sorting and usability testing. This helps ensure that the terminology resonates with them and supports their tasks effectively. Regularly review and update the labeling system to reflect changes in user behavior, industry standards, and content evolution.

Effective labeling systems enhance the findability and usability of content, making it easier for users to navigate and locate information. By focusing on clear naming conventions and appropriate terminology, you create a cohesive and user-friendly information architecture that improves the overall user experience.

11.2.3 Navigation Systems: Menus, Links, and Breadcrumb Trails

Navigation systems, which include menus, links, and breadcrumb trails, are essential for guiding users through a website or application effectively. Menus serve as the primary navigation tool, providing users with a structured overview of available content and helping them access different sections with ease. They can be designed as horizontal bars, vertical lists, or drop-down menus, depending on the site's layout and user needs.

Links are integral to navigation, connecting different pieces of content and allowing users to move seamlessly between related pages. Effective use of internal links can enhance user experience by providing additional information and context, while external links can direct users to valuable resources outside the site.

Breadcrumb trails offer a secondary navigation path, showing users their location within the site's hierarchy and allowing them to backtrack to previous pages or higher-level sections. This feature is particularly useful for websites with deep or complex structures, as it helps users understand their current position and navigate more intuitively.

To create effective navigation systems, begin by understanding your users' needs and behaviors through user research and usability testing. Design menus that are clear, concise, and logically organized, grouping related items together and using familiar labels. Ensure links are descriptive and relevant, providing users with clear expectations of where they will lead. Implement breadcrumb trails on all pages except the homepage to aid navigation and reduce the likelihood of users feeling lost.

Regularly evaluate and update the navigation system based on user feedback and analytics to ensure it continues to meet users' needs and expectations. By focusing on menus, links, and breadcrumb trails, you create a cohesive and user-friendly navigation system that enhances the overall user experience and supports efficient content discovery.

11.2.4 Search Systems: Search Bars, Filters, and Advanced Search Options

Search systems, which encompass search bars, filters, and advanced search options, are vital for helping users quickly locate specific information on a website or application. Search bars are the most straightforward tool, allowing users to enter keywords or phrases to find relevant content. To enhance their effectiveness, ensure that the search bar is prominently placed, easy to use, and equipped with features like auto-suggestions and spell-check.

Filters refine search results by narrowing down options based on specific criteria such as category, date, price, or other attributes. This functionality is particularly useful on e-commerce sites, where users can filter products by size, color, brand, and other specifications to quickly find what they are looking for.

Advanced search options offer even more granular control, allowing users to specify multiple parameters simultaneously. These options can include Boolean operators (AND, OR, NOT), exact phrase matching, and field-specific searches (e.g., searching within titles or descriptions). Providing a clear and user-friendly interface for advanced search options can significantly enhance user experience, especially for users with complex search needs.

To implement effective search systems, start by analyzing user behavior and common search patterns to understand what users typically look for and how they search. Design the search bar to be easily accessible and ensure it provides relevant suggestions and corrections. Develop filters that align with the key attributes of your content and make them easily adjustable. For advanced search options, create a clear and intuitive interface that guides users in formulating precise queries.

Regularly test and refine the search functionality based on user feedback and search analytics to ensure it continues to meet users' needs. By integrating well-designed search bars, filters, and advanced search options, you can significantly improve content discoverability and user satisfaction.

11.2.5 Interaction Design: User Interface and Experience Considerations

Interaction design focuses on creating engaging interfaces with well-thought-out behaviors and actions to facilitate user interactions. A primary aspect is ensuring the user interface (UI) is intuitive and easy to navigate. This involves designing clear and consistent navigation elements, such as buttons and icons, which guide users seamlessly through the site or application.

User experience (UX) considerations include making sure the interface responds predictably to user inputs and provides immediate feedback. This can be achieved through visual cues like hover effects, loading animations, and confirmation messages, which help users understand that their actions have been acknowledged and are being processed.

Another critical component is affordance, which refers to the design aspects that suggest how an object should be used. For example, a button should look clickable, and a slider should look draggable. Good affordance reduces the learning curve and increases user satisfaction.

Accessibility is also vital, ensuring that the design is usable by people with various disabilities. This involves using proper color contrasts, providing text alternatives for non-text content, and enabling keyboard navigation.

Finally, usability testing is crucial in interaction design. This involves observing real users as they interact with the interface to identify any issues or areas for improvement. Iterative testing and feedback loops help refine the design to better meet user needs and enhance overall usability.

Incorporating these elements into interaction design ensures that the UI is not only visually appealing but also functional, accessible, and user-friendly, ultimately leading to a positive user experience.

11.2.6 The Example with Our Sports Shoes Company

To create an effective website for the sports shoes company, it is essential to implement robust information architecture. This can be achieved through the following:[2]

Organization systems: Products are organized into taxonomies and categories such as "Running Shoes," "Casual Sneakers," and "Sports Sandals." Each category is tagged with relevant metadata, like brand, size, and color, to facilitate accurate product filtering.

Labeling systems: Naming conventions ensure consistency and clarity. For instance, product labels like "Men's Running Shoes" and "Women's Training Sneakers" are used. Terminology is kept simple and customer-centric to enhance understanding and searchability.

Navigation systems: The site uses intuitive menus and links, with primary navigation including categories like "Men," "Women," "Kids," and "Sale." Breadcrumb trails are implemented to help users keep track of their navigation path, enhancing their browsing experience.

Search systems: A prominent search bar is available on every page, equipped with filters for narrowing down results by size, brand, and price. Advanced search options allow users to find specific models or features, such as "water-resistant running shoes."

Interaction design: The user interface is designed for ease of use, with clear call-to-action buttons like "Add to Cart" and "Buy Now." Visual cues, such as highlighted hover effects on product images, provide immediate feedback to user interactions. Accessibility features ensure that the website is usable by people with disabilities, including keyboard navigation and text-to-speech compatibility.

By integrating these components, the sports shoes company's website can offer a seamless and engaging user experience, facilitating easy product discovery, and efficient navigation, ultimately driving higher customer satisfaction and conversion rates, as outlined in Fig. 11.1.

The diagram illustrates the different components of information architecture and their interrelationships. It starts with organization systems, which include taxonomy, categorization, and metadata, fundamental for structuring information. Labeling systems involve naming conventions and terminology to ensure clarity and usability. Navigation systems comprise menus, links, and breadcrumb trails, facilitating user navigation. The search systems section highlights search bars, filters, and advanced search options for efficient information retrieval. Finally, interaction

[2] Verified using ChatGPT 4 (June 2024).

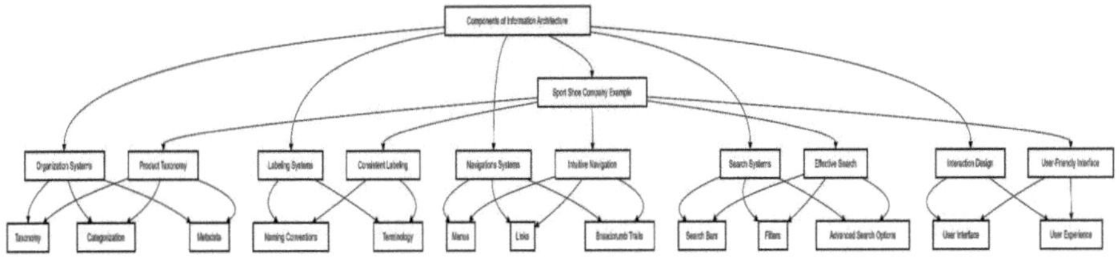

Fig. 11.1 Components of information architecture and their relationship

design focuses on user interface and experience, ensuring accessibility and ease of use.

The example with the sports shoes company integrates these components to enhance user experience and customer satisfaction.

11.3 Principles and Best Practices

11.3.1 User-Centered Design: Understanding User Needs and Behaviors

User-centered design focuses on placing the user at the heart of the design process by thoroughly understanding their needs, behaviors, and preferences. This involves conducting user research through methods such as surveys, interviews, and usability testing to gather insights into how users interact with a product or website. By analyzing this data, designers can create more intuitive and effective interfaces that cater specifically to user expectations and requirements. It is essential to develop personas representing different user types and their goals to guide design decisions. Additionally, iterating designs based on continuous user feedback ensures that the final product is user-friendly, engaging, and meets the users' needs effectively.

11.3.2 Consistency: Maintaining Uniformity in Structure and Labels

Consistency in information architecture involves maintaining uniformity in the structure, labels, and design elements across a website or application. This practice helps users navigate the site more easily, as they can predict where information is located and what actions to take. To achieve consistency, use standardized naming conventions for categories and labels, ensuring that similar content is grouped and labeled in the same way throughout the site. Apply a cohesive visual design, including fonts, colors, and button styles, to create a seamless user experience. Regularly review and update your content and design elements to ensure they adhere to established guidelines, which reinforces user familiarity and trust. Consistency not only enhances usability but also contributes to a professional and polished appearance, improving overall user satisfaction.

11.3.3 Findability: Ensuring Information Is Easily Searchable and Navigable

Findability is crucial for information architecture, as it ensures users can easily locate and access the information they need. This can be achieved by implementing intuitive navigation systems, such as clear menus, well-structured links, and breadcrumb trails that guide users through the website. Incorporating a robust search system, with features like search bars, filters, and advanced search options, helps users quickly find specific content. Organizing content logically through taxonomy and categorization also enhances findability by grouping similar items together, making them easier to discover. Regularly reviewing and updating the information architecture based on user feedback and analytics ensures that the structure remains user-friendly and effective. By focusing on findability, websites can improve user experience, reduce frustration, and increase overall engagement.

11.3.4 Accessibility: Making Content Accessible to All Users, Including Those with Disabilities

Accessibility in information architecture ensures that content is usable by everyone, including individuals with disabilities. This involves adhering to web accessibility standards, such as the Web Content Accessibility Guidelines (WCAG), which provide a framework for making web content more accessible. Key practices include providing text alternatives for non-text content, such as images and videos, to support screen readers used by visually impaired users. Ensuring sufficient color contrast and using clear, readable fonts enhance the visual accessibility of content. Navigation should be keyboard-friendly, allowing users to move through the site without a mouse. Regular accessibility audits and user testing with people who have disabilities help identify and address any barriers, ensuring a more inclusive user experience. By prioritizing accessibility, websites can reach a broader audience and provide a more equitable digital environment.

11.4 Tools and Techniques

11.4.1 Card Sorting: Method for Understanding How Users Categorize Information

Card sorting is a user research technique that helps understand how users organize information. Participants are given cards, each labeled with a piece of content or functionality, and asked to group them in a way that makes sense to them. This process reveals users' mental models and can inform the structure of a website or application. By analyzing the groupings, designers can create an information architecture that aligns with users' expectations and improves usability. Card sorting can be conducted in-person with physical cards or online using software tools, providing valuable insights into how to categorize and label content effectively.

11.4.2 Wireframing: Creating Basic Layouts to Visualize IA

Wireframing involves creating simplified sketches or blueprints of a website or application's layout. These basic visual representations outline the structure, placement of elements, and navigation paths without focusing on design details like color or typography. Wireframes help stakeholders and designers visualize the information architecture and user flow, ensuring that all necessary components are included and logically arranged. They serve as a foundation for developing more detailed prototypes and final designs. Tools like Sketch, Figma, and Adobe XD are commonly used for wireframing, allowing for easy adjustments and collaboration.

11.4.3 User Testing: Techniques to Validate IA with Real Users

User testing involves evaluating the effectiveness of information architecture by observing real users as they interact with a website or application. Techniques such as usability testing, where users are asked to complete specific tasks while being observed, help identify any issues or areas for improvement in the IA. Feedback from user testing provides actionable insights into how users navigate and find information, highlighting any confusion or inefficiencies. Regular user testing throughout the design process ensures that the IA meets users' needs and expectations, leading to a more user-friendly and successful product. Tools like UsabilityHub, UserTesting, and Optimal Workshop can facilitate user testing sessions and data analysis.

11.5 Principles of Information Architecture

Within information architecture, there are eight principles that architects should focus on to create a structure, often illustrated with maps and flowcharts (Klancar, 2020):

1. The principle of objects: Content should be treated as a living, breathing entity with lifecycles, behaviors, and attributes.
2. The principle of choices: Less is more. Keep the number of choices to a minimum.
3. The principle of disclosure: Show a preview of information to help users understand what kind of information is hidden if they dig deeper.
4. The principle of exemplars: Show examples of content when describing categories to help users identify what they are looking for.
5. The principle of front doors: Assume that at least 50% of users will enter the site through a different page than the homepage. Every page should include some information to reassure users that they are on the right website.
6. The principle of multiple classifications: Offer users several different classification schemes to browse the site's content.
7. The principle of focused navigation: Keep navigation simple, and never mix different elements.
8. The principle of growth: Assume that the website's content will grow, and ensure it is scalable (Babich, 2017).

Before applying these principles, the architect needs to have a thorough understanding of the site and a complete inventory of its content. Since there is no single right way to structure content, IA involves not only technical knowledge but also a form of art (Bradley, 2010).

Given the complexity and importance of IA, companies risk failure if they do not implement it effectively. With companies like Google and Facebook blocking low-value content websites, producing valuable content that can be discovered through good IA is crucial (Klancar, 2020).

11.6 Value for the User

In today's world of instant gratification and information overload, delivering the right content quickly is essential. If a user's experience is too complicated or slow, they will simply abandon the process (Klancar, 2020).

IA should revolve around the user's needs. Businesses often focus on their own goals rather than the consumer's needs. Effective navigation should be based on how users want to find information (c).

Peter Morville and Louis Rosenfeld categorize user needs into four types:

1. Known-item seeking: Users search for something specific.
2. Exploratory seeking: Users look for inspiration without a clear idea.

3. Exhaustive research: Users seek as much information as possible.
4. Re-finding: Users look for previously accessed items (Klancar, 2020).

A good information architecture greatly enhances user experience. The quicker users find what they are looking for, the more satisfied they will be. Understanding user needs allows for prioritizing architectural components, leading to better user interface success (Klancar, 2020).

11.7 Information Architecture: Key Takeaways for Managers

Here are some suggestions for how to understand and what to keep an eye on when it comes to managers, recaptioning some of what has already been mentioned:

1. **Definition and importance**: Information architecture (IA) involves organizing and structuring content to facilitate easy navigation and understanding, much like how a traditional architect designs buildings.
2. **Core components**: IA consists of organization systems, labeling systems, navigation systems, search systems, and interaction design, each playing a crucial role in creating an intuitive user experience.
3. **Organization systems**: Effective taxonomy, categorization, and metadata are essential for structuring information logically, enhancing discoverability, and improving content management.
4. **Labeling systems**: Consistent and meaningful naming conventions and terminology help users quickly understand and navigate content, making the website more user-friendly.
5. **Navigation systems**: Well-designed menus, links, and breadcrumb trails guide users through the website, providing a clear path and preventing them from getting lost.
6. **Search systems**: Prominent and efficient search bars, filters, and advanced search options are vital for helping users quickly find specific information on the website.
7. **Interaction design**: An intuitive user interface and experience, with clear navigation elements and responsive feedback, ensure a seamless and satisfying interaction for users.
8. **User-centered design**: Focusing on understanding user needs and behaviors through research and testing leads to more effective and user-friendly information architecture.
9. **Consistency**: Maintaining uniformity in structure, labels, and design elements across the website helps users navigate more easily and enhances the overall user experience.
10. **Findability and accessibility**: Ensuring information is easily searchable and navigable while making content accessible to all users, including those with disabilities, enhances user satisfaction, and broadens the website's reach.

At the end of the day, IA is about finding what you are searching for on a website. As a company selling online, we cannot accept a situation where we have a product, but the customer leaves because he cannot find it. Thus, understanding and implementing effective information architecture (IA) are crucial for creating user-friendly digital environments. By focusing on organization, labeling, navigation, search systems, and interaction design, managers can ensure their websites are intuitive and accessible and provide a seamless user experience.

References

Babich, N. (2017). *The principles of navigation: Designing clear and intuitive navigation systems.* Retrieved from https://uxplanet.org/the-principles-of-navigation-designing-clear-and-intuitive-navigation-systems-973a1e0e12a1

Bradley, M. (2010). *Designing user experiences: Principles and practices.* Retrieved from https://www.smashingmagazine.com/2010/07/ux-design-essentials/

Klancar, M. (2020). *The importance of information architecture in digital marketing.* Retrieved from https://www.linkedin.com/pulse/importance-information-architecture-digital-marketing-milan-klancar

Morville, P. (2006). *Information architecture for the World Wide Web: Designing large-scale web sites.* O'Reilly Media.

Further Reading

Information Architecture Institute. (n.d.). *Definition of information architecture.* Retrieved from informationarchitecture.org.

Rosenfeld, L., Morville, P., & Arango, J. (2015). *Information architecture: For the web and beyond.* O'Reilly Media.

Building an Attractive Site Structure 12

12.1 Background

In this chapter, we will explore how to build an attractive site structure, focusing on important components and the overall process. This book is more for marketers, not first designers or creatives, so we will not delve into details about colors, fonts, and images used in websites. Instead, we will examine various general aspects of web design that contribute to creating an engaging site, including site maps, visual design, hierarchy, visitor engagement, and visual usability tools.

Building an attractive website is not merely about technology or following trends. It should not be created just because it is expected or because everyone else has one. Instead, it should be developed to address a specific need with clear, defined goals in mind. An attractive website is often simple, easy to use, and informative. Websites are also done differently in different countries, and cultures have different ways of expressing what they find attractive and interesting, like the use of strong red and golden colors in China, which companies in the Western world might consider looking a bit kitsch.

Design and trust are closely related. Your site needs to be up-to-date, not only in content and functionality but also in appearance and operation. In a brick-and-mortar store, you build trust by engaging personally with customers face-to-face. They see your building and know they can come back to you during opening hours if something is wrong. Online, you do not have that opportunity, so you start from a trust deficit. Design and functionality on the website are parts of what it takes to compensate for that lack of trust. Simply put, you need to build trust in a different way, by design and functionalities.

K. Solberg Söilen, *Digital Marketing*, Springer Texts in Business and Economics, https://doi.org/10.1007/978-3-031-69518-6_12

For example, the sports shoes company can enhance trust by ensuring its website is visually appealing and user-friendly. High-quality images of products, clear and concise descriptions, and easy navigation help customers feel confident about their purchases. Adding customer reviews and testimonials can provide social proof, further building trust. Moreover, implementing secure payment options and clearly displaying security badges can reassure customers about the safety of their transactions. Finally, offering excellent customer service through live chat, easy-to-find contact information, and prompt responses to inquiries can replicate the personal touch found in physical stores, thereby enhancing trust online.

The focus of this chapter will be on practical steps and techniques for creating a visually appealing and functional website structure. We will guide you through planning the site structure, designing it, implementing it, testing and launching it, and, finally, maintenance and iteration, as can be seen in Fig. 12.1.

Defining objectives is a crucial first step in creating an effective website. This process involves clearly articulating the purpose of the site and identifying the specific goals it aims to achieve. Begin by asking fundamental questions such as, What is the primary function of the site? Who is the target audience? What actions do you want users to take? For example, the objectives could include increasing sales, building brand awareness, or providing information and support.

To define objectives, gather input from key stakeholders through meetings or surveys to understand their expectations and requirements. Prioritize these goals to focus on the most critical outcomes. Ensure that the objectives are specific, measurable, achievable, relevant, and time-bound (SMART) to facilitate effective planning and assessment. Document these objectives clearly and use them as a guide throughout the site development process to maintain alignment with your overall strategy.

By setting well-defined objectives, you create a foundation that informs all subsequent decisions, from design and content creation to user experience and marketing efforts. This clarity helps ensure that the website effectively serves its intended purpose and meets the needs of its audience.

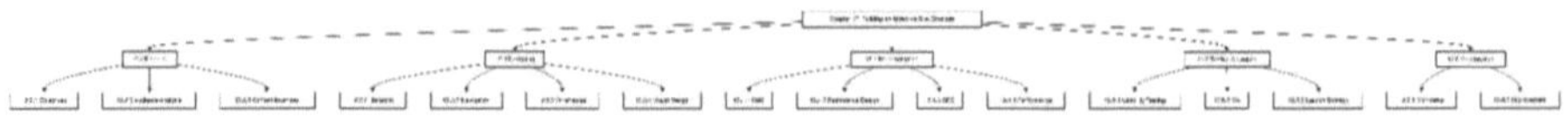

Fig. 12.1 Working process for building site structure

12.2 Site Structure Analysis

12.2.1 Audience Analysis: Understanding the Target Audience and Their Needs

Audience analysis involves identifying and understanding the specific groups of people your website aims to serve. This process begins with demographic research, such as age, gender, location, income level, and education, to paint a clear picture of your target audience. Psychographic data, including interests, values, and lifestyle choices, further refines this understanding.

To perform an effective audience analysis, use tools like surveys, focus groups, and interviews to gather firsthand information about your audience's preferences, challenges, and needs. Analyzing website analytics and social media insights can provide valuable data on user behavior and engagement patterns.

Create detailed audience personas that encapsulate the characteristics and behaviors of different user segments. These personas help in designing user-centric experiences by highlighting the specific needs and motivations of each segment.

Regularly updating the audience analysis ensures that your website stays relevant and continues to meet the evolving needs of its users. Understanding your audience deeply allows you to tailor content, design, and functionality to provide a more engaging and satisfying user experience. This alignment between user needs and site offerings is crucial for achieving your website's objectives and enhancing user satisfaction.

12.2.2 Content Inventory: Listing All the Content and Its Intended Organization

A content inventory involves compiling a comprehensive list of all content on your website, such as text, images, videos, documents, and interactive elements. Start by using tools like content audit software or spreadsheets to catalog each piece of content, including its location (URL), format, and metadata.

The inventory should include detailed information about each content item, such as its title, description, author, publication date, and any relevant tags or categories. This helps in understanding the current state of your content and identifying any gaps or redundancies.

Organize the content based on its type, purpose, and audience relevance. This can involve grouping similar content together and determining the hierarchy and structure that make the most sense for your users. Ensure that the organization aligns with your website's overall objectives and user needs.

Conduct a content audit to evaluate the quality and performance of each content piece. This involves assessing metrics like page views, bounce rates, and user engagement to determine which content is effective and which may need updating or removal.

The content inventory serves as a foundation for developing a content strategy, ensuring that your website offers a coherent and user-friendly experience. Regularly updating the inventory helps maintain content relevance and quality, supporting ongoing site improvements and strategic planning. By thoroughly organizing and understanding your content, you can enhance navigation, searchability, and overall user satisfaction.

12.3 Designing the Site Structure

12.3.1 Hierarchical Structures: Organizing Content in a Clear, Logical Way

Creating a hierarchical structure involves organizing website content in a way that is intuitive and logical for users. Start by identifying the main categories and subcategories based on user needs and business goals. This top-down approach ensures that the most critical content is easily accessible.

Information architects use three main types of content structures:

1. Hierarchical: A tree-like structure with main topics branching into subtopics (Fig. 12.2).
2. Sequential: A step-by-step process guiding users through tasks, as used in the diagrams throughout much of this book.
3. Matrix: Allows users to create their own navigation paths, suitable for more complex information (Fig. 12.3).

We want to use card sorting exercises to determine how users naturally group information. This user-centered method helps in designing a hierarchy that aligns with user expectations. Ensure each level of the hierarchy is clearly defined and that content flows logically from general to specific.

We want to visualize the hierarchy with sitemaps or tree diagrams, showing the relationships between pages and sections. This helps in planning the structure and identifying any potential issues or areas of confusion.

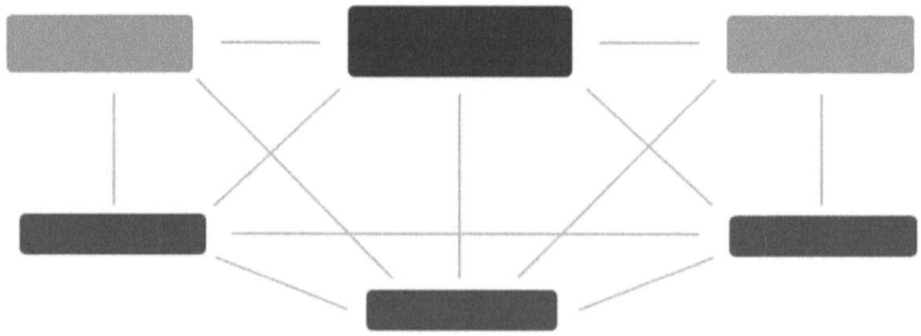

Fig. 12.2 Navigation paths, hierarchical structure

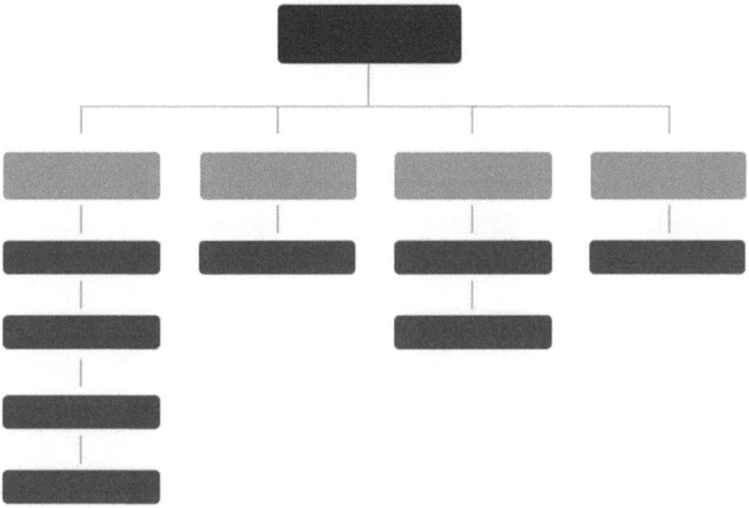

Fig. 12.3 More complex matrix navigation path

A sitemap is a file where you provide information about the various parts of the site, such as pages, videos, and other files, and the connections between them. This helps search engines crawl your site more intelligently. A sitemap, as in Fig. 12.4, indicates to the crawler which files you consider important and provides valuable information about them, such as pages recently updated, the frequency of changes, and alternate language versions.

Maintain consistency in naming conventions and categorization to avoid user confusion. Regularly review and adjust the hierarchy based on user feedback and content performance analytics. The hierarchy should support easy navigation and findability, enhancing the overall user experience by providing a clear path through the site's content.

12.3.2 Navigation Design: Creating Intuitive and User-Friendly Navigation Menus

Make things simple. Do not have more than seven boxes horizontally in your navigation panels. Designing intuitive navigation menus involves creating clear, easily accessible pathways for users to find content.

Start by defining primary, secondary, and tertiary navigation elements based on the site's content hierarchy. Primary navigation usually includes the main categories, while secondary and tertiary levels provide more detailed options.

Use clear, descriptive labels for navigation items to ensure users understand where each link will take them. Avoid jargon, and ensure that labels are consistent throughout the site.

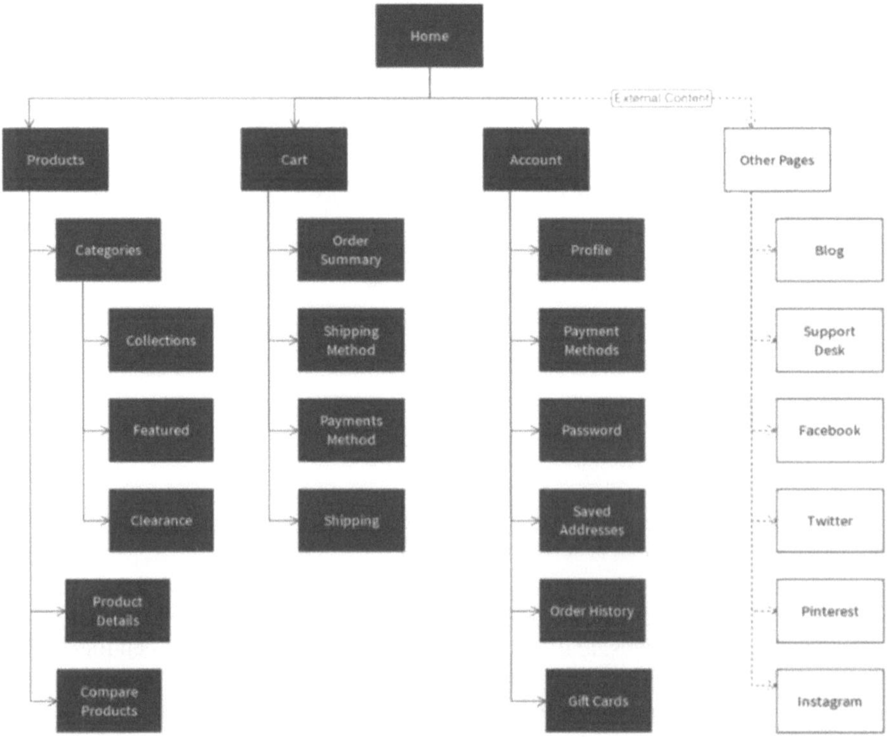

Fig. 12.4 Example of sitemap

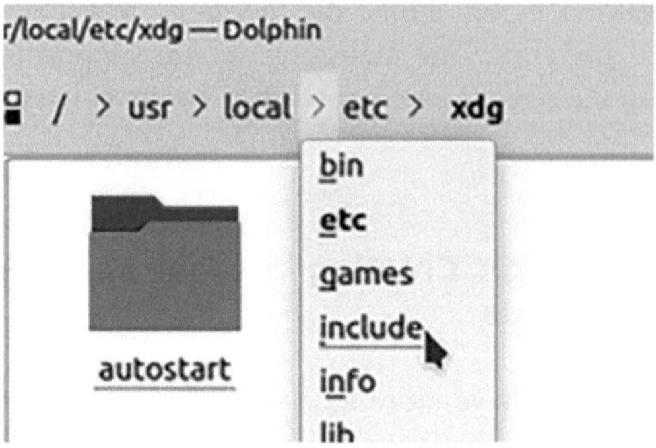

Fig. 12.5 Breadcrumb trails

Incorporate responsive design principles so that navigation menus work seamlessly on all devices, from desktops to smartphones. Use dropdown menus, mega menus, or sidebar menus based on the site's complexity and user needs.

Implement breadcrumb trails, illustrated in Fig. 12.5, to help users understand their current location within the site's structure and easily backtrack if needed.

Conduct usability testing to ensure the navigation design meets user expectations and allows for efficient content discovery. Regularly update the navigation structure based on user feedback and changing content needs.

There are basically three types or kinds of navigation, as shown in Fig. 12.6:

1. **Structural navigation:** This type of navigation helps users understand the overall structure of a website by organizing content in a hierarchical manner. It typically includes primary and secondary menus that allow users to systematically move through different sections and pages of the site.
2. **Associative navigation:** Associative navigation connects related pieces of content through links embedded within the content itself, such as related articles, tags, or categories. This method helps users discover additional relevant information without following the primary site hierarchy.
3. **Utility navigation:** Utility navigation provides access to important tools and services that are not directly related to the main content of the site, such as search bars, login links, or language selection options. These elements are usually found in the header or footer of a website.

12.3.2.1 Main Navigation

Main navigation represents top-level pages in the site's structure and usually includes the site logo and utility navigation. It should be consistent across all pages.

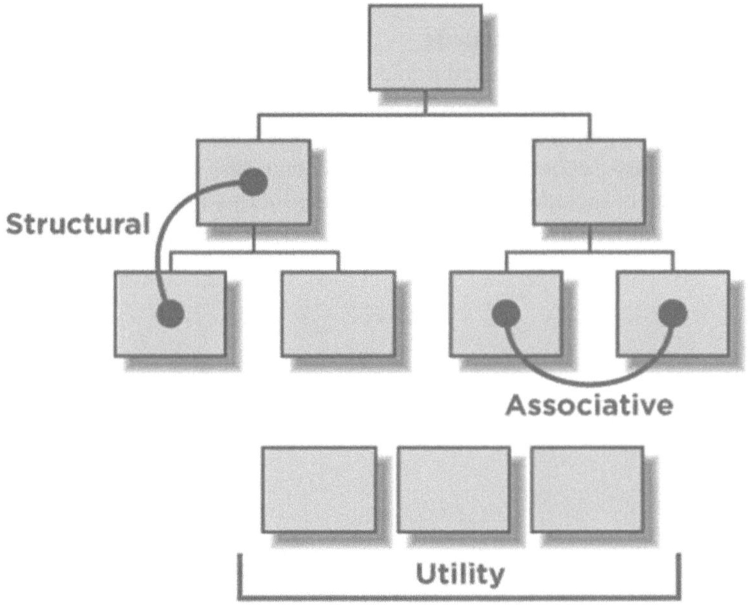

Fig. 12.6 Types of navigation

12.3.2.2 Local Navigation

Local navigation accesses lower levels in the structure, showing options at the same level and below the current page. It often works with global navigation and varies more frequently.

Common arrangements of local and main navigation include, as shown in Fig. 12.7, the following:

- Inverted-L: Global navigation at the top, local navigation on the left.
- Horizontal: Second row of options under global navigation.
- Embedded vertical: Local navigation within a vertical menu.

Associative Navigation

Associative navigation connects pages with similar topics and content, crossing structural boundaries. Common types include contextual navigation, quick links, and footer navigation.

12.3.2.3 Contextual Navigation

Contextual menus provide relevant options based on where you click, similar to a streamlined menu bar.

12.3.2.4 Quick Links

Quick links, as exemplified in Fig. 12.8, are unstructured links placed prominently on a page, providing easy access to important commands. The figure shows some examples.

12.3.2.5 Finding Your Keywords

The search terms people use to find things on a website are called keywords. To create a comprehensive list of keywords, start with brainstorming, and use tools like Google Keyword Planner to find popular terms and variations. Organize these keywords into primary, secondary, and long-tail categories, and map them to specific pages on your site. Include synonyms and related terms in your content to capture searches using different terminology. Optimize your content and meta tags with

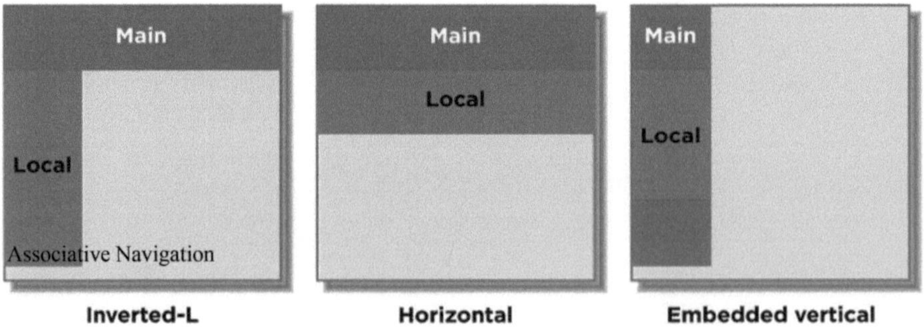

Fig. 12.7 Navigation models

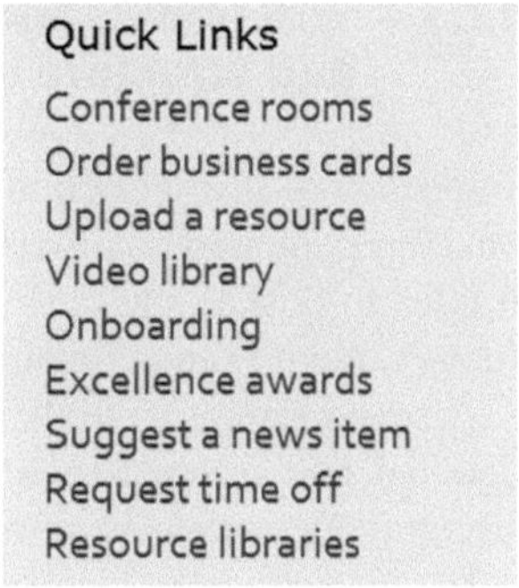

Fig. 12.8 Quick links

these keywords to improve search engine visibility. Implement autocomplete and synonym recognition in your site's search functionality to help users find relevant content easily, even if they use different words. This approach enhances user experience and improves search engine rankings.

12.3.2.6 Footer Navigation

Footer navigation is located at the bottom of the website, usually including company information and basic navigation links.

12.3.2.7 Utility Navigation

Utility navigation includes tools and features that help visitors use the site, such as search, sign-in, and subscribe options.

12.3.3 Colors, Font Size, and Typography in Site Design

Good typography plays a crucial role in site design by enhancing readability, establishing visual hierarchy, and reinforcing brand identity. Proper use of fonts and typographic elements ensures that content is easily digestible, guiding users through the information seamlessly. Consistent and thoughtful typography also helps create a professional and cohesive appearance, making the site more engaging and esthetically pleasing.

When choosing colors for a website, consider your brand identity and the emotions you want to evoke in your audience. Use color psychology to select hues that align with your brand message; for example, blue often conveys trust and professionalism, while red can evoke excitement and urgency. Ensure sufficient contrast between text and background colors for readability and accessibility. Additionally, limit your palette to a few key colors to maintain visual coherence and avoid overwhelming visitors. A good way to start to experiment with colors and fonts is to make quick mockups of wireframes.

12.3.4 Wireframes and Mockups: Visualizing the Layout and Structure of the Site

Wireframing involves creating simplified sketches of the website's layout, focusing on the arrangement of content and navigation elements. Start with low-fidelity wireframes to outline the basic structure and placement of key elements like headers, footers, menus, and content areas. An example is shown in Fig. 12.9.

Use wireframing tools such as Sketch, Figma, or Adobe XD to create more detailed and interactive wireframes. This helps stakeholders visualize the site's structure and provides a foundation for further design iterations.

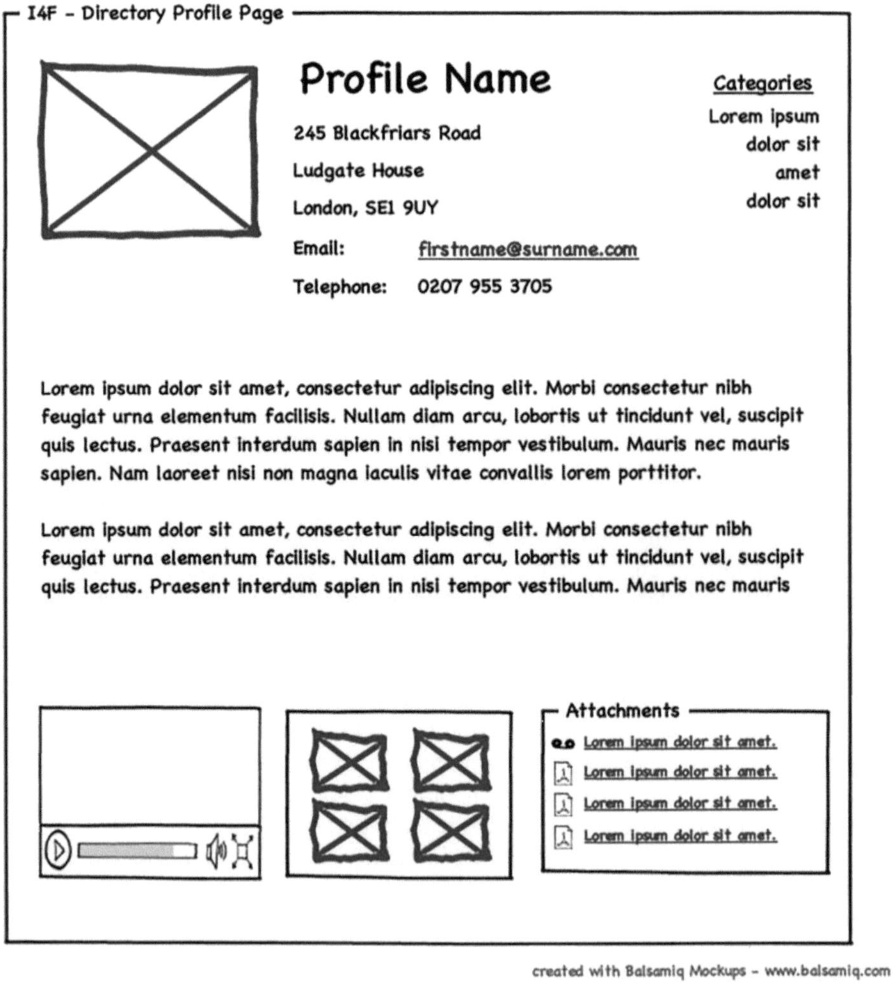

Fig. 12.9 Wireframe example

Develop mockups to add visual details like colors, typography, and images. Mockups give a more accurate representation of the final design, allowing for better evaluation and feedback.

Ensure that wireframes and mockups adhere to the established hierarchical structure and navigation design. They should also consider user interface (UI) best practices to enhance usability and accessibility.

Test wireframes and mockups with users to gather feedback on the layout and structure. Iterate on the design based on this feedback to ensure it meets user needs and expectations.

12.3.5 Visual Hierarchy

Visual hierarchy is the arrangement of elements to indicate their importance. It helps guide users through the website, ensuring they notice important information first.

There are six core principles of visual hierarchy:

1. Size: Larger elements draw more attention.
2. Color: Bright colors highlight important information.
3. Patterns: Use common viewing patterns like F-pattern and Z-pattern.
4. Spacing: Adequate space around elements makes them more visible.
5. Typeface: Contrasting typefaces create a typographic hierarchy.
6. Alignment: Aligning elements indicates their relationship and importance (Singhwal, 2020).

Font size actually matters for what we read and in what order, as is illustrated in Fig. 12.10, which is commonly used in the industry.

12.3.6 Visual Design Principles: Applying Color Theory, Typography, and Layout Techniques

Visual design principles involve using color theory, typography, and layout techniques to create an esthetically pleasing and functional website. Start by choosing a color

Fig. 12.10 Size matters. This is found in multiple locations for example at https://it.pinterest.com/pin/267682771588956819/

palette that aligns with the brand's identity and evokes the desired emotions in users. Use complementary colors to highlight key elements and create a visual hierarchy.

Select typography that is legible and aligns with the overall design esthetic. Combine different font weights and sizes to create contrast and guide users' attention to important content. Ensure that the chosen fonts are web-safe and accessible on all devices.

Use layout techniques such as grids and whitespace to organize content effectively. A well-structured layout improves readability and guides users through the site's content in a logical flow.

Incorporate responsive design principles to ensure the visual design adapts seamlessly across different screen sizes and devices. Test the design on various devices to ensure it maintains its effectiveness and visual appeal.

Regularly review and update the visual design based on user feedback and emerging design trends. A visually appealing and well-structured website enhances user engagement and satisfaction.

Marketers often do not feel conformable doing this esthetical choice so will typically outsource this work to an advertising agency. Outsourcing esthetic choices to an advertising agency can pose several risks. Firstly, it may lead to a disconnect between the company's core values and the marketing messages being created, as the agency might not fully understand or prioritize the company's unique brand identity. Secondly, there's a risk of misalignment in accountability, where ethical or esthetic missteps by the agency could damage the company's reputation without necessarily affecting the agency directly. Additionally, relying on an external agency can dilute internal expertise and understanding, making the company less capable of independently managing these critical aspects in the future. Finally, there may be a lack of transparency and control over how esthetic decisions are handled, potentially leading to inconsistencies in brand messaging and trust issues.

12.4 Implementation

12.4.1 Using Content Management Systems (CMS): Setting Up and Organizing Content in a CMS

Implementing a CMS involves selecting a platform that fits the site's needs, such as WordPress, Joomla, or Drupal. Start by installing the CMS on your web server and conFigureing it according to your site's requirements. Organize your content into categories and tags to ensure it is easily manageable and searchable.

Set up user roles and permissions to control who can add, edit, and manage content. This helps maintain content integrity and workflow efficiency. Use the CMS's built-in tools and plugins to enhance functionality, such as SEO optimization, social media integration, and analytics tracking.

Regularly update the CMS and its plugins to ensure security and functionality. Backup content periodically to prevent data loss and maintain site integrity. The CMS should streamline content management, making it easy to update and maintain the site's content over time.

12.4.2 Responsive Design: Ensuring the Site Is Mobile-Friendly and Adaptable to Different Screen Sizes

Responsive design ensures that a website adapts to various screen sizes and devices, providing an optimal viewing experience. Use flexible grid layouts, scalable images, and CSS media queries to create a responsive design.

Start by designing the site for mobile devices first, and then, gradually enhance it for larger screens (mobile-first approach). This ensures that the site performs well on all devices, from smartphones to desktops. Test the site on various devices and screen sizes to identify and fix any issues related to layout, navigation, and functionality.

Incorporate touch-friendly elements, such as larger buttons and touch gestures, to improve usability on mobile devices. Optimize images and media to reduce load times on slower mobile networks. A responsive design enhances user experience, reduces bounce rates, and improves overall site accessibility.

12.4.3 SEO Considerations: Structuring the Site to be Search Engine-Friendly

SEO considerations involve structuring the site to improve its visibility in search engine results. Start by conducting keyword research to identify terms and phrases relevant to your content. Incorporate these keywords into your site's meta tags, headings, URLs, and content.

Ensure the site has a clear and logical structure, with a well-defined hierarchy that search engines can easily crawl and index. Use descriptive and keyword-rich titles and meta descriptions to improve click-through rates from search engine results.

Implement clean, SEO-friendly URLs that are easy for users and search engines to understand. Use internal linking to connect related content and help search engines understand the site's structure. Optimize images with descriptive file names and alt tags to improve their visibility in image search results.

Regularly update the site with fresh, high-quality content to keep users and search engines engaged. Use tools like Google Analytics and Google Search Console to monitor site performance and identify areas for improvement. A well-optimized site improves search engine rankings, driving more organic traffic to the site.

12.4.4 Performance Optimization: Techniques to Ensure the Site Loads Quickly and Efficiently

Performance optimization involves techniques to ensure the site loads quickly and efficiently, enhancing user experience and search engine rankings. Start by optimizing images and media files to reduce their size without compromising quality. Use tools like compression algorithms and content delivery networks (CDNs) to speed up content delivery.

Minimize the use of heavy scripts and plugins that can slow down the site. Combine and minify CSS and JavaScript files to reduce the number of requests made to the server. Implement browser caching to store frequently accessed files locally on users' devices, reducing load times for repeat visitors.

Optimize the server environment by using fast hosting services and conFigureing server settings for optimal performance. Regularly monitor site performance using tools like Google PageSpeed Insights or GTmetrix to identify and fix performance issues.

Ensure the site is mobile-friendly, as mobile users often experience slower network speeds. By focusing on performance optimization, you can provide a faster, more efficient browsing experience, improving user satisfaction and site engagement.

12.5 Testing and Launch

12.5.1 Usability Testing: Assessing How Real Users Interact with the Site

Usability testing involves evaluating the site by observing how real users interact with it. We may say it is the oxygen of a website. With no visitors, a web page is simply dead. It is a bit like posting on X (formerly Twitter): we think we are communicating because we are on a big platform or on the Internet, where everyone in the whole world is, but there is no one there.

Begin by recruiting participants who represent your target audience. Set up tasks for them to complete, such as finding a specific product or checking out, to assess how intuitively they navigate the site.

Use tools like heatmaps and session recordings to gain insights into user behavior. Collect feedback through surveys or interviews to understand their experience and identify pain points. Analyze the results to pinpoint issues such as confusing navigation, unclear labeling, or slow loading times.

Iterate on the design based on the feedback, making necessary adjustments to improve usability. Conduct multiple rounds of testing to ensure that the changes have addressed the issues. Usability testing helps create a user-friendly site that meets user expectations and enhances satisfaction.

12.5.2 Quality Assurance: Ensuring All Links, Media, and Features Work Correctly

Quality assurance (QA) is a critical step to ensure all site elements function as intended. Develop a comprehensive QA checklist that includes testing all links, media files, forms, and interactive features.

Test the site across different browsers and devices to ensure compatibility and responsiveness. Check for broken links, missing images, and incorrect media files. Validate forms and interactive features to ensure they work correctly and provide appropriate feedback to users.

Conduct performance testing to identify any issues with site speed and loading times. Use automated tools for repetitive tasks and manual testing for more complex scenarios. QA helps ensure a smooth and error-free user experience, enhancing overall site reliability and user satisfaction.

There is nothing more devastating than a dead link. Many think it is not a big deal, but it is, as it sends a strong message to anyone visiting our site that we do not care, we do not have the technological competence, or we are outright sloppy. So check all links regularly, and set up a system to report errors.

12.5.3 Launch Strategy: Planning and Executing a Successful Site Launch

A well-planned launch strategy is crucial for a successful site launch. Start by setting a launch date and preparing a timeline with all necessary tasks and milestones. Develop a marketing plan to build anticipation and awareness, using channels such as email newsletters, social media, and press releases.

Ensure that all content is finalized, tested, and approved before the launch. Conduct a final round of testing to identify and fix any last-minute issues. Prepare a contingency plan to address any potential problems that may arise during the launch.

Coordinate with all stakeholders, including developers, designers, marketers, and customer support, to ensure a smooth launch process. Monitor the site closely during the initial hours and days post-launch to quickly address any issues that users may encounter. A well-executed launch strategy helps ensure a positive initial user experience and sets the stage for long-term site success.

12.6 Maintenance and Iteration

12.6.1 Monitoring Site Performance: Using Analytics to Track User Behavior and Site Performance

Monitoring site performance involves using analytics tools to track how users interact with your site and how well the site performs. Implement tools like Google Analytics, Hotjar, or Adobe Analytics to gather data on user behavior, such as page views, time on site, and bounce rates. Regularly review this data to identify trends, popular content, and potential issues.

Track key performance indicators (KPIs) like load times, server response times, and error rates to ensure the site runs smoothly. Set up alerts for critical metrics to quickly respond to performance issues. Analyzing this data helps identify areas for improvement and ensures the site meets user expectations and business goals.

12.6.2 Continuous Improvement: Regular Updates and Improvements Based on User Feedback and Data

Continuous improvement involves making regular updates to your site based on user feedback and performance data. Collect feedback through surveys, user testing, and direct user interactions to understand user needs and preferences. Use this feedback to prioritize updates and enhancements that will have the most significant impact on user experience.

Moreover, always respond to reviews on third-party sites. Always strive to be correct and polite. Try not to escalate any bad blood or animosities. If necessary, ask the person to contact you by email and settle the differences offline. There was a time when many companies did not answer criticism. Not answering criticism means that you do not disagree with the criticism raised, and it risks creating more criticism of the same sort. Do not turn off comments unless you absolutely have to. Turning off comments implies that you expect criticism and negative feedback.

Implement a schedule for regular content updates, feature enhancements, and performance optimizations. Use A/B testing to validate the effectiveness of changes, and ensure they improve site performance. Regularly review and update your SEO strategies to keep up with search engine algorithm changes and maintain visibility.

Maintain a backlog of improvement ideas, and prioritize them based on user needs and business goals. This iterative approach helps ensure the site remains relevant, user-friendly, and aligned with evolving user expectations and technological advancements. Continuous improvement fosters a dynamic and engaging user experience, driving long-term success.

If you follow this plan, you should be on your way to creating an attractive website with stickiness.

12.7 Definition Expanded

The most commonly used terms in this chapter, besides those already defined, are as follows[1]:

1. **Sitemap**: A file where you provide information about the pages, videos, and other files on your site, and the relationships between them.
2. **Navigation**: The tool that helps visitors get around the website. Good navigation and structure on the website attract users and contribute to an attractive and professional impression.
3. **Visual hierarchy**: The order in which we process the information on a website. Its function is to give users an easy understanding of the information presented. By adding different visual characteristics to sections of information, a developer can influence what a visitor perceives next.

[1] Verified using ChatGPT 4 (June 2024).

4. **Wireframe**: A visual guide that represents the skeletal framework of a website. It helps in planning the layout and interaction of the site's interface without focusing on design elements like color and fonts.
5. **Mockup**: A high-fidelity static design representation of a website. It includes the visual design aspects and provides a detailed look at the appearance and functionality of the final product.
6. **Prototype**: An interactive representation of a website or application used to simulate the user experience and functionality before final development. It allows testing and refinement of design ideas.
7. **Responsive design**: An approach to web design that ensures web pages render well on a variety of devices and window or screen sizes. It emphasizes flexible layouts, images, and CSS media queries.
8. **Content management system (CMS)**: Software used to create, manage, and modify digital content without the need for specialized technical knowledge. Examples include WordPress, Joomla, and Drupal.
9. **User experience (UX)**: The overall experience of a person using a website or application, particularly in terms of how easy or pleasing it is to use. It encompasses usability, accessibility, performance, and esthetics.
10. **Call-to-action (CTA)**: A prompt on a website that tells the user to take some specified action, such as "Buy Now" or "Sign Up." CTAs are critical for guiding users toward desired outcomes.
11. **Breadcrumb trail**: A navigation aid that allows users to keep track of their locations within programs, documents, or websites. It helps users understand the relationship between the pages they are on and the site's hierarchy.
12. **Card sorting**: A method used to help design or evaluate the information architecture of a site. Participants organize topics into categories that make sense to them, which tells how to structure and label the content.
13. **Usability testing**: A technique used to evaluate a product by testing it on users. It helps identify usability problems, gather qualitative and quantitative data, and determine the participant's satisfaction with the product.
14. **Search engine optimization (SEO)**: The practice of increasing the quantity and quality of traffic to your website through organic search engine results. It involves optimizing content and structure for search engines.
15. **Performance optimization**: Techniques to ensure the website loads quickly and efficiently, improving the user experience. This includes optimizing images, leveraging browser caching, and minimizing HTTP requests.
16. **Analytics**: The systematic computational analysis of data or statistics. In the context of web design, it involves tracking and analyzing user behavior and site performance to inform decisions.

12.8 Key Takeaways

Easy navigation on a website is crucial. A highly creative and complex website is pointless if visitors cannot find the information they need. Navigation plays a major role in building the website, using sitemaps that are carefully designed.

A well-designed sitemap helps create a structured visual hierarchy on the website. This allows control over where visitors should navigate first and what makes the first impression. The right theme, color, interface, and size of visible elements contribute to this.

Keeping the page structure simple and easily navigated with good flow will help visitors find the page attractive, increasing the likelihood of repeat visits.

Here are some quick takeaways for managers from this chapter:

1. Defining objectives: Clearly articulate the purpose and goals of the site to guide all subsequent decisions and ensure alignment with business strategies.
2. Audience analysis: Understand the target audience deeply through demographic and psychographic research to tailor the site to their needs and preferences.
3. Content inventory: Conduct a thorough content inventory to organize and manage website content effectively, ensuring coherence and relevance.
4. Hierarchical structures: Design a clear and logical content hierarchy to enhance user navigation and content discoverability.
5. Navigation design: Create intuitive and user-friendly navigation menus that facilitate easy access to content and improve user experience.
6. Wireframes and mockups: Use wireframes and mockups to visualize the site structure and layout, allowing for better planning and stakeholder feedback.
7. Responsive design: Implement responsive design to ensure the site is mobile-friendly and performs well on various devices.
8. SEO considerations: Optimize the site structure for search engines to improve visibility and drive organic traffic.
9. Usability testing: Regularly conduct usability testing to gather user feedback and make iterative improvements to the site.
10. Continuous improvement: Use analytics and user feedback to monitor site performance and make ongoing updates to enhance the user experience and achieve business goals.

An attractive site structure is vital for engaging users and ensuring a seamless online experience. By carefully planning, designing, implementing, testing, and maintaining the website, you can create a user-friendly and visually appealing site that meets your business goals. Regular updates and continuous improvement based on user feedback and performance analytics are essential for sustaining a successful website.

Reference

Singhwal, S. (2020). Digital marketing strategies in the age of artificial intelligence. *Journal of Digital Marketing, 8*(3), 245–256.

Further Reading

Beaird, J., & George, J. (2014). *The principles of beautiful web design*. SitePoint.

Krug, S. (2014). *Don't make me think, revisited: A common sense approach to web usability*. New Riders Publishing.

Nielsen, J. (2000). *Designing web usability: The practice of simplicity*. New Riders Publishing.

Mobile Interface Is All

13

13.1 Introduction

You don't need a laptop to do digital marketing today; a phone will often suffice. The amount of content accessible from the web is virtually the same on a phone. Instagram marketing, for instance, works exceptionally well on a phone, as does TikTok. These platforms are designed primarily for mobile use, which is a significant reason for their popularity. Many young users, who might not own laptops, experience the digital world exclusively through their phones. Phones are optimized for creating short videos and selfies, with cameras on modern phones often surpassing those of standalone cameras. Apps like Canva and Adobe Lightroom are excellent for creating and editing content directly on your phone. However, the phone's utility is limited for more advanced tasks such as running social media campaigns, performing SEO, and coding. Phones are best for checking dashboards, reviews, and sending short emails. The key is to ensure that your customers can interact with you via their phones, even if performing advanced operations on your end may be more challenging.

This chapter aims to provide a better understanding of mobile interface design and its importance. The mobile user interface (UI) encompasses everything a user interacts with on a mobile device, including the touch display that allows users to engage with applications or mobile sites. The mobile interface design is a valuable tool for marketers and businesses, crucial for success given the increasing internet access and growing popularity of mobile phones. It's important for marketers to understand how to leverage the mobile interface and its advantages. UI establishes a relationship between the user and the device, making it essential for all types of businesses.

Good UI design improves the user experience (UX), often leading to loyal and engaged customers. A well-designed UI provides greater opportunities for both retaining customers and developing new relationships. The return on investment in UI design is significant, but developing a well-designed UI is complex, requiring adaptation to different users and anticipation of customer behavior. The interface

K. Solberg Söilen, *Digital Marketing*, Springer Texts in Business and Economics, https://doi.org/10.1007/978-3-031-69518-6_13

helps customers navigate the site and find call-to-action buttons. Mobile sites differ significantly from desktop versions and require adapted interface design to meet new challenges. Additionally, UI design must consider the diversity of users in terms of culture, needs, and behavior. It allows adaptation to different user needs, contributing to a better UX, which fosters loyalty and engagement. Well-developed UI also leads to lower costs, more effective call-to-action elements, and increased traffic to your mobile site.

13.2 Differences Between Desktop and Mobile

Mobile devices fall into various categories, but focusing on their features simplifies understanding. A mobile device is personal; owners choose which applications to download and customize the visual theme. Unlike desktops, which can be accessed in various locations, a mobile device is used by the same person in different settings. Mobile devices are portable, allowing users to take them everywhere. They are quick and easy to use compared to computers, which need to be set up. Mobile device users are always connected to the internet while the PC is mainly on during work hours. This makes a world of difference when it comes to customers' availability.

The differences between desktop and mobile devices extend beyond the devices themselves to include user attitudes. Mobile users are often on the go, interacting with their devices in varied environments such as commuting, waiting for a meeting, or conversing with others. Therefore, mobile UI design must consider these dynamic environments.

Mobile screens are smaller and have fewer pixels compared to computer screens, limiting the amount of information visible at one time. Users often have to zoom in to read content and important information should be placed at the top of the page. Mobile processors are slower, affecting page loading times, and mobile devices typically have lower bandwidth. Therefore, mobile sites need to be bandwidth-efficient and avoid JavaScript-heavy designs.

Mobile devices are touch-based, offering less precision than desktop mouse interactions. Users use gestures such as swiping and pinching to interact with the interface. Due to the lack of precision in touch compared to mouse devices, mobile UI designs must include clear information layouts, simplified forms, and larger UI elements. Mobile keyboards are small, making typing less pleasant, so using smaller URL links and easy navigation is essential.

Desktops support multitasking with multiple applications or sites open simultaneously, a feature limited to mobile devices. Including sharing buttons on every page makes it easier for users to share content without switching windows.

13.3 Different Mobile Users

Designing UI requires considering the diversity of users. Cultural differences affect how symbols, icons, and colors are perceived. Elderly users may have specific needs due to changes in color vision and information processing speed. Disabilities, such as visual, auditory, and motor impairments, also influence interaction with devices.

Mobile users themselves vary significantly. Younger, higher-earning individuals tend to use iPhones, while Android users view more content but are less engaged. Purchases are more often made from iPhones than Android devices, highlighting differences in the mobile ecosystem.

13.4 Different Mobile Uses

There are global differences in mobile phone usage based on location and circumstances. For example, some individuals track their daily activities with their phones, while others seek to limit their digital footprint. Several groups seek to limit their digital footprint for various reasons. Privacy-conscious individuals often do so to protect their personal data from being collected and exploited by corporations for marketing purposes or sold to third parties. Activists and journalists may limit their digital footprint to avoid surveillance and protect their sources, particularly when working in regions with restrictive governments or where freedom of speech is threatened. Additionally, individuals concerned about cybercrime and identity theft may reduce their online presence to mitigate the risk of personal information being stolen or misused. Finally, some people choose to minimize their digital footprint to maintain a clear distinction between their personal and professional lives, ensuring that their private activities remain confidential. Mobile phones are often seen as intimate devices, sometimes more frequently touched than humans.

When I was at CES in 2009 the conference had three messages to visitors: mobile, mobile and mobile. In 2011, smartphones outsold desktops for the first time, marking a significant shift in consumer behavior. Today, mobile phones are the most common consumer devices, incorporating features like alarm clocks, personal calendars, and games. They also serve as powerful communication tools, enabling voice and video calls, instant messaging, and social media interactions. Mobile phones have become essential for navigation, with GPS capabilities providing real-time directions and location-based services. Additionally, they function as portable entertainment centers, offering streaming services for music, movies, and TV shows and access to e-books and audiobooks. Furthermore, smartphones support various applications that cater to health and fitness tracking, online shopping, mobile banking, and professional productivity tools like email, document editing, and cloud storage.

13.4.1 Application Versus Mobile Web

Applications account for 90% of the average American's mobile consumption, with users spending over three hours daily on apps (eMarketer, 2021). Despite the growing dominance of apps, mobile websites remain essential due to their accessibility and ease of use across various devices without needing installation. However, phone applications have limitations, such as screen size and processing capabilities, which can affect user experience and functionality.

Creating an application requires generating user interest to ensure it is chosen over web alternatives. Developers must focus on providing unique value, seamless user experience, and efficient performance to attract and retain users. Additionally, successful apps often leverage push notifications, personalized content, and offline capabilities to enhance user engagement. It's also crucial for developers to keep apps updated and address user feedback promptly to maintain relevance and satisfaction.

While apps offer a more controlled environment and richer interactions, mobile websites provide broader reach and easier maintenance. Businesses must consider their target audience and specific needs when deciding between developing a mobile app or enhancing their mobile web presence.

13.5 User Interface Definition

UI is defined as everything a user can see or interact with, which is crucial for business success. UI design involves the interaction between the application and the user, focusing on how an application works, not just how it looks.

UI design elements include buttons, lists, toggles, icons, and tags. The relationship between the device and the user involves presenting information, facilitating interactions, and guiding users through the site. A successful UI design ensures users enjoy the site.

Berezhnoi (2019) describes UI design as involving three main elements:

- Visual design: Enhancing the site's elegance without compromising functionality and content, including choosing colors, images, and fonts.
- Interactive design: Anticipating user interactions and developing functions accordingly.
- Information architecture: Organizing and labeling the interface to make information accessible and easy to find.

The interactive design also includes providing feedback, such as changing button colors to confirm interaction.

For an interface to be usable, it should be easy to navigate and feel familiar, even on the first visit. Good UI design guides users smoothly through tasks, such as booking a ticket, and ensures they can recall the interface for future visits. Effective

UI design helps steer customers toward desired actions, improving engagement and conversion rates.

13.6 The Web Design Process

Effective web design and interface are critical for engaging customers and ensuring they choose your website over competitors. The process of developing a website remains solid despite technological advancements. Initially, it's essential to determine the website's objective: informational or transactional. Informational sites provide information, while transactional sites encourage purchases. Marketers should be involved in the interface process to ensure customer needs are considered.

Interface design begins after establishing the company's position and objectives. For instance, a company valuing customer service must reflect this on its website. Consistency across all channels is crucial.

Responsive web design ensures the website is accessible on all devices, enhancing cross-channel and cross-device experiences. Understanding different customer search behaviors across devices is vital for successful web design and marketing strategies.

13.7 Target Audience

Defining the target market helps customize the website for the ideal user. Market segmentation divides users into groups based on lifestyle or demographics to understand their behavior and needs. The concept of personas, which provides a deeper understanding of potential customers, is also valuable. This approach helps create user-friendly interfaces that enhance UX.

Content customization is crucial, regardless of the definition of the target market. Start by identifying the target market and setting objectives. Content site navigation is essential in designing interfaces.

13.8 Typical Behavior

Eyeball tracking studies help marketers understand user behavior on websites. The "golden triangle" describes the most viewed area, typically the upper left-hand corner. "Above the fold" refers to the visible part of the page without scrolling.

Web design must consider cognitive effort, as users prefer intuitive navigation. Consistent design helps users understand how to navigate and complete tasks. Flexible navigation options, such as search tools and categories, cater to different user preferences.

Designing for diverse user needs, including cultural differences, age, and impairments, is essential. Offering optional tutorials can help users with varying knowledge levels.

13.9 Testing

Usability testing ensures the site meets user expectations. Applications perceived as user-friendly and easy to learn are favored. Usability testing provides insights for improvement, helping achieve marketing objectives.

Testing different aspects based on the website's objectives is crucial. For transactional sites, ease of checkout and shopping cart abandonment rates are important metrics. User feedback is invaluable for improving UI and ensuring customer satisfaction. Effective UI design minimizes customer support needs, reducing costs and enhancing brand equity.

13.10 Organizing Content

When designing for desktops, web pages typically use multiple columns to organize content, enhancing the web experience. However, this approach is not suitable for mobile interfaces. Mobile users prefer not to scroll through extensive content. Designing a linear story with essential content is more effective for mobile.

Keeping content limited and focused improves the user experience on mobile interfaces. Simplifying the message and information enhances usability and engagement.

13.11 Technical Aspects

Mobile applications connect to the internet or web browsers, often using embedded web views. Cross-browser compatibility is essential for a stable mobile interface. Ensuring your site functions well across different browsers is critical for usability.

Viewing your site from a mobile device helps identify and resolve issues that may not appear on desktops, such as loading times or display problems. Optimizing your site for mobile ensures a positive user experience, increasing the likelihood of conversions.

Building a mobile experience is more complex than developing for desktops due to the need to balance UX and UI design. Each change impacts the overall user experience, requiring careful planning and execution.

13.12 Hyperlinking

Hyperlinks are useful on desktops but less on mobile devices due to smaller screens and less comfortable navigation. On mobile, the experience is more linear, and too many links can overwhelm users. Designing with a clear vision of the mobile experience is crucial.

The limited screen size on mobile devices necessitates a more streamlined approach. Avoid overcrowding the screen with information and focus on guiding the user through the essential steps to complete their tasks.

13.13 Benefits of Mobile UI

An effective mobile UI design helps users understand how to navigate an application, leading to better engagement. Successful UI elements include:

1. Clarity: Clear language and visuals prevent confusion and ensure users understand how to use the application.
2. Familiarity: Using familiar icons, symbols, and colors enhances user recognition and efficiency.
3. Responsiveness: Fast response times keep users engaged and informed, such as confirming actions with feedback.
4. Consistency: Consistent design helps users learn and apply their knowledge across different functions.
5. Aesthetics: Attractive design enhances user enjoyment and satisfaction.

Good UI design attracts and retains users, leading to positive word-of-mouth and increased traffic. Small UI changes can significantly impact user experience and engagement, making it essential to focus on visual details and intuitive navigation.

A well-designed UI enhances UX, driving higher conversion rates and customer loyalty. Positive user experiences lead to increased sales and a growing customer base. Conversely, negative experiences can harm growth prospects.

Investing in good UI design reduces the need for traditional marketing methods like cold calls or flyers, as users are more likely to stay and engage with a well-designed site. In today's fast-paced world, efficient and easy-to-understand interfaces are crucial for success.

The return on investment for UX strategies is significant, with studies showing a high ROI for every dollar spent. Good UX leads to lower bounce rates and higher customer satisfaction, directly impacting sales and growth.

Creating a successful UI requires transparency and adaptability to different user needs. Engaging and intuitive interfaces foster loyalty, which is essential in a competitive market. Loyal customers are more cost-effective to retain than acquiring new ones, emphasizing the importance of good UI design.

UI design helps users quickly find information and engage with the site's content, increasing the likelihood of conversions. Understanding user preferences and designing accordingly enhances the overall experience, driving growth and customer satisfaction.

Good UI design is a fundamental part of building a successful online presence. It ensures users can easily navigate the site, complete desired actions, and have a positive overall experience, leading to long-term loyalty and business success.

13.14 Getting the Metrics Right

Metrics apply to all kinds of devices, not just mobile. Metrics are quantitative measures used to track and assess the performance of various aspects of digital marketing efforts. They are significant because they provide data-driven insights that help marketers understand how well their campaigns are performing. By analyzing metrics, marketers can identify strengths and weaknesses in their strategies, allowing them to make informed decisions to optimize their efforts. Common metrics include website traffic, conversion rates, click-through rates, and return on investment (ROI). These metrics help determine the effectiveness of marketing tactics, such as SEO, social media, and email campaigns.

Working with metrics involves collecting data through tools like Google Analytics, social media insights, and email marketing platforms. Marketers then analyze this data to identify trends and patterns, which can guide adjustments in strategy. For example, if a high bounce rate is detected, it may indicate that the website content needs improvement. Regularly monitoring and interpreting metrics enables marketers to refine their approaches, allocate resources more effectively, and ultimately achieve better results. Table 13.1 shows what some common metrics are and how to work with them:

The main challenges in digital marketing metrics include data accuracy, integrating data from various sources, and keeping up with changing algorithms. Takeaways are the importance of regular monitoring, the need for actionable insights, and the necessity of adapting strategies based on data analysis. Effective use of metrics requires consistent evaluation and adjustment to improve marketing outcomes.

When considering metrics for mobile devices as opposed to laptops, it's important to account for differences in user behavior and interaction patterns. Mobile users often have shorter attention spans and engage with content in quick, fragmented sessions, making metrics like bounce rate and page load time even more critical. Additionally, mobile metrics should include tracking user interactions with mobile-specific features such as tap events, swipe gestures, and in-app behaviors, which are not present in desktop usage. Understanding the context in which mobile users access your site—often on the go or in a multitasking environment—can also influence the interpretation of engagement metrics. By tailoring your approach to the unique aspects of mobile user behavior, you can gain more accurate insights and optimize your digital marketing efforts accordingly.

13.15 Managerial Takeaways

Here are some key takeaways for managers from this chapter:

1. Prioritize mobile UI design: Effective mobile UI design is crucial for enhancing user experience, increasing customer loyalty, and driving engagement. Understanding the unique needs of mobile users helps in creating intuitive and efficient interfaces.

Table 13.1 How to measure metrics in digital marketing [Verified using ChatGPT 4 (June 2024)]

Metric	Description	How to check
Website Traffic	Number of visitors to your website	Google Analytics, web server logs
Conversion Rate	Percentage of visitors who take a desired action (e.g., make a purchase, sign up)	Google Analytics, conversion tracking tools
Bounce Rate	Percentage of visitors who leave the site after viewing only one page	Google Analytics, web analytics tools
Click-Through Rate (CTR)	Ratio of users who click on a link to the number of total users who view a page, email, or ad	Google Ads, email marketing platforms
Cost Per Click (CPC)	Amount paid for each click on a digital ad	Google Ads, social media ad platforms
Cost Per Acquisition (CPA)	Cost to acquire a customer	Google Analytics, advertising platforms
Return on Investment (ROI)	Profitability measure (revenue—cost)/cost	Google Analytics, financial tracking software
Customer Lifetime Value (CLV)	Prediction of the net profit attributed to the entire future relationship with a customer	CRM systems, predictive analytics tools
Social Media Engagement	Measures likes, shares, comments, and overall interaction on social media platforms	Social media analytics tools (Facebook Insights, etc.)
Email Open Rate	Percentage of email recipients who open a given email	Email marketing platforms (Mailchimp, etc.)
Email Click-Through Rate	Percentage of email recipients who clicked on one or more links contained in a given email	Email marketing platforms
Organic Search Traffic	Number of visitors to your website who found it via a search engine	Google Analytics, SEO tools (Ahrefs, SEMrush)
Paid Search Traffic	Number of visitors to your website who found it via paid search ads	Google Ads, Bing Ads
Mobile Traffic	Number of visitors accessing your website via mobile devices	Google Analytics, web analytics tools
Page Load Time	Time it takes for a webpage to fully load	Google PageSpeed Insights, web analytics tools

2. Adapt to mobile user behavior: Mobile users often interact with their devices on the go. Design interfaces that are easy to use in dynamic environments, considering touch-based navigation and smaller screen sizes.
3. Leverage mobile applications and websites: Both mobile apps and mobile websites are essential. Apps provide a controlled environment and richer interactions, while mobile websites offer broader reach and accessibility.
4. Ensure responsiveness: Responsive web design ensures that your website is accessible and functional across all devices, enhancing cross-channel and cross-device user experiences.
5. Focus on user diversity: Consider the varied cultural, demographic, and behavioral characteristics of mobile users. Design adaptable and user-friendly interfaces to cater to different user needs.

6. Optimize for performance: Mobile devices often have slower processors and lower bandwidth. Ensure your site is bandwidth-efficient and avoid heavy JavaScript designs to improve loading times.
7. Enhance user experience with UI elements: Use clear visuals, familiar symbols, and consistent design to improve user satisfaction. Aesthetics and responsiveness are key to keeping users engaged.
8. Incorporate analytics and feedback: Regular usability testing and analytics are essential for understanding user behavior and improving UI design. Collect user feedback to refine interfaces and enhance user satisfaction.
9. Understand technical constraints: Mobile devices have limitations that desktops do not. Optimize your site for mobile by ensuring cross-browser compatibility and addressing issues like loading times and display problems.
10. Invest in UI and UX: A well-designed UI leads to higher conversion rates, customer loyalty, and business success. Investing in good UI design reduces the need for traditional marketing methods and enhances the overall user experience.

People expect to be able to do almost everything using their mobile phone. Therefore, the mobile interface is essential in digital marketing due to the increasing reliance on mobile devices for internet access. Effective mobile UI design will significantly enhance user experience, driving customer loyalty and engagement. Investing in responsive, user-friendly interfaces and optimizing for mobile-specific constraints are crucial for business success in the digital age.

References

Berezhnoi, R. (2019). What is UI Design and why is it important. F5 Studio. Last modified April, 12.

eMarketer. (2021, June 1). US time spent with mobile 2021. https://www.emarketer.com/content/us-time-spentwith-mobile-2021

Further Reading

Krug, S. (2010). *Rocket surgery made easy: The do-it-yourself guide to finding and fixing usability problems*. New Riders.

Nielsen, J., & Budiu, R. (2012). *Mobile usability*. New Riders.

Rubin, J., & Chisnell, D. (2008). *Handbook of usability testing: How to plan, design, and conduct effective tests*. Wiley.

Sauro, J., & Lewis, J. R. (2016). *Quantifying the user experience: Practical statistics for user research*. Morgan Kaufmann.

Tullis, T., & Albert, B. (2013). *Measuring the user experience: Collecting, analyzing, and presenting usability metrics*. Morgan Kaufmann.

14 The Role of Influencers, Celebrity Endorsements, and Identifying Opinion Leaders

14.1 Background

Over the last century, various marketing strategies have evolved, including the use of influencers, celebrity endorsements, and opinion leaders. These strategies leverage the influence of individuals who express their feelings and thoughts about different products or services, helping companies reach and engage consumers more effectively. This chapter delves into the different types of marketing strategies and provides guidance on selecting the appropriate approach for a company.

14.2 Definitions

Influencers, celebrity endorsements, and opinion leaders, as presented in Table 14.1, each play pivotal roles in digital marketing. With their dedicated social media followings, influencers build trust and authenticity, engaging audiences through relatable and persuasive content. Celebrity endorsements leverage the broad reach and credibility of famous personalities, enhancing brand appeal and attracting larger audiences. Opinion leaders, known for their expertise within specific communities or industries, provide authoritative recommendations that resonate deeply with niche audiences. Together, these strategies help brands build trust, increase engagement, and drive consumer behavior, making them essential elements of a successful marketing strategy.

K. Solberg Söilen, *Digital Marketing*, Springer Texts in Business and Economics, https://doi.org/10.1007/978-3-031-69518-6_14

Table 14.1 Influencers, celebrity endorsements, and opinion leaders

Aspect	Influencers	Celebrity endorsements	Opinion leaders	Example with sports shoe company
Definition	Individuals with significant social media followings and influence	Famous personalities endorsing a brand	Experts or authorities in a specific field	Partnering with a fitness influencer to review and showcase new sports shoe releases
Audience	Niche or broad, depending on the influencer's focus	Wide, often mainstream	Specific, industry-focused	Signing a deal with a famous athlete, like Serena Williams, to endorse the sports shoes
Credibility	Built through authenticity and engagement	Leveraged from fame and public image	Based on expertise and knowledge	Collaborating with a renowned sports podiatrist to discuss the benefits of the shoe's design
Engagement	High engagement with followers	High visibility, may have lower engagement	High trust within specific communities	Fitness influencer creates engaging content, such as workout videos, featuring the latest running shoes
Content type	Personalized, often user-generated content	Professional, polished advertisements	Informative, educational content	Famous athlete appears in polished ads showcasing the sports shoes
Cost	Generally lower than celebrity endorsements	Typically very high	Varies, often moderate	Opinion leader writes articles and creates videos explaining technical benefits of the shoe design
Example	Partnering with a fitness influencer to review and showcase new sports shoe releases	Signing a deal with a famous athlete, like Serena Williams, to endorse the sports shoes	Collaborating with a renowned sports podiatrist to discuss the benefits of the shoe's design	Partnering with a fitness influencer to review and showcase new sports shoe releases; signing a deal with a famous athlete like Serena Williams to endorse the sports shoes; collaborating with a renowned sports podiatrist to discuss the benefits of the shoe's design

I have used the Sports Shoe Company as an example above. There are many real-life examples from this industry that make it particularly relevant. Many sports shoe companies have successfully leveraged influencers, celebrity endorsements, and opinion leaders to boost their brands:

Nike is renowned for its partnerships with celebrities and athletes, such as Michael Jordan, whose "Air Jordan" line has become iconic in both sports and fashion.

Adidas has collaborated with influencers like Kanye West, whose Yeezy brand has been highly influential.

Puma partnered with pop star Rihanna, leading to the successful Fenty Puma line. Under Armour gained prominence with endorsements from athletes like Stephen Curry, enhancing their brand credibility.

Reebok has used fitness influencers to promote their products, leveraging social media to reach niche audiences.

New Balance has often collaborated with opinion leaders in the running community to highlight the technical aspects of their shoes.

ASICS has worked with sports scientists and professional athletes to emphasize the performance and health benefits of their footwear.

Each of these strategies has helped these brands connect with different audiences, from mainstream consumers to specialized sports communities.

According to the websites "Front Office Sports" and "33 square" Michael Jordan's endorsement deal with Nike, initially signed in 1984, was worth $2.5 million over 5 years plus royalties. This partnership has become lucrative, with Jordan reportedly earning around $256.1 million in 2022 alone from his 5% cut of Jordan Brand sales, which totaled $5.1 billion that year. Nike's sales increased significantly due to this deal, with the Air Jordan line generating over $100 million in its first year alone. Over the decades, the Jordan Brand has continued to grow, contributing to Nike's dominance in the athletic footwear market. Still we see in Fig. 14.1 how small these costs are relative to Nike's income in the period and over time:

The graph shows that the endorsement payments to Michael Jordan were just a fraction of the total endorsement payments made by Nike. Other stars who have received significant endorsement payments from Nike during the same period include LeBron James, who signed a lifetime contract with Nike in 2015, reportedly worth over $1 billion. Cristiano Ronaldo also has a lifetime deal with Nike, valued at around $1 billion. Kevin Durant has a lucrative deal with Nike, including his own signature shoe line, making him one of the highest-paid athletes under the Nike brand. Other notable endorsements include Tiger Woods, Serena Williams, Kobe Bryant, and Rafael Nadal, all of whom have significantly contributed to Nike's overall marketing and endorsement expenditure. The point is, even though the size of these payments seems exaggerated they make perfect economic sense for the sports shoe company.

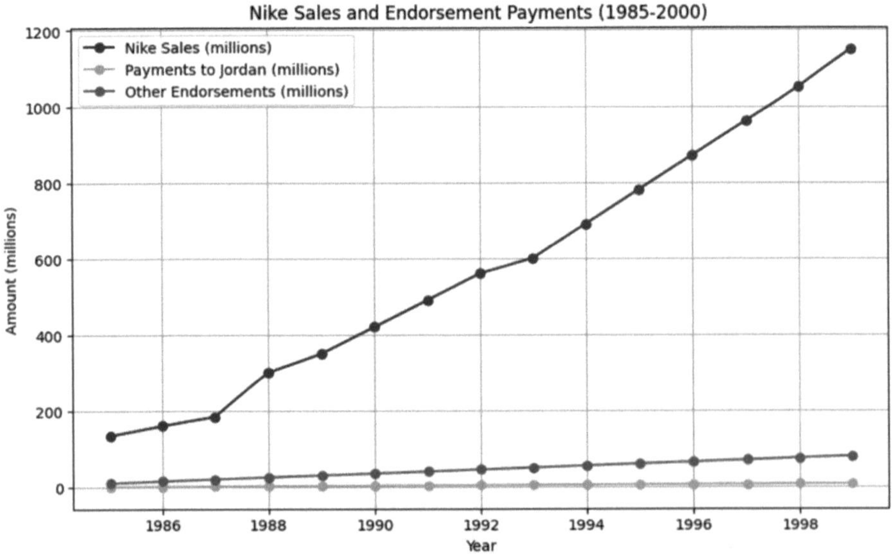

Fig. 14.1 Nike sales as compared to the cost of endorsement payments. This is created by author but based on multiple sources of data information from the web

14.3 Influencers

14.3.1 Influencers ABCC

Now, how do companies like Nike know which stars to endorse? Influencers ABCC (Authenticity, Brand Fit, Community, and Content) framework is a set of criteria used to evaluate and select the right influencers for brand partnerships. Here's a brief explanation of each component:[1]

1. Authenticity: This refers to the genuine nature and credibility of the influencer. An authentic influencer is trusted by their followers because they are perceived as genuine and sincere in their endorsements. Their content feels real and relatable, which helps build a strong connection with their audience.
2. Brand Fit: This is about how well the influencer's persona, values, and content align with the brand's image and values. An influencer who fits well with the brand will naturally integrate the brand's products or services into their content, making the promotion feel seamless and authentic to their followers.
3. Community: This refers to the influencer's follower base and the level of engagement and interaction they have with their audience. A strong community means

[1] Verified using ChatGPT 4 (June 2024).

the influencer has a dedicated and engaged following that values their opinions and recommendations, which can lead to higher impact and conversion rates for the brand.

4. Content: This involves the quality, creativity, and style of the influencer's content. High-quality content that is visually appealing and engaging can significantly enhance the brand's image and attract the target audience. It's important that the influencer's content aligns with the brand's aesthetic and messaging.

By considering these four factors, brands can choose influencers who are not only popular but also effective in promoting their products in a way that resonates with the target audience.

14.3.2 Different Types of Influencers

There may be said to be three main types of influencers, as demonstrated in Table 14.2:

These main types can again be broken into a series of sub-types, as in Table 14.3:

Influencers can be categorized into several types based on their reach and impact. Mega-influencers, like Kylie Jenner, have millions of followers and significant influence but are often expensive and less accessible. In contrast, micro-influencers, such as fitness enthusiasts with 50,000 followers, are seen as more authentic and relatable, making them valuable for niche markets and targeted campaigns. Nano-influencers, with very small but loyal follower bases, are ideal for hyper-targeted marketing due to their cost-effectiveness and influence within their small communities.

Table 14.2 3 Main types of influencers

Simplified category	Detailed type	Relation	Example
Celebrity influencers	Mega-influencers	Both have vast reach and influence, often celebrities with millions of followers.	Kylie Jenner promoting beauty products.
Category influencers	Macro-influencers, industry experts/ thought leaders, bloggers/vloggers	These are experts in specific niches, respected for their knowledge and insights. They build trust within their category.	Isabella Löwengrip for personal branding.
Micro-influencers	Micro-influencers, nano-influencers	These have smaller but highly engaged and trusted followings. They are influential within their community.	A local fitness enthusiast with 10,000 followers promoting health supplements.

Table 14.3 Detailed list of influencers

Type of influencers	Importance	Example
Mega-influencers	Mega-influencers have a vast reach with millions of followers. They are often celebrities and have significant influence but can be less accessible and more expensive.	Kylie Jenner promoting beauty products.
Macro-influencers	Macro-influencers have a large but more niche following compared to mega-influencers. They are important for reaching broader audiences with high engagement.	A popular YouTube tech reviewer like Marques Brownlee.
Micro-influencers	Micro-influencers have a smaller, highly engaged follower base. They are often seen as more authentic and relatable, making them valuable for niche markets and targeted campaigns.	A fitness enthusiast with 50,000 followers promoting health supplements.
Nano-influencers	Nano-influencers have a very small but loyal follower base. They are often regular consumers who are very influential within their small community. They are cost-effective and ideal for hyper-targeted marketing.	A local foodie with 1000 followers sharing restaurant recommendations.
Industry experts/thought leaders	These influencers are highly respected within their field. Their endorsements are seen as credible and authoritative, making them crucial for B2B marketing and industries requiring expert opinions.	Neil Patel for digital marketing insights.
Bloggers/vloggers	Bloggers and vloggers create detailed content and can provide in-depth reviews and tutorials. They are important for content marketing and SEO.	A travel blogger like Nomadic Matt.
Social media stars	These influencers are highly active on social media platforms and have built their following through engaging content. They are essential for brand visibility and engagement on social media.	A TikTok star like Charli D'Amelio.

14.3.3 Different Types of Platforms for Influencers

Influencers can be used in various ways beyond specific platforms to enhance brand visibility and credibility. They can participate in product launches or events, generating buzz and attracting media attention. Collaborating with influencers for guest blog posts or podcast interviews can reach new audiences through different content formats. Additionally, co-creating products or limited-edition items with influencers can leverage their personal brand to drive sales and create a sense of exclusivity. Still, it is the internet platforms that are dominating, and we need to know not only what they are, but when to choose which one. Table 14.4 also shows the number of users for each of the more popular platforms popular in the Western world:

Table 14.4 Types of platforms for influencers

Platform	Description	Number of users	Headquarters
Instagram	A photo- and video-sharing social media platform. Influencers use it to share lifestyle, fashion, travel, and fitness content.	1.5 billion (as of 2023)	Menlo Park, California, USA
YouTube	A video-sharing platform where influencers create and share videos on various topics, from tutorials to vlogs.	2.1 billion (monthly active users as of 2023)	San Bruno, California, USA
TikTok	A short-form video platform where influencers create engaging and viral content, often using music and trends.	1 billion (as of 2023)	Culver City, California, USA
Facebook	A social networking site where influencers can share posts, images, and videos and engage with followers through pages and groups.	2.96 billion (as of 2023)	Menlo Park, California, USA
Twitter	A microblogging platform where influencers share short updates and opinions and engage in real-time conversations.	353 million (as of 2023)	San Francisco, California, USA
LinkedIn	A professional networking platform where industry experts and business influencers share professional content and insights.	900 million (as of 2023)	Sunnyvale, California, USA
Pinterest	A visual discovery and bookmarking platform where influencers share ideas and inspirations through images and boards.	445 million (as of 2023)	San Francisco, California, USA
Snapchat	A multimedia messaging app where influencers create short, ephemeral content, including photos and videos.	332 million (daily active users as of 2023)	Santa Monica, California, USA
Twitch	A live streaming platform primarily for gamers, where influencers broadcast live gameplay and interact with viewers in real time.	140 million (monthly active users as of 2023)	San Francisco, California, USA
Reddit	A social news aggregation and discussion website where influencers engage in niche communities to share content and insights.	430 million (as of 2023)	San Francisco, California, USA

Choosing the right platform for influencer marketing depends not first of all on the number of total views or subscribers but on the target audience, product type, and marketing goals. For lifestyle, fashion, and beauty products, Instagram is ideal due to its visually driven nature and large audience of young adults. If the product involves tutorials or detailed demonstrations, such as tech gadgets or makeup, YouTube is a better choice for its long-form video content and educational potential.

To reach a younger audience with trendy, engaging content, TikTok is effective, especially for products like fashion, fitness, and entertainment. Facebook is suitable for a broad demographic, making it ideal for mainstream consumer goods and services. A study published in 2017 shows that Twitter is best for real-time engagement and promoting events, news, or updates, suitable for tech products and news-related content. Professional users are aware that tweets are being manipulated by communication departments, so they adjust for this in their understanding of the content that is being delivered. Twitter is seen as valuable alongside other social media software (additional software solutions) and used directly together with other software (integrated software solutions). As a stand-alone service, it is found to be of less value to experienced users, and there are no signs that Twitter is seen as a valuable tool for learning.[2] If there is a difference now that Twitter has become X and is under new ownership, it should be addressed in new studies.

LinkedIn is the go-to platform for B2B marketing, professional services, and industry-specific products, catering to a professional audience. Pinterest is excellent for products related to home decor, DIY projects, and wedding planning due to its focus on inspiration and ideas. Snapchat appeals to a younger audience with ephemeral content, making it suitable for brands targeting teens and young adults with trendy or limited-time offers. Lastly, Twitch is perfect for gaming-related products and services, as it directly engages the gaming community through live streaming.

14.3.4 Working with Influencers

Selecting influencers involves identifying those who align with your brand values, target audience, and campaign goals. Start by researching influencers who have a genuine connection with your industry and a substantial following that matches your target demographic. Evaluate their engagement rates, content quality, and authenticity. Once selected, establish clear expectations and objectives for the collaboration, ensuring both parties understand the desired outcomes.

Work with influencers by providing them with detailed briefs that outline your campaign goals, key messages, and creative guidelines. Maintain open communication throughout the partnership, offering support and feedback as needed. Monitor the progress and performance of the campaign, adjusting strategies if necessary to maximize impact. Finally, analyze the results to measure the success of the collaboration and gather insights for future influencer partnerships.

Working with influencers online does carry risks, so it's crucial to be prepared to end the relationship quickly if necessary. To deal with potential issues, establish clear contractual agreements that include clauses for behavior, brand representation, and grounds for termination. Monitor the influencer's online activity regularly to stay informed about any controversial behavior or statements. If an incident occurs, act swiftly by issuing a public statement to distance your brand from the influencer's actions and outline your steps to address the situation.

Communicate directly with the influencer to discuss the issue and decide on the appropriate course of action, whether it's issuing an apology, retracting the collaboration, or terminating the partnership. Maintain transparency with your audience

---

[2] Söilen, K. S., Tontini, G., Aagerup, U., (2017).

throughout the process to uphold trust and show commitment to your brand values. Finally, have a crisis management plan in place to handle any fallout effectively and mitigate damage to your brand's reputation.

14.4 Endorsements

Endorsements involve partnering with celebrities or well-known Figures to promote a brand or product. This strategy leverages the fame and influence of the endorser to enhance brand visibility, credibility, and appeal.

The main difference between working with influencers and endorsements lies in the scope and nature of their influence. Influencers typically have a niche following and build their reputation through consistent content creation and engagement within specific communities. In contrast, endorsements involve high-profile celebrities or public figures whose influence spans a broader audience, leveraging their fame to promote products. Influencer collaborations often focus on authentic, grassroots connections with their audience, whereas endorsements capitalize on the celebrity's widespread recognition and status. The strategies and approaches for managing these relationships also differ, with influencers requiring more personalized and community-driven interactions compared to the more formal and high-stakes nature of celebrity endorsements.

Just like influencers, endorsements can be evaluated using the ABCC framework (Authenticity, Brand Fit, Community, and Content).

14.4.1 Different Types of Endorsers

Endorsers can be categorized similarly to influencers, with some nuances:

1. **Celebrity endorsers:** Well-known public Figures such as actors, athletes, and musicians. Example: Michael Jordan for Nike.
2. **Industry experts:** Respected professionals in a specific field whose endorsement adds credibility. Example: Dr. Oz for health-related products.
3. **Micro-celebrities:** Individuals who have gained fame within a specific niche or community. Example: A well-known fitness trainer promoting sports equipment.

14.4.2 Different Types of Channels for Endorsements

When working with endorsements for a Sports Shoe Company, the focus should be on high-profile channels and platforms that broadcast major sports events and tournaments. Key channels include ESPN, Fox Sports, and NBC Sports, which cover a wide range of sports, including basketball, football, soccer, and athletics. Global sports networks like Sky Sports and Eurosport are also essential for reaching international audiences.

Major tournaments and events to consider include the Olympics, FIFA World Cup, UEFA Champions League, NBA Finals, Super Bowl, and Wimbledon. These events attract massive global viewership and provide excellent opportunities for showcasing endorsed athletes. Additionally, merchandising plays a crucial role in spreading the popularity of endorsed stars. Partnering with retail giants like Foot Locker, Dick's Sporting Goods, and online platforms like Amazon can enhance the visibility and sales of endorsed products.

Leveraging social media platforms to amplify endorsements and creating exclusive, limited-edition merchandise tied to major events can further boost engagement and brand loyalty. Engaging with fans through live events, meet-and-greets, and exclusive content on channels where the endorsed stars are featured can also enhance the effectiveness of the endorsement strategy.

Whatever sports we are talking about, we need to know what the major leagues and associations are associated with it and what networks are able to buy the rights to show their competitions, as depicted in Table 14.5:

As a Sports Shoe Company, we should leverage our endorsed athletes' appearances and performances on major channels by collaborating with these broadcasters to create integrated marketing campaigns. Approach these channels with a proposal that highlights mutual benefits, such as exclusive content featuring our endorsed athletes, co-branded promotions, and sponsored segments during key events. Develop business relationships by offering value through cross-promotional opportunities and shared audiences, ensuring our brand gains visibility and credibility. Additionally, negotiate placement of our products in relevant programming and events, and explore opportunities for joint sponsorship deals. By aligning our brand with both the athletes and the channels that showcase them, we can amplify our reach and impact.

14.4.3 The Special Case of Political Endorsement

Endorsements in the context of US Congress involve public support from influential Figures or organizations, such as politicians, interest groups, or media outlets. These endorsements signal to voters that a candidate has the backing of respected or powerful entities, potentially swaying public opinion and increasing voter trust. Endorsements work by leveraging the endorser's credibility and influence to enhance the candidate's image, often resulting in increased media coverage and campaign donations. The effects can be significant, helping to legitimize lesser-known candidates, mobilize voter bases, and shape the political narrative. However, there are risks associated with endorsements, such as potential backlash if the

Table 14.5 Sports, leagues and channels important for our sports shoe company (Verified using ChatGPT 4 (June 2024))

Sport	Major leagues/associations	Key channels covering events
Basketball	NBA (National Basketball Association), FIBA (International Basketball Federation)	ESPN, TNT, ABC, NBA TV
Soccer	FIFA (Fédération Internationale de Football Association), UEFA (Union of European Football Associations), MLS (Major League Soccer)	ESPN, Fox Sports, NBC Sports, Sky Sports, beIN Sports
Athletics	IAAF (International Association of Athletics Federations), Diamond League	NBC Sports, BBC, Eurosport
Tennis	ATP (Association of Tennis Professionals), WTA (Women's Tennis Association), ITF (International Tennis Federation)	ESPN, Tennis Channel, NBC Sports, Eurosport
Running/marathons	World Marathon Majors (e.g., Boston Marathon, New York City Marathon)	NBC Sports, ABC, BBC, Eurosport
American football	NFL (National Football League)	ESPN, NBC Sports, Fox Sports, CBS Sports
Baseball	MLB (Major League Baseball)	ESPN, Fox Sports, TBS, MLB Network
Rugby	World Rugby, Six Nations Championship, Super Rugby	ESPN, NBC Sports, Sky Sports, Fox Sports
Cricket	ICC (International Cricket Council), IPL (Indian Premier League)	ESPN, Star Sports, Sky Sports, Willow TV
Golf	PGA (Professional Golfers' Association), LPGA (Ladies Professional Golf Association), The Masters	ESPN, NBC Sports, CBS Sports, Golf Channel

endorser is controversial or unpopular with certain voter segments. Additionally, relying heavily on endorsements may lead to perceptions of a candidate being overly influenced by special interests, potentially undermining their authenticity and appeal to independent voters. Overall, while endorsements can provide a crucial boost to political campaigns, they must be managed carefully to avoid negative repercussions.

14.4.4 Handling Risks with Endorsements

Working with endorsers comes with risks, especially if the endorser's behavior becomes problematic. To manage such situations, it's crucial to monitor the endorser's public activity regularly to stay ahead of potential issues. If a scandal arises, act swiftly by issuing a public statement to distance your brand from the behavior and outlining the steps you are taking. Engage in direct communication with the endorser to discuss the issue and decide on appropriate actions, which might include issuing an apology or terminating the partnership. Transparency with your audience is essential; maintain open communication to uphold trust and show commitment to your brand values. Additionally, have a pre-established crisis management plan to handle and mitigate the fallout from any incidents, ensuring minimal impact on your brand's reputation.

For example, when faced with Tiger Woods' alcohol abuse, reckless driving, and wife abuse incidents, Nike initially stood by the athlete but distanced themselves as the situation escalated. They issued public statements expressing concern and disappointment, emphasizing their commitment to ethical conduct. Nike reduced the visibility of Woods in their marketing campaigns and eventually restructured the endorsement deal. They maintained transparency with their audience, reassuring them of their dedication to upholding brand values. The company also implemented a crisis management plan to address any potential damage to its reputation.

14.5 Opinion Leaders

Opinion leaders are individuals whose views and advice are respected and followed within a particular community or industry. They wield influence due to their expertise, credibility, and the trust they have built with their audience. Engaging with opinion leaders can significantly enhance a brand's reputation and reach.

The biggest difference between opinion leaders, compared to influencers and endorsements, is their primary source of influence. Opinion leaders typically gain authority through expertise and knowledge in a particular field, rather than popularity or celebrity status. They are trusted for their insights and advice rather than their promotional reach or endorsement deals. While influencers and endorsers leverage their broad appeal and social media presence, opinion leaders are valued for their credibility and the trust they inspire in their specific areas of expertise.

We can use the same ABCC frameworks when selecting opinion leaders.

14.5.1 Different Types of Opinion Leaders

Opinion leaders can be categorized based on their influence and platforms. A list is provided in Table 14.6:

Opinion leaders vary in influence and the platforms they use, ranging from industry experts to media personalities. Industry experts and thought leaders are respected for their credibility and innovative ideas, shaping trends and opinions within their fields. Community and political leaders hold sway within specific groups, with their advice and endorsements being highly trusted. Academic leaders and media personalities provide authoritative insights and have significant followings, influencing public opinion through their expertise and media presence. The platforms they use are similar to those of influencers but also very different.

Table 14.6 Types of opinion leaders

Type of opinion leaders	Importance	Example
Industry experts	Highly respected within their field; their endorsements are seen as credible and authoritative.	A renowned digital marketing consultant.
Thought leaders	Known for their innovative ideas and insights, they shape industry trends and opinions.	A leading technology futurist.
Community leaders	Influential Figures within specific communities or groups; their advice is highly trusted.	A prominent local environmental activist.
Academic leaders	Scholars and researchers who provide expert opinions based on their academic knowledge.	A respected economics professor.
Media personalities	Journalists and media hosts with a significant following and influence in their niche.	A popular news anchor or podcast host.
Political leaders	Politicians or activists who influence public opinion and policy.	A well-known senator or public advocate.

14.5.2 Different Types of Platforms for Opinion Leaders

Opinion leaders use various platforms to share their insights and influence their audience. Table 14.7 shows some examples:

Choosing the right platform depends on the target audience, the nature of the opinion leader's expertise, and the brand's marketing goals. For professional and B2B marketing, LinkedIn is ideal. For broader audience engagement and visual content, YouTube and Instagram are effective.

14.5.3 Working with Opinion Leaders

Selecting opinion leaders involves identifying those whose expertise and influence align with your brand values and objectives. Start by researching opinion leaders in your industry and evaluating their engagement rates, credibility, and relevance. Establish clear expectations and objectives for the collaboration, ensuring both parties understand the desired outcomes.

Work with opinion leaders by providing them with detailed briefs that outline your campaign goals and key messages. Maintain open communication throughout the partnership, offering support and feedback as needed. Monitor the progress and performance of the campaign, adjusting strategies if necessary to maximize impact. Analyze the results to measure the success of the collaboration and gather insights for future partnerships. The process is quite similar to that of influencers.

Working with opinion leaders online carries risks, so be prepared to address any issues quickly. Establish clear contractual agreements, monitor the opinion leader's activity, and act swiftly if any problems arise. Transparency with your audience and a crisis management plan are essential to uphold your brand's reputation and mitigate any negative impact.

Table 14.7 Types of platforms for opinion leaders

Platform	Description	Number of users	Headquarters
LinkedIn	A professional networking platform where industry experts share professional content and insights.	900 million (as of 2023)	Sunnyvale, California, USA
Twitter	A microblogging platform for sharing short updates and opinions and engaging in real-time conversations.	353 million (as of 2023)	San Francisco, California, USA
YouTube	A video-sharing platform where thought leaders create and share detailed videos on various topics.	2.1 billion (monthly active)	San Bruno, California, USA
Medium	An online publishing platform where experts write in-depth articles and share their knowledge.	100 million (as of 2023)	San Francisco, California, USA
Facebook	A social networking site where community leaders engage with followers through posts, images, and videos.	2.96 billion (as of 2023)	Menlo Park, California, USA
Instagram	A photo- and video-sharing platform used by media personalities to share engaging content.	1.5 billion (as of 2023)	Menlo Park, California, USA
Academic Journals	Publications where academic leaders publish their research and insights.	N/A	Various locations globally

14.6 Key Takeaways

Here are some takeaways from Chap. 14:

- Understanding the role of influencers, celebrity endorsements, and opinion leaders is crucial for modern marketing. These strategies leverage the influence of trusted individuals to effectively engage and reach consumers.
- Influencers build trust and authenticity through their dedicated social media followings, making them valuable for engaging audiences with relatable content. Celebrity endorsements leverage fame to enhance brand appeal, attracting larger audiences despite higher costs.
- Opinion leaders, known for their expertise within specific communities or industries, provide authoritative recommendations that resonate deeply with niche audiences. Their endorsements are seen as credible and authoritative, making them essential for B2B marketing.
- Mega-influencers, like Kylie Jenner, have millions of followers and significant influence but are often less accessible and more expensive. Micro-influencers, with smaller but highly engaged followings, are seen as more authentic and relatable, making them valuable for niche markets and targeted campaigns.
- Nano-influencers have a very small but loyal follower base, making them ideal for hyper-targeted marketing due to their cost-effectiveness. They often influence within their small communities, providing a personal touch that larger influencers might lack.

- Celebrity endorsements involve high-profile Figures whose influence spans a broad audience, leveraging their fame to promote products. This strategy can significantly boost brand visibility but requires careful management to avoid potential backlash from controversial Figures.
- The ABCC framework (Authenticity, Brand Fit, Community, Content) is essential for selecting the right influencers, ensuring their values align with the brand and their content resonates with the target audience. This helps in creating authentic and effective marketing campaigns.
- Different types of influencers and platforms serve various marketing goals. For instance, Instagram is ideal for visually-driven products like fashion, while YouTube suits detailed tutorials and tech reviews.
- Working with influencers and opinion leaders requires clear communication and expectations. Providing detailed briefs and maintaining open communication ensures both parties understand the campaign goals, maximizing the impact and success of the collaboration.
- Managing risks associated with endorsements and influencer partnerships involves regular monitoring and swift action in case of controversies. Transparency with the audience and having a crisis management plan are crucial to maintaining brand reputation and trust.

Generation Z is almost obsessed with influencers; sometimes, it can seem like a teacher. What we have tried to show here is that this is not just hype or damaging. Many companies have even been able to make a comeback by shifting to more use of influencers, as it is considered good value for money. One such example is Abercrombie & Fitch, which, a year ago, was in big trouble but has managed to find a way out with the help of influencer marketing, at least for now.

Further Reading

Boyle, J. S. (2012). Marketing in the digital age. *Marketing Today, 12*, 23–35.

Dahl, D. W., & Moreau, P. (2007). Thinking inside the box: Why consumers enjoy constrained creative experiences. *Journal of Marketing Research, 44*(3), 357–369.

Dekimpe, M. G., & Hanssens, D. M. (2004). Persistence modeling for assessing marketing strategy performance. *Marketing Science, 23*(2), 225–238.

Edelman, D. C. (2010). Branding in the digital age: You're spending your money in all the wrong places. *Harvard Business Review, 88*(12), 62–69.

Keller, K. L. (2009). Building strong brands in a modern marketing communications environment. *Journal of Marketing Communications, 15*(2-3), 139–155.

Leeflang, P. S. H., Verhoef, P. C., Dahlström, P., & Freundt, T. (2014). Challenges and solutions for marketing in a digital era. *European Management Journal, 32*(1), 1–12.

Luo, X., & Donthu, N. (2006). Marketing's credibility: A longitudinal investigation of marketing communication productivity and shareholder value. *Journal of Marketing, 70*(4), 70–91.

Shankar, V., & Malthouse, E. C. (2009). A peek into the future of interactive marketing. *Journal of Interactive Marketing, 23*(1), 1–3.

Storytelling in Marketing 15

15.1 Background

The human mind is naturally inclined to enjoy a good story. Stories are not just for entertainment; they help us understand complex concepts and evoke emotional responses. A common mistake marketers make is believing that customers connect with brands rather than the people behind them. To build stronger connections with customers, marketers must make brands more personal. By giving a brand a personal touch, you can foster loyalty towards your products and services. Effective marketing is about telling compelling stories that people remember for years. With the advent of social media, storytelling has become an even more powerful tool to reach customers. However, this also means that companies must stand out in their storytelling efforts to capture and retain their audience's attention.

15.2 The Power of Storytelling

Storytelling is a powerful marketing tool because it can touch people emotionally, stimulate imagination, communicate messages effectively, and entertain. A good story can reach a diverse audience, including different age groups and interests. The five main advantages of storytelling in marketing are:

1. **Provide an overview**: A story can give the audience a comprehensive understanding of your business, simplifying complex ideas by allowing the audience to fill in the gaps.
2. **Effectiveness**: Using characters and symbols in stories makes communication more effective and easier to understand.
3. **Increased credibility**: A credible story adds trustworthiness to your message.
4. **Memorability**: A well-told story stays in people's minds longer, whether through facts, visuals, or emotions.

K. Solberg Söilen, *Digital Marketing*, Springer Texts in Business and Economics, https://doi.org/10.1007/978-3-031-69518-6_15

5. **Metaphor usage**: Metaphors can enhance the value of the message and help explain it more clearly.

Most customers prefer advertising in story form. A well-told story can create an emotional connection between the customer and the company, fostering a loyal customer base.

15.3 A Short History of Storytelling in Marketing

Storytelling has always been a vital tool for companies to sell their products or services. One early adopter was Coca-Cola, which hired an illustrator in 1931 to create the first image of Santa Claus, associating the brand with the warm, festive feelings of Christmas. The modern concept of digital storytelling began in the 1990s with Dana Atchley, who created short digital stories during his travels across the United States. His work laid the foundation for digital storytelling, influencing platforms like Storytelling.com.

With the rise of social media platforms like Facebook (founded in 2004), marketing opportunities expanded significantly. Today, companies use various social media channels, including Instagram, X (former Twitter), Snapchat, and LinkedIn, to build brand awareness, drive website traffic, and engage customers. Social media facilitates personal dialogue between customers and companies, creating closer relationships.

15.4 Key Elements in Digital Storytelling

Digital storytelling involves seven key elements.

15.4.1 Point of View: The Central Message or Point of the Story

The point of view in storytelling is crucial as it conveys the central message or theme of the story. It serves as the foundation upon which the entire narrative is built, guiding the direction and purpose of the tale. A clear point of view helps the audience understand the core values and intentions behind the story, making it more impactful and memorable. For example, in a marketing context, the point of view could emphasize innovation, trust, or community, which aligns with the brand's mission and goals.

15.4.2 Dramaturgy: The Story Must Be Engaging, with a Key Question Answered by the End

Dramaturgy refers to the structure and composition of the story, ensuring it captivates the audience from beginning to end. An engaging story typically follows a narrative arc with a clear beginning, middle, and end, often presenting a key question or conflict that keeps the audience intrigued. By the conclusion, this question is answered, or the conflict is resolved, providing a satisfying and meaningful resolution. This approach not only maintains the audience's interest but also reinforces the central message of the story.

15.4.3 Emotional Connection: The Story Should Create Recognition and Evoke Emotions to Engage the Audience

Creating an emotional connection is essential for effective storytelling, as it helps the audience relate to the characters and events on a personal level. By evoking emotions such as joy, sadness, excitement, or empathy, the story becomes more memorable and impactful. Emotional engagement can be achieved through relatable characters, compelling plots, and authentic experiences that resonate with the audience's own lives. This connection fosters a deeper understanding and appreciation of the story's message, enhancing its overall effectiveness.

15.4.4 The Gift of Voice: The Storyteller's Voice Can Strengthen the Message

The storyteller's voice plays a vital role in conveying the message with authenticity and conviction. A unique and genuine voice can make the story more relatable and persuasive, drawing the audience in and keeping them engaged. The storyteller's tone, style, and delivery should reflect the essence of the story and resonate with the audience's expectations and emotions. A strong, consistent voice can significantly enhance the credibility and impact of the narrative, making it more memorable and effective.

15.4.5 Soundtrack: Music Can Enhance the Emotional Impact But Must Be Used Carefully to Avoid Distraction

A well-chosen soundtrack can greatly enhance the emotional impact of a story by setting the mood and reinforcing the narrative's themes. Music can evoke specific feelings, amplify dramatic moments, and create a more immersive experience for the audience. However, it is crucial to use music judiciously, ensuring it complements rather than overwhelms the storytelling. Overuse or inappropriate selection of music can distract the audience and detract from the core message, so balance and relevance are key.

15.4.6 Economy: The Story Should Not Contain Too Much Information, Allowing the Audience to Fill in Gaps

Economy in storytelling involves presenting information concisely, leaving room for the audience to infer and imagine. By avoiding excessive details, the story remains focused and easier to follow while engaging the audience's creativity and personal interpretation. This approach helps maintain interest and prevents the narrative from becoming overwhelming or tedious. Striking the right balance between information and suggestion ensures the story is both compelling and thought-provoking.

15.4.7 Pacing: The Rhythm of the Story Is Crucial to Maintaining the Audience's Focus

Pacing refers to the speed and flow of the narrative, which is crucial for keeping the audience engaged and focused. A well-paced story balances moments of action and reflection, building tension and providing relief at appropriate intervals. Proper pacing ensures that the audience remains interested without feeling rushed or bored, enhancing their overall experience. By carefully managing the story's rhythm, storytellers can guide the audience's emotional journey and effectively reinforce the central message.

15.5 The Working Process of Making the Story

To start with, we can imagine a general working process for how storytelling in marketing fits in marketing communication, as illustrated in Fig. 15.1:

To create an effective story, start by defining your audience to understand their preferences and interests. Identify the core message you want to communicate, ensuring it aligns with your audience's values. Develop a compelling narrative that includes engaging elements like characters, conflict, and resolution. Choose the right channels to reach your audience, focusing on the platforms where they are most active. Create high-quality content that effectively tells your story through text, images, videos, or other media. Distribute and promote your content across these channels to reach a broader audience. Engage with your audience by responding to comments, fostering discussions, and analyzing feedback and results to refine and improve your storytelling efforts.

Figure 15.2 depicts how a compelling story can be made.

To craft a compelling marketing story, start by researching and understanding your audience. Gather data to comprehend their preferences, interests, and pain

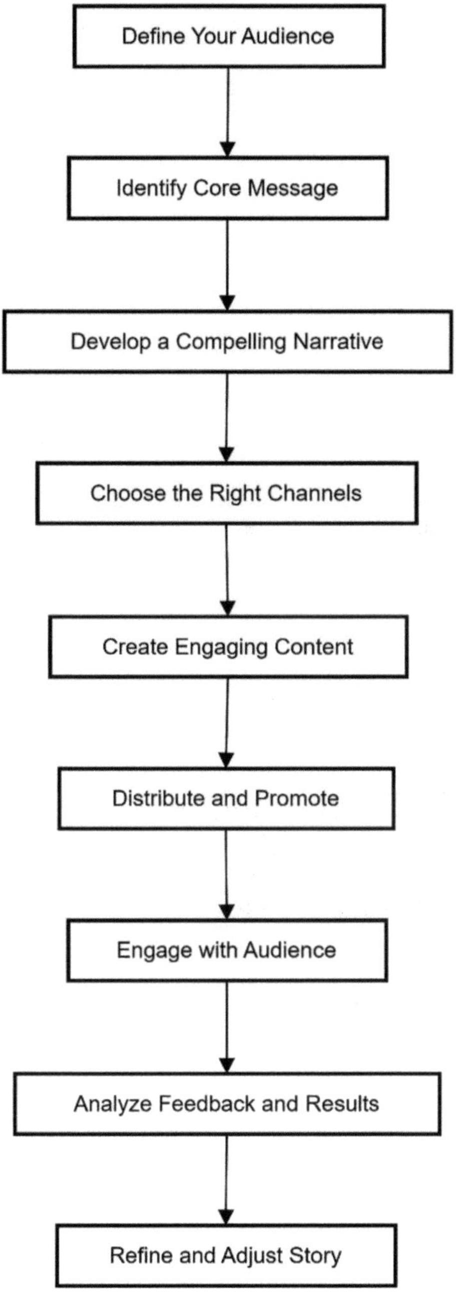

Fig. 15.1 The working process of how to create an effective story

points. Next, identify the key message or value proposition you want to convey through your story. Then, brainstorm potential story ideas that align with this message and resonate with your audience.

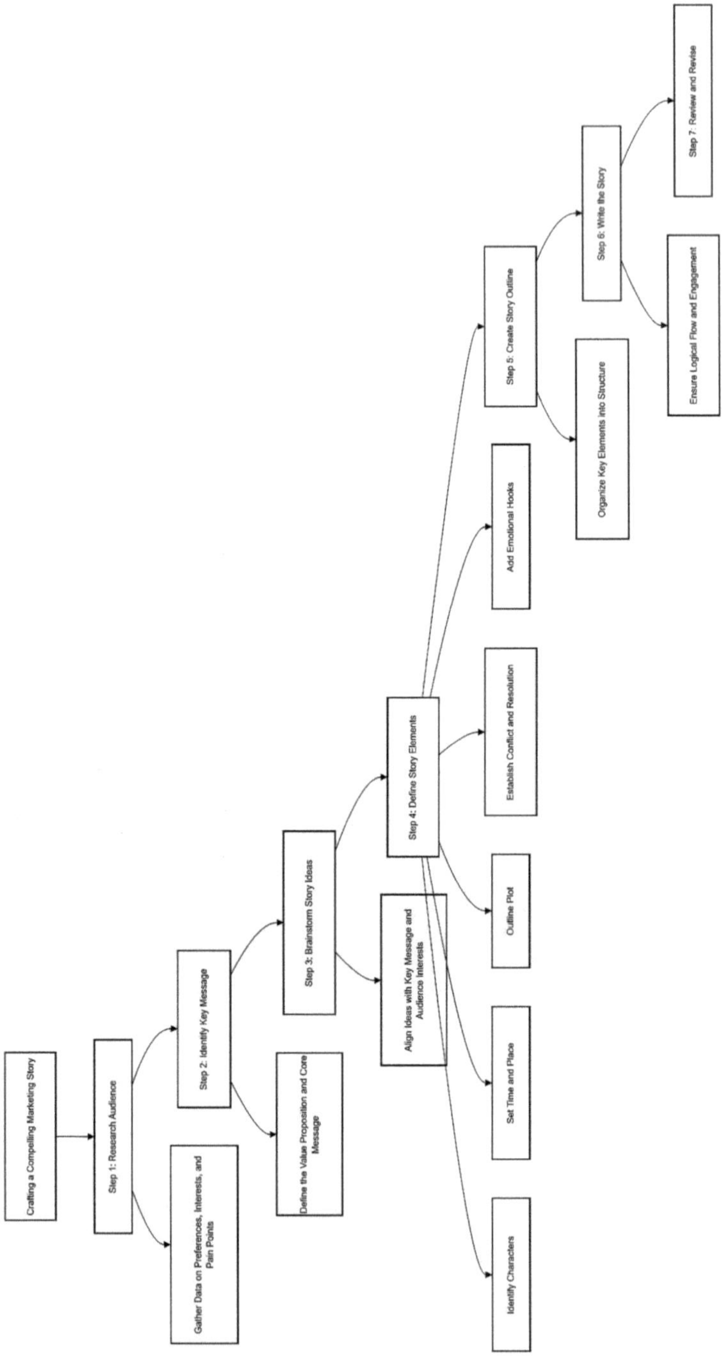

Fig. 15.2 The process of crafting a compelling marketing story

Define the essential elements of your story, including the characters, setting, plot, conflict, and resolution. Identify the main characters and decide on the time and place where your story will unfold. Outline the sequence of events that make up your plot, determine the main conflict and how it will be resolved, and identify emotional hooks to engage your audience.

Create a detailed story outline, organizing these key elements into a coherent structure. Write the full story, ensuring it flows logically and maintains interest. Review and revise the story to enhance clarity, coherence, and impact. Add relevant visuals and media, such as images, videos, or infographics, to complement and enhance the narrative. Finally, complete the story, ensuring all elements are polished and ready for distribution. This detailed approach focuses on the key elements and steps involved in effective storytelling for marketing.

15.6 Competences in Storytelling

Competences in storytelling for marketing include creativity and imagination, which are crucial for crafting engaging and original narratives that capture the audience's attention. Strong writing skills are essential to communicate the story clearly and effectively, ensuring it resonates with the target audience. Understanding the audience is critical, as it allows marketers to tailor stories to their interests, needs, and emotional triggers. Visual communication skills are also important, as incorporating visuals like images, videos, and graphics can enhance the story's impact. Analytical skills help assess the effectiveness of storytelling efforts and make data-driven adjustments. To write a good story, it's an advantage to have read some history and literature and know your geography, too, as good stories will often build on this knowledge. Lastly, strategic thinking is necessary to align the story with broader marketing goals and brand messaging.

15.7 Social Media Storytelling Strategies

15.7.1 Authenticity

Authenticity is important in storytelling as it builds trust with customers. Brands must avoid being fake because customers can easily detect inauthenticity, which can lead to significant backlash and loss of trust. A notable example is the 2015 Volkswagen "Dieselgate" scandal, where the company faced severe consequences for falsifying emissions data, resulting in a loss of trust and billions in fines. To reinforce authenticity, brands should support genuine projects and collaborate with trusted influencers. This approach can lead to increased customer loyalty and higher spending.

15.7.2 Showcase the Employees

Humanizing the brand by showcasing employees can make storytelling more personal and relatable. Customers build stronger relationships with people rather than just the brand itself. For example, Marriott International uses its Instagram account (@Marriottcareers) to share behind-the-scenes stories and highlight employees' perspectives on social issues. This strategy creates a personal connection with followers, making the brand more approachable and trustworthy.

15.7.3 The Customers' Stories

Sharing customer stories can be a powerful storytelling tool that resonates emotionally with the audience. In 2019, Nike's Instagram campaign featured real people's weight loss journeys, which emotionally connected with the audience and showcased the brand's impact on individuals' lives. Similarly, Airbnb uses customer experiences and photos to tell personal stories about their stays, focusing on the people and their experiences rather than just the places. This approach helps create a deeper connection with the audience by highlighting real-life stories and testimonials.

15.7.4 Know Your Audience and Your Marketing Position

Understanding your audience is fundamental for effective storytelling. Brands should speak the customer's language and engage them in dialogue through polls, idea proposals, and challenges. By knowing the customer, companies can create relevant content that fosters engagement and commitment. Additionally, understanding the company's relationship with the customer, whether as peers or former customers, can guide the storytelling approach. This ensures that the content is not only engaging but also resonates deeply with the audience.

15.7.5 Build a Brand Character

Creating a brand character involves developing a personality that embodies the brand's values and resonates with the target audience. This character can be real or fictional and should align with the ideal customer profile. The character's traits, such as excitement, ruggedness, competence, sophistication, or sincerity, help convey the brand's attributes effectively. A well-developed brand character can make the brand more relatable and memorable for customers, enhancing their connection to the brand.

By following these strategies, companies can effectively use storytelling to build stronger connections with their audience, enhance brand loyalty, and ultimately drive business success. When done authentically and thoughtfully, storytelling can transform a brand's presence on social media and create lasting relationships with customers.

15.7.6 The Marketing Story for Our Sports Shoe Company

Based on this, we could imagine two different stories for our Sports Shoes Company, one more modest that could be true and one more flamboyant:

Modest Story (Could be True)

In 1985, a group of passionate athletes in a small town in Sweden decided to create a sports shoe that would provide unmatched comfort and support. They started experimenting in a local workshop, testing various materials and designs. After countless trials and feedback from local runners, they developed a unique shoe that combined durability with excellent cushioning. The shoes quickly gained popularity among local sports enthusiasts, leading to the establishment of our sports shoe company, which they called NordicStride. Today, our shoes are worn by athletes across Sweden and in large parts of Europe, known for their quality and performance. Despite our growth, we remain committed to our roots, ensuring every shoe is crafted with the same dedication and passion. Our mission is to empower athletes of all levels to achieve their best, with footwear they can trust.

Detailed Story (Fictional)

In 1922, Lars M. Bergström, a Swedish adventurer and inventor related to the great Swedish explorer in the nineteenth century, returned home after years of exploring the rugged terrains of South America. Inspired by the resilience of the indigenous people and their handcrafted footwear, he set out to create the perfect sports shoe in his small Swedish village which he called HeritageStride. What he found was that Indians had solved the riddle of how to make perfectly comfortable shoes that are easy to move around in. Lars worked tirelessly, incorporating traditional techniques with innovative designs, eventually crafting a shoe that combined the strength of South American craftsmanship with Scandinavian precision. His breakthrough came when he met Jesse Owens, a legendary Olympic athlete, during a hike in the Alps, who tested and praised the shoes' unparalleled comfort and support. This athlete's endorsement catapulted the brand into international fame, leading to its adoption by elite sportsmen and explorers worldwide. To this day, our shoes honor Lars's legacy, blending historical craftsmanship with modern technology to support athletes in their greatest endeavors. Each pair tells a story of adventure, innovation, and the relentless pursuit of excellence.

Now, if you were a marketer, which story would you go with and why?

15.8 Untrue or False Marketing Stories

Do marketing stories need to be true? Is telling false stories bad marketing, leading to lower sales? While the intuitive answer might be yes, the reality is more complex.

Consider the case of Hollister. Despite its "Since 1922" claim, Hollister was actually founded in 2000 by Abercrombie & Fitch, not in California. The year 1922 and the California origin story are entirely fictional, crafted to align with the brand's laid-back, beach-inspired aesthetic. This fabricated history has successfully contributed to the brand's identity and appeal. According to the story, John M. Hollister, Sr., founded the company in 1922 after traveling from New York to the South Pacific, where he fell in love with the lifestyle and brought it back to California.

The story of "Eight & Bob" perfume centers around a fictional historical anecdote involving Albert Fouquet, a Parisian aristocrat, who supposedly created the fragrance in the 1930s. According to the tale, Fouquet met a young John F. Kennedy during a summer on the Côte d'Azur and gave him a sample of the perfume, which Kennedy later asked for more of, referring to it as "Eight & Bob." The narrative includes elements of glamour and intrigue, such as secret formulas and evading the Nazis during World War II. In reality, the brand was re-established in the twenty-first century, and the story is a marketing tool to add a layer of sophistication and allure. Despite its fictional nature, the tale successfully enhances the brand's prestige and mystique.

The story of "Eight & Bob" is almost too good to be true, featuring the Kennedy family, the Côte d'Azur, and the Nazis—all elements that make it captivating but also highly suspect. For a long time, the company did not openly admit the story was fabricated, but after inquiries, including those from my students, they now acknowledge its fictional nature. This raises another question: given that a story is not true, should a company admit this somewhere on its webpage, or should it maintain the mystique by staying silent?

In my opinion, transparency is crucial. While crafting an engaging, albeit fictional, narrative is possible, it is important to be honest about it when asked; it's the difference between a fake story and one that is simply untrue. Acknowledging the fictional nature of the story can preserve the brand's integrity and build trust with consumers.

15.9 Managerial Takeaways

Here are some suggestions for key takeaway for this chapter:

1. **Understand your audience**: Research your target audience to grasp their preferences and pain points, ensuring your story resonates with their interests and needs. Knowing your audience helps tailor the narrative to engage them effectively.

2. **Craft a clear core message**: Identify the central message or value proposition of your story to maintain focus and coherence. This core message should align with your brand's mission and goals, making the story impactful and memorable.
3. **Develop engaging story elements**: Create compelling characters, settings, and plots that capture the audience's attention. Incorporate conflict and resolution to maintain interest and ensure the story has a meaningful conclusion.
4. **Use authenticity**: Build trust with your audience by telling authentic stories. Avoid fabricating details that can be easily disproven, as authenticity strengthens brand credibility and loyalty.
5. **Incorporate emotional hooks**: Engage your audience emotionally by including relatable experiences and genuine emotions in your story. Emotional connections make stories more memorable and impactful.
6. **Leverage visuals and media**: Enhance your story with relevant visuals, such as images, videos, and infographics. Visual elements can make your narrative more engaging and easier to understand.
7. **Optimize for different channels**: Choose the right platforms to distribute your story based on where your audience is most active. Tailor your content to fit the characteristics and best practices of each channel.
8. **Maintain clear pacing**: Ensure your story flows well, balancing moments of action and reflection to keep the audience engaged. Proper pacing prevents the narrative from feeling rushed or dragging on.
9. **Monitor and adjust**: Continuously analyze feedback and results to understand what works and what doesn't. Use these insights to refine your storytelling approach for future campaigns.
10. **Be transparent**: If your story includes fictional elements, be honest about it when asked. Transparency can preserve your brand's integrity and build trust with your audience, distinguishing between creative storytelling and deception.

Creating false stories can be risky, although sometimes companies manage to get away with it. Abercrombie & Fitch has taken a high-risk approach to storytelling, particularly with the creation of the Hollister brand and with Abercrombie itself, aiming to achieve prestige through exclusivity. This strategy involved literally excluding a large number of customers and body types from their selection.

Further Reading

Aaker, D. A. (1991). *Managing brand equity: Capitalizing on the value of a brand name*. Free Press.

Brodie, R. J., Hollebeek, L. D., Jurić, B., & Ilić, A. (2011). Customer engagement: Conceptual domain, fundamental propositions, and implications for research. *Journal of Service Research, 14*(3), 252–271.

Christodoulides, G., & De Chernatony, L. (2010). Consumer-based brand equity conceptualization and measurement. *International Journal of Market Research, 52*(1), 43–66.

Keller, K. L. (1993). Conceptualizing, measuring, and managing customer-based brand equity. *Journal of Marketing, 57*(1), 1–22.

Kotler, P., & Keller, K. L. (2012). *Marketing management* (14th ed.). Prentice Hall.

Lemon, K. N., & Verhoef, P. C. (2016). Understanding customer experience throughout the customer journey. *Journal of Marketing, 80*(6), 69–96.
Rust, R. T., Zeithaml, V. A., & Lemon, K. N. (2004). Customer-centered brand management. *Harvard Business Review, 82*(9), 110–118.
Srivastava, R. K., Shervani, T. A., & Fahey, L. (1998). Market-based assets and shareholder value: A framework for analysis. *Journal of Marketing, 62*(1), 2–18.

Stealth Marketing on Social Media 16

16.1 Background

Stealth marketing is a technique where products are advertised to people without them realizing it. Typically used for new product launches, it creates a "buzz" by subtly introducing products to select individuals rather than using direct, aggressive advertising. This strategy relies heavily on word of mouth (WOM), making customers feel like they discovered the product or service themselves and encouraging them to speak positively about it. Stealth marketing is a low-cost, effective strategy that aims to build excitement and interest, making consumers more receptive to direct advertising later in the book.

16.2 Definitions

Here are some of the key terms used in this chapter:

- **WOM (word of mouth)**: Free promotion through satisfied customers who speak positively about a product or brand.
- **Buzz**: Maximizing WOM potential for a product or campaign through conversations on social media and other platforms.
- **Viral stealth videos (VSVs)**: Subtly include a product in videos, creating positive associations without direct advertisement.
- **SNS (social network service)**: Online platforms like Facebook and Instagram where people connect and interact.
- **Guerrilla marketing**: An unconventional marketing strategy that aims to achieve maximum exposure and engagement with minimal resources, often through surprise and creativity.
- **Product placement**: The practice of subtly placing products in movies, TV shows, or other media to promote them without direct advertising.

K. Solberg Söilen, *Digital Marketing*, Springer Texts in Business and Economics, https://doi.org/10.1007/978-3-031-69518-6_16

- **Influencer seeding**: The process of providing influencers with free products or services in hopes they will share positive experiences with their followers.
- **Undercover Marketing**: A tactic where marketers interact with potential customers without revealing their true intent, creating authentic-looking recommendations or experiences.
- **Native advertising**: Advertising that matches the form and function of the platform on which it appears, blending in with regular content to avoid disrupting the user experience.
- **Astroturfing**: The practice of creating fake grassroots campaigns to generate buzz and influence public perception, often through fake reviews or testimonials.
- **Ambush marketing**: A strategy where a brand associates itself with a particular event or campaign without paying for sponsorship, gaining exposure and recognition.
- **Micro-influencers**: Influencers with smaller, highly engaged followings who can provide authentic endorsements and reach niche audiences effectively.
- **Content seeding**: Distributing content across various platforms and channels to maximize visibility and encourage organic sharing and engagement.
- **Brand advocates**: Loyal customers who voluntarily promote a brand through word of mouth, social media posts, and personal recommendations, often incentivized by the company.
- **Buzz agents**: Individuals recruited to create buzz around a product or service, often through social media posts, blog entries, and word of mouth.

These terms provide a comprehensive understanding of the various tactics and elements involved in stealth marketing on social media.

16.3 Social Media Marketing

Social media platforms enable interactive and participatory marketing, contrasting traditional media like TV and radio. Stealth marketing leverages owned, paid, and earned media on platforms such as Facebook, Instagram, and X (formerly Twitter). So, we have:

- **Owned media:** Company-controlled media like websites and social profiles.
- **Paid media:** Direct payments for ads and sponsorships.
- **Earned media:** Free exposure gained through publicity and influencer endorsements.

Stealth marketing can overlap with paid, earned, and owned media, but it is characterized by its subtlety and indirect approach, which distinguishes it from traditional marketing strategies. Here is how stealth marketing can intersect with these categories:

1. Paid media:
   (a) Stealth marketing can involve paid media when a company pays influencers, actors, or other individuals to subtly promote a product without making it

obvious that they are being compensated. For example, an influencer might casually mention or use a product in their content without explicitly stating it is an advertisement.

2. Earned media:
   (a) Stealth marketing can generate earned media when the subtle promotion leads to organic word of mouth or media coverage. For example, if a product placement in a popular TV show or movie catches the public's attention, it may lead to discussions, reviews, and mentions in various media outlets, all of which are earned.
3. Owned media:
   (a) Stealth marketing can be integrated into owned media through content that subtly promotes a product without being overt. For example, a company blog might share a story or article that includes the product in a natural, non-intrusive way, or a social media post might feature the product in a lifestyle context rather than as a direct advertisement.

In essence, stealth marketing is a tactic that can be used within paid, earned, and owned media frameworks, as shown in Fig. 16.1. Its defining characteristic is the subtlety and indirect nature of the promotion, aiming to create buzz and interest without the audience immediately recognizing it as marketing.

Stealth marketing is shown as a central node connecting to paid, earned, and owned media. Underpaid media, examples include influencer compensation and subtle product placement. Under earned media, examples include organic word of mouth and media coverage. Under owned media, examples include company blogs and social media posts. Each example is further illustrated with specific scenarios to clarify how stealth marketing operates within these media categories.

16.4 Stealth Marketing for the Sport Shoe Company

Stealth marketing aims to subtly promote products, often linked to new product launches. Influencers, celebrities, and brand pushers use social media to create awareness. Behavioral targeting collects consumer data to push relevant ads, making them appear more organic and personalized.

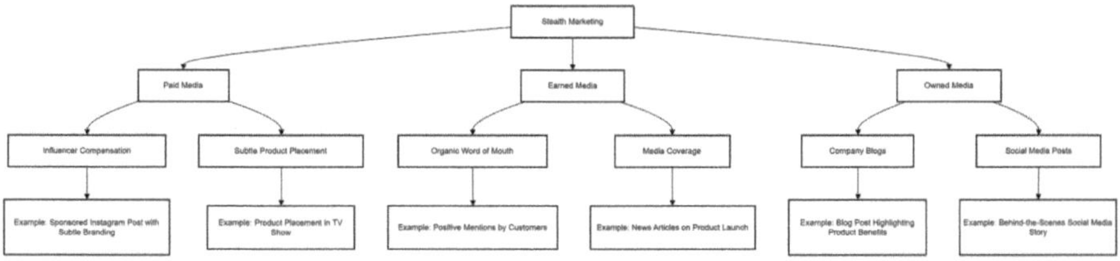

Fig. 16.1 Stealth marketing as relates to owned, paid and earned media

Our sports shoe company can implement stealth marketing through the following example:

Consider this scenario:

- Influencer seeding: Identify a group of local fitness influencers with a dedicated but not overly large following. These influencers are known for their authenticity and engagement with their audience.
- Subtle product placement: Provide these influencers with our latest sports shoes, encouraging them to wear the shoes during their regular workout routines, runs, or fitness classes. Ensure that they don't explicitly advertise the shoes but naturally incorporate them into their content.
- Content creation: The influencers create content such as workout videos, photos, and stories, where the shoes are visibly worn but not overtly promoted. They might mention how comfortable and supportive their workout gear is without directly stating that it is a sponsored post.
- Engagement and interaction: The influencers engage with their followers, answering questions and discussing their fitness routines. When followers inquire about their gear, they can casually mention the shoes and share their genuine experience.
- Owned media integration: Share the influencers' content on our company's social media channels and website, positioning it as user-generated content. Highlight the authentic and organic nature of the posts without making them seem like paid advertisements.

Example post by an influencer:

> Just finished an intense morning run! 🏃 ♀ Loving my workout routine these days and feeling super energized. Btw, these shoes have been amazing—they've really helped with my form and comfort. ✸ #FitnessJourney #MorningRun

Using this approach, our sports shoe company can subtly introduce the product to potential customers through trusted influencers, creating a buzz and encouraging organic word-of-mouth promotion.

16.5 Different Types of Stealth Marketing Strategies

16.5.1 Celebrity Marketing: Leveraging Influential Figures to Subtly Promote Products

Celebrity marketing involves engaging well-known personalities to use or mention a product without making it obvious that it's a paid promotion. This strategy relies on the celebrity's influence and the natural trust their audience has in them. For instance, a popular athlete might wear our sports shoes during their regular activities and subtly mention how they enjoy their performance. The key is that the endorsement appears genuine and unforced, leading the audience to develop a positive association with the product. This approach can significantly boost brand visibility and credibility without the overt feel of traditional advertisements.

16.5.2 Brand Pushers: Hiring People to Organically Mention Products in Everyday Conversations

Brand pushers are individuals hired to casually incorporate product mentions into their daily interactions. They might discuss the product's benefits with friends, family, or acquaintances in a natural and authentic manner.

For example, brand pushers for our sports shoe company might talk about how comfortable and supportive their shoes are during casual chats at the gym or social gatherings. The goal is to create organic buzz and word-of-mouth promotion by making the product seem like a natural choice for everyday use. This strategy helps in building a grassroots level of brand awareness and trust among potential customers.

16.5.3 Viral Marketing: Spreading Product Information Quickly Through Social Media

Viral marketing aims to create content that is so engaging that it is rapidly shared across social media platforms. This can include videos, memes, or challenges that feature the product subtly yet effectively. For our sports shoe company, we could create a viral challenge where people showcase their unique workout routines while wearing our shoes, encouraging others to participate and share their videos. The viral nature of the content helps in reaching a wide audience quickly and inexpensively. By leveraging the power of social media sharing, the brand can achieve significant exposure and engagement.

16.5.4 Bait-and-Tease Marketing: Attracting Customers with Enticing Offers That Lead to Upsells

Bait-and-tease marketing involves attracting customers with an appealing offer that piques their interest and leads them to explore more expensive or premium products. For instance, our sports shoe company might promote a limited-time discount on entry-level shoes, encouraging customers to visit our store or website. Once there, customers are presented with higher-end options and additional accessories that complement the initial purchase. This strategy not only drives initial traffic but also increases the likelihood of upselling and cross-selling, enhancing overall sales. The key is to create an irresistible initial offer and then guide customers toward more profitable products.

16.5.5 Video Game Marketing: Incorporating Brand Ads in Video Games for Repeated Exposure

Video game marketing involves placing brand advertisements within video games to ensure repeated exposure to players. This can be done through in-game billboards, character gear, or even storyline integrations. For our sports shoe company, we could partner with popular sports or fitness games to feature our shoes as part of the game's equipment options. Players would see the brand consistently as they engage with the game, reinforcing brand recognition and recall. This strategy is particularly effective for reaching younger audiences and avid gamers who spend significant time interacting with these digital environments.

16.5.6 Music Marketing: Embedding Brand Mentions in Popular Songs to Increase Product Visibility

Music marketing entails collaborating with artists to incorporate brand mentions or product placements within their songs or music videos. This strategy leverages the wide reach and emotional impact of music to subtly promote the brand.

For our sports shoe company, we could partner with a popular musician to mention our shoes in their lyrics or feature them in a music video. This creates a lasting impression on the audience, as they associate the brand with the positive emotions and memories tied to the music. By embedding the brand in a cultural and entertaining context, music marketing can enhance visibility and appeal.

16.6 Attitudes Toward Stealth Marketing on Social Media

Consumer attitudes toward stealth marketing vary widely. Positive attitudes arise when consumers find the ads informative, interesting, or entertaining, often appreciating the subtle and engaging approach. Negative attitudes develop when ads are perceived as deceptive or intrusive, leading to a breach of trust and potential backlash. Transparency and authenticity are crucial to maintaining positive consumer relationships and avoiding the pitfalls of stealth marketing. When consumers feel misled, it can result in a damaged brand reputation and loss of loyalty. On the other hand, well-executed stealth marketing that respects the audience's intelligence can enhance brand perception and foster a deeper connection. Ultimately, the success of stealth marketing depends on the delicate balance between creativity and honesty, ensuring that promotional efforts are both subtle and sincere.

16.7 Ethics and Legal Considerations in Stealth Marketing

Ethical concerns in stealth marketing include transparency, consumer trust, and the impact on vulnerable populations. It is important for companies to consider how their tactics might deceive or manipulate consumers, potentially eroding trust. Legal considerations involve disclosure requirements, truth in advertising, and data privacy, ensuring that all promotional activities comply with regulations. Companies must navigate these carefully to avoid backlash and legal issues, as failure to do so can result in significant penalties and a damaged reputation. Ethical practices help in maintaining a positive brand image and fostering long-term customer loyalty. Legal compliance not only protects the company but also ensures that consumers are treated fairly and respectfully. Balancing ethical concerns with effective marketing strategies is essential for sustainable business success in the long run.

16.8 Best Practices for Stealth Marketing on Social Media

Here is a list of takeaways and best practices from this chapter on stealth marketing:

1. **Maintain transparency**: Clearly disclose paid partnerships and sponsored content. Transparency builds trust with consumers and ensures compliance with legal regulations, avoiding potential backlash and penalties.

2. **Build authentic relationships**: Choose influencers who genuinely align with your brand values and messaging. Authentic partnerships create more believable and relatable content, enhancing the credibility and effectiveness of the marketing campaign.
3. **Respect consumer privacy**: Comply with data protection laws and be transparent about data usage. Protecting consumer privacy fosters trust and loyalty, demonstrating that the company values and respects its audience's personal information.
4. **Create value-driven content**: Develop content that provides value to the audience and avoids overly promotional messages. Focus on storytelling, informative content, and engaging experiences that resonate with consumers and encourage organic sharing.
5. **Monitor and respond**: Actively engage with consumer feedback and be prepared to address concerns promptly. Monitoring responses allows for quick adjustments to the campaign and shows consumers that their opinions are valued, enhancing brand reputation.
6. **Leverage subtlety**: Ensure that promotional content is integrated naturally into the audience's daily activities and media consumption. Subtlety helps avoid the perception of being overly sales-driven, making the marketing feel more authentic and trustworthy.
7. **Use influencers wisely**: Select influencers who have a strong, engaged following that matches your target demographic. Influencers with genuine connections to their audience can create more impactful and credible endorsements for your brand.
8. **Measure impact**: Use analytics tools to track the performance of stealth marketing campaigns. Measuring the impact helps in understanding what strategies work best and allows for data-driven improvements in future campaigns.
9. **Ensure legal compliance**: Stay updated on advertising laws and regulations to ensure all marketing practices are compliant. Legal compliance protects the company from fines and lawsuits and ensures that marketing efforts are ethical.
10. **Adapt to feedback**: Be flexible and willing to adjust strategies based on consumer feedback and campaign performance. Continuous improvement based on real-time data ensures that marketing efforts remain effective and relevant.

Consumers are becoming increasingly accustomed to new technologies and services, reducing the impact of flashy effects. Therefore, it becomes crucial to consistently evaluate the actual value these innovations provide. Engaging in shock tactics for publicity is unsustainable and can exhaust marketers and audiences alike. However, this doesn't mean marketers should pass up opportunities to generate buzz and earn free publicity when they arise. By focusing on genuine value and strategically leveraging moments that naturally attract attention, marketers can create meaningful and lasting impressions.

Further Reading

Ahuja, R. D., Michels, T. A., Walker, M. M., & Weissbuch, M. (2007). Teen perceptions of disclosure in buzz marketing. *Journal of Consumer Marketing, 24*(3), 151–159.

Bambauer-Sachse, S., & Mangold, S. (2011). Brand equity dilution through negative online word-of-mouth communication. *Journal of Retailing and Consumer Services, 18*(1), 38–45.

Berger, J., & Schwartz, E. M. (2011). What drives immediate and ongoing word of mouth? *Journal of Marketing Research, 48*(5), 869–880.

Chevalier, J. A., & Mayzlin, D. (2006). The effect of word of mouth on sales: Online book reviews. *Journal of Marketing Research, 43*(3), 345–354.

Dellarocas, C. (2003). The digitization of word of mouth: Promise and challenges of online feedback mechanisms. *Management Science, 49*(10), 1407–1424.

Godes, D., & Mayzlin, D. (2004). Using online conversations to study word-of-mouth communication. *Marketing Science, 23*(4), 545–560.

Liu, Y. (2006). Word of mouth for movies: Its dynamics and impact on box office revenue. *Journal of Marketing, 70*(3), 74–89.

Trusov, M., Bucklin, R. E., & Pauwels, K. (2009). Effects of word-of-mouth versus traditional marketing: Findings from an internet social networking site. *Journal of Marketing, 73*(5), 90–102.

17 The Video-First World: How Everything Is Video and Evaluated in Seconds

17.1 Background

This chapter explores the rapid rise of video in social media marketing. The preference for video content has surged in recent years, with predictions that video marketing will dominate digital marketing channels. Over the past few years, this trend has become apparent due to three key factors. Firstly, social media has driven a new type of video consumption, where videos are often watched without sound, making text and scripting crucial. Secondly, companies no longer need expensive equipment to create high-quality videos; smartphones and simple tools suffice. Thirdly, consumers' demand for video content has grown, as moving images are more engaging and shareable.

The landscape of digital marketing has transformed significantly with the rise of video content. Platforms like TikTok, Instagram Reels, YouTube, and Facebook Watch have redefined how brands connect with their audiences. The shift towards video is driven by its ability to capture attention quickly and convey messages more effectively than text or static images. Research shows that video content generates higher engagement rates, with viewers spending more time interacting with videos compared to other types of content.

Example 1: TikTok's explosive growth: TikTok, a platform dedicated entirely to short-form videos, has seen explosive growth since its launch. Brands like Guess and Chipotle have successfully Used TikTok to create viral content that resonates with younger audiences. For instance, Guess launched the #InMyDenim challenge, encouraging users to showcase their style transformation using Guess denim, which resulted in millions of user-generated videos.

Example 2: Instagram Reels for engagement: Instagram Reels offers another powerful tool for brands to engage with their followers. Reels allows users to create 15- to 60-s videos set to music, which can be edited with various effects and text overlays. Brands like Sephora use Reels to provide quick makeup

K. Solberg Söilen, *Digital Marketing*, Springer Texts in Business and Economics, https://doi.org/10.1007/978-3-031-69518-6_17

tutorials, product showcases, and behind-the-scenes glimpses, effectively reaching their audience in a dynamic and visually appealing format.

17.2 Key Factors Driving the Shift to Video

Several key factors have contributed to the increasing dominance of video in social media marketing:

Silent video consumption: Many social media users watch videos without sound, relying on subtitles and visual storytelling. This trend has necessitated the inclusion of clear text and compelling visuals to convey the message effectively. Facebook's auto-play feature, which defaults to mute, has particularly influenced this behavior.

Accessible technology: Advancements in smartphone technology have democratized video production. High-quality cameras and editing apps available on smartphones enable businesses of all sizes to produce professional-looking videos without significant investment. Tools like Canva and Adobe Spark simplify the video creation process, making it accessible even for those with limited technical skills.

Consumer preference: Consumers increasingly prefer video content because it is more engaging and easier to digest. Videos can convey complex information quickly and memorably, making them ideal for tutorials, product demonstrations, and storytelling. A HubSpot study found that 54% of consumers want to see more video content from brands they support.

17.3 Developing a Video Marketing Strategy

For brands, adopting a video marketing strategy is now essential. This approach is not new, but its importance has escalated significantly. Video marketing dominates social media, with research indicating that the majority of popular social channels are video-centric. Authenticity in video content resonates more with consumers, meaning that videos can be raw and straightforward.

Live streaming: Live streaming has become a powerful tool for real-time engagement. Platforms like Instagram Live and Facebook Live allow brands to interact with their audience directly, answering questions and providing live demonstrations. For example, fitness brands often use live streaming for workout sessions, allowing users to follow along and engage in real time.

Content planning: Companies must first address fundamental content questions: Why are we doing this? Who are we targeting? What is the video's purpose? What message do we want to convey? Without clear answers to these questions, creating impactful videos is challenging.

Product tutorials and how-to's: Educational content such as tutorials and how-to videos are extremely popular. Brands like Home Depot create detailed DIY project videos that not only promote their products but also provide value to their customers by helping them complete home improvement projects.

17.4 Types of Videos and Choosing the Right Channels

There are various types of videos, and it's crucial for brands to select the right type and channel based on their target audience. Each platform and video type serves a different purpose and reaches different segments of the audience.

Product demonstrations: Short, informative videos that show how a product works can be highly effective on platforms like Instagram and Facebook. For example, Dyson uses product demonstration videos to highlight the features and benefits of their vacuum cleaners and other home appliances.

Behind-the-scenes: Giving audiences a glimpse behind the scenes can humanize a brand and build a stronger connection. For instance, fashion brands often use behind-the-scenes videos during photoshoots or events to show the effort and creativity involved in their processes.

User-generated content (UGC): Encouraging customers to create and share their own videos featuring a brand's products can amplify reach and credibility. Brands like GoPro leverage UGC by sharing videos shot by their users, showcasing the versatility and performance of their cameras in real-life scenarios.

Brand storytelling: Videos that tell a brand's story, including its history, mission, and values, can foster a deeper emotional connection with the audience. An example is the video series by Ben & Jerry's that highlights their commitment to social justice and environmental sustainability.

Influencer collaborations: Partnering with influencers to create authentic content can boost credibility and reach. Influencers can produce videos that naturally incorporate the brand's products into their content, such as a fitness influencer demonstrating a workout using specific athletic gear.

The rise of video in social media marketing is undeniable. As platforms continue to prioritize video content, brands must adapt by developing comprehensive video marketing strategies that align with their goals and resonate with their audience. By leveraging various types of videos and the strengths of different social media channels, companies can enhance their engagement, build stronger connections, and drive better results.

17.5 The Challenge of Deep Fakes in Video Authenticity

One attractive aspect of the video is that it has traditionally been difficult to fake; when you are online with sound and video, you are immediately exposed, and whether the content you produce is good or bad, it will be detected quickly, bringing the moment of truth sooner. This immediacy has made video a trustworthy medium, as authenticity can be assessed in real time by viewers. However, we are entering a period where deep fakes will pose a significant problem, potentially undermining the credibility of video content. Deep fakes use advanced AI to create highly realistic but fake videos, making it harder to distinguish between genuine and manipulated footage. This emerging challenge threatens the reliability of video as a medium for truth and authenticity. How we will solve this issue remains to be seen, but it will likely involve technological advancements in detection and verification, as well as new regulations and ethical standards.

17.6 Types of Videos

Video content can take many forms, depending on the message and the audience. Marketers must consider what they want to communicate and how to best reach their target audience. Videos can range from text-based and press releases to blog posts and more. According to industry sources, video content can be categorized into three main areas: awareness, engagement, and education.

17.6.1 Awareness Videos

Awareness videos aim to attract attention and should be entertaining and appealing. These videos are designed to introduce a brand or product to a broad audience. They often focus on storytelling, humor, or visually stunning content to capture viewers' interest. Examples include brand introduction videos, viral marketing campaigns, and teaser trailers for upcoming products or events. The goal is to create a memorable first impression that encourages viewers to learn more about the brand.

17.6.2 Engagement Videos

Engagement videos seek to elicit reactions and shares, appealing to viewers' emotions. These videos are crafted to foster interaction, whether through likes, comments, or shares on social media. Content that sparks conversations or evokes strong emotional responses, such as heartfelt stories, challenges, or interactive videos, falls into this category. An example is Dove's "Real Beauty Sketches" campaign, which engaged viewers by challenging societal beauty standards and encouraging personal reflection and sharing.

17.6.3 Educational Videos

Educational videos aim to inform and teach viewers, often targeting current or potential customers. These videos can cover a wide range of topics, from how-to guides and tutorials to explainer videos and in-depth product demonstrations. They are particularly effective in building authority and trust, as they provide valuable information that helps viewers solve problems or understand complex concepts. An example is HubSpot's video tutorials on digital marketing strategies, which offer practical advice and insights to their audience.

17.6.4 Testimonial Videos

Testimonial videos feature individuals giving testimonials about a company's product or service. They can be celebrity endorsements or customer testimonials. Celebrity endorsements leverage the influence of well-known personalities to sway consumer behavior. Customer testimonials, on the other hand, can trigger word-of-mouth effects, building trust among new customers by showcasing real-life experiences and satisfaction. For instance, fitness brands often use testimonial videos from athletes and regular users to highlight the effectiveness of their products.

17.6.5 Social Media Videos

These videos are designed to be shared on social media platforms and include interviews, behind-the-scenes footage, product features, live videos, and tutorials. Social media videos are typically short, engaging, and tailored to each platform's audience. For example, Instagram Reels or TikTok videos often feature quick tips, fun challenges, or brief product highlights to capture the short attention spans of users. The aim is to create content that is easily consumable and shareable, maximizing reach and engagement.

17.6.6 First Page Video

Including videos on a company's landing page can improve search engine rankings and increase visitor engagement. Videos on landing pages can lead to higher conversion rates and longer visitor durations. These videos typically provide an overview of the product or service, highlight key benefits, and include calls to action. A well-crafted landing page video can significantly boost a site's effectiveness by making the content more dynamic and engaging, encouraging visitors to stay longer and explore further.

17.6.7 Vlogs

Vlogs, or video blogs, are another form of video content that can be highly engaging. They can cover a wide range of topics, from personal stories to professional advice. Vlogs can be personal, live broadcasts, informative, or even designed to provoke discussion. They offer a more informal and authentic way to connect with the audience, as the vlogger often shares their thoughts, experiences, and expertise directly. For example, a tech company might use vlogs to provide product updates, industry insights, or behind-the-scenes looks at their development process.

17.6.8 Webinars

Webinars are online seminars that can be used for a variety of purposes, including product demonstrations, educational sessions, and marketing research. They are typically longer than other types of video content and are more targeted. Webinars allow for in-depth exploration of topics and often include interactive elements such as Q&A sessions, polls, and live chat. They are an excellent way for companies to engage with their audience on a deeper level, providing valuable information and fostering direct interaction.

17.7 Key Terms and Definitions

There are many terms that are related to this chapter on vide in digital marketing. Here is a list of the more common ones and what they mean[1]:

1. **Video-first strategy**: A marketing approach that prioritizes video content over other types of media to engage and communicate with audiences more effectively.
2. **Engagement rate**: The level of interaction that video content receives from viewers, including likes, shares, comments, and views.
3. **Short-form video**: Video content that is typically under one minute in length, designed for quick consumption and high engagement on social media platforms like TikTok and Instagram Reels.
4. **Live streaming**: Broadcasting video content in -time over the internet, allowing for immediate viewer interaction and engagement.
5. **User-generated content (UGC)**: Videos created by consumers rather than brands, which can be shared on social media to build authenticity and community around a product or service.
6. **Deep fakes**: AI-generated videos that manipulate appearances and voices to create highly realistic but false representations, posing challenges for verifying authenticity.
7. **Subtitles and closed captions**: Text overlays that transcribe the audio content of videos, making them accessible to viewers who watch without sound or have hearing impairments.
8. **Video SEO (search engine optimization)**: Strategies to improve the visibility and ranking of video content in search engine results, making it easier for audiences to discover.
9. **Viral content**: Videos that rapidly gain popularity and widespread sharing across social media platforms due to their engaging and relatable nature.
10. **Interactive video**: Videos that incorporate interactive elements like clickable areas, quizzes, or decision-making paths, enhancing viewer engagement and participation.

[1] Verified using ChatGPT 4 (June 2024).

11. **Influencer collaborations**: Partnerships between brands and social media influencers to create video content that promotes products or services in a relatable and authentic manner.
12. **Video analytics**: Tools and metrics used to measure the performance of video content, including views, watch time, engagement, and conversion rates.
13. **Authenticity**: The perception that video content is genuine, honest, and relatable, which is crucial for building trust with audiences.
14. **360-degree video**: Immersive video content that allows viewers to explore the scene in all directions, enhancing the interactive experience
15. **Ephemeral content**: Videos that are only available for a short period, like Instagram Stories and Snapchat, creating a sense of urgency and exclusivity.
16. **Brand storytelling**: Using video content to convey a brand's values, mission, and history in a compelling and engaging way, fostering deeper connections with audiences.
17. **Motion graphics**: Animated visual elements used in video content to explain complex information quickly and clearly, often used in explainer videos and infographics.
18. **B-roll footage**: Supplementary video footage that supports the main content, often used to provide context or additional visual interest in a video.
19. **Video editing software**: Tools used to cut, enhance, and assemble video footage into a polished final product, such as Adobe Premiere Pro and Final Cut Pro.
20. **Content calendar**: A scheduling tool that helps plan and organize the release of video content to ensure consistent posting and strategic timing.

Video has become all-encompassing. More than any other platform, YouTube has become the go-to place for all kinds of video content, including news, movies, and how-to clips. As the interest in becoming a YouTuber increases, so does the difficulty of breaking through and achieving those 100,000 views necessary to earn some good money and fulfill the dream of becoming a professional YouTuber.

17.8 Key Takeaways for Managers

Some key takeaways from this chapter include:

1. **Embrace the shift to video**: Managers must recognize the rapid rise of video content as a dominant force in social media marketing. Video engages audiences more effectively than text or static images, making it essential for modern digital strategies.
2. **Leverage accessible technology**: The advancements in smartphone technology and editing apps allow companies of all sizes to produce high-quality videos. Managers should invest in these accessible tools to create professional content without significant financial investment.
3. **Optimize for silent video consumption**: Many users watch videos without sound, making subtitles and visual storytelling crucial. Managers need to ensure

their videos are effective even when viewed on mute by incorporating clear text and compelling visuals.
4. **Develop a comprehensive video strategy**: Crafting a video marketing strategy involves answering fundamental questions about the target audience, purpose, and messaging. Managers must plan content that aligns with these objectives to maximize impact.
5. **Use different types of videos**: There are various types of videos—awareness, engagement, educational, testimonial, social media, and more. Managers should select the right type and channel based on their target audience and marketing goals.
6. **Capitalize on user-generated content**: Encouraging customers to create and share videos featuring the brand can amplify reach and credibility. Managers should foster an environment that promotes user-generated content to enhance authenticity and community engagement.
7. **Address the challenge of deep fakes**: As deep fake technology advances, maintaining video authenticity becomes critical. Managers must stay informed about detection and verification methods to protect their brand's credibility.
8. **Monitor and analyze video performance**: Utilizing video analytics tools to measure engagement, views, and conversion rates is essential. Managers should regularly analyze this data to refine their strategies and improve future video content.

Video content is a critical moment of truth for organizations and individuals, offering viewers an immediate impression of who you are and what you represent, often within seconds. Unlike written expressions, video conveys authenticity and personality, making it difficult to fake—until the advent of deepfake technology. This new capability allows for the creation of highly realistic, but entirely fabricated, video content, raising concerns about its potential uses and impacts. The future of video authenticity and trust will be shaped by how we address and regulate deepfake technology.

Further Reading

Demers, J. (2015). *7 Tips for an effective video marketing campaign*. Inc.com. Retrieved from https://www.inc.com/jayson-demers/7-tips-for-an-effective-video-marketing-campaign.html

Hansson, L., Wrangmo, A., & Solberg Söilen, K. (2013). Optimal ways for companies to use Facebook as a marketing channel. *Journal of Information, Communication and Ethics in Society, 11*(2), 112–126.

Hollander, E. (2018). *The importance of video marketing*. Forbes. Retrieved from https://www.forbes.com/sites/forbesagencycouncil/2018/11/02/the-importance-of-video-marketing-in-2018/?sh=53f1d7483e57

Martin, T. (2017). *The power of video marketing in today's world*. Business2Community. Retrieved from https://www.business2community.com/video-marketing/the-power-of-video-marketing-in-todays-world-01893995

Patel, N. (2019). *How to develop a video marketing strategy*. Neil Patel. Retrieved from https://neilpatel.com/blog/develop-video-marketing-strategy/

Smith, A. (2020). *Video marketing: The future of content marketing*. Social Media Examiner. Retrieved from https://www.socialmediaexaminer.com/video-marketing-future-content-marketing/

Why Music Matters in Digital Marketing 18

18.1 Background

This chapter examines the significance of music in digital marketing, its impact on consumer behavior, and the history of its use in marketing strategies. Combining branding with music allows organizations to communicate creatively with their target audience. Music uniquely affects the brain, particularly in terms of memory, making it highly effective for branding. Emotions generated by music create a more personal connection with the audience than written advertisements.

Music advertisements tell a story, connecting with the listener on a deeper level. This emotional strategy helps differentiate the brand and convey its values. Music in advertising aids memorability and product recall, making it an optimal strategy. The combination of sound in music advertisements influences the consumer's emotional state and attitude, enhancing the overall impact of the marketing effort. Music for use in marketing and advertising comes in many forms, as shown in Table 18.1:

These types of music can be strategically chosen and used to enhance marketing efforts, create deeper emotional connections, and improve overall brand recognition and recall.

18.2 Definitions

Music: Scientifically, music is a combination of wave movements producing sounds at different frequencies. These sounds are perceived as music when arranged in a way that is pleasing to the listener. The process involves vibrations in the eardrum, transmitted through the auditory bones to the brain, where the sound is interpreted. Music evokes emotions, and these responses can vary from person to person.

Emotional marketing: A marketing approach that leverages the emotional responses elicited by music to create a strong connection between the brand and the consumer.

K. Solberg Söilen, *Digital Marketing*, Springer Texts in Business and Economics, https://doi.org/10.1007/978-3-031-69518-6_18

Table 18.1 Types of music used in digital marketing and their use

Type of music	Use	Examples
Jingles	Short, catchy tunes designed to be memorable and enhance brand recall.	McDonald's "I'm Lovin' It," Intel's "Intel Inside"
Background music	Sets the mood and enhances the consumer experience in retail environments or videos.	Classical music in luxury stores, instrumental tracks in explainer videos
Popular music	Leverages the popularity and fan base of existing songs to connect with target audiences.	Pepsi's collaboration with Beyoncé, Nike ads featuring popular songs
Custom compositions	Original music created specifically for a brand or campaign to ensure uniqueness and alignment with brand identity.	Coca-Cola's "Taste the Feeling," Intel's jingle
Licensed tracks	Uses well-known songs by purchasing rights for use in advertisements to tap into their cultural resonance.	Apple's use of "There Goes My Hero" by Foo Fighters, Levi's "Stand By Me" by Ben E. King
Ambient music	Creates a subtle and immersive background sound that enhances the overall atmosphere without distracting.	Starbucks' in-store playlists, spa and wellness centers' ambient tracks
User-generated music content	Encourages customers to create and share videos featuring the brand, using specific music tracks or themes.	TikTok challenges like Chipotle's #GuacDance, GoPro's user-shared adventure videos with music
Live music performances	Engages audiences through live events, concerts, or performances sponsored by the brand.	Heineken's sponsorship of Coachella, Red Bull's live music events
Mood music	Tailors the music to fit specific moods or emotions to enhance the emotional impact of the marketing content.	Spotify's mood-based playlists for brands, "inspirational" tracks in motivational ads
Brand anthems	Full-length songs created specifically for a brand, often reflecting the brand's values and ethos.	The "We Are Young" campaign by Taco Bell, the "Hello Tomorrow" anthem by Emirates
Thematic music	Music that aligns with a particular theme or campaign to create a cohesive marketing narrative.	John Lewis Christmas ads, Nike's "Dream Crazy" campaign with thematic music
Cultural or regional music	Uses music that reflects specific cultural or regional influences to connect with local markets.	Toyota's use of traditional Japanese music in local ads, Pepsi India's Bollywood-inspired campaigns

Stimulus-response: A theory in sensory marketing focusing on how sensory inputs, like music, influence consumer behavior and decision-making.

Popular music in advertising: The use of well-known songs or artists in marketing campaigns to leverage their existing fan base and cultural significance.

18.3 Strategies for Using Music in Digital Marketing

18.3.1 Emotional Marketing

Traditionally, advertisements were not designed to evoke emotions. Today, emotional marketing is common because products and services are often similar, making it difficult to differentiate them based on price or features alone. Emotional intelligence in marketing involves perceiving, interpreting, and expressing emotions, eliciting emotions to facilitate understanding, comprehending the information conveyed by emotions, and controlling emotions to promote development. This approach allows companies to create a brand identity that resonates emotionally with consumers.

McDonald's "I'm lovin' it" campaign used a catchy jingle to embed the brand into popular culture. The campaign, featuring a song by Justin Timberlake and produced by Pharrell Williams, significantly boosted McDonald's brand recognition and sales.

18.3.2 Stimulus-Response

Sensory marketing focuses on the impact of sensations on the customer's product experience. Visual and auditory stimuli, such as video and music, engage the brain in ways written text cannot. Videos stimulate imagination, thought processes, and emotional responses, making them powerful tools in digital marketing.

Coca-Cola's use of the song "Taste the Feeling" in its advertising campaigns effectively created a sensory and emotional connection with its audience, enhancing brand recall and loyalty.

18.3.3 Music Makes Us Feel Something

Music elicits emotions and captures attention, influencing mood and behavior. Studies show that sound waves trigger reactions in the brain's Heschel's Gyrus, lighting up this area and creating emotional responses. Marketers use familiar music or specific artists to target certain demographics, enhancing the effectiveness of their campaigns.

Nike's use of inspirational music in its commercials, such as the song "Dream On" by Aerosmith, creates an emotional uplift that resonates with viewers and reinforces the brand's motivational message.

18.3.4 Music to Affect Decision Making

Background music in retail stores aims to enhance the shopping experience and influence purchasing decisions. The type of music played can create a sense of affinity with the customer, distracting the brain and making spontaneous purchases more likely. Muzak, a form of background music, is used to calm and stimulate consumers, though its effectiveness in increasing sales is debated.

Studies have shown that playing classical music in high-end retail stores can increase sales by creating an upscale atmosphere that encourages customers to spend more.

18.3.5 Popular Music in Advertising

The use of popular music in advertising has grown, with musicians increasingly relying on advertisements for income and exposure. This trend has created a new relationship between popular music and advertising. Companies like Pepsi and Coca-Cola have positioned themselves as music culture enthusiasts, using music to promote their products and connect with consumers.

Pepsi's collaboration with Beyoncé for the "Pepsi Super Bowl Halftime Show" promoted the brand and leveraged the artist's massive following to enhance its reach and impact.

18.4 Getting Permission to Use Music in Digital Marketing

To use music in a video, a company must get the proper licenses. First, they need to identify the copyright holders of the song, which typically includes the songwriter, the publisher, and the recording artist or label. Next, the company should contact these rights holders to negotiate the terms of use and secure the necessary permissions. This process involves obtaining a synchronization license, which allows the company to use the music in a video, and a master use license, which permits using a specific recording. It's advisable to work with a music licensing agency or legal professional to navigate the complexities and ensure all legal requirements are met. The company must also be prepared to pay licensing fees, which can vary widely depending on the popularity of the song and the scope of its use. Once all agreements are in place, the company should keep detailed records of the licenses and permissions granted to avoid potential legal issues in the future. Companies that want to use specific music need to deal with the rights holders, as listed in Table 18.2:

18.5 Music Marketing in Practice

Music marketing has become essential due to its powerful emotional and cultural impact. Brands use music to create memorable experiences, drive engagement, and build loyalty. Here are some effective strategies:

Integration with social media: Music videos and clips are widely shared on platforms like Instagram, TikTok, and YouTube. Brands can create catchy jingles or partner with artists to produce viral music videos. For example, the TikTok

Table 18.2 List of rights holders to music and their portfolio size

Rights holder	Example of artists	HQ	Number of artists in the portfolio
Universal Music Group (UMG)	Taylor Swift, Billie Eilish, Drake	Santa Monica, California, USA	10,000+
Sony Music Entertainment	Beyoncé, Adele, Travis Scott	New York, New York, USA	8000+
Warner Music Group (WMG)	Ed Sheeran, Bruno Mars, Cardi B	New York, New York, USA	6000+
BMG Rights Management	The Rolling Stones, Kylie Minogue	Berlin, Germany	3000+
Kobalt Music Group	Paul McCartney, The Weekend	New York, New York, USA	2000+
Concord Music Publishing	Daft Punk, Phil Collins	Nashville, Tennessee, USA	1000+
Primary Wave	Bob Marley, Whitney Houston	New York, New York, USA	800+
Downtown Music Holdings	John Lennon, OneRepublic	New York, New York, USA	700+
Hipgnosis Songs Fund	Shakira, Neil Young	London, UK	500+
Reservoir Media	Sheryl Crow, Offset	New York, New York, USA	400+

campaign for the song "Old Town Road" by Lil Nas X used a combination of user-generated content and brand-sponsored posts to make the song a viral sensation, ultimately leading to its massive commercial success.

Playlists and streaming services: Brands can create playlists on streaming services like Spotify and Apple Music that reflect their brand identity. These playlists can be shared with customers, creating an ongoing brand presence in their daily lives. Starbucks curates playlists on Spotify that align with its in-store atmosphere, reinforcing the brand experience both in and outside of its cafes.

Concert sponsorships and music festivals: Sponsoring concerts and music festivals can increase brand visibility and connect with target audiences in a dynamic, engaging environment. Heineken's long-standing sponsorship of the Coachella Music Festival has helped the brand maintain a strong presence among young, music-loving consumers.

Custom music production: Brands can produce original music for their advertising campaigns to ensure that their messaging is unique and memorable. Intel's iconic "Intel Inside" jingle is an example of how a simple, custom-produced sound can become synonymous with a brand.

Collaborations with musicians: Partnering with popular artists for endorsements or co-branded music projects can significantly boost a brand's appeal. Adidas's collaboration with Kanye West for the Yeezy sneaker line combined music and fashion, resulting in a highly successful product launch that capitalized on the artist's influence.

18.6 Key Takeaways for Managers from the Chapter: Why Music Matters in Digital Marketing

Here are some takeaways from this chapter:

1. **Harness emotional marketing:** Use music to evoke emotions that create a strong, personal connection between your brand and consumers. This can help differentiate your brand and convey its values more effectively than text alone.
2. **Leverage popular music:** Incorporate well-known songs or artists in your marketing campaigns to tap into their existing fan base and cultural significance. This can enhance brand recall and connect with a wider audience.
3. **Use custom compositions:** Create original music specifically for your brand to ensure uniqueness and alignment with your brand identity. This approach can make your marketing more memorable and impactful.
4. **Implement stimulus-response theory:** Use sensory inputs like music to influence consumer behavior and decision-making. Background music in retail stores, for example, can enhance the shopping experience and increase sales.
5. **Optimize social media integration:** Share music videos and clips on platforms like Instagram, TikTok, and YouTube to engage with audiences and create viral content. Social media campaigns involving music can significantly boost brand visibility and engagement.
6. **Create playlists and use streaming services:** Develop branded playlists on services like Spotify and Apple Music to maintain a presence in consumers' daily lives. Curated playlists that reflect your brand's identity can reinforce your brand experience.
7. **Sponsor concerts and music festivals:** Increase brand visibility and connect with target audiences by sponsoring live music events. Engaging with consumers in dynamic environments like concerts and festivals can build a stronger brand association.
8. **Collaborate with musicians:** Partner with popular artists for endorsements or co-branded music projects. These collaborations can enhance your brand's appeal and reach, leveraging the influence of well-known musicians.

In recent years, the use of video content and photos often comes with accompanying music. This powerful combination has become easier to implement due to advancements in streaming services for music. By understanding and leveraging the power of music in digital marketing, companies can create more engaging, memorable, and effective campaigns that resonate deeply with their audience. Integrating music with video content enhances emotional connections, reinforces brand messaging, and captures viewers' attention more effectively than visuals alone. This strategic use of music helps brands stand out in a crowded digital landscape and fosters a stronger emotional bond with their audience.

Further Reading

Ali, A. (2019). The role of music in marketing. *MarketingProfs*. Retrieved from https://www.marketingprofs.com/articles/2019/42079/the-role-of-music-in-marketing

Bradley, D. (2018). How music influences the way we shop. *BBC Future*. Retrieved from https://www.bbc.com/future/article/20181112-how-music-influences-the-way-we-shop

Jansson-Boyd, C. (2019). How music affects shopping behavior. *Psychology Today*. Retrieved from https://www.psychologytoday.com/us/blog/consumer-behavior/201903/how-music-affects-shopping-behavior

North, A. C., & Hargreaves, D. J. (1998). The impact of music on shopping behavior. *Journal of Applied Social Psychology, 28*(1), 53–66.

Rentfrow, P. J., & Gosling, S. D. (2003). The do Re Mi's of everyday life: The structure and personality correlates of music preferences. *Journal of Personality and Social Psychology, 84*(6), 1236–1256.

Drafting the Storyline; Expected Emotions 19

19.1 Background

A storyline in digital marketing is the structured narrative that a brand uses to communicate its message and values to its target audience. It consists of a beginning, middle, and end, designed to engage, evoke emotions, and guide the audience toward a desired action. By crafting compelling storylines, brands can create memorable connections and foster long-term relationships with their customers.

A compelling storyline is crucial in digital marketing to engage the target audience effectively. The ultimate goal of any marketing strategy is to build long-term relationships with customers and partners, and a well-crafted story can connect, evoke emotions, and provide solutions. Crafting a storyline for social media marketing involves careful planning and execution to ensure it resonates with the audience and enhances brand trust and loyalty.

19.2 Development of Storytelling in Marketing

The evolution of storytelling in marketing has roots in the earliest forms of advertising but gained significant traction with the rise of digital media. Brands recognized the potential of storytelling to create deeper emotional connections with consumers. Over time, storytelling became a pivotal element in marketing strategies, with companies using various platforms to share their narratives and engage with audiences on a more personal level.

K. Solberg Söilen, *Digital Marketing*, Springer Texts in Business and Economics, https://doi.org/10.1007/978-3-031-69518-6_19

Taking our Sports Shoes Company and say we decided to go with story number two with "Lars M. Bergström, a Swedish adventurer and inventor related to the great Swedish explorer in the 19th century," here are some examples of storylines:

19.2.1 Example 1: "The Explorer's Legacy"

Lars M. Bergström's journey begins in the dense forests of South America, where he learns the secrets of the indigenous people's craftsmanship. The storyline follows his return to Sweden, where he works day and night in his small village workshop to perfect the design of HeritageStride shoes. The climax of the story is his encounter with Jesse Owens in the Alps, highlighting the athlete's immediate admiration for the shoes' comfort and support. The narrative concludes with the shoes gaining international fame, symbolizing the blend of adventure, tradition, and innovation.

19.2.2 Example 2: "From the Andes to the Alps"

This storyline emphasizes the geographical and cultural journey of HeritageStride shoes. It starts with Lars's adventures in the Andes, where he gains inspiration from indigenous footwear. The plot then shifts to his meticulous design process back in Sweden, showcasing the fusion of South American techniques and Scandinavian precision. The turning point is Jesse Owens's discovery of the shoes during a mountain hike in the Alps, leading to the shoes becoming a global sensation among athletes and explorers.

19.2.3 Example 3: "A Shoe for Every Journey"

The storyline focuses on the versatility and durability of HeritageStride shoes, crafted for adventurers and athletes alike. It traces Lars's journey from South America to Sweden, illustrating his dedication to creating a shoe that can withstand any terrain. The story highlights various testimonials from early users, culminating in Jesse Owens's endorsement. The narrative ends by showcasing modern-day athletes and adventurers who continue to rely on HeritageStride for their toughest challenges.

19.2.4 Example 4: "Endorsement of Excellence"

This storyline revolves around the impact of Jesse Owens's endorsement. It begins with Lars's initial struggles and eventual success in designing the perfect shoe, followed by a detailed account of his meeting with Owens. The story focuses on how Owens's praise and subsequent public endorsement catapulted HeritageStride into the spotlight, leading to its adoption by top athletes worldwide. The narrative emphasizes the ongoing legacy of excellence and performance associated with the brand.

19.2.5 Example 5: "Crafted by Tradition, Perfected by Technology"

This storyline contrasts the traditional techniques Lars learned in South America with the modern technologies he incorporated in Sweden. It starts with his exploration and learning phase in the rugged terrains, followed by his innovative design process back home. The story highlights the unique features of the shoes and their rigorous testing by Jesse Owens. The conclusion focuses on how HeritageStride continues to evolve, integrating the latest technology while honoring its rich heritage.

What we have done here is divide the entire story of the brand into smaller subsections that are more easily manageable and with which we can create entire series of messages, creating not only a sense of continuity but also of recognition.

19.3 Drafting the Storyline

How can we draft a storyline? One suggestion is to follow what is called the 7 Elements Message: The first step is to have a clear message and strategy for what the audience should think, feel, and do after engaging with the story. The goal should include a call to action (CTA) to guide the audience's next steps. For example, if the goal is to increase conversions on a whitepaper landing page, the story should make readers want to learn more about the brand and trust the company. The message should be singular and clear, possibly supported by three to four submessages with statistics and examples to reinforce the core message.

Dramaturgy: Build an exciting story with a beginning, middle, and end. This structure should be planned before creating the content to avoid issues. Creating a storyboard and writing a script is essential. Involving team members who work closely with customers in the script review process can provide valuable insights.

Emotion: The story must evoke an emotional response to keep the audience engaged. Triggering an emotional reaction at the beginning helps capture attention. Emotional marketing is effective because it creates a lasting first impression and drives decision-making. Emotions such as happiness, sadness, fear, and anger can inspire different actions, like sharing, giving, loyalty, or virality.

Voice: The narrator's voice is crucial for delivering the message effectively. The voice should be clear, articulate, and genuine, matching the story's tone and content. The right voice can guide the audience and enhance their emotional connection to the story.

Soundtrack: The soundtrack should complement the story without distracting from it. Music can set the mood and create the right perception, adding an extra layer of information to the narrative content.

Economy: The length of the story should be kept concise to maintain the audience's attention. Ideally, stories should be no longer than necessary to convey the message effectively. Retention rates improve with concise storytelling, making it possible to keep more readers engaged until the end.

Rhythm and tempo: The story's rhythm and tempo affect audience engagement. A consistent pace with strategic pauses or accelerations can evoke different emotions and maintain interest. Factors like narrative tempo, dialogue rate, and scene transitions influence the story's overall tempo.

19.4 Types of Stories

Different types of stories can be used for marketing on social media:[1]

- Promotion stories: These stories increase awareness of new products, making customers curious and likely to share with others.
- Explainers: These stories show how to use a product, providing helpful tips and solving problems without overtly promoting the product.
- Vlogs: Regular video blogs that delve into specific topics, keeping the target audience engaged with new information.
- Interviews: Quick and easy to produce, these stories build relationships with partners and provide free marketing through shares.
- Event stories: Stories from events make viewers feel included and can inspire attendance at future events.
- Product reviews: Influencers review products, providing trusted recommendations to their followers.

Choosing the best type of story depends on the company's budget, expertise, and the specific message to be conveyed. Stories can answer customer questions, raise brand awareness, or explain product features effectively.

19.5 Platforms Stories

Platform stories can be shared on various social media platforms, including Facebook, Instagram, X (formerly Twitter), LinkedIn, Snapchat, TikTok, and YouTube. Each platform has different recommended story-lengths[2]:

1. Instagram: 15–60 s
2. X (formerly Twitter): 2 min and 20 s
3. Facebook: 1 min

[1] Verified using ChatGPT 4 (June 2024).

[2] Verified using ChatGPT 4 (June 2024).

4. YouTube: 10 min or longer for in-depth content, but 2–3 min for general engagement
5. Snapchat: 10 s per snap, up to 60 seconds per story
6. TikTok: 15–60 s

In 2023, YouTube became the most popular platform for watching online stories, with over 2.1 billion monthly active users. Snapchat has continued to grow significantly, with 332 million daily active users watching 18 billion stories per day. TikTok has also emerged as a major player, with over 1 billion monthly active users consuming short-form video content.

It's essential to tailor story content to the specific platform and audience to maximize engagement. Each platform has its own unique features and audience preferences, so understanding these nuances is crucial for effective storytelling. By leveraging the strengths of each platform and creating content that resonates with the audience, companies can effectively use storytelling to reach and engage their target audience, creating memorable and impactful content.

19.6 Management Takeaways

Here are some of the takeaways from this chapter:

1. **Importance of a compelling storyline**: A well-crafted storyline is crucial in digital marketing to effectively engage the target audience. It helps in creating memorable connections and fostering long-term relationships with customers.
2. **Historical development of storytelling**: Understanding the evolution of storytelling in marketing helps recognize its potential to create deeper emotional connections with consumers. The rise of digital media has amplified the importance of storytelling in engaging audiences on a personal level.
3. **Breaking down the brand story**: Dividing the brand's story into manageable subsections allows for a series of messages that create a sense of continuity and recognition. This approach helps maintain audience interest and reinforces brand identity over time.
4. **Message clarity and strategy**: The storyline should have a clear, singular message supported by sub-messages and a strong call to action (CTA). This strategy ensures that the audience knows exactly what to think, feel, and do after engaging with the story.
5. **Dramaturgy and structure**: Building a storyline with a clear beginning, middle, and end is essential. Planning the structure before creating content, including storyboarding and scripting, helps avoid issues and ensures a coherent narrative.
6. **Emotional engagement**: The story must evoke an emotional response to keep the audience engaged. Emotions like happiness, sadness, fear, and anger can drive actions such as sharing, loyalty, and virality.

7. **Voice and soundtrack**: The narrator's voice should be clear and genuine, matching the story's tone. A well-chosen soundtrack can complement the narrative, setting the mood and enhancing the emotional impact without distracting from the story.
8. **Conciseness and pacing**: Keeping the story concise helps maintain the audience's attention. The rhythm and tempo of the narrative, including strategic pauses and accelerations, influence audience engagement and emotional response.

Everyone loves a good story, but few can tell one convincingly. Sometimes I wonder if we were better at this a generation ago. Regardless, we must never forget this art, as it has always been what binds us together as humans and societies. By understanding and applying these principles, companies can effectively use storytelling to reach and engage their target audience, creating memorable and impactful content that resonates deeply. This strategic use of storytelling not only captures attention but also fosters a stronger emotional connection, making brands more relatable and memorable.

Further Reading

Abrahamson, E. (2013). How to tell your brand's story. *Harvard Business Review*. Retrieved from https://hbr.org/2013/03/how-to-tell-your-brands-story

Denning, S. (2006). Effective storytelling: Strategic business narrative techniques. *Strategy and Leadership, 34*(1), 42–48.

Fog, K., Budtz, C., & Yakaboylu, B. (2005). *Storytelling: Branding in practice*. Springer.

Gill, R. (2015). Why storytelling in marketing works. *Forbes*. Retrieved from https://www.forbes.com/sites/forbesagencycouncil/2015/12/02/why-storytelling-in-marketing-works/?sh=7b905f313d96

Simmons, A. (2006). *The story factor: Inspiration, influence, and persuasion through the art of storytelling*. Basic Books.

Embedding 20

20.1 Background

Embedding in digital marketing involves integrating multimedia elements such as videos, images, and links directly into websites, social media posts, or emails. This practice enhances the visual appeal and interactivity of the content, making it more engaging for the audience. By embedding content from platforms like YouTube or Instagram, marketers can extend their reach, improve user engagement, and track performance metrics effectively.

In today's digital landscape, embedding plays a crucial role in enhancing marketing strategies and engaging customers. Embedding allows for the seamless integration of multimedia content such as images, videos, links, and other digital elements directly into websites, emails, and social media posts. This approach increases user engagement by making content more visually appealing and interactive. Embedding videos on a website, for instance, can significantly boost the time visitors spend on the site, reduce bounce rates, and build trust and credibility with potential customers.

20.2 Evolution of Embedding

The practice of embedding content has evolved alongside advances in web technologies. Initially, websites were primarily text-based, but as internet speeds increased and multimedia capabilities expanded, embedding became a standard practice. The ability to embed videos, images, and interactive elements has transformed how content is consumed and shared online. This shift began with the introduction of HTML embedding tags and has since grown with the rise of platforms like YouTube, which facilitate easy embedding of videos.

K. Solberg Söilen, *Digital Marketing*, Springer Texts in Business and Economics, https://doi.org/10.1007/978-3-031-69518-6_20

20.3 Importance of Embedding in Digital Marketing

Embedding content is essential in digital marketing as it enhances the visual appeal and interactivity of web pages, social media posts, and emails. By embedding videos, images, and interactive elements, marketers can capture audience attention more effectively and provide a richer user experience. This approach not only increases engagement but also helps convey complex information in a more digestible and memorable format.

20.4 Social Video Marketing and Embedding

Social video marketing benefits significantly from embedding, as it allows videos to be easily shared and viewed across multiple platforms. Embedding videos in social media posts, blogs, and emails can amplify their reach and impact.

20.5 Social Video Platforms

20.5.1 Social Video Marketing Platform: YouTube

YouTube facilitates easy embedding, allowing users to share videos across various platforms. By embedding YouTube videos, brands can extend their reach, engage more viewers, and track engagement metrics such as views and shares.

Example: A tech company embeds product demo videos on their website to provide visitors with detailed information about their products, leading to higher engagement and conversion rates.

20.5.2 Social Video Marketing Platform: Instagram

Instagram supports embedding of posts and stories, enabling brands to share engaging visual content on their websites and blogs. This integration helps drive traffic to Instagram profiles and boosts overall engagement.

A fashion brand embeds Instagram posts featuring their latest collection on their website, encouraging visitors to explore more on their Instagram page.

20.5.3 Social Video Marketing Platform: TikTok

TikTok videos can be embedded into websites and blogs, allowing brands to leverage the platform's viral content for broader reach and engagement.

A restaurant embeds TikTok videos of popular menu items on its website to attract younger audiences and boost online orders.

20.6 Advantages of Embedding

Embedding offers several advantages in digital marketing:

1. **Enhanced engagement**: Embedded content, especially videos, captures attention more effectively than text, leading to longer site visits and higher interaction rates.
2. **Improved SEO**: Embedding videos on your website can improve search engine rankings, as search engines prioritize multimedia content.
3. **Increased sharing**: Embedded content is easily shareable across social platforms, extending the reach and impact of your marketing efforts.
4. **Cost-effective**: Embedding videos from platforms like YouTube or Vimeo reduces hosting costs and leverages the platform's infrastructure and audience.

A travel agency embeds customer testimonial videos on their landing pages, resulting in higher trust and increased bookings.

20.7 How to Embed Content

To embed a YouTube video, you can follow these simple steps:

1. Go to the YouTube video you want to embed.
2. Click on the "Share" button below the video.
3. Select the "Embed" option.
4. Copy the HTML code provided.
5. Paste the code into your website's HTML editor.

If you forget, there are always instructional videos on YouTube and other platforms. That goes for almost everything these days.

20.8 Best Practices for Embedding

Here are a number of things to bear in mind when embedding:

- **Ensure relevance**: Embed content that is relevant to your audience and complements the surrounding content.
- **Optimize for load times**: Use compressed media files to ensure that embedded content does not slow down your website.
- **Use clear calls to action**: Encourage viewers to take the next step, such as sharing the content or visiting your social media profiles.
- **Monitor performance**: Track engagement metrics to understand how embedded content is performing and make adjustments as needed.

An online retailer embeds product review videos on their product pages to provide social proof and encourage purchases.

20.9 Takeaways from This Chapter

Embedding is a powerful tool in digital marketing, enhancing content engagement and extending the reach of multimedia elements. By effectively integrating videos, images, and other digital media into websites and social media posts, brands can create more interactive and memorable experiences for their audiences. Implementing best practices for embedding ensures that content remains relevant, engaging, and effective in achieving marketing goals.

1. Embedding enhances engagement by integrating multimedia elements like videos, images, and links directly into websites and social media posts. This visual appeal captures user attention, leading to longer site visits and higher interaction rates.
2. The evolution of embedding has significantly transformed content consumption and sharing online. Starting with simple HTML embedding tags, it has grown with platforms like YouTube, which facilitate easy embedding of videos, boosting the overall user experience.
3. Embedding content is essential in digital marketing as it increases digital platforms' visual appeal and interactivity. By embedding multimedia content, marketers can convey complex information more effectively, making it easier for the audience to understand and remember.
4. Embedding videos on social media platforms like YouTube, Instagram, and TikTok amplify their reach and impact. For example, embedding a product demo video on a website can provide detailed information, leading to higher engagement and conversion rates.
5. Embedding offers several advantages, including enhanced engagement, improved SEO, increased sharing, and cost-effectiveness. By embedding content from platforms like YouTube, businesses can reduce hosting costs while leveraging the platform's infrastructure and audience.

Embedding is all about integrating what content you have. By following these insights, companies can effectively use embedding to enhance their digital marketing strategies, creating more engaging and interactive experiences for their audiences.

Further Reading

Anderson, C. (2006). *The long tail: Why the future of business is selling less of more.* Hyperion.
Brown, L., & Duguid, P. (2000). *The social life of information.* Harvard Business School Press.

Chaffey, D., & Ellis-Chadwick, F. (2019). *Digital marketing: Strategy, implementation and practice* (7th ed.). Pearson.
Smith, A. (2013). Marketing strategies for the digital age. *Marketing Journal, 25*(4), 202–216.

Real-Time Video Editing 21

21.1 Background

Real-time video editing is the process of editing and modifying video content instantly as it is being created or shortly after recording. This involves making changes such as adding effects, filters, music, text, and transitions on the fly, often using web-based platforms or software that support live adjustments. Real-time video editing enables creators to quickly produce polished and engaging videos without extensive delays, making it a valuable tool for live broadcasts, social media updates, and timely marketing campaigns.

This chapter explores the concept of real-time video editing, particularly through platforms like Snapchat and YouTube. Real-time video editing involves creating and modifying video content on the fly, adding effects, filters, music, text, and symbols as needed. Various web-based video editing systems manage video content in segments, stored in different file-based storages for ease of editing. Handling video content from multiple sources can be cumbersome, making real-time editing tools essential for efficiency and creativity.

21.2 Why a Special Chapter on Real-Time Video Editing?

Real-time video editing deserves a special chapter due to its transformative impact on digital marketing and content creation. Here are the key reasons why it is so important:[1]

1. Immediate engagement: Real-time video editing allows for immediate interaction with audiences. This capability is crucial in the fast-paced world of social media, where timely and relevant content can significantly boost engagement

[1] Verified using ChatGPT 4 (June 2024).

K. Solberg Söilen, *Digital Marketing*, Springer Texts in Business and Economics, https://doi.org/10.1007/978-3-031-69518-6_21

and retention. For example, brands can respond to current events or trends with quick, polished video content that resonates with viewers in the moment.
2. Enhanced content quality: With real-time editing tools, creators can enhance the quality of their content on the go, adding professional touches that make videos more appealing. This includes the use of filters, effects, music, and text overlays that can transform a basic video into a visually compelling story.
3. Efficiency and cost-effectiveness: Traditional video editing can be time-consuming and expensive, requiring specialized software and skilled professionals. Real-time video editing tools, often available on social media platforms like Snapchat and YouTube, democratize the process, making it accessible to a broader range of users and reducing the time and cost associated with video production.
4. Increased reach and visibility: Videos edited in real-time can be quickly shared across multiple platforms, maximizing their reach and impact. This immediacy helps in capturing the audience's attention when it matters most, thereby increasing the likelihood of the content being shared and going viral.
5. Adaptive marketing strategies: Real-time editing supports dynamic marketing strategies, allowing brands to adapt their messages based on live feedback and interactions. This flexibility helps marketers refine their approaches and deliver content that is more relevant and engaging to their target audience.
6. Improved user experience: For live events and broadcasts, real-time video editing enhances the viewer's experience by providing a seamless, polished presentation. This level of professionalism helps build trust and credibility with the audience, making them more likely to engage with and support the brand.

In summary, real-time video editing is crucial because it enables brands to produce high-quality, timely content that engages audiences effectively, supports dynamic marketing strategies, and enhances overall user experience. Its role in digital marketing is indispensable, warranting a dedicated chapter to comprehensively explore its benefits and applications.

21.3 Terms and Definitions Specific to Real-Time Video Editing

Real-time video editing is the process of editing and rearranging video content instantly to create new work. This includes tasks such as rearranging clips, applying filters, performing color corrections, and creating transitions, all of which can be done live or during a recording session. So, we must have an understanding of the terms:[2]

1. *Real-time video editing*: The process of editing and enhancing video content as it is being recorded or shortly after, using tools and software that allow for

[2] Verified using ChatGPT 4 (June 2024).

immediate adjustments and refinements. This can include adding filters, effects, text overlays, and music without significant delays.

2. *Live streaming*: The broadcasting of video content in real time over the internet, often with the capability for real-time editing. Platforms like YouTube Live and Instagram Live enable users to interact with their audience immediately, making live adjustments to the video as needed.
3. *Filters*: Pre-set visual effects that can be applied to video content in real time to enhance or alter its appearance. Filters can instantly change the color, contrast, and overall look of the video.
4. *Overlays*: Graphics, text, or images superimposed on a video during editing. In real-time video editing, overlays can be added live to provide additional information, such as captions, logos, or interactive elements.
5. *Effects*: Visual or auditory modifications applied to video content to enhance its appeal. Real-time effects can include transitions, animations, and sound enhancements implemented as the video is recorded or streamed.
6. *Metadata*: Information embedded within video files that describe various attributes of the content, such as titles, descriptions, and tags. In real-time video editing, metadata can be added or adjusted on the fly to improve searchability and organization.
7. *Frame-accurate editing*: The ability to make precise edits at the exact frame level within a video. This is crucial to ensure smooth transitions and exact timing in real-time editing scenarios.
8. *Synchronization*: The process of aligning audio, video, and other multimedia elements in real time to ensure they play seamlessly together. Synchronization is essential in live broadcasts and when adding real-time effects.
9. *Interactive elements*: Components such as polls, quizzes, or clickable links added to videos to engage viewers actively. Real-time video editing tools often include features for integrating interactive elements into live or recorded content.
10. *Streaming protocols*: Technical standards that enable the real-time transmission of video and audio over the internet. Common protocols include RTMP (Real-Time Messaging Protocol) and HLS (HTTP Live Streaming), facilitating smooth live streaming and editing.
11. *User-generated content (UGC)*: Videos and other multimedia content created by users rather than professional content creators. Real-time video editing tools empower users to enhance their UGC with professional-quality effects and features.
12. *Multi-source editing*: The capability to edit and integrate video content from multiple sources simultaneously. This is particularly useful in live broadcasts where feeds from different cameras or locations are combined in real time.
13. *Scene transitions*: Techniques used to switch between different scenes or segments in a video. Real-time video editing tools allow for the seamless application of transitions such as fades, cuts, and wipes during live recording or streaming.

14. *Aspect ratio adjustments*: Changes to the width-to-height ratio of a video. Real-time video editing software can modify aspect ratios on the fly to fit different platforms and viewing devices.
15. *Resolution scaling*: Adjusting the resolution of a video to match the capabilities of the streaming platform or viewing device. Real-time video editing tools can upscale or downscale video quality in real time to ensure optimal viewing experiences.

By understanding these terms and their definitions, users can better navigate the complexities of real-time video editing and leverage.

21.4 How to Do Real-Time Video Editing with HeritageStride Example

In a previous chapter, we decided to go with the story of HeritageStride. In Table 21.1 is an elaborated example of how to do real-time video editing using this example:

By leveraging real-time video editing tools on these platforms, HeritageStride can create engaging, professional, and interactive content that resonates with their audience, enhances brand presence, and drives customer engagement.

21.5 Takeaways

Here is a list of takeaways from this chapter:

1. *Immediate engagement*: Real-time video editing allows brands to interact with audiences instantly, capitalizing on current events and trends to create relevant content. This approach enhances engagement by providing timely and dynamic videos that resonate with viewers.
2. *Enhanced content quality*: Utilizing real-time editing tools enables the addition of professional touches such as filters, effects, and overlays, making the video content more visually appealing and compelling. This enhancement boosts the overall quality and appeal of marketing videos.
3. *Efficiency and cost-effectiveness*: Real-time video editing reduces the need for extensive post-production, saving time and costs associated with traditional video editing. This democratizes video creation, allowing even small businesses to produce high-quality content efficiently.
4. *Increased reach and visibility*: Videos edited in real-time can be quickly shared across multiple platforms, maximizing their exposure and impact. This immediacy helps in capturing the audience attention and encourages wider distribution and sharing of the content.
5. *Adaptive marketing strategies*: Real-time editing supports flexible marketing strategies by allowing brands to adjust their messages based on live feedback

Table 21.1 Real-time video with HeritageStride

Platform	Purpose	Step-by-step real-time video editing process	Example
YouTube	Product launch	1. Start a live stream showcasing the new HeritageStride shoe. 2. Use real-time editing tools to switch between different camera angles showcasing the shoe's features. 3. Add live overlays with key product information, such as material, price, and availability. 4. Integrate live Q&A by displaying questions from the audience on screen and answering them in real time. 5. Conclude with a call to action and link to the purchase page.	Host a live product launch event, demonstrating the shoe's unique features and answering live questions from potential customers.

(continued)

Table 21.1 (continued)

Platform	Purpose	Step-by-step real-time video editing process	Example
Instagram	Behind-the-scenes content	1. Use Instagram Live to stream behind-the-scenes footage from the HeritageStride design studio. 2. Apply real-time filters to enhance the visual quality of the stream. 3. Add text overlays highlighting key design elements and team member introductions. 4. Use the interactive poll feature to get instant feedback from viewers on design preferences. 5. Save the live video to IGTV for future viewing.	Stream a behind-the-scenes look at the design and manufacturing process, engaging viewers with live polls and interactive elements.
TikTok	User-generated content campaign	1. Create a branded TikTok challenge encouraging users to showcase their HeritageStride shoes in action. 2. Edit submissions in real time using TikTok's video editing tools to add branded filters and music. 3. Compile the best user-generated videos into a highlight reel. 4. Add text overlays and call-to-actions to the highlight reel. 5. Share the highlight reel on the HeritageStride TikTok profile.	Launch a #StrideChallenge where users show off their HeritageStride shoes in unique settings, editing the best clips for a branded compilation video.

(continued)

Table 21.1 (continued)

Platform	Purpose	Step-by-step real-time video editing process	Example
Facebook	Customer testimonials	1. Host a live stream featuring satisfied customers talking about their experience with HeritageStride shoes. 2. Use real-time editing to switch between customer testimonials and close-up shots of the shoes. 3. Add live captions and customer names for clarity. 4. Integrate background music to enhance the testimonials. 5. End with a call to action encouraging viewers to share their own testimonials.	Stream live customer testimonials, adding real-time captions and switching between speakers to create an engaging narrative.
LinkedIn	Industry expert interviews	1. Schedule a live interview with an industry expert discussing the benefits of HeritageStride shoes. 2. Use real-time video editing to add lower-thirds graphics introducing the expert. 3. Include slides or visual aids in the stream to support key points. 4. Engage with the audience by displaying live comments and questions on screen. 5. Conclude with professional contact information and links to further resources.	Host a live interview with a sports physiotherapist discussing the ergonomic benefits of HeritageStride shoes, using real-time overlays to highlight key insights.

(continued)

Table 21.1 (continued)

Platform	Purpose	Step-by-step real-time video editing process	Example
Snapchat	Quick tips and tutorials	1. Record short, engaging tutorials on how to style or care for HeritageStride shoes. 2. Use Snapchat's real-time editing tools to add filters, text, and music. 3. Include step-by-step overlays to guide viewers through the tutorial. 4. Post the tutorial to the HeritageStride Snapchat story. 5. Save and share the tutorial on other platforms like Instagram stories and Facebook.	Create a quick tutorial on how to clean and maintain HeritageStride shoes, using real-time editing to add helpful tips and visual instructions.

and interactions. This adaptability ensures that the content remains relevant and engaging to the target audience.

6. *Improved user experience*: For live events and broadcasts, real-time video editing enhances the viewing experience by providing a seamless and polished presentation. This professionalism builds trust and credibility with the audience, fostering a stronger connection to the brand.
7. *Interactive elements*: Real-time video editing tools enable the integration of interactive components like polls, quizzes, and clickable links. These elements engage viewers actively, making the content more interactive and memorable.
8. *Platform optimization*: Different social media platforms offer specific tools and features for real-time video editing, allowing brands to tailor their content to each platform's unique audience and format. This optimization ensures maximum engagement and effectiveness of the videos.
9. *Boosted SEO performance*: Embedding videos on websites and optimizing them for search engines can improve search engine rankings, driving more organic traffic to the site. This strategy enhances visibility and increases the likelihood of audience discovery.
10. *Versatility across platforms*: Real-time video editing can be applied across various platforms, each with its unique strengths and audience. By leveraging these tools on platforms like YouTube, Instagram, TikTok, and LinkedIn, brands can create a cohesive and comprehensive video marketing strategy that reaches diverse audiences effectively.

Real-time video is part of not only our professional lives but, first of all, our social lives, as we use our phones to record family events or entertainment we attend. More and more users are also uploading this material in real time, making it accessible to larger groups.

As we get older, we are going to be the first generation ever to have a considerable amount of video recordings documenting our lives. Two generations ago, only a handful of individuals had 8 mm cameras, and it was too expensive to use them often.

References

Kaplan, A. M., & Haenlein, M. (2010). Users of the world, unite! The challenges and opportunities of social media. *Business Horizons, 53*(1), 59–68.
Kotler, P., & Armstrong, G. (2018). *Principles of marketing* (17th ed.). Pearson.
Weinberg, T. (2009). *The new community rules: Marketing on the social web*. O'Reilly Media.
Zarrella, D. (2010). *The social media marketing book*. O'Reilly Media.

Social CRM

22

22.1 Background

Social Customer Relationship Management (Social CRM) is a modern approach to managing customer relationships that integrates social media channels and customer data. Unlike traditional CRM, which focuses primarily on sales and customer service interactions, Social CRM emphasizes building and nurturing relationships through social engagement. This approach is essential in today's digital landscape, where consumers expect more personalized and interactive experiences with brands. So, we separate between:

- *CRM (customer relationship management)*: A strategy for managing a company's interactions with current and potential customers, involving data analysis to improve business relationships.
- *Social CRM*: An extension of traditional CRM that leverages social media platforms to interact with customers, gather data, and build relationships. It focuses on creating a two-way dialogue between the brand and the customer.

Social CRM differs from traditional CRM by emphasizing quicker, more transparent interactions through social media. It allows for informal, real-time communication and leverages the power of social platforms to enhance customer engagement and brand loyalty. This approach not only fosters stronger customer relationships but also supports positive media coverage and influencer engagement.

22.2 Evolution of Social CRM

Customer relationship management has evolved significantly since the 1970s. Initially focused on automating sales and managing customer data, CRM systems have grown to incorporate comprehensive customer insights and engagement strategies. The introduction of Social CRM in the late 2000s marked a shift towards

K. Solberg Söilen, *Digital Marketing*, Springer Texts in Business and Economics, https://doi.org/10.1007/978-3-031-69518-6_22

integrating social media interactions into CRM systems, enhancing the ability to engage with customers on their preferred platforms.

22.3 The Social CRM Process

The Social CRM process involves several key steps, as illustrated below in Fig. 22.1:

1. *Data collection*: Gathering customer data from various social media platforms using listening tools
2. *Data analysis*: Processing and analyzing the collected data to derive insights about customer preferences and behavior
3. *Engagement*: Interacting with customers through targeted responses, personalized messages, and social media posts
4. *Feedback Loop*: Continuously monitoring customer interactions and feedback to refine engagement strategies and improve customer relationships

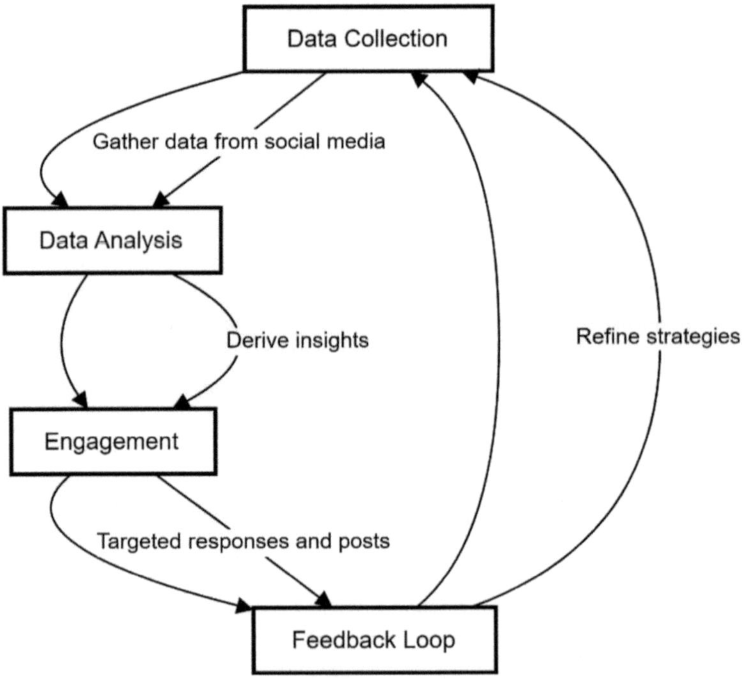

Fig. 22.1 The Social CRM process. Source: Lashgari, Maryam; Sutton-Brady, Catherine; Solberg Søilen, Klaus; Ulfvengren, Pernilla; Johnston, WesleyJ; Johnston, Wesley J (2018). Adoption Strategies of Social Media in B2B: A Multiple Case Study Approach. Journal of Business & Industrial Marketing, (), 00–00. doi:10.1108/JBIM-10-2016-0242

The diagram illustrates the cyclical process of Social CRM, starting with Data Collection from various social media platforms using listening tools, which feeds into Data Analysis to derive insights about customer preferences and behavior. These insights drive targeted Engagement through personalized responses and posts, and the Feedback Loop continuously monitors interactions to refine and improve customer relationship strategies.

22.4 The Technology Behind

Social CRM systems use sophisticated software to collect, analyze, and manage customer data from social media platforms. Popular Social CRM tools include HubSpot CRM, Salesforce CRM, and Zoho CRM, which offer features like social listening, automated responses, and data integration to provide a comprehensive view of customer interactions.

22.5 Social CRM Strategies

A successful Social CRM strategy involves collaboration between marketing, sales, and customer service departments. Key components include social listening to monitor customer conversations, social publishing to engage with customers, and the use of data analytics to personalize interactions.

Applications include:

- *Marketing:* Personalized marketing campaigns based on social media data.
- *Sales:* Identifying and nurturing leads through social engagement.
- *Customer service:* Providing timely support through social media channels.
- *Collaboration:* Enhancing internal communication and collaboration to improve customer experiences.

22.6 Social CRM Metrics

Social CRM metrics help measure the effectiveness of customer engagement strategies. Key metrics include:

- *Building awareness:* Web traffic, search volume trends, and the volume of followers
- *Increasing sales:* Customer visits, social mentions, and repeat visits
- *Assessing industry changes:* Share of voice and market visibility

22.7 Advantages and Disadvantages of Social CRM

22.7.1 Advantages

Here are some of the advantages:

Enhanced customer insights: Social CRM provides a deeper understanding of customer preferences and behavior, allowing companies to tailor their strategies more effectively.
Improved customer engagement: It facilitates real-time interactions and personalized communication, making customers feel valued and heard.
Increased brand loyalty: By fostering consistent and meaningful engagement, Social CRM helps build stronger relationships and enhances customer loyalty.
Better customer service: Social CRM enables quick and effective responses to customer inquiries and issues, improving overall customer satisfaction.

22.7.2 Disadvantages

The disadvantages:

Resource intensive: Implementing Social CRM requires a significant investment in technology and human resources, which can be a burden for some companies.
Data management challenges: Ensuring data accuracy and managing large volumes of information can be complex and demanding.
Potential for negative feedback: Public platforms can amplify negative feedback, which, if not managed properly, can harm the company's reputation.

22.8 Examples of Social CRM in Action

It is always helpful to look at some examples to see what different phenomena in digital marketing are and how they work, as seen in Table 22.1:

These examples illustrate how companies effectively use Social CRM to engage with customers, respond to feedback, and foster brand loyalty. Each company employs specific strategies to enhance customer satisfaction, from personalized interactions and community building to innovative customer-centric platforms and real-time support systems. By leveraging Social CRM tools, these companies are able to provide exceptional customer service and create engaging, relevant content for their audiences.

22.9 Key Takeaways

These are some key takeaways from this chapter:

Table 22.1 Examples of Social CRM

Example	Company	Description
1	Starbucks	Starbucks uses social media to engage with customers, respond to feedback, and promote new products. Through the "My Starbucks Idea" platform, they gather customer suggestions and implement popular ideas, showcasing customer-centric innovation.
2	Dell	Dell employs Social CRM to monitor and respond to customer inquiries and complaints on social media. Their Social Media Listening Command Center tracks conversations across multiple platforms, allowing for timely and effective customer support.
3	Nike	Nike leverages social media to create a community around its brand. Through personalized interactions and engaging content, they foster a loyal customer base that actively participates in brand campaigns and events.
4	Zappos	Zappos is known for its exceptional customer service, which extends to its social media interactions. They use Social CRM to quickly address customer concerns and provide personalized shopping experiences, enhancing customer satisfaction and loyalty.
5	Coca-Cola	Coca-Cola uses Social CRM to create engaging social media campaigns that resonate with their global audience. By leveraging customer data, they tailor their messaging to different demographics, driving higher engagement and brand loyalty.

1. *Immediate engagement:* Social CRM allows for real-time interaction with customers, fostering immediate and meaningful connections that enhance customer satisfaction and loyalty.
2. *Enhanced customer insights:* Leveraging social media data provides deeper insights into customer preferences and behaviors, enabling more personalized and effective marketing strategies.
3. *Improved brand loyalty:* Consistent and meaningful engagement through Social CRM helps build stronger, long-term relationships with customers, increasing brand loyalty.
4. *Cost-effective marketing:* Social CRM can reduce marketing costs by targeting customers more accurately and engaging them through cost-effective social media platforms.
5. *Real-time feedback:* Social CRM enables brands to receive and respond to customer feedback in real time, improving customer service and satisfaction.
6. *Increased sales:* By nurturing leads and engaging with customers on social media, Social CRM can drive higher conversion rates and increase sales.
7. *Enhanced brand reputation:* Proactive and positive engagement on social media helps improve a brand's reputation and can lead to positive word-of-mouth marketing.
8. *Better customer service:* Social CRM tools allow for quick and effective resolution of customer issues, enhancing overall customer experience.
9. *Scalability:* Social CRM systems can scale with a business, supporting the management of growing customer bases and increasing interaction volumes.

10. *Data-driven decisions:* The insights gained from Social CRM data help businesses make informed decisions, improving marketing strategies and business outcomes.

Social CRM and similar software played a crucial role in establishing Oracle as a leader in enterprise solutions. By integrating social media insights with customer relationship management, Oracle provided businesses with powerful tools to enhance customer engagement and streamline communication. This capability allowed companies to personalize their marketing efforts and improve customer satisfaction, leading to increased loyalty and sales. The success and widespread adoption of these solutions significantly contributed to Oracle's growth and reputation in the technology industry.

Further Reading

Evans, D. (2008). *Social media marketing: An hour a day*. Wiley.

Scott, D. M. (2011). *The new rules of marketing & PR: How to use social media, blogs, news releases, online video, and viral marketing to reach buyers directly* (3rd ed.). Wiley.

Stelzner, M. A. (2011). *Launch: How to quickly propel your business beyond the competition*. Wiley.

Tuten, T. L., & Solomon, M. R. (2017). *Social media marketing*. Sage.

Personal Branding 23

23.1 Background

A personal brand is a statement of who someone is and what they stand for. Personal branding is a planned process involving three phases. The first phase is establishing a brand identity; it is essential to stand out in a crowded market while meeting the expectations of a specific target audience. The second phase is developing the positioning of the brand through active communication of the brand identity by managing symbolism, behavior, and communication. The final phase is evaluating the brand image to improve and achieve personal and professional goals. People who use personal marketing expand their human capital by investing in continuous learning and enhance social capital through exposure. This, in turn, leads to economic profitability and financial success. Personal branding requires regular attention, constant intention, and steadfast commitment, but ultimately, it is about being yourself, the best you can always be.

This chapter focuses on personal branding and its use in digital marketing. Since its introduction in 1997 by Tom Peters in the article "The Brand Called You," the term personal branding has gained widespread usage and become a buzzword with both positive and negative connotations. Personal branding is about taking control over how you are perceived by others and strategically managing those perceptions to achieve your goals. Without a specific approach, all you have is a personal image.

Looking at international companies like Coca-Cola or Volvo, they have created a strong association and expectations for themselves and their products over a long period. This creates a strong belief in what customers will receive when they buy the company's product. By communicating effectively and at the right time to their audience, these companies can foster long-lasting relationships with their customers, ensuring they continue to choose their products. Personal branding works similarly, communicating in a way that creates a response with personality, values, and what the person stands for. This response is then used to build even more connections, creating a personal brand that the audience associates with certain attributes. For example, when you watched Michael Jordan play basketball, you knew he

K. Solberg Söilen, *Digital Marketing*, Springer Texts in Business and Economics, https://doi.org/10.1007/978-3-031-69518-6_23

would dominate. Jordan had a powerful attribute that connected him to the brand in people's minds as "the greatest basketball player of all time," which gave him leverage, even though some would argue that other better players have come since.

Furthermore, most cultural icons often hire marketing agencies, publicists, and personal advisors to manage their brands with expertise. Even without prior resources, anyone can create a personal brand.

23.2 Social Media and Other Platforms

23.2.1 Social Media

To grow a personal identity today, social media is the best and easiest way. Practically everyone is online; it is the first place people look when they want to learn about a person and their activities. Therefore, social media is the perfect place for a personal brand to create a reputation and become visible in a specific niche or industry. Generally, branding requires some form of budget for promotion to build awareness, eventually leading to brand loyalty. However, social media has opened new paths for people to promote themselves as brands effectively and cost-efficiently. Today, we live with almost unlimited information, and platforms such as X (formerly Twitter), Facebook, LinkedIn, and Instagram allow us to communicate, publish, and produce content on an entirely new level. In this current environment, social media marketing is a crucial part of the promotional mix in modern brand communication. Social media communication strongly influences brand image, while traditional media substantially impacts brand awareness. For marketers to develop and maintain a close brand-customer relationship and for customers in their decision-making process, social media represents a vital resource. Companies can influence consumers' attitudes, perceptions, and preferences related to their brand through social media efforts by creating a brand image that connects with targeted customers and developing brand awareness. These platforms have created new possibilities for brands to connect with stakeholders and customers, forcing brands to adapt if they want to gain visibility among all customer groups. This has led companies to turn to social media influencers to market their brand and products, a common strategy in industries such as fashion and beauty.

23.2.2 Snapchat

Snapchat is a multimedia app with photo sharing that was launched in 2011 by Reggie Brown, Evan Spiegel, and Bobby Murphy while they were studying at Stanford University. The application allows users to take pictures or record video clips and then add filters, stickers, text, or drawings. These photos or videos can be sent to friends or posted to the user's "story" and are called snaps. Snapchat has approximately 397 million monthly active users and 293 million daily active users, with 4 billion snaps created every day, and on average, people spend 30 min per day on Snapchat. This application is perfect for a personal brand targeting a younger audience, as 78% of internet users aged 18–24 use Snapchat and 90% of Snapchat users are between 13 and 24 years old.

Even though Snapchat's popularity among brands is increasing, there is still less competition on this platform compared to others like Facebook or Instagram, where most brands have profiles, making it harder to connect with users and stand out. Snapchat is different from other social media platforms as it does not have a "like button" and does not allow users to comment or share others' posts. The purpose is to interact with the people you send videos and images to, providing a unique way for personal branding to reach out to their audience. An example of this is CNN, which initially had trouble connecting with millennials but successfully engaged more millennials through Snapchat than through their site. However, Snapchat should not be the main marketing platform for a personal brand; rather, it should be an added source of marketing. Platforms like Facebook or Instagram should be used as the main marketing channels, where customers can share images, leave reviews, and create user-generated content. These platforms offer more features that help brands connect in meaningful ways with their target audience and have more diverse and larger user bases.

A strategy is required for Snapchat marketing, which may differ from strategies used on other platforms. For instance, the frozen yogurt restaurant Sixteen Handles offered a coupon code redeemable in-store in exchange for users sending them snaps of themselves with their frozen yogurt. Similarly, Audi wanted to connect with young, female, millennial-aged, first-time car buyers. They teamed up with ABC's show "Pretty Little Liars," posting exclusive content about the show on Snapchat, giving Audi access to its followers and the show an additional platform. This campaign helped Audi gain over 115,000 followers on Snapchat.

23.2.3 LinkedIn

LinkedIn is a platform that aims to give professionals worldwide the opportunity to connect, be more productive, and successful. Launched on May 5th, 2003, LinkedIn is now the world's largest professional network, with over 930 million users in more than 200 territories and countries. LinkedIn is ideal for establishing a personal brand if users put effort into regularly posting content and updating their profiles. The platform has 310 million active users per month, with 40% signing in every day. However, only three million of these users share content weekly, providing a spotlight for those who want to create their brand. Another advantage of LinkedIn is that 4 out of 5 users drive business decisions globally. LinkedIn offers great opportunities to connect with people outside of one's usual network, helping the brand grow.

23.2.4 Instagram

Instagram is a social media platform that works best as an app on your mobile device, allowing users to share pictures and videos with the public and, in this case, their followers. This platform has become one of the best mobile applications and has found its way into both the young and old people's online lives, especially the young. It was founded in 2010 by Kevin Systrom and Mike Krieger and is now owned by Facebook. Instagram has over one billion active users every month, 90% of all users follow a company, and more than 500 million people use Instagram Stories every day. Instagram Stories is a function that creates the opportunity for users to post photos and videos to a sequential feed, where every post is accessible to others for 24 h each.

With Instagram, the idea and ideals of interaction between brands and consumers have been reconstructed in the twenty-first century. Consumers now expect brands to communicate using visuals, which challenges organizations to become more innovative in their marketing. This platform also gives brands a way to show a unique point of view of themselves to their customers. People use it for many different reasons, such as a source of inspiration, finding great pictures or as a creative outlet. Out of all those people, the individuals that are open to new perspectives, brands, and, in this case, personal brands will not have a problem reaching them.

The profiles that have the most followers on Instagram are celebrities, and in social media marketing, celebrity endorsement is a commonly used strategy. Each celebrity attracts a certain group of people and becomes a sort of reference to many people, forming their values and attitudes. This has made brands, especially those in the fashion sector, partner up with different types of celebrities, including athletes, singers, and models, to gain access to new markets. This leads to the two parties signing a contract, and the celebrity uses their brand to post about the company's brand in exchange for some sort of payment. A study showed that customers who bought a product or service they had seen recommended by a celebrity got higher self-esteem.

Another group of people who uses their brand in the same way as celebrities are influencers. These ultra-connected individuals are the first ones to try out new trends and have the power to introduce other brands to an audience of consumers. Influencers are very sought-after brand ambassadors because they integrate different brands into their lives and show them on Instagram. These personal branders have an important role in the fashion industry, for example. Instagram is the most used platform by influencers because of, among other things, the application's creation of communities. This trend seems to continue in the near future. This explains why about 86% of companies use influencer marketing. Even if the terms between an influencer and a brand often work similarly to those between a celebrity and a brand, influencers seem more personable, credible and easy to relate to because of their shared experiences and showing parts of their life on social media.

23.3 Building a Personal Brand: The Example of Instagram

Building a strong personal brand on Instagram involves several key steps, especially if you are not already a celebrity or an influencer.

First, you need to design the foundation of your brand. Start by defining your target audience, which is the group of people you want to attract and satisfy with your Instagram page. This helps you select a specific topic for your content and makes future marketing easier. Determine your brand's purpose and the story behind it, which will help you define your values and unique voice. Ensure that your brand elicits positive feelings such as excitement and social approval while minimizing negative emotions and never offending anyone. Strive for brand resonance by building a loyal relationship with your audience and analyzing your account activity to gauge emotional connections.

Next, focus on your brand's positioning. You need to position your brand clearly and interestingly in the minds of your consumers to stand out in the competitive market.

Designing a content plan is also crucial. Your content should reflect both your knowledge and personality, demonstrating that you rely on expertise and personal flair.

Building a community around your brand involves actively listening to your audience, meeting their needs, or fulfilling their curiosity. Use Instagram stories and other interactive functions to engage with your followers.

The next step is designing your brand elements. Your brand name should be unique, catchy, short, and easy to read. Provide a short description of your brand, including information about yourself and your goals. Establish a way of communication that builds brand awareness and fosters strong, positive, and unique associations and feelings.

Visual elements are also vital. Your main profile picture should be a clear photo of yourself. Ensure that the colors in your feed are consistent, as this affects the overall aesthetic of your profile. Use highlight covers for your stories to enhance your profile image and maintain a specific style that correlates well with your feed.

Promoting your blog requires more than just creating an Instagram page and waiting for followers. Use both free and commercial advertising to promote your brand effectively.

Finally, consider monetizing your Instagram presence, as exemplified in Fig. 23.1. Once you reach a significant number of followers—often above 10,000 subscribers to be a micro-influencer and 100,000 to be a macro-influencer—advertising companies may approach you for partnerships, turning your online presence into a source of income.

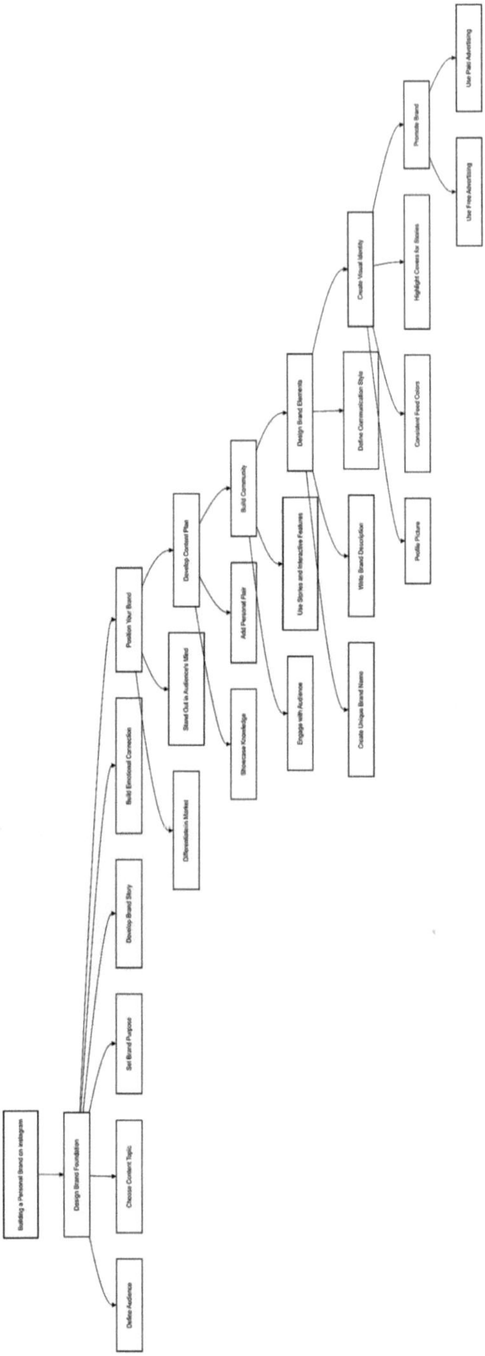

Fig. 23.1 Building a personal brand: the example of Instagram

23.4 Podcasts

A podcast is a series of audio episodes that users can download to personal devices for listening. Podcasts can be found on platforms like iTunes and Spotify. In 2023, businesses spent over $1 billion on podcast advertising, and over 50% of people in the United States have listened to podcasts, which equates to roughly 165 million people. This platform is excellent for connecting with an audience on a deeper level than through text alone, as podcasts often provide a window into who a person really is.

Below in Table 23.1 is a list of the top 15 podcasters worldwide, including the name of the host, number of viewers, nationality, and profile:

Not all content here is of high quality; it is just popular. Much is psychology hodge podge and self-help, but it reflects what people search for and want. Others may react to why there are no Chinese or Indian podcasts at the top. The lists reflect the sources and popularity metrics commonly available in Western media. However, there are popular podcasts in China and India, and they have significant audiences

Table 23.1 Most popular podcasters[a]

Podcast name	Host	Number of viewers	Nationality	Profile
The Joe Rogan Experience	Joe Rogan	11.0 million	American	Comedian, MMA Commentator
Crime Junkie	Ashley Flowers & Brit Prawat	9.0 million	American	True Crime Enthusiasts
The Daily	NYT, Michael Barbaro	8.0 million	American	Journalist
Stuff You Should Know	Josh Clark & Charles W. Bryant	6.0 million	American	Educators
Pod Save America	Jon Favreau, Jon Lovett, Dan Pfeiffer & Tommy Vietor	5.0 million	American	Political Commentators
Call Her Daddy	Alex Cooper	4.0 million	American	Media Personality
My Favorite Murder	Karen Kilgariff & Georgia Hardstark	4.0 million	American	Comedians
Armchair Expert	Dax Shepard	3.0 million	American	Actor, Comedian
The Ben Shapiro Show	Ben Shapiro	3.0 million	American	Political Commentator
The Dave Ramsey Show	Dave Ramsey	2.5 million	American	Financial Advisor
TED Talks Daily	Various	2.0 million	Various	Various
Freakonomics Radio	Stephen J. Dubner	2.0 million	American	Journalist, Author
The Michelle Obama Podcast	Michelle Obama	2.0 million	American	Former First lady, Author
How I Built This	Guy Raz	1.5 million	Amerfigican	Journalist
The Tim Ferriss Show	Tim Ferriss	1.5 million	American	Entrepreneur, Author

[a]Verified using ChatGPT 4 (June 2024)

Table 23.2 Popular political and news pods[a]

Podcast name	Host	Number of viewers	Nationality	Profile
The Joe Rogan Experience	Joe Rogan	11.0 million	American	Comedian, MMA Commentator
The Daily	NYT/Michael Barbaro	8.0 million	American	Journalist
Pod Save America	Jon Favreau, Jon Lovett, Dan Pfeiffer & Tommy Vietor	5.0 million	American	Political Commentators
The Dan Bongino Show	Dan Bongino	4.0 million	American	Political Commentator
Tucker Carlson Today	Tucker Carlson	4.0 million	American	Political Commentator
The NPR Politics Podcast	Various	3.5 million	American	Journalists
The Ben Shapiro Show	Ben Shapiro	3.0 million	American	Political Commentator
The Rachel Maddow Show	Rachel Maddow	3.0 million	American	Journalist
The Daily Zeitgeist	Jack O'Brien & Miles Gray	2.5 million	American	Comedians
The David Pakman Show	David Pakman	2.0 million	American	Political Commentator
The Young Turks	Cenk Uygur & Ana Kasparian	2.0 million	American	Political Commentators
The Rubin Report	Dave Rubin	1.8 million	American	Political Commentator
Left, Right & Center	Josh Barro, Rich Lowry, & Others	1.7 million	American	Journalists
The Breakdown with Shaun King	Shaun King	1.5 million	American	Activist
The Political Gabfest	Emily Bazelon, John Dickerson & David Plotz	1.5 million	American	Journalists
The New Yorker: Politics and More	Various	1.4 million	American	Journalists

[a]Verified using ChatGPT 4 (June 2024)

as well, but finding an accurate viewer number of them is more difficult. The challenge is often that data for non-Western podcasts might not be as readily available or easily comparable due to differences in how viewership is measured and reported.

Below in Table 23.2 is a list of popular political pods:

We can compare this to regular news channels on what we call old media or linear TV, as shown in Table 23.3. The Figures are what the networks say they have themselves and cannot be fully trusted. They are ballpark Figures.

We see that pods are quickly catching up with old-fashioned TV news programs. The phenomenon is also highly country-dependent, where some countries, like the

Table 23.3 Popularity of news programs on linear TV

Rank	TV news program	Network	Country	Number of viewers (worldwide)
1	CCTV Evening News	CCTV	China	135 million
2	NHK News 7	NHK	Japan	10 million
2	Tagesschau	ARD	Germany	10 million
4	BBC News at Ten	BBC	United Kingdom	8 million
5	ABC World News Tonight	ABC	United States	9 million
6	France 2 Le Journal 20H	France 2	France	6 million
7	Vremya	Channel One Russia	Russia	5 million
8	The News with Shepard Smith	CNBC	United States	4 million
9	Newsnight	BBC	United Kingdom	2 million
9	El Noticiero Univision	Univision	United States	2 million

US, have more popular pods, and the population has been exposed to these channels for a longer period of time.

The most interesting phenomenon with podcasters is not that they often attract more viewers than networks but why they do so. They are more popular because they create better content. Viewers are ultimately not interested in big, expensive studios with hundreds of employees working in a large building; they care about what the podcasters have to say. Another phenomenon that should interest everyone is that viewers can sit and listen to a political program for 2–3 h. It was "common knowledge" in the TV business that you had to deliver short and fast snippets of information in just minutes, sometimes seconds, which often turned out to be false. All of this is a victory for content over form and gives reasons for optimism about the internet as a source of news.

On the other side, there is, of course, the problem of biases and objectivity. Established media argue that they are more objective and bound to facts, whereas information on the internet can be dangerous. This is also correct, for the most part. The point is that the good news that can be found on the internet is quite often better than the good news on the old established channels. There is so much erroneous news on the internet primarily because there is so much more news available, and anyone can start a new channel—and too many do. This is truly the democratization of news.

In our living rooms, it suddenly includes everyone's opinion, which can be overwhelming at times. However, you also get really smart people into your living room, such as top university professors who are rarely invited by the big networks or would not accept an invitation. Thus, you have both the best and the worst of worlds at the same time. You also see this same phenomenon on single platforms like X. Most information on X can be very hateful and unpleasant if you don't know who to follow. However, if you have a group of good sources, what they will bring you is typically more valuable information than what you will find anywhere else, and you get it as it happens in real time.

23.5 Strategies and Methods

Expanding a personal brand involves adopting effective models and strategies that highlight your uniqueness and professional strengths. Among the most notable approaches is the framework developed by personal branding pioneer William Arruda, which outlines steps to advance your career through branding basics. These steps include:

1. *Knowing Yourself*
   - Focus on something that drives you with passion and authenticity. This involves deep self-reflection to understand your core values, strengths, and what genuinely makes you unique. It's crucial to gather feedback from others to understand their perception of you, which helps in shaping a positive personal brand.
   - Example: Conduct a personal SWOT analysis (Strengths, Weaknesses, Opportunities, Threats) to gain a comprehensive understanding of your brand identity.
2. *Showing Yourself*
   - Define your personal brand and create a personal brand statement that clearly communicates who you are and what you stand for. Develop career marketing tools such as a professional resume, portfolio, and an engaging social media presence. Create a 3D brand bio that offers a complete and dynamic picture of yourself, highlighting your experiences, skills, and personal values.
   - Example: Design a professional website or blog where you can showcase your work, share insights, and interact with your audience.
3. *Letting Yourself Grow*
   - Build and execute a personal media plan to expand your brand's reach and reinforce your message consistently. This involves integrating your personal brand into your daily activities, networking, and nurturing relationships within your brand community. Continuously seek opportunities for growth and learning to keep your brand relevant and authentic.
   - Example: Regularly publish articles, attend industry conferences, and participate in webinars to stay updated and visible in your field.

Another effective strategy is proactive personal branding, which includes:

- *Checking Your Online Footprint*: Regularly search for your name online to see what information is available about you. This helps in managing your digital presence effectively.
- *Removing Threats*: Identify and remove any negative or outdated information that could harm your personal brand. This might involve contacting websites to remove old content or updating your profiles.

- *Posting Positive Assets*: Continuously create and share positive, high-quality content that aligns with your personal brand. This could include blog posts, social media updates, and professional achievements.
- *Maintaining Credibility*: Ensure that all information you share is accurate and truthful. Building trust with your audience is crucial for a strong personal brand.
- *Adjusting Strategy Based on Results*: Regularly review your branding efforts and their impact. Use analytics and feedback to refine your strategy and ensure it remains effective and aligned with your goals.

23.6 Criticism

Despite the advantages, personal branding has faced criticism, particularly regarding the authenticity and impact of online personas. Critics argue that the nature of online platforms can lead to personal brands that appear insincere or fabricated, driven primarily by personal gain rather than genuine representation. This can result in a disconnect between the brand and reality, where individuals portray an idealized version of themselves that does not reflect their true selves.

Another significant criticism is the influence of social media influencers on their followers. Influencers often showcase a glorified version of their lives, focusing on their successes, luxury lifestyles, and idealized appearances. This can create unrealistic expectations among their followers, who may feel pressured to achieve similar levels of social status and beauty standards. The constant exposure to these idealized images can lead to lower self-esteem and an increased tendency to edit photos to conceal perceived flaws, contributing to a culture of inauthenticity and superficiality.

Moreover, the emphasis on personal branding can sometimes overshadow professional competence, where individuals might prioritize their online image over actual skills and performance. This shift can undermine the importance of genuine expertise and hard work, leading to a superficial approach to career advancement.

In summary, while personal branding offers numerous benefits in terms of career growth and visibility, it is essential to approach it with authenticity and integrity. Balancing self-promotion with genuine representation and focusing on building real value can help mitigate the negative aspects and create a sustainable, trustworthy personal brand.

23.7 Key Takeaways

Here are some of the lessons from the chapter on Personal Branding:

- Establishing Brand Identity: Building a strong personal brand involves clearly defining who you are and what you stand for, ensuring you stand out in a crowded market while meeting the expectations of your target audience.

- Active Brand Positioning: Successful personal branding requires actively communicating your brand identity through consistent symbolism, behavior, and communication strategies to create a memorable impression.
- Continuous Evaluation: Regularly evaluating and refining your brand image is essential to achieving your personal and professional goals, adapting to feedback and market changes.
- Leveraging Social Media: Social media platforms like Instagram, LinkedIn, and Snapchat are crucial for growing a personal brand, offering cost-effective ways to promote yourself and connect with a broad audience.
- Engaging Content Creation: Creating and sharing engaging content that reflects your knowledge and personality is vital for building a loyal community around your brand.
- Authenticity and Consistency: Maintaining authenticity and consistency in your messaging and interactions helps build trust and credibility with your audience.
- Strategic Networking: Actively engaging with your audience and building relationships through social media interactions and community involvement strengthens your brand.
- Proactive Online Presence: Regularly checking and managing your online footprint, posting positive content, and addressing any negative information is critical for maintaining a strong personal brand.
- Balancing Promotion and Substance: While promoting your brand is important, focusing on genuine representation and professional competence ensures long-term success and credibility.
- Addressing Criticism: Be aware of the potential downsides of personal branding, such as the risk of appearing insincere or creating unrealistic expectations, and strive to balance self-promotion with authenticity.

I guess it's fair to say that most human beings work on their brand identity, especially at work, as we are always trying to present ourselves in the best light possible and are constantly occupied with our reputation. Thus, it is very easy for marketers to relate to the concept of personal branding and understand its importance.

Further Reading

Barker, S., & Gensch, D. H. (1978). Does Big Five work? *The Psychological Record, 28*(4), 555–568.

Cavanaugh, J. K., & Frederick, H. H. (1999). Impact of personal branding in higher education. *Journal of Education for Business, 74*(4), 293–298.

Goffman, E. (1959). *The presentation of self in everyday life*. Anchor Books.

Peters, T. (1997). The brand called you. *Fast Company, 10*, 83–90.

Rampersad, H. K. (2008). A new blueprint for powerful and authentic personal branding. *Performance Improvement, 47*(6), 34–37.

Schawbel, D. (2010). *Me 2.0: 4 steps to building your future*. Kaplan Publishing.

Building Brands Online and Brand Identity

24

24.1 Background

Building Brands Online and Brand Identity involves creating a distinctive and memorable digital presence that resonates with target audiences, ensuring consistent messaging and visual elements across all platforms. This process is essential for fostering customer recognition, loyalty, and engagement in a competitive digital marketplace. An extra chapter on this topic is valuable because it delves into the specific strategies and tools necessary to establish a robust online brand, addressing the unique challenges and opportunities presented by the digital environment.

The chapter explores the significance of building an online brand and the key elements contributing to a strong brand identity. A memorable brand name and symbol are crucial as they enhance customer retention by sticking in the customer's mind. Creating a recognizable name and symbol increases the likelihood of returning customers. A brand logo significantly impacts consumer awareness, recognition, and buying behavior. The logo represents the brand's origin, values, and promises, aiming to build trust through positive consumer experiences and satisfaction.

Location is also a vital element for a brand's identity. The location affects the brand's identity and overall consumer experience, influencing behavior and expressions shaped by culture and religion. A strong online brand identity can reduce the need for external advertisements, as exemplified by brands like Zalando, where customers automatically think of them for certain products. The digital world enables brands to reach broader and previously inaccessible audiences, raising awareness and engagement.

The digital proficiency of users, ranging from young to old, enhances the value of online brands. Consumers often define themselves by their products, extending their personality and perception to others. Brands leverage this to capture the importance of their audience and drive engagement. Consumer satisfaction is a key predictor of behavior and repeat purchases, with customers engaging through various platforms like brand websites and social media channels.

K. Solberg Söilen, *Digital Marketing*, Springer Texts in Business and Economics, https://doi.org/10.1007/978-3-031-69518-6_24

Engaging consumers through building communities and fostering e-WOM (electronic word-of-mouth) is crucial. This influences other consumers' brand choices through shared experiences and interactions on platforms like blogs and social media. Utilizing search engines is also essential for brand recognition and engagement.

24.2 Building Brand Identity

Building an online brand and developing a strong brand identity are crucial for capturing consumer attention and fostering loyalty in the digital marketplace. A memorable brand name and symbol enhance customer retention and recognition, making it easier for customers to remember and return to a brand. In the digital age, a strong online brand identity can also reduce the need for external advertisements, as successful brands like the Zalando show.

David Aaker's model identifies four main categories essential for building a brand identity: awareness, loyalty, positioning, and associations. Aaker emphasizes creating a visual and experiential brand identity that resonates with consumers.

Components of Brand Identity
- *Product*: What the brand offers.
- *Organization*: The brand's organizational values.
- *Person*: The brand's personality and customer connection.
- *Symbol*: The brand's visual elements for recognition and memory.

Core identity: It involves the essential associations consumers have with the brand, while *extended identity* includes additional elements like textures and visual forms to complement the core identity.

Naming the brand: A unique and memorable brand name is crucial. It should be easy to pronounce, captivating, and not too similar to existing words or brands to avoid confusion. An effective brand name enhances recognition, recall, and positive consumer attitudes.

Brand logotype: The logo is a visual marker that influences first impressions, recognition, and long-term relationships. A well-designed logo, considering size, color, and shape, enhances memorability and positive associations. The color of the logo is particularly important as it creates distinctions and associations.

Brand location: Brand location affects consumer behavior and perceptions. Effective location-based marketing, using digital devices and platforms, enhances brand visibility and engagement. For example, Starbucks uses location-based data to offer precise and relevant promotions.

Competitor analysis: Understanding competitors' strategies and consumer reactions helps brands differentiate themselves and inform effective brand positioning. Analyzing direct and indirect competitors provides insights into customer preferences and market trends.

Pricing as a distinguishing tool: Pricing influences consumer decisions and brand personality. Effective pricing strategies attract customers and justify higher prices for unique items. Dynamic pricing, as used by Amazon, allows brands to adjust prices based on demand and product availability, optimizing sales and profits.

Psychology of building a brand online: Understanding customer psychology and behavior is crucial for building a trustworthy brand identity online. Consistent and positive experiences across digital touchpoints create powerful market positions in consumers' minds.

Reaching the target audience: Brands interact with consumers through digital devices, platforms, media, data, and technology. Effective online branding requires understanding these interactions to create meaningful connections with the audience.

Choosing the relevant digital environment: Online branding involves selecting the right digital environment to create positive customer experiences and satisfaction. Brands must deliver value and genuine engagement through their online channels.

24.3 Building a Brand Online

Effective online branding strategies encompass various digital channels, including websites, search engine marketing, mobile content, rich media, e-commerce, and email marketing. Utilizing these channels allows brands to engage consumers, fostering loyalty and creating positive brand associations.

Email marketing is an essential component of online branding, involving both outbound and inbound strategies. These strategies include retention, conversion, brand promotion, acquisition, and reactivation. Email marketing is known for its high return on investment (ROI) and cost-effectiveness, making it an excellent method for reaching a wide audience.

SMS marketing offers direct communication with consumers, which is particularly useful for timely promotions and updates. However, it tends to be less favored compared to email marketing due to its intrusive nature.

Content marketing shifts the focus from direct selling to providing valuable information. By creating informative and engaging content, brands can build trust and establish authority. This approach not only enhances search engine rankings but also drives organic traffic to the brand's website.

Native marketing is about creating content that blends seamlessly with the platform on which it appears. This method effectively reaches new audiences by integrating promotional and regular user-generated content, increasing engagement and authenticity.

Affiliate marketing extends a brand's reach through performance-based partnerships. Affiliates promote the brand on their platforms and earn commissions for driving traffic or sales, expanding the brand's audience and market presence.

Remarketing focuses on targeting users who have previously visited a brand's website but did not make a purchase. By serving ads to these potential customers on various platforms, brands can increase the likelihood of conversion and keep the brand top-of-mind.

24.4 Building Brand Loyalty

Building brand loyalty involves consistently delivering high-quality products and services, engaging with customers through personalized communication, and creating a sense of community. Loyal customers are more likely to make repeat purchases, advocate for the brand, and provide valuable feedback.

Brand loyalty can be broken as quickly as it is created, or even faster. Gucci is a good example from the past, and Abercrombie & Fitch is a more recent example. However, the latter company seems to have been able to recover after learning some hard-earned lessons.

24.5 Customer Experience

The customer experience is central to building a successful online brand. Brands must ensure that every touchpoint—from the website and social media to customer service and product delivery—provides a positive and seamless experience. This includes:

- *User-friendly website*: A well-designed, easy-to-navigate website enhances the overall customer experience.
- *Personalization*: Tailoring content and offers to individual customer preferences and behaviors.
- *Responsive customer service*: Providing timely and helpful responses to customer inquiries and issues.
- *Consistent branding*: Ensuring that the brand message and visual identity are consistent across all channels.

24.6 Measuring Success

To gauge the effectiveness of online branding efforts, brands must regularly measure and analyze key performance indicators (KPIs). These can include:

- *Brand awareness*: Metrics such as website traffic, social media followers, and search engine rankings.
- *Customer engagement*: Interaction rates on social media, email open rates, and content shares.
- *Conversion rates*: The percentage of website visitors who make a purchase or complete a desired action.
- *Customer retention*: The rate at which customers return to make repeat purchases.

- *Customer satisfaction*: Feedback collected through surveys, reviews, and customer service interactions.

Brand awareness can be measured through metrics such as website traffic, social media followers, and search engine rankings. Customer engagement is gauged by interaction rates on social media, email open rates, and content shares. Conversion rates refer to the percentage of website visitors who make a purchase or complete a desired action. Customer retention measures the rate at which customers return to make repeat purchases. Customer satisfaction is assessed through feedback collected from surveys, reviews, and customer service interactions.

24.7 Adapting to Trends

Staying ahead in the digital marketplace requires brands to adapt to emerging trends and technologies. This includes:

- *Mobile optimization*: Ensuring that all digital content is accessible and user-friendly on mobile devices.
- *Social commerce*: Leveraging social media platforms to facilitate direct purchases.
- *Video content*: Using video to engage and inform customers, as video consumption continues to rise.
- *Influencer partnerships*: Collaborating with influencers to reach new audiences and build credibility.
- *Data analytics*: Utilizing data to gain insights into customer behavior and preferences, enabling more effective marketing strategies.

Mobile optimization involves making sure that all digital content is accessible and user-friendly on mobile devices. Social commerce leverages social media platforms to facilitate direct purchases, making it easier for customers to buy products. Video content is increasingly important for engaging and informing customers, given the rising consumption of video media. Collaborating with influencers helps brands reach new audiences and build credibility. Utilizing data analytics provides insights into customer behavior and preferences, allowing for more effective marketing strategies.

24.8 Key Takeaways

Here are some Key takeaways from this chapter:

1. *Importance of brand identity*: Establishing a strong brand identity is crucial for recognition and customer loyalty. This involves creating a memorable logo, a distinctive brand name, and consistent visual elements.

2. *Role of digital media*: Leveraging digital media, including social media, email marketing, and search engine marketing, is essential for building and maintaining a strong online brand presence.
3. *Customer-centric approach*: Building a brand online requires a focus on the customer experience. This includes providing personalized interactions, responsive customer service, and a user-friendly website.
4. *Content marketing*: Providing valuable and informative content helps build trust and authority. High-quality content improves search engine rankings and drives organic traffic.
5. *Native and affiliate marketing*: Native marketing blends promotional content with user-generated content for authenticity, while affiliate marketing expands reach through performance-based partnerships.
6. *Remarketing*: Targeting users who have previously interacted with your brand increases the likelihood of conversion and keeps your brand top-of-mind.
7. *Building brand loyalty*: Consistently delivering high-quality products and services and engaging with customers through personalized communication helps build loyalty and advocacy.
8. *Measuring success*: Regularly measuring KPIs such as brand awareness, customer engagement, conversion rates, and customer satisfaction helps gauge the effectiveness of branding efforts.
9. *Adapting to trends*: Staying ahead of emerging trends and technologies, such as mobile optimization and social commerce, ensures continued relevance and competitive edge in the digital marketplace.
10. *Long-term strategy*: Building and maintaining a strong online brand identity requires a comprehensive, adaptable approach that integrates various digital marketing strategies and focuses on creating lasting customer relationships.

Creating a brand is as much an art as it is a science. Many organizations think they must constantly change the brand or its colors to be up to date. In my experience, it's much more important to care for it and use it consistently. If what the company does is good, customers will come to associate the brand with quality, almost no matter how it looks.

Further Reading

Aaker, D. A. (1996). *Building strong brands*. Free Press.

Kapferer, J. N. (2008). *The new strategic brand management: Creating and sustaining brand equity long term*. Kogan Page Publishers.

Keller, K. L. (1993). Conceptualizing, measuring, and managing customer-based brand equity. *Journal of Marketing, 57*(1), 1–22.

Kotler, P., & Keller, K. L. (2012). *Marketing management* (14th ed.). Pearson Education.

Park, C. W., Jaworski, B. J., & MacInnis, D. J. (1986). Strategic brand concept-image management. *Journal of Marketing, 50*(4), 135–145.

Online Partnerships 25

25.1 Background

A partnership is an arrangement where different parties collaborate for mutual benefit. In the context of online partnerships, companies work together through various online channels to promote their services and products, thereby creating a buzz around their brand. Main forms of online partnerships include link-building (SEO), affiliate marketing, online sponsorship, aggregators such as price comparison sites, co-branding, co-marketing, and influencer outreach. These partnerships are integral to structured and well-planned online marketing strategies, particularly in e-commerce.

This chapter focuses on online partnerships, exploring various strategies and methods used in this domain. Recognizing the importance of relationships in digital marketing, partnerships have become a critical element in expanding the reach of digital marketers and building relationships between different parties. These partnerships are essential in both online and offline marketing, varying in approach based on the size of the company. Large companies often have dedicated staff and resources for managing online partnerships, whereas smaller companies may face challenges in fully leveraging these opportunities.

25.2 Importance of Online Partnerships

Online partnerships are essential because they help brands increase visibility, build credibility, and reach broader audiences. Through strategic alliances, businesses can leverage each other's strengths and resources to achieve common goals. Online partnerships also facilitate cost-effective marketing, enhance SEO efforts, and drive higher engagement and conversion rates.

K. Solberg Söilen, *Digital Marketing*, Springer Texts in Business and Economics, https://doi.org/10.1007/978-3-031-69518-6_25

25.3 Types of Online Partnerships

25.3.1 Affiliate Marketing

Enables companies (affiliates) to earn money by directing customers to e-commerce sites (advertisers). Advertisers aim to increase online sales, while affiliates earn commissions by promoting products or services. This performance-based model is effective in driving high-quality traffic with low financial risk for advertisers.

25.3.2 Search Engine Optimization (SEO)

Involves optimizing websites to rank higher in search engine results. SEO can be divided into on-page and off-page optimization. On-page optimization enhances website content and structure, while off-page optimization focuses on external factors like link building to improve reputation and authority.

25.3.3 Online Sponsorships

Involves a brand linking with related content to create brand awareness and strengthen appeal. Sponsorships can include logos, articles, videos, and other advertising methods, enhancing credibility through association with a trusted online presence.

25.3.4 Co-Branding

A collaboration where two or more companies display content together, sharing marketing efforts and brand logos. Co-branding enhances consumer awareness and creates a new, composite brand, benefiting both parties, especially when the brands are complementary but not competitive.

25.4 Implementing Online Partnerships

A process of how to succeed with online partnership may look something like this:

Identifying potential partners: The first step is identifying potential partners who align with your brand values and objectives. Look for companies, influencers, or organizations that complement your business and have a similar target audience.

Setting clear goals and expectations: Define what each party aims to achieve and how success will be measured. Establishing these parameters helps in creating a focused and effective partnership strategy.

Creating a partnership agreement: Formalizing the partnership with a written agreement ensures that all parties understand their roles, responsibilities, and benefits. The agreement should outline the scope of the partnership, deliverables, timelines, and any financial arrangements.

Developing joint marketing strategies: Collaborate with partners to develop joint marketing strategies leveraging each other's strengths. This could include co-branded content, shared social media campaigns, joint events, or bundled product offerings.

Leveraging technology: Use technology to manage and optimize the partnership. Tools for project management, communication, and analytics can help streamline processes and track the performance of partnership activities.

Monitoring and evaluation: Regularly monitor the progress of the partnership and evaluate its performance against set goals. Use metrics such as traffic, engagement, conversion rates, and revenue to assess the impact of the partnership.

Building strong relationships: Maintain open communication with your partners and address any issues promptly. Celebrate joint successes and recognize each other's contributions, fostering long-term collaborations and opportunities for future partnerships.

We can illustrate the same process in a diagram, as in Fig. 25.1:

25.5 Examples of Successful Online Partnerships

Some Online partnerships have proven to be happy marriages, but it is very rare that they last forever:

Amazon and Visa: Amazon partnered with Visa to offer exclusive discounts to customers using Visa cards for purchases. This partnership drove sales for Amazon and increased transaction volumes for Visa through co-branded marketing campaigns and special offers.

Uber and Spotify: Uber and Spotify teamed up to allow passengers to control the music during their ride through the Spotify app, enhancing the customer experience. This unique collaboration drove user engagement and brand loyalty.

Nike and Apple: Nike and Apple collaborated to create the Nike+ line of products, integrating Apple's technology with Nike's athletic gear. The partnership resulted in a successful product line appealing to fitness enthusiasts.

25.6 Future Trends in Online Partnerships

There are a number of identified trends in the literature on online partnerships:

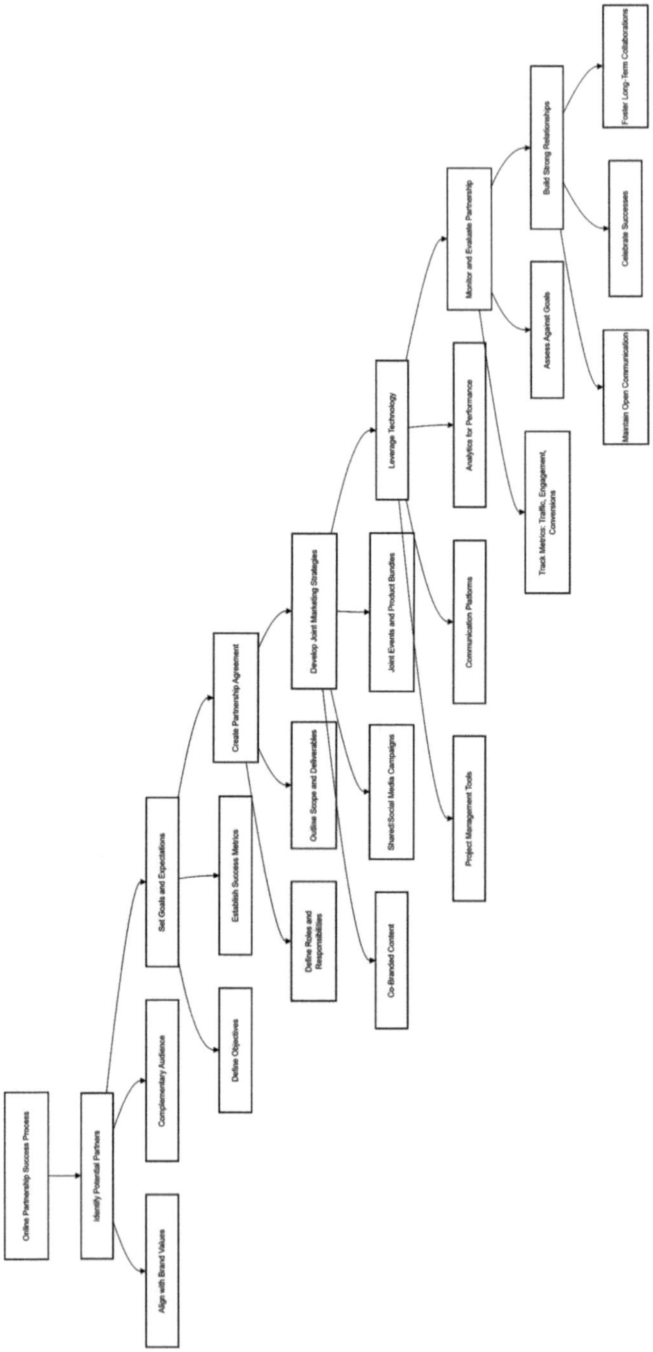

Fig. 25.1 Steps in implementing online partnerships

Influencer partnerships: Brands are increasingly partnering with social media influencers for targeted audience reach. These partnerships are evolving into long-term collaborations and co-created content.

Data-driven partnerships: Brands are using data analytics and artificial intelligence to identify potential partners, personalize marketing efforts, and measure collaboration effectiveness.

Cross-industry collaborations: Brands are exploring partnerships beyond their traditional industry boundaries, creating innovative products and services and reaching new customer segments.

Sustainability-focused partnerships: Brands are forming partnerships focused on sustainability, promoting eco-friendly products and practices to enhance reputation and appeal to socially conscious consumers.

The logic behind these partnerships is simple: if you bring together two quality brands, you get something new, something additional, and something more than what you had before. This technique has been used for a long time in the music industry, where you have different famous artists appear together.

For example, the Live Aid concerts in 1985 featured collaborations between legends like Queen, David Bowie, and U2. Another example is the recording of "We Are the World" in 1985, which brought together artists like Michael Jackson, Lionel Richie, and Stevie Wonder. More recently, the Coachella music festival has seen surprise collaborations, such as Beyoncé performing with Destiny's Child in 2018.

25.7 Key Takeaways

Here are some takeaways from this chapter:

- Online partnerships enhance brand visibility, drive sales, and create customer value.
- Identifying the right partners is crucial for successful collaborations.
- Clear goals and expectations help in creating focused partnership strategies.
- Leveraging technology can optimize partnership management and performance tracking.
- Continuous monitoring and evaluation ensure partnership effectiveness.
- Building strong relationships with partners fosters long-term collaborations.
- Successful case studies provide valuable insights for developing your own strategies.
- Future trends include influencer partnerships, data-driven collaborations, cross-industry partnerships, and sustainability-focused initiatives.
- Online partnerships are essential for achieving marketing goals and ensuring long-term growth in the digital landscape.
- Implementing strategic and well-structured online partnerships can significantly enhance brand success and customer engagement.

Partnerships between companies can vary widely in duration, with some lasting for decades and others dissolving after only a few years. Successful partnerships typically have clear, mutual benefits and a strong alignment of goals, allowing them to endure over time. However, partnerships can also face challenges such as changing market conditions, shifts in strategic direction, or conflicts of interest, which may lead to their termination. In many cases, companies seek to renegotiate or reframe their partnerships to adapt to evolving business landscapes, ensuring continued relevance and value.

Further Reading

Anderson, C. (2009). *Free: The future of a radical price*. Hyperion.

Clemons, E. K. (2009). The complex problem of monetizing virtual electronic social networks. *Decision Support Systems, 48*(1), 46–56.

Halpern, M. (2010). *The power of social networking: Using the Internet to build your business*. Entrepreneur Press.

Kumar, V., & Shah, D. (2004). Building and sustaining profitable customer loyalty for the 21st century. *Journal of Retailing, 80*(4), 317–330.

Srinivasan, R., Anderson, R., & Ponnavolu, K. (2002). Customer loyalty in e-commerce: An exploration of its antecedents and consequences. *Journal of Retailing, 78*(1), 41–50.

Omnichannel Marketing 26

26.1 Definition and Importance

Omnichannel marketing is a strategy where all of a company's channels are centered around the customer, creating a seamless and personalized buying experience. This approach fully integrates physical and digital channels, allowing synchronized marketing across all customer touchpoints. The goal is to deliver relevant content and marketing at the right time, using unified data to understand individual consumer behavior. Studying omnichannel marketing is crucial because it allows businesses to adapt to changing consumer behaviors and expectations, ensuring a consistent and engaging customer experience across all platforms.

Omnichannel marketing is closely related to multichannel marketing, customer experience (CX), digital transformation, customer relationship management (CRM), and data analytics. While multichannel marketing uses separate channels to reach customers, omnichannel marketing integrates all channels to provide a seamless and consistent customer experience. This integration enhances customer experience by ensuring consistency, personalization, and convenience across all touchpoints. Digital transformation is essential for omnichannel marketing, as it involves adopting digital tools and processes to create a unified customer journey. CRM systems play a crucial role in omnichannel marketing by collecting and utilizing customer data from various channels to deliver personalized experiences. Data analytics provides the insights needed to understand customer behavior, track performance metrics, and optimize marketing strategies across different channels. Together, these elements work to create a cohesive and efficient omnichannel marketing strategy that enhances customer satisfaction and drives business growth.

K. Solberg Söilen, *Digital Marketing*, Springer Texts in Business and Economics, https://doi.org/10.1007/978-3-031-69518-6_26

26.2 Background

Over the past decade, the consumer shopping journey and retail business have evolved significantly. The shift from physical stores to a comprehensive buying process encompassing multiple channels has reshaped the industry. New digital channels such as mobile platforms and social media have influenced business models and strategies, changing the retail mix and consumer buying behavior. As a result, retail companies have moved from brand-centric to customer-centric strategies, known as omnichannel marketing, which views the relationship between all of a company's channels and how consumers interact with and Use them.

26.3 Evolution of Retail Sales Channels

Sales channels are the methods through which retailers sell goods or services to consumers. The variety of marketing and sales channels has expanded significantly due to new technologies. Initially, many retail companies applied multichannel strategies, keeping their sales channels separate. However, consumers now use multiple channels during their buying process, making it essential to integrate physical stores with e-commerce, mobile platforms, social media, and other digital tools to provide a seamless consumer experience. Consumers expect uniform service, information, and pricing across all channels, as well as prompt feedback, particularly from online platforms.

26.4 Omnichannel Marketing Explained

The term "omni" comes from Latin and means "everything" or "every." In marketing, omnichannel refers to a strategy where all of a company's channels are centered around the customer. This strategy integrates physical and digital channels, ensuring a consistent and seamless experience across all touchpoints. It addresses the increased mobility and connectivity of modern consumers, who now expect uniform product ranges, pricing, and service across all channels. Companies must blur the lines between digital and physical interactions to offer a unified customer experience.

26.4.1 From Multichannel to Omnichannel

Companies can integrate their channels in various ways:

1. Multichannel: Separate channels used for different tasks. Consumers may use different devices and platforms during their purchase journey.
2. Cross-channel: Combines aspects of multichannel and omnichannel marketing. Some channels are integrated, creating synergies but lacking full data integration.

3. Omnichannel: Seamlessly integrates all channels, allowing for smooth transitions and unified data collection. Provides a complete view of customer behavior and enables personalized marketing.

The evolution from multichannel to omnichannel has been driven by changes in consumer behavior, technological advancements, and increased competition. Companies must adapt to this new approach to remain competitive, requiring significant investment in resources, time, and structural changes.

26.5 Technological Development

Transitioning to an omnichannel strategy requires significant technological investment. Companies need integrated systems that link product and customer data across all channels. Advanced IT solutions are essential for merging digital and physical channels, offering features like free Wi-Fi in stores, interactive screens, augmented reality, virtual mirrors, self-scanning, and mobile payment options. Overcoming silo management structures is crucial for successful omnichannel implementation, requiring integration of all departments, creating common goals, and fostering collaboration.

26.6 The Consumer in the Center

In today's retail environment, the customer plays a central role. Implementing omnichannel solutions allows companies to create a seamless, value-driven shopping experience across all channels. This approach leads to increased customer loyalty and competitive advantages. The shift from mass marketing to personalized marketing focuses on creating meaningful and interactive experiences for consumers. Omnichannel strategies enable companies to use unified data for tailored marketing, respecting consumer privacy and balancing personalization with consumer integrity.

26.7 Key Takeaways

Here are some takeaways from the chapter:

1. Omnichannel marketing centers on creating a seamless and personalized customer experience across all channels.
2. The shift from multichannel to omnichannel marketing has been driven by changes in consumer behavior and technological advancements.
3. Integrated systems linking product and customer data across channels are essential for successful omnichannel strategies.

4. Overcoming silo management structures and fostering collaboration among departments are crucial for implementation.
5. Omnichannel strategies enable companies to use unified data for personalized marketing.
6. Customers remain at the center of omnichannel marketing, driving loyalty and competitive advantages.
7. Technological investments and organizational restructuring are vital for developing effective omnichannel strategies.

The whole reason why we are able to build advanced omnichannel marketing is because information is tied together by new technological platforms, and what we have today is only the beginning. In the next step, all of these integrations will be controlled by AI-run algorithms.

Further Reading

Chaffey, D., & Ellis-Chadwick, F. (2019). *Digital marketing: Strategy, implementation, and practice*. Pearson.

Verhoef, P. C., Kannan, P. K., & Inman, J. J. (2015). From multichannel retailing to omni-channel retailing: Introduction to the special issue on multichannel retailing. *Journal of Retailing, 91*(2), 174–181.

Brynjolfsson, E., Hu, Y. J., & Rahman, M. S. (2013). Competing in the age of omnichannel retailing. *MIT Sloan Management Review, 54*(4), 23.

27 Gamification Strategies

27.1 Background

Gamification is the process of adding game elements to non-game contexts to encourage participation and engagement. It is simply a very smart pedagogical method as we all like games, so turning things into games makes sense. It involves incorporating data-driven techniques and game mechanics into applications, online communities, and other platforms to motivate users. The goal is to enhance user experience, whether the users are customers, employees, or students. Application creators, businesses, and advertisers use gamification to drive interest and improve returns on investment by tapping into human competitiveness and the desire to succeed.

A critical distinction must be made between gamification and actual games. Games are self-contained with specific rules, players, progression, and other elements that define the experience. Bernard Suits describes games as activities directed towards achieving specific states of affairs using permitted means defined by rules. Players accept these rules to create an experience distinct from the real world, where they can win, lose, perform well or poorly, and derive enjoyment or frustration.[1]

While games might have educational or persuasive goals outside the game itself, gamification integrates with real-world interactions, requiring some form of engagement beyond just playing. For example, the game Chore Wars motivates players to do household chores by rewarding them with in-game experience points, but players are not forced to perform these tasks outside the game context.

In contrast, gamification aims to motivate and encourage specific behaviors through the application's design. An example is Pokémon Go, where users explore their surroundings to catch virtual creatures, incorporating real-world exploration as part of the game's mechanics.

[1] Suits (2005).

K. Solberg Söilen, *Digital Marketing*, Springer Texts in Business and Economics, https://doi.org/10.1007/978-3-031-69518-6_27

Game elements or mechanics are techniques developers use to make games engaging. These include point systems, rewards, leaderboards, and levels, all of which play a crucial role in motivating users within gamified applications.

27.2 Development of Gamification

Gamification gained significant traction in 2002 when Nick Pelling coined the term while developing game-like interfaces for ATMs and vending machines. Despite initial setbacks, the concept grew, with companies like Bunchball pioneering the use of game mechanics as a service in 2007. Bunchball's projects, such as the Dunder Mifflin Infinity social network, showed the potential of gamification to boost user engagement. Since then, many companies have adopted gamification. Codecademy, for example, uses gamification to make learning to code engaging by incorporating game mechanics into their educational platform.

27.3 The Psychology Behind Gamification

B.J. Fogg's Behavior Model explains the psychological principles behind gamification. The model posits that Motivation, Ability, and Trigger must converge for a behavior to occur. Motivation is the drive to perform a behavior, Ability is the ease with which the behavior can be performed, and Trigger is the cue that initiates the behavior. If any of these elements are missing, the desired behavior will not occur.

27.4 Game Mechanics

Gamification relies on several core game mechanics, including:

- Avatars: Visual representations of players that increase engagement and commitment
- Points: Basic units of reward that provide immediate feedback and motivation
- Badges: Visual representations of achievements that confirm progress and set goals
- Levels: Structured stages that guide users through progression, enhancing motivation and curiosity
- Leaderboards: Rankings that show users' standings relative to peers, fostering competition and engagement

27.5 Game Dynamics: Implementing Gamification

Michael Wu defines Game Dynamics as the temporal evolution and patterns of both the game and the players that enhance enjoyment. Richard Bartle identifies four gaming personalities—Achiever, Explorer, Socializer, and Killer—each requiring different game dynamics for motivation. Understanding these dynamics is crucial for successful gamification.

27.6 Where and How to Use Gamification

Gamification can be applied across various contexts, including B2C, B2B, and G2C. Examples include Garmin's use of leaderboards and challenges to motivate users in fitness activities, Salesforce's use of badges and leaderboards to enhance customer relationship management, and Stockholm's speed camera lottery to encourage safe driving.

27.7 Gamification to Gather Data

Beyond motivation and engagement, gamification helps gather quantitative data from users, which companies can use to identify potential improvements and better target their efforts. Data collection through gamification can range from psychographic to geographic information, providing valuable insights for businesses.

27.8 Limitations of Gamification

One of the primary limitations of gamification is the potential for it to become repetitive and predictable. When users start to recognize patterns and predict the gamified elements, the novelty wears off, and the experience can feel more like a chore than an engaging activity. It's essential to strike a balance between introducing new elements and maintaining the core mechanics that make the experience enjoyable.

Additionally, gamification can sometimes lead to unintended consequences, such as fostering unhealthy competition or encouraging behaviors that prioritize game mechanics over actual learning or productivity. Companies must carefully design their gamified systems to ensure they promote positive behaviors and outcomes.

Another challenge is ensuring that the gamification strategies align with the intrinsic motivations of users. While extrinsic rewards like points and badges can be effective in the short term, they may not sustain long-term engagement if they don't resonate with users' intrinsic motivations. Therefore, it is crucial to understand the target audience and design gamification elements that appeal to their deeper motivations.

27.9 Practical Applications of Gamification

27.9.1 Education

In education, gamification has been used to enhance student engagement and motivation. By incorporating game elements such as points, badges, and leaderboards, educators can create a more interactive and rewarding learning experience. For instance, platforms like Duolingo use gamification to make language learning fun and engaging, encouraging users to complete lessons and achieve milestones.

27.9.2 Corporate Training

Corporate training programs have also benefited from gamification. Companies use gamified learning modules to train employees on new skills and procedures. This approach not only makes training more enjoyable but also improves retention and application of knowledge. For example, Deloitte uses gamification in its leadership training programs, incorporating elements like missions, levels, and badges to motivate employees.

27.9.3 Health and Fitness

Gamification has made significant inroads in the health and fitness industry. Applications like Fitbit and MyFitnessPal use game mechanics to encourage users to adopt healthier lifestyles. By setting goals, tracking progress, and rewarding achievements, these apps help users stay motivated and accountable. Challenges and social sharing features further enhance the experience by fostering a sense of community and competition.

27.9.4 Marketing and Customer Engagement

Businesses use gamification to engage customers and build brand loyalty. Reward programs, interactive campaigns, and branded games are common strategies. Starbucks, for example, has a highly successful loyalty program that uses gamification elements like stars and rewards to encourage repeat purchases. Similarly, Nike's Nike+ app gamifies running by tracking performance, offering challenges, and allowing users to compete with friends.

27.9.5 Environmental Sustainability

Gamification can also promote environmental sustainability by encouraging eco-friendly behaviors. Apps like Recyclebank reward users for recycling and making sustainable choices. By earning points for actions like reducing waste and conserving energy, users are motivated to adopt greener habits.

27.10 The Case of HeritageStride Using Gamification

Using our Sports Shoe company, Table 27.1 shows how gamification can be used for digital marketing for the sport shoes company HeritageStride:

This table outlines how gamification strategies can be effectively applied to various aspects of digital marketing for HeritageStride, enhancing customer engagement, loyalty, and overall brand experience.

27.11 The Future of Gamification

The future of gamification holds immense potential as technology continues to evolve. With advancements in artificial intelligence, virtual reality, and augmented reality, gamified experiences can become even more immersive and personalized. AI can tailor gamification elements to individual users' preferences and behaviors, enhancing engagement and effectiveness.

Virtual and augmented reality can create more interactive and realistic gamified environments. For instance, VR can be used in education to simulate real-world scenarios, providing hands-on learning experiences. AR can enhance marketing campaigns by creating interactive and engaging customer experiences.

Moreover, as data analytics become more sophisticated, companies can gain deeper insights into user behavior and preferences. This data can be used to refine gamification strategies and create more targeted and effective interventions.

27.12 Key Takeaways

Here are some of the takeaways from this chapter:

1. Gamification leverages game elements in non-game contexts to boost engagement and motivation.
2. It has diverse applications across education, corporate training, health, marketing, and sustainability.

Table 27.1 Using gamification for HeritageStride

Marketing aspect	Gamification strategy	Implementation	Expected outcomes
Customer engagement	Points and rewards system	Introduce a points system where customers earn points for activities like making purchases, writing reviews, and sharing on social media.	Increased customer interaction and engagement, encouraging repeat purchases and brand advocacy.
Social media campaigns	Social media challenges	Launch social media challenges where customers post pictures or videos of themselves wearing HeritageStride shoes during workouts.	Enhanced brand visibility on social media platforms, creating a sense of community and promoting user-generated content.
Product promotion	Limited-time badges	Offer limited-time badges for customers who purchase new product releases within a specific timeframe.	Increased sales during product launches, fostering a sense of urgency and exclusivity.
Customer loyalty	Tiered loyalty program	Implement a tiered loyalty program where customers unlock new tiers and rewards based on their cumulative points.	Strengthened customer loyalty and retention, encouraging customers to stay engaged with the brand for longer periods.
Fitness tracking	Integrated fitness app	Develop a fitness app that tracks workouts and steps, rewarding users with points or discounts for achieving fitness goals.	Increased brand affinity and engagement, positioning HeritageStride as a partner in customers' fitness journeys.
Community building	Leaderboards and competitions	Introduce leaderboards and competitions where customers can compete against each other in fitness challenges.	Fostered community spirit and friendly competition, enhancing customer engagement and loyalty.
Product education	Interactive tutorials and quizzes	Create interactive tutorials and quizzes about shoe care, running techniques, and fitness tips, rewarding participants with points.	Improved customer knowledge and product usage, enhancing the overall customer experience and satisfaction.
Customer feedback	Feedback badges and recognition	Reward customers with badges for providing valuable feedback on products and services.	Increased customer feedback and insights, allowing HeritageStride to improve products and services based on user input.

(continued)

Table 27.1 (continued)

Marketing aspect	Gamification strategy	Implementation	Expected outcomes
Event participation	Virtual events and challenges	Host virtual events and challenges, such as virtual races or fitness classes, where participants earn points and badges.	Enhanced brand presence and engagement through interactive events, encouraging customers to stay connected with the brand.
Sales promotion	Gamified discount offers	Offer gamified discounts where customers can unlock discounts by completing certain activities or challenges.	Increased sales and customer engagement, making the shopping experience more interactive and enjoyable.

3. Effective gamification relies on understanding user motivations and designing engaging game mechanics.
4. The concept has evolved rapidly, with significant contributions from companies like Duolingo and Fitbit.
5. Psychological principles like B.J. Fogg's Behavior Model underpin successful gamification strategies.
6. Challenges include maintaining novelty, aligning with intrinsic motivations, and avoiding negative behaviors.
7. Future advancements in AI, VR, and AR promise even more personalized and immersive gamified experiences.

When games first came out and kids—mostly boys—started to lock themselves in their rooms and play Fortnite and other video games for hours on end, parents started worrying, and rightfully so. But the experience of working with games also has a pedagogical advantage, as it can be applied to solving problems and learning.

Reference

Suits, B. (2005). *The grasshopper: Games, life and utopia*. Broadview Press.

Further Reading

Bartle, R. A. (1996). Hearts, clubs, diamonds, spades: Players who suit MUDs. *Journal of MUD Research, 1*(1) Retrieved from http://mud.co.uk/richard/hcds.htm

Deterding, S., Dixon, D., Khaled, R., & Nacke, L. (2011). From game design elements to gamefulness: Defining "gamification". In *Proceedings of the 15th international academic MindTrek conference: Envisioning future media environments* (pp. 9–15). ACM. https://doi.org/10.1145/2181037.2181040

Fogg, B. J. (2009). A behavior model for persuasive design. In *Proceedings of the 4th international conference on persuasive technology* (pp. 1–7). ACM.

Granquist, C., Strömberg, F., & Solberg Söilen, K. (2015). Games as a marketing channel-The impact on players and spectators. *International Journal of Electronic Business Management, 13*(5), 57–65.

Hamari, J., Koivisto, J., & Sarsa, H. (2014). Does gamification work?—A literature review of empirical studies on gamification. In *Proceedings of the 47th Hawaii international conference on system sciences* (pp. 3025–3034).

Wu, M. (2011). The science behind gamification: Why it works and how to do it. Retrieved from https://community.lithium.com/t5/Science-of-Social-Blog/The-Science-Behind-Gamification-Why-it-works-and-how-to-do-it/ba-p/30447

Zichermann, G., & Cunningham, C. (2011). *Gamification by design: Implementing game mechanics in web and mobile apps*. O'Reilly Media, Inc.

28 Cross-Selling and Upselling

28.1 Definitions and Importance

This chapter explores the concepts of cross-selling and upselling, which are crucial strategies in digital marketing. Cross-selling involves selling an additional product or service to an existing customer, while upselling encourages the buyer to purchase a more expensive item. Both strategies offer significant benefits, such as increasing sales and enhancing customer loyalty.

Cross-selling: Cross-selling is the practice of selling related or complementary products to an existing customer. It generates additional revenue from an already established customer base by offering products that complement the original purchase.

Upselling: Upselling persuades the customer to purchase a more expensive item, upgrade, or add-on to the product they initially intended to buy. This technique is common in both B2B and B2C sales.

Difference between cross-selling and upselling: Cross-selling and upselling are distinct strategies often used together. Cross-selling offers related products to enhance the customer's purchase, while upselling encourages the purchase of a higher-end product. Both aim to increase the average order value and improve customer satisfaction.

28.2 Why the Topic Is of Interest

Cross-selling and upselling are of interest because they maximize the value of existing customer relationships. By leveraging these techniques, businesses can:

- Generate immediate revenue
- Build long-term customer loyalty

K. Solberg Söilen, *Digital Marketing*, Springer Texts in Business and Economics, https://doi.org/10.1007/978-3-031-69518-6_28

- Increase the customer's lifetime value
- Enhance the overall customer experience

One way to start this process is to do a market basket analysis.

28.3 Market Basket Analysis and Product Bundling Strategy

Market basket analysis examines products that customers frequently purchase together. This technique helps identify patterns and relationships between items, enabling businesses to optimize product placement and promotional strategies.

Market Basket Analysis (MBA) is closely related to the product bundling strategy employed by Amazon. Here's how they are connected: Amazon Uses the insights gained from Market Basket Analysis to create effective product bundling strategies.

MBA helps Amazon identify which products are commonly purchased together. For example, if customers often buy a laptop with a mouse and a laptop bag, MBA will highlight this pattern.

Using the data from MBA, Amazon can suggest bundles tailored to individual customers' buying habits. For instance, if a customer is looking at a camera, Amazon might recommend a bundle that includes a camera case and memory card, based on the frequent combinations identified through MBA.

By bundling products that are commonly bought together, Amazon not only increases the average order value but also enhances customer satisfaction by providing a convenient shopping experience. Customers feel they are getting a comprehensive solution to their needs in one purchase.

Amazon can use real-time data to adjust its bundles dynamically. As new purchase patterns emerge, MBA continuously feeds this information back into the system, allowing Amazon to update its bundles to reflect the latest trends and preferences.

Consider a customer looking at a digital camera on Amazon. Based on MBA, Amazon's algorithm knows that customers who bought this camera often also purchased a specific type of lens, a tripod, and a camera bag. Amazon then displays these items as a recommended bundle on the product page, often at a discounted rate compared to buying each item separately. This strategy leverages the insights from MBA to create compelling and relevant product bundles that encourage customers to spend more while feeling that they are getting better value.

In summary, Market Basket Analysis provides the foundational data that tells Amazon's product bundling strategies. By understanding which items are frequently purchased together, Amazon can create highly appealing bundles for customers, thereby increasing the amount of up-selling and cross-selling.

From a more general perspective, we can say that the of identifying these opportunities process goes through four major steps:

1. Know your audience: Understand customer demographics, psychographics, and feedback to tailor cross-sell and upsell offers.
2. Build out customer journeys: Map out customer interactions to identify key points for cross-sell and upsell opportunities.
3. Address problems with solutions: Determine which additional products can solve customer problems or enhance their experience.
4. Practice active listening: Be attentive to customer cues during interactions to identify potential cross-sell or upsell moments.

28.4 Strategies to Effectively Cross-Sell and Upsell

To effectively cross-sell and upsell, we should consider the following strategies:

Remarketing: Remarketing involves targeting customers who have previously shown interest in your products but did not complete a purchase. By sending reminders or tailored ads, you can re-engage these customers and encourage them to complete their purchase or consider additional products.

Product bundling: Product bundling offers customers a combination of related products at a discounted price, which can encourage them to buy more items together. This strategy not only increases the average order value but also enhances the perceived value of the purchase.

Customer case studies: Showcasing customer case studies shows how other clients have benefited from your products or services, building trust and credibility. These success stories can motivate potential customers to make a purchase by seeing real-world applications and results.

Follow-up routine: A consistent follow-up routine involves checking in with customers after their purchase to ensure satisfaction and introduce additional products or services. This practice helps maintain a relationship with the customer and opens opportunities for future cross-selling and upselling.

Reasonable offers: Making reasonable cross-sell and upsell offers means suggesting products that are relevant and within a reasonable price range compared to the original purchase. This approach ensures that customers see the additional products as valuable and not as a hard sell, increasing the likelihood of acceptance.

Customer experience is critical in cross-selling and upselling. Understanding and meeting customer expectations create positive perceptions that foster loyalty. Personalized interactions and attentive service significantly boost these efforts.

28.5 Models for Cross-Selling and Upselling

These are the most common business models used for cross-selling and upselling:

- Propensity-to-buy (PtB): Propensity-to-buy models predict the likelihood of a customer purchasing a product within a predefined time horizon. By analyzing historical purchase data and customer behavior, businesses can identify which

customers are most likely to respond to specific marketing efforts. This helps target marketing resources effectively and increases the chances of making a sale.
- Cross-sell campaign optimization: Cross-sell campaign optimization focuses on maximizing the value of marketing campaigns by targeting the right customers with the most relevant products. This involves analyzing customer data to identify the best cross-sell opportunities and tailoring campaigns to these insights. The goal is to increase the efficiency and ROI of marketing efforts by reaching customers who are most likely to make additional purchases.
- Customer Segmentation: Customer segmentation identifies groups of similar customers based on various criteria such as demographics, purchase history, and behavior. By understanding the characteristics and needs of different segments, businesses can tailor their cross-sell and upsell offers to be more relevant and appealing. This targeted approach enhances the effectiveness of marketing efforts and improves customer satisfaction.
- Customer lifetime value (CLV): Customer lifetime value (CLV) calculates the expected value of future relationships with a customer, helping businesses prioritize high-value customers for cross-selling and upselling efforts. By focusing on customers with the highest potential lifetime value, businesses can maximize long-term profitability. CLV helps allocate resources efficiently and ensures that marketing efforts are directed toward customers who offer the greatest return on investment.

To succeed with our cross-selling and upselling strategies or business models, we will rely on a number of technologies and tools.

28.6 Technology and Tools for Cross-Selling and Upselling

Several tools and technologies enhance cross-selling and upselling strategies:

- Customer relationship management (CRM) systems: Customer relationship management (CRM) systems, like Salesforce and HubSpot, provide comprehensive tools for managing customer interactions and data. These systems help businesses track customer behavior, preferences, and purchase history, which are crucial for identifying cross-sell and upsell opportunities. By centralizing customer information, CRM systems enable personalized marketing efforts and improve customer relationship management.
- Predictive analytics: Predictive analytics tools use machine learning and data mining techniques to forecast future customer behavior. These tools analyze patterns in historical data to predict which customers are most likely to respond to cross-sell and upsell offers. By leveraging these insights, businesses can target their marketing efforts more effectively and increase the chances of successful sales.
- Marketing automation platforms: Marketing automation platforms, such as Marketo and Mailchimp, automate the process of sending personalized market-

ing messages to customers. These platforms can manage email campaigns, track customer interactions, and deliver tailored cross-sell and upsell recommendations based on customer behavior. Automation streamlines marketing efforts, making it easier to scale and manage campaigns efficiently.

- E-commerce platforms: E-commerce platforms like Shopify and Magento often come with built-in tools for cross-selling and upselling. These tools can suggest related products or higher-value alternatives during shopping, enhancing the customer experience and increasing sales. By integrating these features into the online shopping journey, businesses can effectively boost their average order value and improve customer satisfaction.

28.7 Measuring our Cross-Selling and Upselling

Let's consider our Sport Shoe Company, HeritageStride. In Table 28.1 is a detailed description outlining how the company can set up Key Success Factors (KSFs) for cross-selling and upselling and control them using relevant Key Performance Indicators (KPIs):

To achieve all this, we are going to have to do a series of things correctly in the organization.

Table 28.1 KSFs for measuring cross-selling and upselling

Key success factor (KSF)	Description	KPIs	Control measures
Effective cross-selling offers	Creating attractive cross-selling offers that complement the primary purchase.	Average order value (AOV)	Monitor AOV trends, analyze successful cross-sell combinations, and adjust offers based on customer preferences and purchase patterns.
High-value upselling strategies	Encouraging customers to purchase higher-end products or add-ons.	Customer lifetime value (CLV)	Track CLV over time, identify top-selling premium products, and assess the impact of upsell strategies on long-term customer value.
Optimized conversion rates	Ensuring that cross-sell and upsell suggestions effectively convert into sales.	Conversion rate	Measure conversion rates for cross-sell and upsell offers, run A/B tests to optimize suggestions, and refine targeting based on customer segments.
Strong customer retention	Maintaining high customer satisfaction and loyalty through effective cross-sell and upsell efforts.	Customer retention rate	Monitor retention rates, gather customer feedback on cross-sell and upsell experiences, and implement loyalty programs to enhance customer retention.
Customer feedback integration	Using customer feedback to refine cross-sell and upsell strategies.	Feedback and surveys	Collect and analyze customer feedback regularly, conduct surveys post-purchase, and use insights to improve product recommendations and offers.

28.8 Best Practices

Best practices to maximize cross-selling and upselling effectiveness we are going to need to get a series of processes right in the organization:

Personalize offers: Tailor cross-sell and upsell recommendations to each customer's unique preferences and purchase history. By using data analytics and customer insights, you can create highly relevant offers that resonate with individual buyers. Personalized offers increase the likelihood of acceptance and enhance the overall customer experience.

Train your sales team: Ensure that your sales team is well-versed in the benefits and techniques of cross-selling and upselling. Provide comprehensive training on identifying opportunities and presenting additional products or upgrades effectively. A knowledgeable and confident sales team can significantly improve the success rate of these strategies.

Focus on customer needs: Always prioritize the customer's needs and preferences when suggesting cross-sell and upsell options. Understanding the customer's pain points and desires allows you to offer products that genuinely enhance their experience. This customer-centric approach builds trust and increases the likelihood of repeat business.

Monitor and adjust: Continuously track the performance of your cross-selling and upselling efforts through key performance indicators (KPIs). Use this data to identify what is working and where improvements are needed. Regularly adjust your strategies based on insights and feedback to ensure they remain effective and relevant.

Avoid overloading: Be cautious not to overwhelm customers with too many cross-sell and upsell offers at once. Focus on quality over quantity, presenting a few well-chosen recommendations that are most likely to be of interest. This approach prevents decision fatigue and ensures that customers view your suggestions as helpful rather than intrusive.

28.9 Ethical Considerations

There are considerable ethical considerations in cross-selling and upselling. For one thing, most customers don't want and certainly did not intend to buy anything else than what they came searching for.

Transparency: Ensure that all cross-sell and upsell offers are presented with clear and accurate information. Customers should be fully informed about the features, benefits, and costs of additional or upgraded products. Transparency builds trust and helps maintain a positive relationship with your customers.

Honesty: Avoid using manipulative or high-pressure tactics to encourage customers to buy more. Focus on providing genuine value by recommending products that truly enhance the customer's experience or solve their problems. Honesty in your sales approach fosters long-term loyalty and credibility.

Customer consent: Always seek the customer's consent before making additional product recommendations. Customers should feel in control of their purchasing decisions and not be pressured into buying more than they initially intended. Respecting customer consent ensures a positive shopping experience and prevents potential resentment.

Data privacy: Protect customer data and use it responsibly when creating personalized cross-sell and upsell offers. Adhere to data protection regulations and ensure that customers' personal information is handled securely and ethically. Prioritizing data privacy is crucial for maintaining customer trust and complying with legal requirements.

28.10 Future Trends in Cross-Selling and Upselling

The application of AI in digital marketing will see no less than a revolution in the field, not only for customer service but in all processes. In many ways, it's easier to say which processes in digital marketing will not be changed by AI. Future trends to watch include:

Artificial intelligence (AI) and machine learning: AI and machine learning will increasingly play a significant role in predicting customer preferences and behaviors. These technologies can analyze vast amounts of data to provide highly accurate and personalized recommendations. This capability will enhance the effectiveness of cross-selling and upselling efforts by making them more targeted and relevant.

Omni-channel integration: As customers interact with brands across multiple channels, seamless integration of these channels will become crucial. Ensuring a consistent and unified experience across online and offline platforms will enhance cross-selling and upselling opportunities. Businesses that successfully integrate their sales channels can offer a more cohesive and engaging customer journey.

Enhanced personalization: Advances in data analytics will allow for even greater levels of personalization in cross-selling and upselling. By leveraging detailed customer profiles and real-time data, businesses can tailor their offers to meet individual needs and preferences precisely. Enhanced personalization will increase customer satisfaction and conversion rates.

Voice commerce: With the rise of voice-activated devices like smart speakers, voice commerce is becoming more prevalent. Businesses will need to adapt their cross-selling and upselling strategies to cater to voice interactions, offering relevant suggestions through voice assistants. This trend opens new avenues for engaging customers in a hands-free, convenient manner.

Sustainability and ethical selling: As consumers become more conscious of sustainability and ethical practices, businesses will need to align their cross-selling and upselling strategies with these values. Offering eco-friendly or ethically sourced products can enhance customer loyalty and satisfaction. Emphasizing sustainability in marketing efforts will appeal to increasingly aware and socially responsible consumers.

28.11 Managerial Takeaways on Cross-Selling and Upselling

Here are some of the takeaways from this chapter:

1. *Understand definitions and strategies*: Cross-selling and upselling are distinct yet complementary strategies that involve selling additional or higher-end products to existing customers. Knowing the difference helps apply the right technique to effectively enhance sales and customer loyalty.
2. *Importance of cross-selling and upselling*: These strategies are crucial for maximizing the value of existing customer relationships. They not only generate immediate revenue but also build long-term loyalty, increasing the customer's lifetime value.
3. *Use market basket analysis*: Leveraging market basket analysis (MBA) can reveal customer purchase patterns, helping identify effective product bundling opportunities. This approach is exemplified by companies like Amazon, which use MBA to create relevant and appealing product bundles.
4. *Personalize offers for better engagement*: Personalizing cross-sell and upsell offers based on customer preferences and purchase history increases the likelihood of acceptance. Utilizing data analytics to tailor recommendations can significantly enhance customer experience and satisfaction.
5. *Invest in training your sales team*: A well-trained sales team that understands the benefits and techniques of cross-selling and upselling can effectively identify opportunities and present additional products or upgrades. This knowledge translates to higher conversion rates and improved customer interactions.
6. *Focus on customer needs*: Prioritizing the customer's needs and preferences when suggesting additional products ensures that the offers are relevant and valuable. A customer-centric approach builds trust and encourages repeat business.
7. *Monitor and adjust strategies*: Continuously track the performance of cross-selling and upselling efforts through key performance indicators (KPIs) such as Average Order Value (AOV), Customer Lifetime Value (CLV), and conversion rates. Use these insights to make data-driven adjustments to your strategies.
8. *Ethical considerations in selling*: Maintain transparency, honesty, and customer consent in all cross-sell and upsell interactions. Respecting customer data privacy and adhering to ethical selling practices is crucial for building long-term customer trust.
9. *Embrace future trends*: Stay ahead by incorporating emerging trends such as AI and machine learning for predictive analytics, omni-channel integration for a seamless customer experience, and voice commerce for hands-free interactions. These trends can significantly enhance the effectiveness of cross-selling and upselling strategies.

10. *Promote sustainability and ethical practices*: Aligning cross-selling and upselling strategies with sustainability and ethical practices can appeal to socially conscious consumers. Offering eco-friendly or ethically sourced products can strengthen customer loyalty and differentiate your brand in the marketplace.

Cross-selling and up-selling present significant opportunities in almost any sales situation, yet they are often forgotten or overlooked. By integrating these strategies into our business approach, we can effectively boost revenue and enhance customer relationships. Emphasizing the importance of recognizing these opportunities can lead to more successful interactions and long-term customer loyalty.

Further Reading

Davenport, T. H., & Harris, J. G. (2007). *Competing on analytics: The new science of winning*. Harvard Business Review Press.

Wedel, M., & Kannan, P. K. (2016). Marketing analytics for data-rich environments. *Journal of Marketing, 80*(6), 97–121.

Waller, M. A., & Fawcett, S. E. (2013). Data science, predictive analytics, and big data: A revolution that will transform supply chain design and management. *Journal of Business Logistics, 34*(2), 77–84.

AI and Marketing Automation 29

29.1 Definition and Importance

Marketing automation refers to the use of software to automate marketing processes such as customer segmentation, data integration, and campaign management. It enhances decision-making, increases ROI, and boosts customer satisfaction and loyalty by nurturing customers with highly customized content, converting more prospects into paying customers.

AI plays a transformative role in marketing automation by analyzing vast amounts of data to predict customer behavior and preferences, enabling highly personalized marketing campaigns. It automates repetitive tasks such as email marketing, social media posting, and ad management, freeing up time for marketers to focus on strategy and creative work. AI-driven insights allow for real-time adjustments to campaigns, optimizing performance and improving ROI. Additionally, AI enhances customer segmentation by identifying patterns and trends that might be missed by human analysis, ensuring more accurate targeting. As a result, AI significantly enhances the efficiency and effectiveness of digital marketing efforts, leading to better customer engagement and satisfaction.

29.2 Return on Investment (ROI) and Marketing Automation

ROI in marketing automation is measured by the gain from investment minus the cost of investment, divided by the cost of investment. Effective marketing automation provides a higher ROI by nurturing leads, reducing costs, and enhancing customer relationships, resulting in higher conversion rates and reduced costs for sales-ready leads.

Examples of software that companies will typically purchase include Hubspot, Active Campaign, Sendinblue, Pardot, Infusionsoft, Marketo, AutopilotHQ, and GetResponse, which offer different features to suit various budgets and needs, from

K. Solberg Söilen, *Digital Marketing*, Springer Texts in Business and Economics, https://doi.org/10.1007/978-3-031-69518-6_29

basic segmentation and email marketing tools to advanced functionalities for identifying target customers and forecasting ROI.

29.3 Key Components of Marketing Automation

Here is a list of components to consider when performing marketing automation:

Data collection and analysis: Data is collected from various sources, including customer interactions, databases, and web analytics, and then segmented and analyzed to extract valuable information. This enables managers to optimize ROI and achieve other objectives by converting raw data into actionable knowledge.

Management and monitoring interface: Effective marketing automation requires strategic planning and continuous monitoring. Managers must develop well-executed plans based on results and continuously test and learn from data, integrating multiple media channels to ensure messages are customized and delivered through the right medium at the right time.

Segmentation: Customers are segmented based on predefined criteria, such as their position in the sales funnel, allowing for targeted marketing efforts that ensure the right message reaches the right customer at the right time.

Triggers and rules: Triggers are predefined actions that activate marketing responses based on customer behavior, which can be passive (based on past transactions) or active (based on direct interactions). Rules are set to automate these triggers, ensuring timely and relevant marketing actions.

Customized objectives: The primary goal of marketing automation is to create personalized and customized experiences for customers. Objectives are set to optimize various aspects of the marketing process, from content delivery to offer presentation, with insights from data analysis helping refine these objectives.

29.4 GDPR and Marketing Automation

Notice how apps and webpages ask if they can track our location. They are required to do so by law.

The General Data Protection Regulation (GDPR) significantly impacts marketing automation by imposing strict data protection requirements. Companies must ensure data is collected with proper consent, documented, and stored securely, allowing consumers to withdraw their consent and ask for data deletion at any time, maintaining ethical and legal marketing practices.

29.5 Exemplary Applications of Marketing Automation

To make learning easier, here are some examples in the form of scenarios for how marketing automation is used in practice:

Scenario 1: Restaurant franchise application: A franchise restaurant can use a smartphone application to dynamically promote different items based on weather conditions, location, and time of day, increasing customer engagement and sales by offering relevant promotions.

Scenario 2: Cinema personalized marketing: A cinema can track customer purchase history and trigger newsletters when a new movie that matches their interests is released, keeping customers engaged and increasing ticket sales.

Scenario 3: Online travel agency: An online travel agency can customize its website to display destinations based on customer preferences, enhancing the user experience and increasing the likelihood of bookings.

29.6 Differentiation from Related Terms

By now, there are many terms to keep separated in digital marketing, and adding new ones certainly does not help. Still, it's important that we try to grasp their differences.

Customer relationship management (CRM) systems: While CRM systems focus on organizing, tracking, and managing customer data, marketing automation extends beyond CRM by integrating various marketing tools and channels to deliver personalized marketing messages and automate the entire marketing process.

Email campaign management: Email campaign management involves sending bulk emails to a targeted audience, whereas marketing automation integrates email marketing with other channels to provide a holistic approach to customer engagement, ensuring emails are part of a larger, coordinated marketing strategy.

29.7 The Marketing Automation Process

Below is a description and a figure or diagram of the actual working process:[1]

1. *Data collection and segmentation:* Data is collected from various sources such as databases, customer interactions, and web analytics, then segmented based on predefined criteria like customer behavior, demographics, and position in the sales funnel.
2. *Management, analytics, and monitoring:* Effective marketing automation requires strategic planning, continuous monitoring, and analysis to deliver relevant, personalized messages through the right medium at the right time.
3. *Triggers and rules:* Triggers are actions or behaviors that activate automated marketing responses, with rules set to automate these triggers, ensuring timely and relevant marketing actions.

[1] Verified using ChatGPT 4 (June 2024).

4. *Customized objectives:* The primary goal is to create personalized experiences for customers, involving setting specific objectives like optimizing content delivery, presenting customized offers, and enhancing user engagement.
5. *Compliance with GDPR:* Companies must ensure compliance with data protection regulations like GDPR, obtaining proper consent for data collection, documenting data handling practices, and allowing consumers to withdraw their consent and ask for data deletion.

We can express the same process in a diagram as in Fig. 29.1:

The diagram outlines the process of marketing automation, starting with data collection and segmentation, where data from various sources is gathered and categorized based on criteria like customer behavior. This data is then used in management, analytics, and monitoring to strategically plan and deliver personalized marketing messages. The process includes setting triggers and rules to automate responses, establishing customized objectives for personalized customer experiences, and ensuring compliance with GDPR regulations to protect customer data and privacy.

29.7.1 Key Considerations for Implementing Marketing Automation

How can we go about implementing marketing automation? What are some of the things to keep in mind?

Start small: When implementing marketing automation, start with small-scale tests to understand what works before scaling up, ensuring a smoother implementation process and avoiding wasted resources.

Regular monitoring: Continuous monitoring is required to ensure marketing automation functions as intended, with managers regularly checking and updating automation processes to optimize performance.

Integration with multiple channels: Successful marketing automation integrates various channels, including email, social media, and physical marketing strategies, ensuring the marketing message reaches the customer through the most effective medium.

Understanding customer behavior: To create personalized and effective marketing campaigns, analyze customer behavior to identify patterns, preferences, and triggers that drive customer engagement.

29.8 Key Takeaways

Here are some of the key takeaways from this chapter:

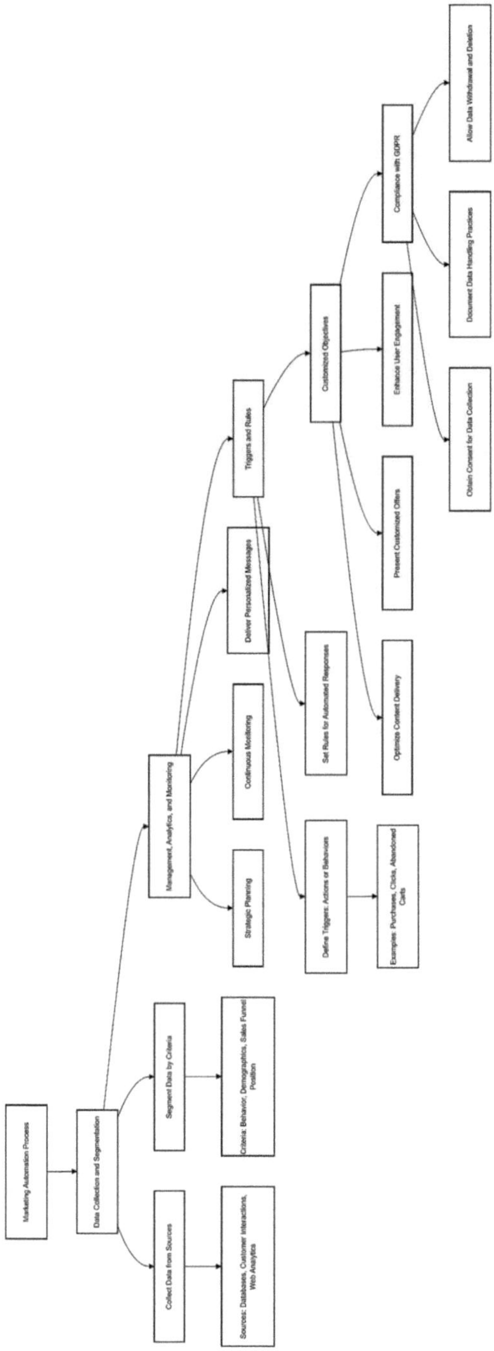

Fig. 29.1 The *marketing automation process*

- Marketing automation transforms the way companies approach marketing by leveraging data and technology to deliver personalized, efficient, and effective campaigns.
- It enhances decision-making, increases ROI, and improves customer satisfaction and loyalty.
- By integrating various marketing tools and channels, companies can create a cohesive and dynamic marketing strategy that resonates with customers.
- Effective implementation requires understanding the challenges, following best practices, and staying ahead of future trends.
- Companies that embrace marketing automation and adapt to its evolving landscape will be better positioned to meet customer needs, drive engagement, and achieve long-term success.
- Data quality and integration, technical expertise, content creation, privacy concerns, measuring effectiveness, and customer engagement are critical challenges to address.
- Best practices include setting clear goals, segmenting the audience, developing quality content, using A/B testing, monitoring and optimizing, ensuring compliance, integrating with other systems, and providing training.
- Future trends include AI and machine learning, predictive analytics, voice search and smart assistants, omnichannel marketing, customer experience focus, and real-time personalization.

Consider the case of a real-life company like Starbucks, which has embraced marketing automation to enhance customer engagement. By leveraging data and technology, Starbucks sends personalized offers to customers through their mobile app, increasing loyalty and boosting sales. This approach not only improves customer satisfaction but also demonstrates how effective marketing automation can drive long-term success.

Further Reading

Davenport, T. H., & Ronanki, R. (2018). Artificial intelligence for the real world. *Harvard Business Review, 96*(1), 108–116.

Jarek, K., & Mazurek, G. (2019). Marketing automation as a supporting tool for online marketing. *Management, 23*(1), 205–222.

King, R. (2018). The future of marketing automation. *Marketing Magazine, 123*(4), 56–59.

Kotler, P., & Armstrong, G. (2018). *Principles of marketing* (17th ed.). Pearson Education.

Paschen, J., Wilson, M., & Ferreira, J. J. (2020). Collaborative intelligence: How human and artificial intelligence create value along the B2B sales funnel. *Business Horizons, 63*(3), 403–414.

Petrovic-Lazarevic, S., & Sohal, A. (2018). The relationship between human and artificial intelligence. *AI & Society, 33*(2), 193–204.

Geolocation of Visitors 30

30.1 Definition and Importance

Geolocation is the process of identifying the geographical location of a device, such as a mobile phone or computer, to determine its physical address at the time of usage. Understanding the location of online visitors is crucial in today's global market as it allows businesses to customize web pages, advertisements, and services based on visitor location, thereby enhancing marketing efforts and potentially increasing sales.

For example, when using Google Maps, if a user is searching for nearby restaurants, Google Maps can send local ads for dining deals and promotions from restaurants in the user's immediate vicinity, effectively targeting potential customers with relevant, location-based offers.

30.2 How to Implement Geolocation

How can we implement geolocation? What are the different ways?

Data collection and segmentation: Data is collected from various sources such as IP addresses, GPS, and cell towers, then segmented based on predefined criteria like customer behavior, demographics, and position in the sales funnel. This segmentation allows businesses like HeritageStride to tailor their marketing strategies to specific customer groups, enhancing the relevance and effectiveness of their campaigns.

Management, analytics, and monitoring: Effective geolocation-based marketing requires strategic planning, continuous monitoring, and data analysis. By using tools like CRM systems and marketing automation software, HeritageStride can deliver relevant, personalized messages through the right medium at the right time, optimizing customer engagement and ROI.

K. Solberg Söilen, *Digital Marketing*, Springer Texts in Business and Economics, https://doi.org/10.1007/978-3-031-69518-6_30

Triggers and rules: Triggers are predefined actions that activate marketing responses based on customer behavior, such as entering a specific geographic area. For example, HeritageStride could send a promotional message to customers who enter a geofenced area around their retail stores, encouraging them to visit and make a purchase.

Customized objectives: The primary goal is to create personalized experiences for customers. HeritageStride can set specific objectives like optimizing content delivery, presenting customized offers, and enhancing user engagement based on geolocation data, thereby improving customer satisfaction and loyalty.

Compliance with GDPR: Companies must ensure compliance with data protection regulations like GDPR. This involves obtaining proper consent for data collection, documenting data handling practices, allowing consumers to withdraw their consent and request data deletion, and ensuring ethical and legal marketing practices.

We can express this process in a diagram, as in Fig. 30.1:

30.3 Applications of Geolocation

Once we have figured out how to do geolocations, we want to outline some examples of applications of Geolocation:

Targeted advertising: Geolocation enables businesses to tailor advertising and content based on visitor location. For instance, HeritageStride can promote weather-appropriate footwear to customers based on their geographic region.

Customer insights: By analyzing location data, businesses can gain insights into customer behavior and preferences. HeritageStride can identify popular products in different regions and adjust their inventory and marketing strategies accordingly.

Rewards for loyal customers: Tracking visitors through geolocation helps marketers identify and reward loyal customers. HeritageStride could offer special discounts or promotions to repeat customers who frequently visit their physical or online stores.

Attracting new clients: Location-based advertising helps companies attract new customers by targeting those most likely to be interested in their products. HeritageStride can use geofencing to target advertisements to potential customers near their stores, encouraging them to visit.

Measurable results: Geolocation provides measurable results that help businesses evaluate the effectiveness of their marketing strategies. HeritageStride can track the impact of location-based campaigns on foot traffic and sales, making data-driven decisions to improve future campaigns.

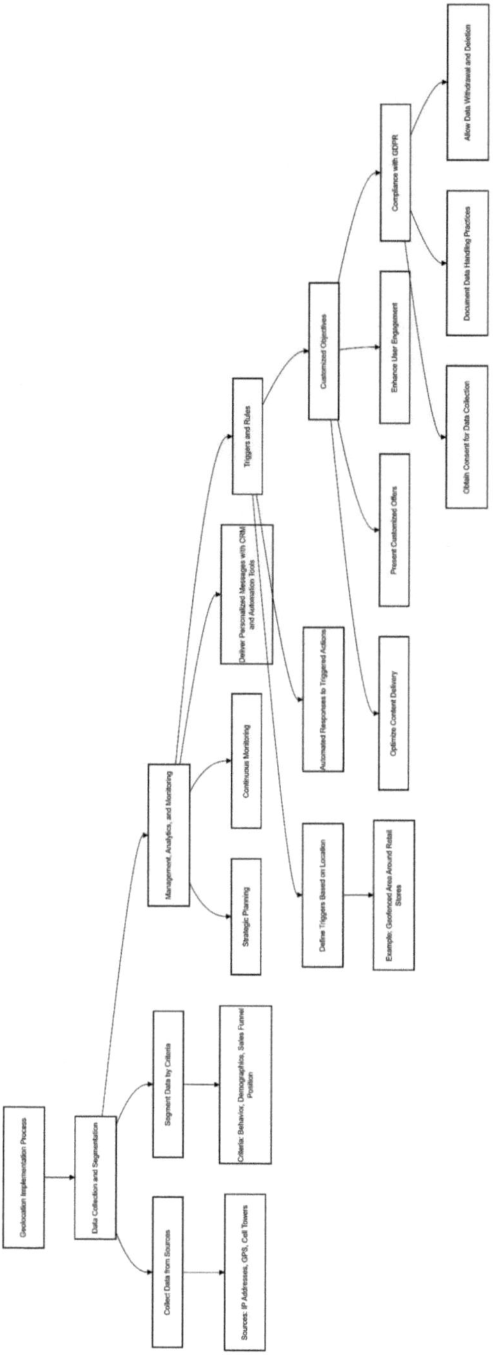

Fig. 30.1 The process of implementing geolocation

30.4 Different Geolocation Marketing Techniques

The main techniques used are as follows:

Geotargeting: Delivers advertising content based on the visitor's precise location, making marketing efforts more relevant and effective. HeritageStride can use geotargeting to show local store promotions to nearby customers.

Geofencing: Creates a virtual perimeter around a real-world geographic area, allowing targeted advertising at specific events or locations. HeritageStride can set up geofences around shopping malls to attract potential customers with real-time promotions.

Beacons: Small Bluetooth transmitters in stores send personalized messages to visitors' devices, enhancing in-store marketing efforts. HeritageStride can use beacons to offer in-store discounts and product recommendations to shoppers.

30.5 Ethics and Legal Considerations

Geolocation raises ethical concerns, such as constant surveillance and unauthorized data sharing. Ensuring user consent and transparency is crucial for ethical geolocation practices.

Various laws protect user privacy and regulate the use of geolocation data. Compliance with regulations like GDPR is essential to maintain trust and legality in marketing practices.

30.5.1 An Example: Governments

Governments use geolocation to restrict content, track criminals, locate people in emergencies, and disseminate information about local hazards. Geolocation is employed by businesses to tailor advertising and content based on visitor location. Governments use it to restrict content, such as gambling or streaming services, to specific regions. Table 30.1 shows a list of some major online gambling companies and their popularity:

Table 30.1 Online gambling companies and their impact

Company	Headquarters	Number of players	Approximate revenue	Number of employees
bet365	England, UK	90 million	$3 billion	5,1
Flutter Entertainment	Dublin, Ireland	18 million	$7 billion	14
888 Holdings	Gibraltar, UK	25 million	$850 million	1,35
Kindred Group	Sliema, Malta	30 million	$1.5 billion	1,6
Entain	Isle of Man, UK	25 million	$5.5 billion	25
William Hill	Gibraltar, UK	3 million	$2 billion	11

Online gambling companies face several major issues. Addiction and problem gambling are significant concerns, as easy access to online platforms can lead to financial and personal distress for individuals. Regulatory and legal challenges arise due to varying laws across different jurisdictions, creating inconsistencies in how these companies operate. Security and fraud are also major issues, as online gambling platforms are often targets for cyberattacks, and users face risks of fraud and identity theft. Ensuring that minors don't access gambling sites is a persistent challenge, with underage gambling being a serious problem. Fair play concerns exist, with some players questioning the integrity and transparency of the games offered by these companies. Additionally, online gambling can be exploited for financial crimes such as money laundering. Finally, the social impact of gambling proliferation can lead to broader societal issues, including increased rates of gambling addiction and related social problems.

A second example is geofencing. Geofencing is explored for traffic management and safety improvements, enhancing transportation efficiency and reducing environmental impact.

30.6 Future Prospects and Recommendations for Businesses

The future of geolocation technology holds immense potential with advancements in augmented reality (AR) and the Internet of Things (IoT). These innovations will further integrate geolocation into everyday life, providing even more personalized and context-aware services.

Recommendations for businesses include:

- *Embrace geolocation technology:* Integrate geolocation into marketing strategies to target customers more effectively and personalize offerings.
- *Ensure compliance:* Adhere to legal standards and get explicit user consent for data collection and usage to maintain trust and comply with regulations such as GDPR.
- *Invest in security:* Protect geolocation data from unauthorized access and breaches to safeguard user privacy.
- *Leverage advanced tools:* Use the latest geolocation tools and platforms to enhance marketing efforts and improve customer insights.
- *Monitor and adapt:* Regularly review geolocation strategies and adapt them based on performance metrics and changing consumer behaviors.

30.7 Managerial Takeaways

Here are some managerial takeaways from this chapter:

- Leverage geolocation for targeted marketing: Use geolocation to deliver personalized advertisements and content based on visitor location, enhancing marketing relevance and effectiveness.

- Enhance customer insights: Analyze location data to gain valuable insights into customer behavior and preferences, allowing for better inventory and marketing strategy adjustments.
- Reward loyal customers: Use geolocation to identify and reward loyal customers with special discounts or promotions, promoting customer retention and satisfaction.
- Attract new customers: Implement location-based advertising to target potential new customers near your stores, increasing foot traffic and sales opportunities.
- Measure campaign effectiveness: Track the impact of geolocation-based marketing campaigns on metrics such as foot traffic and sales, making data-driven decisions to refine future strategies.
- Implement various geolocation techniques: Employ geotargeting, geofencing, and beacons to enhance marketing efforts, delivering relevant and timely messages to customers based on their location.
- Maintain ethical practices: Ensure transparency and get user consent for data collection, addressing ethical concerns related to surveillance and data sharing.
- Ensure legal compliance: Adhere to regulations like GDPR to protect user privacy and maintain legal compliance in geolocation data usage.
- Invest in security: Protect geolocation data from unauthorized access and breaches to safeguard user privacy and build trust.
- Adapt to future trends: Stay ahead of advancements in geolocation technology, such as augmented reality (AR) and the Internet of Things (IoT), to provide even more personalized and context-aware services.

By following these recommendations, businesses like HeritageStride can harness the power of geolocation to drive growth, improve customer satisfaction, and stay ahead in the competitive market.

When asked on our mobile devices if we allow geographic tracking, we should consider the benefits of personalized services and local recommendations we could receive, such as nearby restaurant deals or traffic updates. However, we must also weigh the privacy implications and potential data security risks associated with sharing our location. Ultimately, we should make an informed decision based on our comfort level with these trade-offs.

Further Reading

Chang, H. H., & Chen, S. W. (2008). The impact of online store environment cues on purchase intention: Trust and perceived risk as a mediator. *Online Information Review, 32*(6), 818–841.

Demirkan, H., & Delen, D. (2013). Leveraging the capabilities of service-oriented decision support systems: Putting analytics and big data in cloud. *Decision Support Systems, 55*(1), 412–421.

Dong, X., & Triche, J. (2021). Analyzing geolocation data in retail: Leveraging big data for business outcomes. *Journal of Retail Analytics, 15*(2), 234–247.

Petersen, J. A., & Kumar, V. (2009). Are product returns a necessary evil? The role of online shopping experiences. *Journal of Marketing, 73*(3), 35–50.

Van Dijk, J., & Hacker, K. (2018). The digital divide as a complex and dynamic phenomenon. *The Information Society, 34*(1), 36–42.

31 Dropshipping

31.1 Definition and Importance

Dropshipping is a supply chain management method where retailers do not keep goods in stock but transfer customer orders and shipment details to a manufacturer, another retailer, or a wholesaler, who then ships the goods directly to the customer. This method is crucial in today's e-commerce landscape as it allows businesses to expand their product offerings without the need for large capital investments in inventory, making it easier to scale and adapt to market demands. It also causes frequent problems, such as when both the customer and the seller think that the order will be shipped right away and arrive quickly without really understanding or being in control of the process.

31.2 How to Implement Dropshipping

A good way to learn about dropshipping is to ask how it can be done, following a procedure:

Data collection and segmentation: Data is collected from various sources such as IP addresses, GPS, and cell towers, then segmented based on predefined criteria like customer behavior, demographics, and position in the sales funnel. This segmentation allows businesses like HeritageStride to tailor their marketing strategies to specific customer groups, enhancing the relevance and effectiveness of their campaigns.

Management, analytics, and monitoring: Effective geolocation-based marketing requires strategic planning, continuous monitoring, and data analysis. By using tools like CRM systems and marketing automation software, HeritageStride can deliver relevant, personalized messages through the right medium at the right time, optimizing customer engagement and ROI.

K. Solberg Söilen, *Digital Marketing*, Springer Texts in Business and Economics, https://doi.org/10.1007/978-3-031-69518-6_31

Triggers and rules: Triggers are predefined actions that activate marketing responses based on customer behavior, such as entering a specific geographic area. For example, HeritageStride could send a promotional message to customers who enter a geofenced area around their retail stores, encouraging them to visit and make a purchase.

Customized objectives: The primary goal is to create personalized experiences for customers. HeritageStride can set specific objectives, such as optimizing content delivery, presenting customized offers, and enhancing user engagement based on geolocation data, to improve customer satisfaction and loyalty.

Compliance with GDPR: Companies must ensure compliance with data protection regulations like GDPR. This involves obtaining proper consent for data collection, documenting data handling practices, and allowing consumers to withdraw their consent and ask for data deletion, ensuring ethical and legal marketing practices.

We may illustrate this process in a diagram, as in Fig. 31.1.

But, what does this mean for our Sports Shoes Company? How can they practice dropshipping? How should they think about this opportunity?

HeritageStride, a sports shoe retailer, can leverage dropshipping to expand its product offerings and efficiently meet customer demands without significant capital investment. They can partner with various manufacturers and wholesalers to list a wide range of sports shoes on their online store without needing to stock these products physically. This allows them to offer the latest styles and brands, keeping their inventory dynamic and appealing to a broad customer base. By utilizing dropshipping, HeritageStride can eliminate the need for warehousing and inventory management, reducing overhead costs. This reduction in overhead costs means they can allocate more resources to marketing, customer service, and improving their online store's user experience. With dropshipping, HeritageStride can focus on marketing and sales rather than logistics. When a customer places an order, HeritageStride can forward the order details to the dropshipping supplier, who will then ship the product directly to the customer, ensuring quick order fulfillment and delivery. Dropshipping also allows HeritageStride to scale its business quickly and respond swiftly to market trends and seasonal demands. HeritageStride can use data from customer orders to analyze trends and preferences, creating targeted marketing campaigns to promote popular or seasonal sports shoes to specific customer segments. By freeing up resources typically tied up in inventory management, HeritageStride can enhance its customer service and improve overall customer

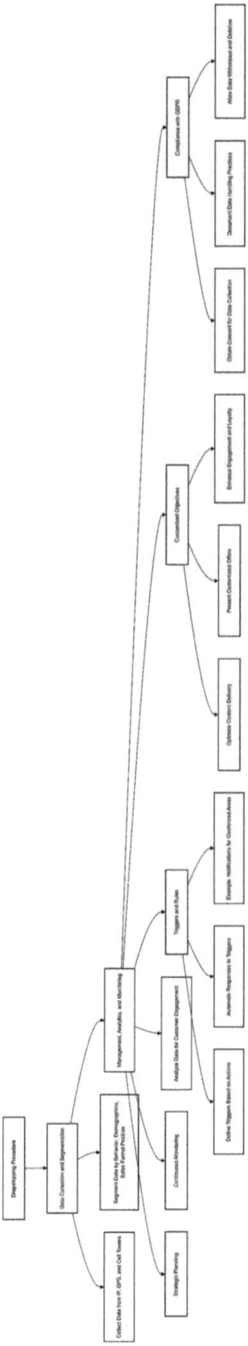

Fig. 31.1 Dropshipping procedure

Table 31.1 Dropshipping in practice for HeritageStride

Aspect	Description
Expand product range	Partner with various manufacturers and wholesalers to list a wide range of sports shoes on the online store without needing to stock these products physically.
Reduce overhead costs	Eliminating the need for warehousing and inventory management will allow more resources to be allocated to marketing, customer service, and improving the online store.
Streamline operations	Focus on marketing and sales rather than logistics by forwarding customer orders to dropshipping suppliers who ship products directly to customers.
Scalability	Easily add new products to the online store without worrying about storage space or inventory risks, enabling swift response to market trends and seasonal demands.
Targeted marketing campaigns	Use data from customer orders to analyze trends and preferences, creating targeted marketing campaigns to promote popular or seasonal sports shoes to specific segments.
Focus on customer experience	Enhance customer service by offering personalized shopping experiences, quick responses to inquiries.

satisfaction. This strategy enables HeritageStride to offer a broader product selection, reduce operational complexities, and deliver an exceptional customer experience.

We summarize these points in Table 31.1 below.

Let's take what we have learned so far and define a dropshipping model.

31.3 A Dropshipping Model

The successful implementation of the dropshipping model involves establishing efficient services such as payment methods, return policies, and packaging strategies. Retailers often receive payments upon order placement, but they must manage their accounts with manufacturers to maintain a surplus of funds. Return policies should clearly define responsibilities and procedures for handling returned products. Packaging costs may increase due to the use of various materials by different manufacturers.

A key aspect of successful dropshipping is designing compatible information systems to ensure seamless communication between manufacturers and retailers. Retailers must quickly forward customer orders to manufacturers to avoid delivery delays. The single-period model framework, which aims to maximize product profit under probabilistic demand, is often used to manage inventory and capacity effectively. Figure 31.2 shows how elements necessary to build a successful dropshipping function:

The next question to ask would be how we can use this model and what its applications are.

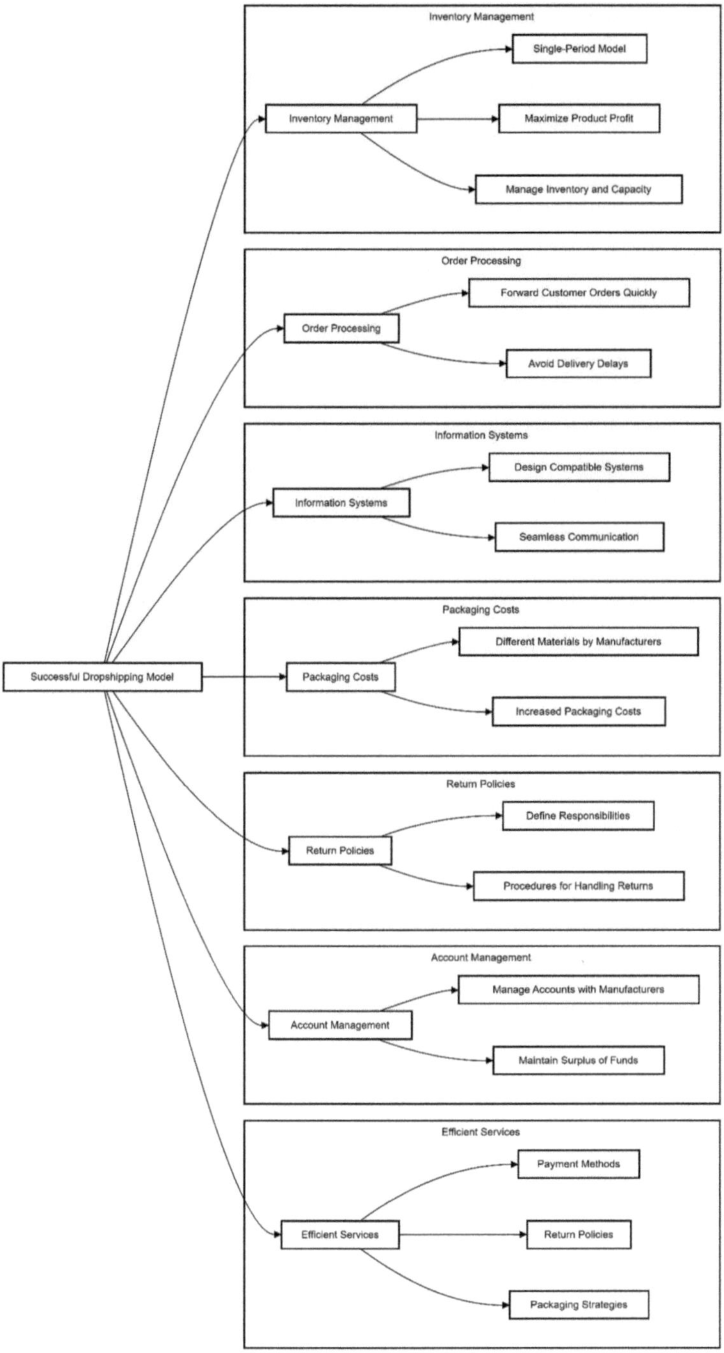

Fig. 31.2 A successful dropshipping model

31.4 Applications of Dropshipping

Dropshipping has a number of quite different applications:[1]

Targeted advertising: Geolocation enables businesses to tailor advertising and content based on visitor location. For instance, HeritageStride can promote weather-appropriate footwear to customers based on their geographic region.

Customer insights: By analyzing location data, businesses can gain insights into customer behavior and preferences. HeritageStride can identify popular products in different regions and adjust its inventory and marketing strategies accordingly.

Rewards for loyal customers: Tracking visitors through geolocation helps marketers identify and reward loyal customers. HeritageStride could offer special discounts or promotions to repeat customers who frequently visit their physical or online stores.

Attracting new clients: Location-based advertising helps companies attract new customers by targeting those most likely to be interested in their products. HeritageStride can use geofencing to target advertisements to potential customers near their stores, encouraging them to visit.

Measurable results: Geolocation provides measurable results that help businesses evaluate the effectiveness of their marketing strategies. HeritageStride can track the impact of location-based campaigns on foot traffic and sales, making data-driven decisions to improve future campaigns.

31.5 Different Geolocation Marketing Techniques

We talked about geofencing earlier, so what are the different geolocation marketing techniques?

Geotargeting: Delivers advertising content based on the visitor's precise location, making marketing efforts more relevant and effective. HeritageStride can use geotargeting to show local store promotions to nearby customers.

Geofencing: Creates a virtual perimeter around a real-world geographic area, allowing targeted advertising at specific events or locations. HeritageStride can set up geofences around shopping malls to attract potential customers with real-time promotions.

Beacons: Small Bluetooth transmitters in stores send personalized messages to visitors' devices, enhancing in-store marketing efforts. HeritageStride can use beacons to offer in-store discounts and product recommendations to shoppers.

[1] Verified using ChatGPT 4 (June 2024).

31.6 Ethics and Legal Considerations

Geolocation raises a number of ethical concerns, such as constant surveillance and unauthorized data sharing. Do we think this is ok? Are we even willing to pass on and sell this data to other providers? Where do our ethical limits go in this concern, as a company and also as individual employees? Ensuring user consent and transparency is crucial for ethical geolocation practices.

Laws protect user privacy and regulate the use of geolocation data. Compliance with regulations like GDPR is essential to maintain trust and legality in marketing practices.

31.7 Future Prospects and Recommendations for Businesses

The future of geolocation technology holds immense potential with advancements in augmented reality (AR) and the Internet of Things (IoT). These innovations will further integrate geolocation into everyday life, providing even more personalized and context-aware services.

Here are some recommendations for businesses:

- *Embrace geolocation technology:* Integrate geolocation into marketing strategies to target customers more effectively and personalize offerings.
- *Ensure compliance:* Adhere to legal standards and get explicit user consent for data collection and usage to maintain trust and comply with regulations such as GDPR.
- *Invest in security:* Protect geolocation data from unauthorized access and breaches to safeguard user privacy.
- *Leverage advanced tools:* Use the latest geolocation tools and platforms to enhance marketing efforts and improve customer insights.
- *Monitor and adapt:* Regularly review geolocation strategies and adapt them based on performance metrics and changing consumer behaviors.

31.8 Key Takeaways

Here are some of the managerial takeaways from this chapter:

- Dropshipping has revolutionized the e-commerce industry, providing a viable business model for retailers to offer a wide range of products without the burden of inventory management.
- While it presents challenges such as lower profit margins and inventory issues, careful planning, reliable suppliers, and excellent customer service can mitigate these challenges.
- As the e-commerce landscape continues to evolve, dropshipping businesses must stay abreast of emerging trends and technologies.
- Dropshipping businesses can thrive in the competitive online marketplace by leveraging AI, embracing sustainability, exploring global markets, enhancing customer experiences, and targeting niche markets.

- Understanding the intricacies of dropshipping and implementing best practices will enable retailers to build successful and sustainable businesses in the ever-expanding world of e-commerce.
- Targeted advertising based on geolocation can significantly enhance the relevance and effectiveness of marketing campaigns.
- Analyzing location data provides valuable insights into customer behavior, helping businesses adjust their strategies accordingly.
- Rewarding loyal customers through geolocation tracking can increase customer retention and satisfaction.
- Location-based advertising is an effective way to attract new customers and drive foot traffic to physical stores.
- Measuring the impact of geolocation-based campaigns is crucial for making data-driven decisions and improving future marketing efforts.

Dropshipping is tempting for our sports shoe company because of its low upfront costs and ease of implementation. However, we must ensure we can trust the supply chain and verify that the goods will arrive on time. For instance, if a customer needs a pair of shoes for an upcoming competition and the order arrives late, the purpose of buying the shoes is defeated, and we risk damaging our relationship with that customer. Ensuring timely and reliable delivery is crucial to maintaining customer trust and satisfaction.

Further Reading

Davies, G. (2017). The rise of dropshipping: E-commerce revolution or passing fad? *E-Commerce Times, 26*(4), 14–18.

Graham, G. (2020). *Dropshipping for beginners: A step-by-step guide to create a passive income stream*. Amazon Digital Services.

Huang, G. Q., Lau, J. S. K., & Mak, K. L. (2003). The impacts of sharing production information on supply chain dynamics: A review of the literature. *International Journal of Production Research, 41*(7), 1483–1517.

Jang, Y., & Klein, R. (2020). Supply chain decisions in dropshipping operations. *Journal of Supply Chain Management, 56*(2), 45–60.

Lim, W. S. (2021). Dropshipping and its impact on global e-commerce. *International Journal of Retail & Distribution Management, 49*(1), 45–61.

Sanders, N. R., & Ritzman, L. P. (2004). *Supply chain management: A global perspective*. Wiley.

Browsing and Purchasing Online 32

32.1 Definition and Importance

Browsing and purchasing online involve the steps consumers take to find, evaluate, and buy products through the Internet. Understanding how and why consumers use the Internet for shopping is essential for businesses to adapt their marketing strategies, build customer loyalty, and remain competitive in the digital marketplace. This chapter focuses on the browsing and purchasing stages, examining how consumers search for information and make purchase decisions.

We want to understand what thought processes go through the mind of a customer browsing, as depicted in Fig. 32.1.

This diagram illustrates the thought process of a customer when browsing and purchasing online. It starts with the *Stimulus*, which is the initial awareness of a product. This leads to the *Zero Moment of Truth (ZMOT)* that we talked about earlier, where the customer researches products, reads reviews, and compares prices. During the *Consideration* phase, the customer evaluates different options and seeks recommendations. This is followed by the *Intent* phase, where the customer decides and checks for any discounts. Once a decision is made, the customer proceeds to the *Purchase* phase. Finally, if satisfied, the customer enters the *Loyalty* phase, leading to repeat purchases and recommendations to others.

32.2 How to Implement Browsing and Purchasing Strategies

To implement effective browsing and purchasing strategies, start with data collection and segmentation. Gather data from sources such as search engines, social media, and customer interactions. Segment this data based on behavior, demographics, and purchase intent, which helps businesses tailor their marketing strategies to specific customer groups, thereby improving the relevance and effectiveness of their campaigns.

K. Solberg Söilen, *Digital Marketing*, Springer Texts in Business and Economics, https://doi.org/10.1007/978-3-031-69518-6_32

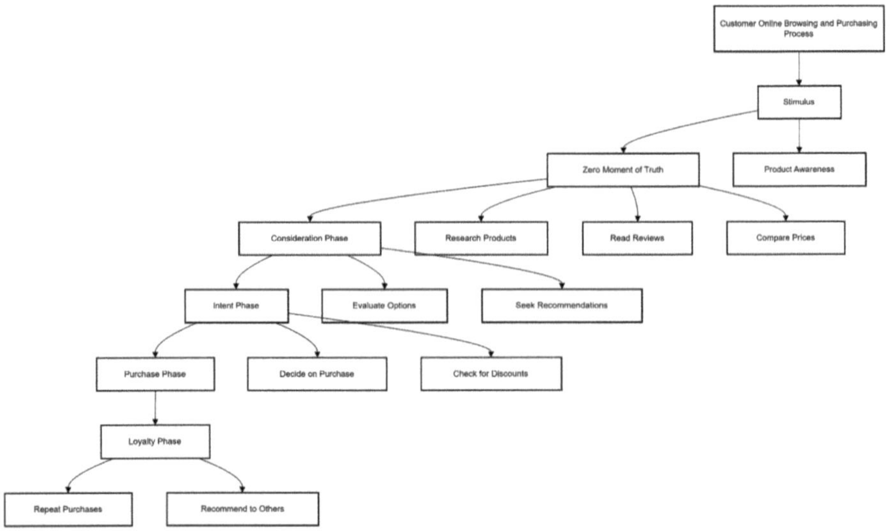

Fig. 32.1 Thinking process for the customer when browsing online

Next, use management, analytics, and monitoring tools. Use web analytics, CRM systems, and social media analytics to gather insights into consumer behavior. Continuous monitoring and strategic planning allow businesses to deliver personalized messages and optimize customer engagement and return on investment.

Set up triggers and rules to guide consumer actions. Predefined actions can activate marketing responses based on consumer behavior, such as viewing specific products or adding items to a cart. These triggers help guide consumers through the purchase process and encourage conversions.

Define customized objectives to drive marketing efforts. Set clear goals for personalized marketing, such as optimizing content delivery, offering customized deals, and enhancing user engagement. These objectives help improve customer satisfaction and loyalty.

Finally, ensure compliance with GDPR. Make sure all data collection and marketing practices comply with data protection regulations. Get proper consent, document data handling procedures, and provide options for consumers to manage their data. This approach ensures ethical and legal marketing practices.

32.3 The Online Browsing Process

We have basically two kinds of search:

Internal search: Consumers recall their own knowledge and experiences when looking for everyday, inexpensive items they are familiar with. This internal search is quick and relies on memory.

External search: For more expensive or high-risk purchases, consumers seek additional information online or offline. They compare different brands, read reviews, and look for detailed product information to make an informed decision.

32.4 Understanding Consumer Behavior Through Browsing and Purchasing

To effectively implement data analysis, businesses should analyze browsing data to understand consumer behavior, preferences, and trends. This involves using tools like Google Analytics, social media insights, and CRM systems to gather valuable information. By examining this data, businesses can identify patterns in how consumers interact with their online presence.

Gaining customer insights is crucial for tailoring marketing strategies. Understanding what drives consumer decisions, such as price sensitivity, product features, and brand loyalty, helps businesses create more targeted and effective campaigns. For example, if data shows that consumers are highly sensitive to price changes, a company might focus on offering competitive pricing or special discounts.

Customer insights also reveal which product features are most important to different segments of the market. This information allows businesses to highlight these features in their marketing efforts, increasing the likelihood of attracting interested customers. Additionally, understanding brand loyalty can help businesses develop strategies to retain their most valuable customers.

Overall, using data analysis and customer insights enables businesses to make informed decisions, optimize their marketing efforts, and ultimately improve customer satisfaction and loyalty. This data-driven approach helps companies stay competitive in a rapidly changing market.

32.5 Key Considerations for Online Success

To starting think about how to achieve online success we may consider what is called the Four Cs of Companies: Competitors, Customers, Culture, and Content. These elements are essential for online success. Understanding competitors, knowing customer preferences, adapting to online culture, and providing valuable content help differentiate a business.

In the same way, we have the four Cs of Customers: Customers look for products that are Cheap, Customized, Convenient, and Compelling. Meeting these expectations can drive sales and build loyalty.

We should also consider E-loyalty: Building a loyal online customer base requires excellent service and long-term relationship building. Trust and reputation are crucial for gaining e-loyalty, as consumers value authentic and reliable brands.

32.6 Overcoming Limitations of E-Commerce

To overcome the limitations of e-commerce, businesses must address security concerns by implementing robust data protection measures. Ensuring secure transactions and protecting customer information from breaches are essential steps to build trust with online shoppers. By prioritizing security, companies can mitigate the risks associated with online shopping and reassure customers that their data is safe.

In addition to security, offering competitive shipping and return policies is crucial for attracting and retaining customers. Businesses should strive to balance the costs of these services with the benefits of increased customer satisfaction. Competitive shipping options can enhance the overall shopping experience by providing faster delivery times and reliable service.

Effective return policies are equally important, as they provide customers with confidence in their purchases. By making the return process simple and hassle-free, businesses can encourage repeat purchases and foster customer loyalty. Overall, addressing security and optimizing shipping and return policies are key strategies for overcoming the limitations of e-commerce.

32.7 Combining Offline and Online Strategies

To create synergy between channels, we should integrate online and offline strategies to ensure a seamless customer experience. We should make sure that product listings are easily searchable online, providing comprehensive information that mirrors what is available in physical stores. This approach helps customers find the products they need, whether they start their search online or offline. Additionally, provide detailed store information, such as locations, hours, and in-store availability, to enhance convenience for shoppers. Using strong SEO practices is crucial to attract and convert customers, driving traffic to both online and brick-and-mortar locations.

32.8 Future Trends in Online Browsing and Purchasing

Here is a list of future trends to consider:

Artificial intelligence and machine learning enhance personalization, predictive analytics, and customer service automation. These technologies provide deeper insights and improve marketing effectiveness.

Optimize for voice search as smart speakers and assistants become more prevalent. This trend requires adapting SEO strategies to capture voice queries effectively.

Augmented reality and virtual reality technologies offer immersive shopping experiences. These technologies allow customers to visualize products before purchasing.

Optimize the mobile shopping experience with mobile-friendly websites, apps, and payment options as mobile usage continues to grow.

Show commitment to sustainability and ethical practices to attract environmentally conscious consumers. This approach can help businesses connect with a growing segment of the market that values sustainability and ethics.

32.9 Key Takeaways

In the end, here are the managerial takeaways from this chapter:

1. Understanding the online browsing and purchasing process is essential for businesses to adapt their marketing strategies and build customer loyalty.
2. The online buying process involves several stages, including stimulus, research, consideration, intent, purchase, and loyalty.
3. Effective data collection and segmentation help businesses tailor their marketing strategies to specific customer groups, improving relevance and effectiveness.
4. Utilizing tools like web analytics, CRM systems, and social media insights allows businesses to gather valuable consumer behavior data.
5. Setting up triggers and rules can guide consumer actions and encourage conversions throughout the purchase process.
6. Defining clear, customized objectives for marketing efforts helps improve customer satisfaction and loyalty.
7. Ensuring compliance with data protection regulations like GDPR is crucial for ethical and legal marketing practices.
8. Gaining customer insights through data analysis helps businesses understand what drives consumer decisions and tailor their marketing strategies accordingly.
9. Integrating online and offline strategies creates a seamless customer experience, enhancing convenience and driving traffic to both channels.
10. Staying ahead of future trends, such as AI, voice search, AR/VR, mobile commerce, and sustainability, can give businesses a competitive edge in the digital marketplace.

A slow browser is a cardinal sin in the world of digital marketing. All the effort put into creating engaging content and seamless experiences can be undone by a poor connection. It's like building only a magnificent structure to see it crumble because of a weak foundation. In the fast-paced world of e-commerce, the only thing that should be moving faster than your customers' preferences is their Internet connection! Ensuring swift and reliable connectivity is essential to keeping up with customer expectations and maintaining a competitive edge.

Further Reading

Anderson, C. (2004). *The long tail: Why the future of business is selling less of more*. Hyperion.
Brynjolfsson, E., Hu, Y. J., & Rahman, M. S. (2013). Competing in the age of omnichannel retailing. *MIT Sloan Management Review, 54*(4), 23–29.
Grewal, D., Roggeveen, A. L., & Nordfält, J. (2017). The future of retailing. *Journal of Retailing, 93*(1), 1–6.
Rigby, D. (2011). The future of shopping. *Harvard Business Review, 89*(12), 65–76.

B2B Digital Marketing 33

33.1 Background

This chapter focuses on business-to-business digital marketing (B2B digital). Generally, marketing discipline is about showing how to sell products to consumers, known as business-to-consumer marketing (B2C). However, B2B transactions significantly surpass B2C in sales volume, making them crucial for employment and economic growth. Figure 33.1 shows an example of a working process in B2B marketing.

Despite high sales volumes, B2B marketing activities are not necessarily more extensive. Many industries remain highly competitive, where technical quality and price primarily determine relationships, especially lower in the supply chain where margins are smaller. For example, the mobile phone industry produced approximately 1.17 billion devices in 2023, maintaining its status as one of the largest industries, though it is not the most profitable. In contrast, industries such as accounting, tax services, legal services, and oil and gas are known for higher profitability. Within the communication sector, service providers often earn the most revenue.

In 2023, smartphone components accounted for significant portions of exports from several Asian countries: 33% from Taiwan, 17% from Malaysia, and 16% from Singapore. Apple, a major player in the smartphone industry, relies on a network of key suppliers, with Foxconn (Hon Hai Precision Industry) being one of the most prominent partners. Foxconn is the world's largest contract electronics manufacturer, producing a significant portion of Apple's products and about 40% of all consumer electronics sold worldwide.

Despite this, carriers tend to capture the greatest value in terms of gross profit from each handset, followed by handset manufacturers, with suppliers earning significantly less. As of 2023, Foxconn remains a crucial player in the industry, reflecting the complex dynamics and varying profitability across different segments of the supply chain.

K. Solberg Söilen, *Digital Marketing*, Springer Texts in Business and Economics, https://doi.org/10.1007/978-3-031-69518-6_33

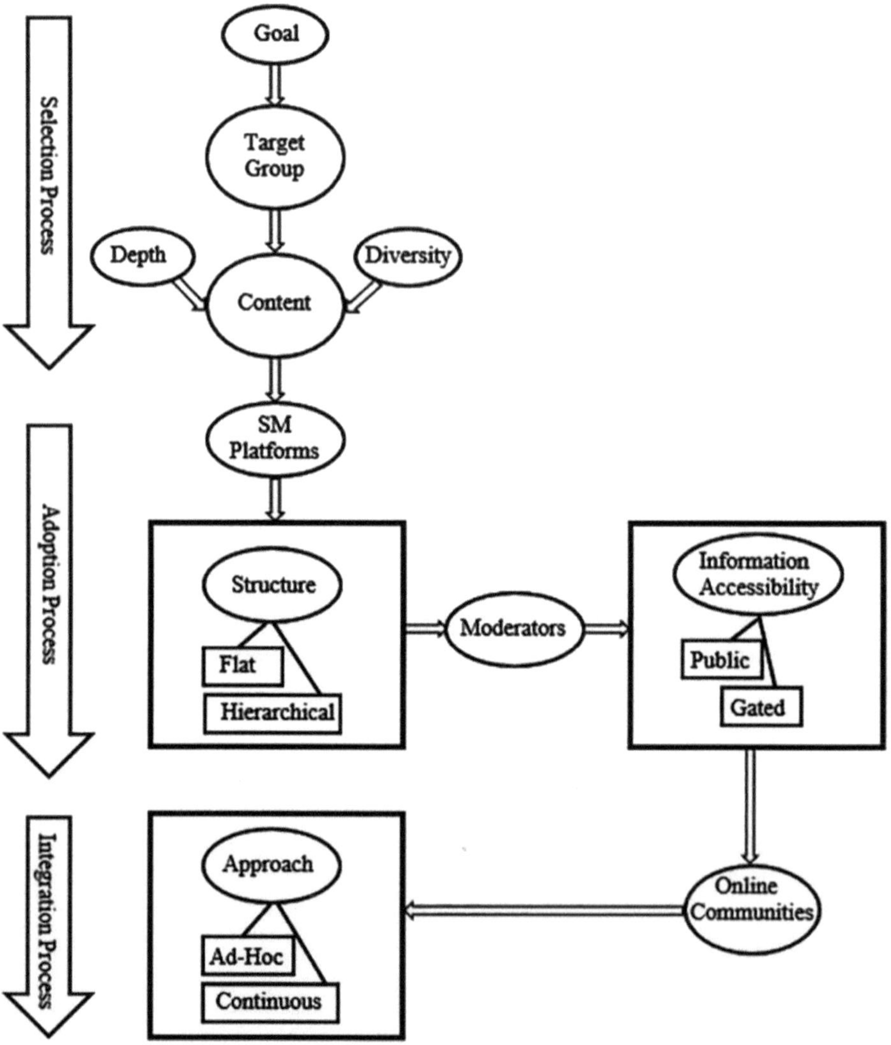

Fig. 33.1 Working process in B2B marketing

33.2 The Objective of B2B Digital Marketing

B2B digital marketing tackles two main challenges: finding customers generating interest in products (B2B digital segmentation and B2B digital communication) and making transactions more efficient (B2B e-commerce). The Internet offers solutions for both new software and hardware technologies. This chapter focuses primarily on marketing aspects, assuming the reader has a basic understanding of B2B marketing. We will briefly touch on the nature of B2B and its differences from B2C, emphasizing the new aspects of B2B digital marketing.

B2B digital marketing is a new framework for studying and practicing marketing. It allows mass customization, tailoring orders to demand, and remembering numerous customer relationships. It also shifts focus from push marketing to pull marketing, emphasizing noninvasiveness and responsible data use. Cold calls and aggressive sales tactics are no longer effective; today's buyers are less loyal and more informed. Knowledge and trust are crucial in B2B marketing. Buyers spend most of their time evaluating information about suppliers and competitors online, completing up to 60% of purchasing decisions before contacting a supplier. Sellers must show knowledge and expertise to be considered.

Existing customers tend to focus on finding new customers rather than deepening existing relationships, overestimating their loyalty. We have moved from a "seller-dominated" to a "buyer-dominated" marketplace, where buyers complete most of the sales cycle before contacting sellers. This shift means sellers must focus on building stronger brands, though this is challenging in B2B due to the many different decision-makers and influencers involved.

Strong B2B brands are built through consistent, successful deliveries over time. Understanding the customer journey, as discussed in a previous chapter, helps us understand this process better.

33.3 Definitions

Business-to-business digital marketing (B2B digital) involves using information and communications technology (ICT) to find customers, persuade them to purchase products, and ensure repeat business. B2B e-commerce involves selling products online through a digital sales portal. B2B digital segmentation defines groups of people interested in products by creating personas with specific traits. Advances in IT allow for larger numbers of segments. B2B digital communication involves using ICT to convey information to potential and existing customers to generate interest in products. Content marketing involves creating, publishing, and distributing valuable information to a targeted online audience. In B2B, valuable information includes basic knowledge (the why) and practical knowledge or skills (the how) to solve business problems. The term buyer refers to the entire selling process before an actual purchase, after which the buyer becomes a customer. A potential customer is used synonymously with the buyer. Other definitions will be provided throughout the chapter as needed. Table 33.1 shows the more important definitions for this chapter.

33.4 The B2B Digital Marketing Process

B2B marketing has always focused on creating leads and building relationships, but the methods have evolved. Over the past two decades, we have transitioned from display ads to search ads and editorial content in online advertising. Unlike B2C, creating leads in B2B is a long process that involves building trust over time.

Table 33.1 Key definitions in B2B digital marketing

Term	Definition
B2B digital	Use of ICT to find, persuade, and serve customers
B2B e-commerce	Selling products online via a digital sales portal
B2B digital segmentation	Defining groups of people interested in products by creating personas
B2B digital communication	Using ICT to convey information to potential and existing customers
Content marketing	Creating, publishing, and distributing valuable information to a targeted online audience
Buyer	Refers to the entire selling process before an actual purchase
Potential customer	Synonym for buyer

Companies achieve this by producing quality whitepapers, thought leadership articles, webinars, and other research-based content, making it available to target markets. Email newsletters, blog posts, and infographics are also used to provide value to potential and existing customers. This groundwork leads to sales calls and demos, forming the essence of effective B2B digital marketing today.

The process can be illustrated in Fig. 33.2.

Surrounding this process are various software solutions requiring new skills, including search engine optimization, data analysis, big data, data mining, user experience design, and cybersecurity. These topics are discussed in separate chapters.

Understanding who is interested in our content and what they are looking for is crucial. To gather this information, we ask users for contact details and their interests before giving them access to valuable information like whitepapers. Knowing the "who" and "what" helps us understand the "why," making it easier to deliver the best-suited products and identify opportunities for upselling and cross-selling.

Throughout the process, the focus should be on demonstrating knowledge and value, not on aggressive sales tactics. Buyers are sensitive to pushy behavior and value their privacy. Thus, we use call-back requests and live chat functions to engage with potential customers.

Box 33.1 Contact Forms or Email Addresses?

Contact forms are preferred by sellers as they streamline the process and allow for targeted responses. However, users often find them cumbersome and prefer email for its ease of use and recordkeeping. Despite the potential for spam, providing an email address can improve customer satisfaction, unless offering something like a whitepaper or webinar sign-up.

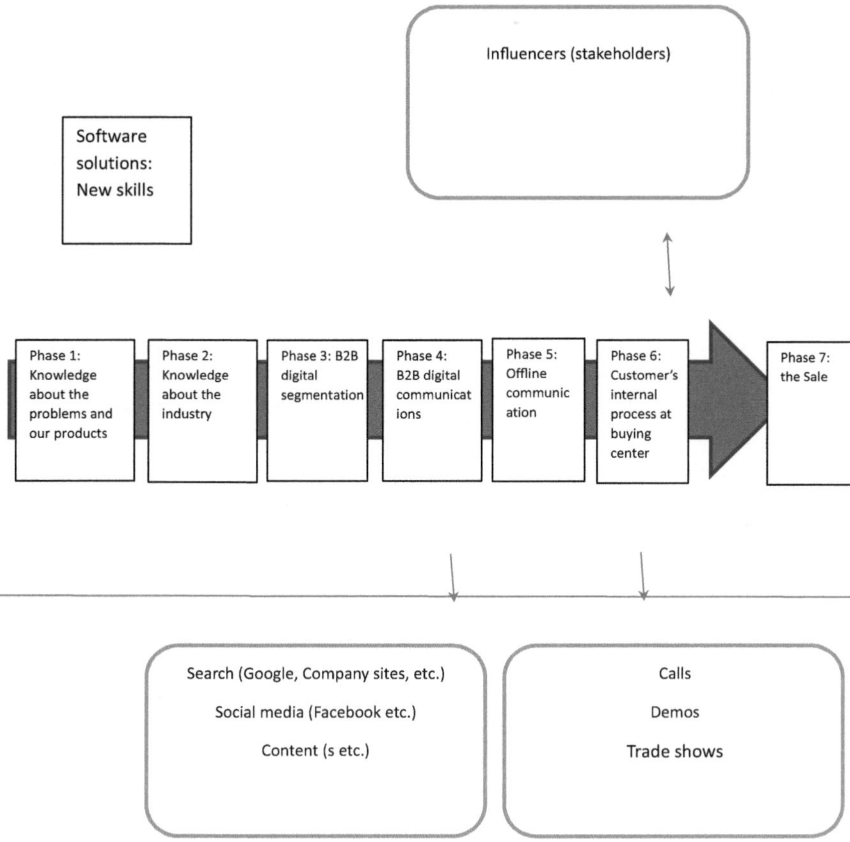

Fig. 33.2 An overview of B2B digital marketing

33.5 B2B Digital Content Marketing

A significant portion of B2B marketers in North America have established dedicated content marketing groups within their organizations. Although B2B marketers have used Internet applications for over two decades, the adoption of B2B digital marketing was initially slow. American companies have traditionally led in social media B2B marketing, positioning themselves as "thought leaders" and building relationships with all stakeholders. However, in recent years, European and Asian companies have been catching up.

B2B digital content marketing involves creating, distributing, and sharing relevant, valuable, and timely content to aid customers in their purchasing process. This builds a relationship based on trust, which is a function of knowledge and quality, not just cost.

Content marketing consists of various messages or meanings. The content can be in the form of text (reviews, chats, link pages, case studies, client testimonials, Q&As (soon to be replaced by AI), newsletters, white papers, articles, e-books, tweets, quizzes, polls, news releases, PR announcements), images (infographics, photos, cartoons, maps), videos (memes, interviews, vlogs), and audio (podcasts) in different forms and combinations (slide-shares, online games, social media postings, webinars, QR codes, Wikis). The content vehicle refers to specific services used, such as X (former Twitter) or Facebook. The channel is more general and refers to where the product is marketed, such as to the producer, wholesaler, retailer, or customer. It includes people, activities, and organizations and is also known as the distribution channel, corresponding to the term place in marketing. In digital marketing, this can be a platform, which sometimes also refers to an interface serving as the base for various media and vehicles, including social media, display ads, websites, mobile, and search. The terms channel and media are often used interchangeably in the literature. A marketing vehicle is a specific tool for delivering a message to a target audience, and for each medium, there are several vehicles.

The purpose of good content is to draw traffic to a website. To achieve this, we must perform Search Engine Optimization (SEO), ensuring the site appears high on search engine results. Good SEO results from understanding how major search engines like Google, Bing, and Baidu rank information based on user utility. These companies provide guidelines for advertisers on how to succeed in this process (good SEO) but discourage manipulation of the system (bad or black hat SEO).

Content marketing is central to B2B digital. Along with SEO, it is considered one of the most important tools in digital marketing. From a marketing perspective, content marketing involves anticipating and meeting an existing customer's need for information. It requires marketers to think about the type of content they want to use, whether in e-magazines, blog texts, social media posts, webinars, pictures, videos, animations, e-books, white papers, podcasts, or infographics. From a company perspective, creating content involves deciding what to say, to whom, and where. In B2B digital, the focus is not primarily on selling the product but on providing valuable information related to the industry.

B2B remains about building relationships, but the methods have changed. Online, new actors such as community moderators and social media influencers play a role. In traditional or offline marketing, the audience is mostly passive. In digital marketing, the audience is active, engaging in social media, giving reviews, and discussing products on blogs. Buyers prefer to read customer reviews over glossy brochures as they are perceived to have higher integrity. They critically assess reviews, analyzing variables such as the number of reviews and their timing. Photos uploaded by customers are also scrutinized for authenticity.

33.5.1 User-Generated Content and User-Created Content

Much of the content delivered by sellers is dynamic, allowing others to change it either directly (as with a wiki) or indirectly (by adding comments). This can be risky for the seller if the content receives heavy criticism or is manipulated by trolls. Removing altered content can lead to a larger wave of protests. The audience has become part of the content production process, often referred to as user-generated content (UGC) or user-created content (UCC). UGC includes any form of content posted online and may or may not be controlled by a gatekeeper like a web moderator.

The OECD defines three requirements for text to be considered UGC: it must be published on the web (publication requirement), collaborators must add value to the content (creative effort), and it should be created outside professional routines and practices.

Control over content creation is a major concern for companies as a single post can cause significant negative publicity. Removing a post can be difficult and may worsen the situation if recorded by the community. The Internet reflects society's diverse groups and ideas, governed by a spirit of fairness, honesty, and democracy among experienced users. These users, when united, can quickly damage a company's reputation and operations online. Security and damage control are crucial in both B2C and B2B marketing.

33.5.2 What Content and in Which Form?

Research suggests that companies should tell their stories rather than just list products and key selling points. The story should be unique to distinguish it from others and strengthen the brand. However, ensuring the content is relevant and valuable to the customer is essential. Companies should understand the information buyers seek about their business or industry. This might include industry trends, best practices, roles of various actors, and solutions to common business challenges.

Companies must balance using their existing competencies and acquiring new knowledge to address these information needs. This approach represents a shift from the traditional focus on what companies want to tell buyers to address what buyers want to know. Early research showed that empathy was crucial in selling, but sales meetings often focused on targets rather than developing personal traits like empathy in personnel. In B2C, push techniques might target "Phools," customers who may be tricked into purchasing a product, but such customers are rare in B2B.

Many B2B buyers have end-users or consumers at the end of their value chain. If a company's customers are B2C companies, this requires broader industry knowledge. Companies must address issues across the entire value chain, from raw materials to recycling. In the next part, we will define the different types of users present in the value chain.

33.6 Users of B2B Digital

It is beneficial to distinguish between different types of users for marketing purposes, as they have varying objectives and behaviors. Social media users can be divided into six groups: creators, critics, collectors, joiners, spectators, and inactives.

These are summarized in Table 33.2 below.

Table 33.2 Users of social media

#	User type	Behavior
1	Creators	Add new content
2	Critics	React to content
3	Collectors	Organize content and/or reactions
4	Joiners	Are registered but do not visit content often
5	Spectators	Are registered and visit content often
6	Inactives	Are registered but never visit the content

Creators can be subdivided based on their profile, expertise, and the frequency of their contributions. Critics range from experts (less biased) to trolls (highly biased). Collectors can be anyone from users sharing links to researchers analyzing postings and reactions for campaigns. The remaining categories depend on activity levels: joiners, spectators, and inactives.

A decade ago, there were many newbies, but they have largely disappeared in the Western world and much of Asia. Other models include lurkers, who surf around mostly out of curiosity or looking for deals. Lead members often feel ownership of social media, forums, or hashtags and act protectively.

In B2B, users can be corporate or noncorporate and can include any class of stakeholders relevant to the industry, such as government users, employees, customers, suppliers, creditors, communities, trade unions, owners, and investors. Understanding the content and users helps define B2B digital strategies and plans for conducting B2B digital marketing, which involves making a series of decisions and alternatives.

33.7 B2B Digital Strategies

Companies need strategies to show the direction for gaining a competitive advantage and to track their progress. A company without a strategy is like a sailing boat without a keel; it moves unpredictably and risks capsizing. Ignoring a digital strategy risks the company being overtaken by others. Back in 2017, many companies realized that future growth would be online. For instance, H&M lacked a digital strategy, causing its stock to fall substantially, whereas IKEA adapted quickly by hiring employees with digital skills.

There are two primary B2B models: vertical and horizontal. In a classic vertical B2B model, relationships are built within the same industry, either upstream or downstream. In a horizontal B2B model, companies from various industries do business with each other, also either upstream or downstream.

Relationships between companies may involve intermediaries. Research shows that in many cases, buyers from large companies rely on advisors, consultants, or colleagues to identify and evaluate suppliers. This implies that marketing efforts might be directed towards facilitators rather than directly to customer companies.

There are three B2B models based on the strength of the relationship between suppliers and buyers: manufacturing-driven businesses (supplier-oriented), buyer-oriented businesses, and intermediary models where the power balance is more equal. These models apply to the online world as well.

B2B relationships are often organized in hubs or networks, either vertically within a specific industry or horizontally along a business process. The success of vertical hubs depends on factors such as fragmentation among buyers and suppliers, inefficiencies in the supply chain, critical mass of key players, domain knowledge, creating master catalogs, and adjacent vertical markets. Horizontal hubs succeed based on process standardization, process knowledge, workflow automation, deep content integration, and customization to industry-specific differences.

Today, business software often matches companies automatically based on criteria of interest and industry. Barter models match parties with reciprocal assets to minimize currency risk.

33.7.1 Choosing Engagement Strategies

Digital strategies related to social media involve who can share what and where within the organization. Engagement strategies can be categorized as shown in the Table 33.3 below.

In a top-down strategy, stricter control is either preferred or left to certain management members to decide in communication. These individuals have the competence and trust of top management. In a bottom-up strategy, staff are either given direction and rules for how to contribute or are freely allowed to contribute using their judgment.

The effectiveness of these strategies depends on the employees' competencies and the competitive environment, varying from one organization to another. Organizations with educated personnel may empower staff, while those with diverse educational backgrounds may prefer tighter control. Companies with trade secrets and in competitive environments might limit online communication to a few designated personnel. Without an engagement strategy, organizations risk miscommunication, inconsistencies, media scandals, and loss of customers.

Table 33.3 Engagement strategies

	Top-down	Bottom-up
Tighter control	Strict rules for who says what and when	Everyone should know how to contribute
Empowerment of staff	Trusting in management to contribute	Everyone can contribute

33.7.2 Choosing Pricing Strategies

Another strategic decision involves pricing content on the Internet. Generally, there are four pricing strategies: exchange for personal information, item-based pricing, subscriptions, and contracts/licenses.

In exchange for personal information, digital content is often free or available in return for the visitor's contact information. Additional questions about the user's needs or how they found the content may be asked. This information helps improve marketing efforts. Item-based pricing is used for elaborate and expensive whitepapers, which might be sold at a price with a discount for personal information. Coupons may also be used based on previous engagements or targeting specific buyer segments. Subscriptions apply to regular information like newsletters or reports. Contracts and licenses are used for access to large datasets or software, such as libraries forming consortia for journal access. Different bundling techniques from publishers offer opportunities for upselling.

33.7.3 Choosing the Purpose of the Content

Creating valuable and timely content to help customers in their purchasing process can be divided into four main types: educating content, persuading content, converting content, and entertaining content (the latter being more common in B2C but also present in B2B).

When we want to entertain, we send messages with a strong emotional appeal to make them more shareable. Educating content is intended for a wider audience, particularly those who may not yet be familiar with our products or services. This content must also be shareable and packaged in a format that facilitates sharing. For example, when sharing text on Facebook, it is better to include an image and a link to the full information.

Persuading content uses emotional appeals to gradually change the buyer's mind. Converting content is more rational, focusing on facts and data. Generally, B2B content is more rational, but nuances exist depending on the organization and the audience (e.g., technical vs. nontechnical personnel) and the platform used. Different strategies might be employed at various stages of the purchasing process, starting with emotional content to raise awareness and moving towards rational content as potential customers inquire about our offerings. After purchase, it might be beneficial to revert to emotional messages, such as thank you notes, before starting the process again. This planning can be organized in a spreadsheet for all products and services, highlighting the complexity of choosing the purpose of each message before forming the actual messages and selecting vehicles. The formation of content should be based on a knowledge gap analysis.

33.7.4 Identifying the Customer's Knowledge Gap

Identifying the customer's knowledge gaps involves understanding what the customer wants and needs to know. Often, the customer knows what they want to know and will ask for it (solicited knowledge), but sometimes they do not know what they need and therefore do not ask (unsolicited knowledge). Sometimes, customers are unaware of their need for certain information until it is presented to them.

Solicited knowledge typically involves information the customer actively seeks, tracked through web analytics or direct inquiries. Unsolicited knowledge is what we think the customer needs to know, deduced by understanding the company's activities and comparing them to industry trends. Although some assumptions are made, even minor inaccuracies are generally acceptable as long as the information is not excessive or spam-like.

Combining solicited and unsolicited knowledge forms the customer's knowledge gap. The larger the gap, the greater the opportunity to add value. In B2B, where potential customers are often highly knowledgeable, there is increased pressure to perform well.

Some might argue that having a good product at a good price is sufficient. While this might be true in exceptional cases, even the best products need to be well-presented online to be found by potential buyers. An outdated website can create a negative impression, suggesting that the company and its products are also outdated. Trust in the Internet is built by demonstrating mastery of current technology and design.

Knowledge gaps can be categorized into four main types: gaps about products, services, the industry, and the competitive environment and external factors. Companies often seek information about their competitors, but sharing such information can be sensitive if the competitor is also a customer.

33.7.5 Who Should Form and Communicate the Content

The person responsible for forming and communicating content significantly influences the message and its reception. There are three basic strategies involving different combinations of content producers (who create the messages) and content presenters (who deliver the messages). Serious companies prefer knowledgeable personnel, whether in-house or external, to create content. Communicating the messages can be done by the same knowledgeable person, an available staff member, or a hired celebrity spokesperson. Table 33.4 below summarizes these options.

The cost of the communicator often depends on the importance of the message. The most knowledgeable person might be too expensive or unsuitable for other reasons, such as being introverted or needed elsewhere in the organization.

Companies often collaborate with well-known externals, such as authors, celebrities, or authorities, to attract more attention and engagement. Celebrity branding or endorsement uses social status to promote a product. In B2B, customer referencing (testimonials) is common when buyers seek peer advice on high-value products

Table 33.4 Content producers and presenters

Production of content	Communication of messages	Cost
Knowledgeable personnel	Celebrity spokesperson	High
Knowledgeable personnel	Knowledgeable personnel	Medium
Knowledgeable personnel	Available personnel	Low

and services. Customer Reference Programs (CRPs) streamline finding suitable customer references and make the sales process more effective.

While B2C practices in celebrity endorsement cannot be directly copied, they can be adapted for B2B. Influencers in B2B are recognized for their industry knowledge rather than entertaining content. B2B influencers often stay relevant longer but face high pressure, leading to burnout. Marketing influencers are highly paid communication tools whose careers typically last a few years.

Studies suggest that celebrity endorsement generates more attention, desire, and action than online customer reviews. However, reviews are better remembered, and consumers are more likely to search for products and share attitudes from reviews. Future strategies will likely combine celebrity endorsements and reviews based on the company's marketing goals.

33.7.6 Other Strategies for B2B

Numerous strategic decisions are relevant for B2B digital marketing. Content timing is crucial and depends on when users visit different platforms. For instance, posting a link to a whitepaper on LinkedIn should consider office hours and avoid busy times like Mondays or Fridays. Time zones must also be considered to reach international customers. Content timing involves deciding when to publish, considering events like trade shows or product launches, and how often to send reminders.

Other strategic choices include the amount of content published, the degree of controversy (high controversy attracts attention but is risky), consistency of content (striving for high consistency), and choice of words (using less-selling language).

Building trust is a key B2B strategy. Trust is earned over time through consistent behavior and frequent publication of valuable material, such as market research, reports, case studies, whitepapers, and e-books. This helps build long-term relationships and credibility with customers.

In the next part, we will discuss different media or vehicles in more detail as examples of marketing media.

33.8 B2B Digital Media and Vehicles

In this section, we focus on different types of content (media) and the actual platforms where content can be published (vehicles). We will not cover all media and vehicles, and it should be remembered that they are constantly evolving. Examples of media include whitepapers, webinars, and vlogs. Vehicles include Gmail, Facebook, X (former Twitter), and LinkedIn.

Both media and vehicles can be used in collaborative forms, allowing for questions and comments. For example, a whitepaper can be uploaded to a forum where comments are possible, while a vlog is often sent out as a single, ready-made file with no opportunity for collaboration but with the possibility to contact the creator. One advantage of noncollaborative formats is that files can be smaller and easier to share, potentially reaching a larger audience. Webinars are often targeted at a smaller audience, while vlogs are more often used as marketing tools for a broader audience. The type of media used depends largely on the target audience and platform.

In B2C, companies seek publishers (YouTube stars and influencers) with millions of subscribers to promote their products. In B2B, the focus is more on content and thought leadership than on mass distribution. Bloggers who engage in brand partnership deals are more relevant than large-scale influencers. B2B influencers need to stay relevant for longer periods and avoid scandals, which often attract attention in B2C. In B2B, gaining attention involves saying something insightful and demonstrating knowledge in an engaging and pleasant manner.

The B2B audience consists of executives seeking new business ideas or understanding their peers' perspectives. They are not necessarily looking for one correct answer but want to see arguments for different positions due to the complexity of topics. They are not looking to buy immediately and will leave a site if they sense overt marketing unless it is very subtle. The underlying contract is to provide valuable content in exchange for the executive's time, eventually leading to trust through repeated valuable interactions.

Knowledge is becoming more important in B2B marketing, but companies have less time to become knowledgeable. Marketers now have less time for research, and buyers have less time to read about potential purchases, shifting towards mobile-friendly formats and interactive content. This does not mean abandoning text for video entirely, but there is a trend towards shorter presentations. Buyers seek more case studies to benchmark their experiences against others, and they value influencer content, peer reviews, third-party publications, and user-generated feedback.

Executives need to understand that content marketing is not just another campaign but a shift in mentality and culture. Companies now find themselves in both their primary industry and the publishing business, needing to produce their own knowledge rather than just distributing others' content. Producing knowledge does not necessarily mean conducting primary research, but companies should still aim to provide valuable, original insights.

Digital marketing allows for effective measurement of marketing activities, from counting "likes" to analyzing customer reviews. This helps in adjusting marketing efforts that do not lead to more sales. Customer responses can be translated into degrees of appreciation, allowing companies to gauge the effectiveness of their marketing activities. Table 33.5 illustrates what is here called measuring expected responses to a survey report:

"Likes" are akin to a thank you, while user registration indicates the expectation of valuable content. Selling a report signifies a high degree of expected appreciation. Measuring actual appreciation requires analyzing customer feedback and reviewing post-publication actions.

33.8.1 Email Marketing

Email marketing is often considered spam, but when used correctly, it is an effective way of delivering good content, surpassing social media, company websites, and blogs. The key is proper market targeting, identifying, and sending emails only to those who will appreciate them. Poorly targeted emails not only miss the mark but also annoy potential future customers.

Spam results from bulk emails, whereas opt-in emails are more targeted. The real issue is that most users find solicited emails irrelevant. Companies often bypass spam filters and make it hard to unsubscribe, further irritating users. It is crucial to empathize with the receiver and test campaigns from their perspective before sending.

Effective email marketing involves producing valuable content, maintaining professional design, and avoiding hyperbolic language or push marketing. Developing a quality subscriber list and encouraging interaction helps improve content. Unsubscribing should be easy, and the initial email should show how to do it. Limit the number of emails sent and analyze the results using web analytics. Tools like Google Analytics can track how each email drives traffic to the landing site and monitor visitor behavior.

A chat function on the website can help if visitors have questions or need assistance. It should be properly staffed with competent personnel to be effective. Chatbots are also used, but they must be advanced enough to understand and respond accurately to avoid frustrating users.

Most people dislike no-reply emails and bounced emails. GDPR regulations require companies to make it easy for users to contact them and ask for data deletion. Immediate contact through chat functions can be a good solution if reply emails are not feasible.

Table 33.5 Measuring expected responses to a survey report

Response types	Equivalent to	Appreciation
Likes, retweets, comments	"Thank you."	Low
User registration	Leave contact information (except sales calls)	Medium
Selling the report (e-com)	Pay for it	High

Email marketing often includes text content directly in the email, attachments, or links to downloadable files. The most common content is a report or a whitepaper.

33.8.2 The Whitepaper

A whitepaper is an authoritative report designed to fill a knowledge gap, helping potential and existing customers understand complex issues and demonstrating industry knowledge. Whitepapers are often problem-oriented, as readers seek solutions or support for decision-making.

Originally, whitepapers were British government documents outlining policies before legislation. In business, they are well-founded documents that help solve or clarify issues, known as gray literature. Good whitepapers are educational rather than promotional and should be tailored to the audience. Consider writing multiple versions for different stakeholders.

Attention must be captured quickly, showing mastery of the subject. Good graphics enhance content, and professional authors can improve quality. Subtlety is key; overt advertising within the paper can undermine its effectiveness.

Once completed, whitepapers can be uploaded to the website, emailed to prospects, posted on social media, and shared in industry portals. They can be sent to the media with a press release, broken into smaller pieces for teasers, and cited in articles for trade journals. Physical copies can be printed for conferences and trade shows, and they can also be used for internal training.

Whitepapers pair well with other media, such as web conferences, offering a rational and personal tone combination. Webinars can discuss whitepaper content, creating multiple touchpoints with the customer.

33.8.3 Web Conferencing and Webinars

Web conferencing includes various online collaborative services like webinars, webcasts, and peer-level web meetings. Definitions vary as technologies evolve. A webinar is a type of web conference akin to an online seminar, usually lasting 30–60 min.

Companies use webinars for education, product demonstrations, and gathering customer information for marketing research. Webinars attract potential customers by addressing hot topics, creating an engaging and less demanding alternative to reading whitepapers. Combining webinars and whitepapers creates numerous touchpoints with customers.

Touchpoints are well understood in marketing. Meeting potential customers at different junctions creates the impression of a significant, serious supplier. Webinars offer a low-barrier first contact, which can be followed by physical meetings at conferences, creating a full circle of interaction. Successful webinars feature attractive visuals, minimal text, and positive, energetic voices. The best times for webinars are mid-week, avoiding busy Mondays and winding down Fridays. While video is more entertaining, the focus should be on delivering valuable content.

Webinars allow customers to learn about products, trends, and industry topics, showcasing the company's expertise. A poorly executed webinar can harm reputation, so content should be tested and edited before release.

Webinars differ from vlogs in that they target a smaller, more private audience, whereas vlogs aim for wider dissemination.

33.8.4 Vlogs

A video blog or video log (vlog) is, as the name suggests, a blog where the medium is video and sound. It is often spread via a link and watched as a form of video television on the Internet. Much of this material ends up on YouTube, where it is easily accessible and gets both faster and larger spread. A major difference between a webinar and a vlog is that the latter tends to be more noncollaborative. A vlog is often shorter and more entertaining, though differences sometimes blur.

There are personal vlogs and corporate vlogs. YouTube previously ran live-broadcasting vlogs called YouTube Live, which have now been replaced by a live-streaming service called the YouTube Live section. The service makes no distinction between vlogs and seminars. Live-streaming gives the impression of immediacy and can be variously collaborative, such as by inviting Skype calls and tweets into the broadcast. This helps turn vlogs or webinars into popular events.

Skype, an example of IP telephony (Voice over Internet Protocol), transfers voice communications and multimedia sessions over the Internet. When transferred via the public switched telephone network (PSTN), it is referred to as videotelephony. Both technologies are used for video podcasts (vodcasts), ranging from low-budget video clips to big-production web television series.

Other forms of video and audio logs also exist, including the more traditional audio podcast, discussed next. One special form of vlogs is vlogumentaries, which are documentaries created by combining several vlogs.

33.8.5 Podcasts

A podcast is an audio recording that can be downloaded on a computer or mobile application. Individual programs or pods are used for broadcasting longer content on any Internet-connected device. Pods are often made for people on the go and are excellent for commuters. They are powerful for B2B, as they present an opportunity to engage a manager for half an hour before work distractions begin. The average length of a pod is over 45 min. In B2B, pods are better for longer lectures, as opposed to shorter and more entertaining vlogs or webinars. In style and tone, they are like a good radio program, informative but entertaining. With mobile screens and widespread broadband, pods are great for listening in cars or on bikes, where visual attention is needed elsewhere.

Podcasts hold the audience's attention for longer periods and encourage regular returns, like a series of lectures.

33.8.6 Photoblog (Photolog)

Another alternative to video or audio media is sharing photos on platforms like Instagram, WordPress, or Pinterest. With better digital cameras on mobile phones and direct photo uploads, the popularity of photos has increased. The real-time quality of this medium has made it particularly popular at trade shows and other events where potential customers want to see what is happening immediately. Blogs, in general, are also good for SEO, as Google values their contribution to good content.

Photoblogs should tell a story and share a journey, requiring consistency in visual language and message. Photos must be aesthetic and coherent, with a clear purpose and perspective. Good portraits or close-ups have significant value. Visitors to our booth may want access to copies of their photos, which they can use in their work, creating valuable content if we succeed in taking better photos than they have of themselves.

33.8.7 Social Media Marketing

Businesses once avoided social media, but today, they use platforms like Facebook and Messenger to communicate with other businesses and customers. They follow influencers on X (former Twitter) and search for competitors on LinkedIn.

Examples of popular social media sites include Google+, Facebook, X (former Twitter), QZone, Instagram, Weibo, Habbo, VK, Tumblr, LinkedIn, Renren, Bebo, and hi5. While LinkedIn is most popular in B2B, marketers use services like Facebook, X (former Twitter), Google+, YouTube, and Pinterest.

The choice of social media services depends on the location and preferences of the target audience. For example, Hi5 is popular in Latin America, while Weibo is popular in China. Companies must evaluate the cost and customer preferences in their target locations to choose the most effective social media platform.

Social media sites can quickly lose popularity. Myspace, for example, was the most popular site from 2005 to 2009 but has since fallen significantly in ranking. Vine, a video-sharing platform, shut down in 2017, with companies now experimenting with longer video formats. Instagram has increased video lengths to up to 10 min in multi-video posts. As of 2024, the most popular social media platforms include Facebook, with over 3 billion users; YouTube, with 2.5 billion users; and Instagram, with 2 billion users. Platforms like BeReal have also seen significant growth, though their long-term sustainability remains uncertain.

B2B digital content marketing delivers value through information. This "publishing approach" to marketing engages and builds trust, allowing users to co-produce content. The web is a pull marketing environment where companies attract customers through search engine optimization and social media. Inbound marketing views customers as partners or co-creators of value, shifting from selling to helping customers.

A model for implementing social media in B2B marketing identifies coordination as a major issue. Companies must avoid dilution of brand, double work, inefficiencies, and inconsistencies. Achieving a balance between engagement and maintaining functional positioning requires careful management.

Most B2B websites focus on the company, products, and services, which are neither educational nor entertaining. Companies aim to build trusted authority through content marketing. Customers expect educational or entertaining content, which may not directly relate to the product being sold. Key elements for creating trust include shared values, interdependence, quality communication, and nonopportunistic behavior.

In digital marketing, various forms of customer feedback are used daily. On X (former Twitter), users can comment, retweet, like, or send messages. On Facebook, reactions include love, haha, wow, sad, and angry, with each emotion represented by an emoticon. Interpreting these reactions accurately requires understanding the context.

33.8.7.1 Facebook

Facebook (FB) is of interest to marketers due to its massive Internet traffic. It is where people are now, although its popularity may have peaked. Some believe FB will remain dominant, while others point to its declining popularity among teenagers and young adults.

According to Statista, as of 2024, Facebook has approximately 3 billion monthly active users, with around 2 billion users accessing the platform daily. Of these daily users, 56.8% are male, and 43.2% are female. Users primarily access Facebook through mobile devices, with 68.7% using only smartphones to log in.

A recent study revealed that Americans check their phones on average every 12 min, amounting to about 80 times per day. Millennials check their phones even more frequently, averaging 150 times per day. Direct calls are often not appreciated unless a relationship is established, so companies are advised to engage customers through mobile applications instead.

Many companies use Facebook Messenger for customer contacts and set up private groups for specific topics. Some smaller businesses rely entirely on FB, finding it easier to manage and free.

Research shows that the best strategy for companies on FB is to focus on delivering quality and value rather than quantity of information. Proper handling of criticism on FB can enhance credibility while ignoring or mishandling it can damage reputation. Shutting down the company page during overwhelming negative reactions can be a temporary solution.

To optimize FB use in marketing, companies should create a profile consistent with their overall design and messages. Involvement and up-to-date information are crucial. Combining LinkedIn, X (former Twitter), and FB can broaden social media engagement. Photos and status updates should have clear purposes and be well thought out. Negative comments should be taken seriously.

33.8.7.2 LinkedIn

LinkedIn is considered the most important social media for B2B, despite lower average user engagement compared to other platforms. LinkedIn generates higher visitor-to-lead conversion rates than X (former Twitter) and Facebook, and it attracts professionals, making it ideal for business hours.

LinkedIn allows targeted advertising campaigns by location, industry, profession, and position. While some criticize LinkedIn for low engagement and inauthentic connections, it remains valuable for building contacts and providing information.

33.8.7.3 X (Former Twitter)

X functions like a modern newswire, allowing users to send small messages (tweets), forward others' tweets (retweets), follow users, and like tweets. It is useful for spreading information quickly but can be dangerous if tweets are not carefully considered. Retweets, comments, and likes help gauge tweet effectiveness.

For B2B, tweets often summarize longer texts with links. Companies use X to communicate with a targeted audience, sharing ideas and updates. While many tweets go unnoticed, entertaining, educational, and transparent content tends to gain more attention.

33.8.7.4 Other Social Networking Sites

Other social networking sites include regional platforms like Hi5 in Latin America and Weibo in China. These platforms offer unique advantages and should be explored for their ability to generate Internet traffic and attract target audiences.

In digital B2B, the focus is on using social media sites for their marketing potential rather than adhering to specific platforms. Next, we will discuss the use of exchanges in B2B digital marketing.

33.9 B2B Digital Exchanges

Digital marketing platforms consist of digital marketing media and digital marketing exchanges. These are platforms where customers and suppliers come together to make or facilitate transactions. Just like in social media marketing, marketing exchanges are part of what we call marketing automation. These are software platforms and technologies designed to effectively market on multiple channels online and automate repetitive tasks. Digital marketing exchanges use electronic data interchange (EDI), developed in the 1960s and 1970s, to share information with suppliers by soft orders.

To meet customer requirements, companies tend to align all their channels in a synchronized operating model, sometimes called omnichannel retailing. EDI systems, as well as electronic point of sale (EPOS) systems, provide valuable historical data to make quick, cooperative operations in an omnichannel retailing strategy. EDI is used worldwide despite its risks. Electronic data exchange can lead to greater interdependence and unexpected collaborations, like when competing airlines join reservation hubs to fend off rivals in other industries.

EDI has been introduced globally, coming to China in the 1990s. Today, up to 95% of the top 500 enterprises worldwide use EDI technology to process trade and business documents with their partners, rebuilding business models and management modes accordingly. EDI has become the dominant mode of international trade in developed countries and will become essential for entering the international market, much like containers and bar codes were previously. It is already becoming a network, an information society, and a paperless society, with continuous spread.

33.9.1 Display Advertising

The most common transaction in B2B is display advertising, which involves advertising on websites, apps, or social media through banners or other ad formats. Companies looking to place an ad on the Internet have three main options: direct ad placements by contacting publishers, indirect ad placement through advertising networks like Infolinks, Revenue Hits, and Adblade, or automated ad placement through Ad Exchanges, similar to a stock market where buyers and sellers meet. Examples of Ad Exchanges are DoubleClick (Google), OpenX, and AppNexus. To place ads, users need a demand-side platform (DSP), software that allows buyers of digital advertising inventory to manage multiple ad exchanges and data exchange accounts through one interface. This enables sophisticated segmentation and target marketing. Examples are Adobe Media Optimizer, Adform, and Google Marketing Platform. On the supply side, advertisers need a platform to manage their advertising space inventory, fill it with ads, and receive revenue, known as the sell-side platform (SSP).

Contracts on ad exchanges are made through real-time bidding (RTB), where advertising inventory is bought and sold on a per-impression basis within milliseconds.

To help companies combine all their market data, data management platforms (DMPs) are used for collecting and managing data, mainly for digital marketing purposes. DMPs organize and activate first-, second-, and third-party audience data from various sources, making cross-channel marketing easier. A company's data often exists in silos like CRM databases, call center data, online site behavior, or points of sale (POS). These are referred to as first party data. Other silos contain data from partner organizations (second party data) and from external sources like market data companies (third party data). Effective DMPs combine all three, using Big Data and artificial intelligence algorithms to process these large data sets.

Advertising servers (ad servers) are similar to DMPs but on the supply side. They centrally manage and run online advertising campaigns, handling creatives generated by art directors, creative directors, and copywriters in advertising agencies. Examples of ad servers are Adzerk, DoubleClick for Publishers (DFP), and OpenX Ad Server.

An ad server can also be seen as an ad exchange, facilitating the buying and selling of media advertising inventory from multiple ad networks where prices are determined through a system of bids.

Demand side platforms (DSPs) are automated software used by advertisers to purchase digital advertising space in real time. These platforms enable advertisers to manage and optimize ad campaigns across multiple exchanges, ensuring ads are placed in front of the right audience. DSPs Use data to make informed decisions on ad placements, allowing for more precise targeting and efficient spending. This technology streamlines the ad-buying process, making it more effective and cost-efficient compared to traditional methods.

33.9.2 Auction and Exchange Models

B2B digital markets employ various market mechanisms, either fixed-price models like purchasing from a catalog or dynamic pricing models like auctions, exchanges, or barter systems. The fixed-price model works best in markets where buyers and sellers are fragmented, often purchasing small amounts. This model is ideal where most purchasing occurs with prequalified suppliers and predefined business rules, where demand is predictable, and prices do not fluctuate frequently.

Auction models create value by matching buyers and sellers using specially designed software, primarily through the Internet. This model works best in markets where the perception of value varies greatly, such as capital equipment, used products/antiquities, unsalable returned products, and hard-to-find products.

Exchange models are built on real-time bid-ask matching processes, market-wide price determination, and settlement and clearing mechanisms. Leading B2B exchanges include Amazon Business, Alibaba, ThomasNet.com, EC21, Joor, and IndiaMart.

33.9.3 Types of Marketplaces

There are three types of e-marketplaces: vertical marketplaces around specific industry sectors, horizontal marketplaces around products and services that cut across several industries, and marketplaces focused on different functions.

At the turn of the century, there were many exchanges for B2B, but since then, rapid consolidation in the industry has eliminated many vendors. The first wave disappeared with the dot com bubble in 2000–2002. Digital markets held great promise because B2B customers faced enormous organizational costs for procurement, purchasing, and inventory maintenance. Online systems that could reduce these costs and improve efficiencies were highly anticipated.

However, most companies struggle more with getting the right product delivered at the right time than with searching for many suppliers. This problem was solved by better logistics, which developed in the 1990s. Today, private exchanges are more stable, with safer proprietary information and optimized logistical arrangements. Companies are more concerned about controlling their entire supply chain than saving a few extra dollars on purchasing.

Many entrants overestimated the importance of zero marginal costs and underestimated the need for a critical mass of vendors and buyers. Now, each industry has one or two large public exchanges. Although the digital part did not initially work for banks, there has been rapid progress in the B2B banking sector. Improvements in payment and checkout functions, ease of registration, and shipping options are seen almost weekly. When old banks cannot adapt to the new digital environment, new actors like PayPal and Klarna emerge. The competitive environment is rapidly evolving, with improvements in one exchange leading to changes in the next as buyers can change suppliers in minutes, and all are trying to learn from customer feedback.

33.9.4 Trading Models for B2B Digital Exchanges

There are four types of B2B exchanges:

1. *Catalog aggregators*: These must be neutral, independent sites operated by a third party to bring many competing sellers together and earn buyers' trust in the site's information.
2. *Post and browse*: This is like a private members' room, creating a virtual community where people interested in buying or selling a particular product connect through a web-based bulletin board.
3. *Auction markets*: These allow multiple buyers and sellers to collectively set prices for a wide range of products and services, representing a departure from the fixed-price model.
4. *Continuous auto-execution systems*: These work only for standardized products with high liquidity.

33.9.5 Enterprise Resource Planning (ERP) for B2B Digital

Enterprise resource planning (ERP) is the integrated management of core business processes, often in real-time, mediated by software and technology. Integrated e-commerce is often acknowledged by the supplier of the back-end system, such as SAP ERP or Microsoft Dynamics. While many B2B e-commerce suppliers claim to be integrated, most web stores are interfaced. With integrated e-commerce, the software solution is installed on top of the back-end system, manually setting up the connection between business logic and the back-end database.

33.9.6 Marketing Automation

Marketing automation is defined as software designed to automate marketing actions. It has become more popular as marketing departments seek to automate repetitive tasks such as emails, social media, and website actions.

However, there are negative effects when organizations view marketing automation as a quick fix to their challenges. Instead of generating good leads themselves, companies often buy lists of email addresses or ready-made reports, giving a false sense of security. Marketing automation should be used to increase effectiveness, not as a shortcut.

Content marketing should be highly specialized. For most companies, it is a way to save time and be more effective in pushing communication with customers. No-reply emails and slow responses indicate a lack of real dialog. Customer support is a balance between service cost and market credibility.

Table 33.6 shows common forms of marketing automation B2B.

Marketing automation works in B2B but requires more care and special attention than in B2C. Success is measured through bibliometrics, analyzing visitor numbers, site visits, and conversion rates.

When setting up complex automation processes, it is crucial to test them from the customer interface. Small errors can lead to no sales, such as a nonfunctioning coupon code or address input issue. Companies often discover these mistakes too late, resulting in lost sales. Continuous testing is essential.

Marketing automation addresses the issue that most sales leads are never contacted. Sales in B2B follow similar sales funnel frameworks as in B2C, moving from suspects (potential buyers), to prospects/leads (interested and qualified buyers), to customers/deals. Marketing automation solves the problem of long

Table 33.6 Ten examples of marketing automation in B2B

#	B2B	B2C	Explanation
1	Welcome programs		The welcome email sent after registration
2	Repurchase programs		Gathering customer feedback and up- and cross-selling options. Gives the customer an opportunity to leave a review, share a photo, or purchase suggestions
3		Reminder programs	A reminder to people who didn't click on our first email, possibly with an extra offer
4		Multichannel programs	Reaching the customer through different channels without being perceived as spam
5		Winback programs/	Trying to get back a customer who has been inactive, perhaps by reminding them of items left in the basket or making special offers
		Retargeting programs	
6	Treatment programs		Separating customers according to their buyer status and sending customized offers
7	Test offers		Testing new offers to a few customers at a time to see what works
8	One-off, multistep		Building excitement around an upcoming event with a series of timely offers and information
	Campaigns		
9		Transactional programs	Sending offers automatically based on customer

follow-up times. Research shows that contacting a customer within an hour increases the chances of making a sale sevenfold, while the average response time is 42 h.

33.10 Other Topics in B2B Digital Marketing

33.10.1 Social Selling, Social Monitoring, and Skillsets for B2B Digital

With digital marketing, we are witnessing the renaissance of social selling. Social selling is the preferred way for B2B to develop relationships to achieve sales. What is new today are the many new and more effective ways of sharing relevant content and interacting directly with potential buyers. Digital marketing also offers new opportunities for personal branding, defined as "a perception or emotion, maintained by somebody other than you, that describes the total experience of having a relationship with you.[1]" To measure the results of social selling and personal branding, we use social monitoring (social listening). Social monitoring involves tracking content on social media sites with the help of software to find out what people are saying about us, our customers, competitors, or the industry. Intelligence gathered is used to reshape our strategy. Examples of software used include Google Alerts, Hootsuite, and Social Mention.

As digital marketing is substantially different from traditional brick-and-mortar marketing, the skills needed and the education required to fill these functions are also new. The digital marketing employee must be an expert in data analysis, capable of extracting, analyzing, and translating important data from the company's computer systems. They must be knowledgeable about mobile technology and able to navigate the landscape of user experience design (UX, UXD, UED, or XD), which enhances user satisfaction by improving usability, accessibility, and pleasure in product interaction. Additionally, the employee must have a solid understanding of cybersecurity to protect computer systems from theft or damage, avoiding major risks and costs for the company.

33.10.2 Co-Creation for B2B Digital

Businesses are reviewed and evaluated online, meaning we do not directly control much of the information created about us and shared online. We can indirectly control this by ensuring that our products fulfill customers' expectations, a phenomenon referred to as nonintended co-creation. This can be both valuable and damaging for a company, depending on how it plays out.

Another form of co-creation is inviting third parties to add information to existing platforms, such as blogs and forums. Companies can create open-access documents that can be expanded, much like wikis. This is referred to as intended

[1] See McNally and Speak (2002).

co-creation. Again, the effects can be valuable or damaging. Together, these four forms of co-creation contribute to our brand image.

33.10.3 E-Procurements

E-procurement, or electronic procurement, is the process of purchasing goods and services using digital methods and technologies. It automates and streamlines the procurement process through electronic systems, facilitating efficient management of purchasing activities and supplier relationships. An overview of E-procurement in B2B is presented in Table 33.7.

Electronic data interchange (EDI) focuses on automating business transactions using standardized formats for secure transmission. Common examples include the exchange of purchase orders and invoices. Supplier web portals enable direct interaction with suppliers, offering real-time updates that are specific to each supplier. These portals often manage inventory and track orders.

Electronic catalogs centralize product information, making it searchable and customizable. They are used for catalog-based purchasing and can be integrated with enterprise resource planning (ERP) systems. Online auctions involve competitive bidding, featuring dynamic pricing and time-limited bidding periods. Reverse auctions for procurement are a typical example.

Table 33.7 E-procurement in B2B

E-Procurement method	Focus	Features	Examples
Electronic data interchange (EDI)	Automating business transactions	Standardized format, secure transmission	Exchanging purchase orders, invoices
Supplier web portals	Direct supplier interaction	Supplier-specific, real-time updates	Supplier-managed inventory, order tracking
Electronic catalogs	Centralizing product information	Searchable, customizable catalogs	Catalog-based purchasing, integration with ERP
Online auctions	Competitive bidding	Dynamic pricing, time-limited bidding	Reverse auctions for procurement
e-tendering	Soliciting and evaluating bids	Secure bid submission, automated evaluation	Government tenders, large-scale contracts
e-RFQ (ask for quote)	Gathering price and service information	Standardized forms, automated quote comparison	Price discovery, supplier selection
e-purchasing	Automating purchase orders	Streamlined ordering, order history management	Recurrent orders, office supplies
e-invoicing	Digitizing invoice processing	Automated matching, reduced processing time	Electronic payment, invoice approval workflows

E-tendering is used to solicit and evaluate bids securely, with automated bid submission and evaluation processes. This method is often used for government tenders and large-scale contracts. The e-Request for Quote (e-RFQ) method gathers price and service information using standardized forms, allowing for automated comparison of quotes. This is useful for price discovery and supplier selection.

E-purchasing automates the process of creating and managing purchase orders, streamlining ordering and maintaining order histories. It is commonly used for recurrent orders, such as office supplies. Lastly, e-invoicing digitizes the processing of invoices, automating matching and reducing processing time. This method is often used for electronic payments and invoice approval workflows.

33.10.4 B2B Portals

B2B portals, or business-to-business portals, are online platforms that facilitate commerce between businesses. These portals provide a digital space where companies can find and connect with suppliers, manufacturers, wholesalers, and other businesses to procure goods and services. B2B portals, as shown in Table 33.8, streamline and enhance various aspects of the procurement and sales processes by offering a range of features and functionalities.

The table provides a structured overview of B2B portals, highlighting their features, benefits, and some prominent examples.

33.11 Managerial Takeaways from Chapter on B2B Digital Marketing

This is a long chapter, so here are just a few of the takeaways:

1. *Adapt to competitive markets:* Understand that technical quality and price are crucial in highly competitive B2B markets.
2. *Emphasize profitability in service industries:* Recognize that industries like accounting, legal services, and oil and gas are often more profitable than manufacturing sectors.
3. *Focus on digital marketing strategies:* Use digital marketing to improve customer acquisition and retention.
4. *Leverage B2B E-commerce:* Implement B2B e-commerce to streamline transactions and reduce costs.
5. *Use data for segmentation:* Collect and segment data to tailor marketing strategies for specific customer groups.
6. *Optimize customer engagement:* Use CRM systems and analytics tools to enhance customer engagement and ROI.
7. *Implement marketing automation:* Automate marketing tasks to increase efficiency and effectiveness.

Table 33.8 B2B portals

Variable	Description	Examples	Benefits
Product listings and catalogs	Detailed information about products and services including descriptions, images, specifications, and pricing	Alibaba.com, GlobalSources.com, ThomasNet.com, IndiaMART.com, Amazon Business	Easier product comparison, informed decision making
Search and navigation	Advanced search options and filters to find specific products or suppliers quickly	Alibaba.com, GlobalSources.com, ThomasNet.com, IndiaMART.com, Amazon Business	Saves time, enhances user experience
Ordering and purchasing	Integrated systems for placing orders, shopping carts, order tracking, and payment processing	Alibaba.com, GlobalSources.com, ThomasNet.com, IndiaMART.com, Amazon Business	Streamlines procurement process, secure transactions
Supplier and buyer profiles	Detailed company information including products, services, certifications, and contact details	Alibaba.com, GlobalSources.com, ThomasNet.com, IndiaMART.com, Amazon Business	Builds trust, facilitates reliable partnerships
RFQ and tendering	Systems for submitting and evaluating requests for quotations and tenders	Alibaba.com, GlobalSources.com, ThomasNet.com, IndiaMART.com	Competitive pricing, better supplier options
Communication and collaboration	Messaging, chat functionalities, document sharing, project management, and discussion forums	Alibaba.com, GlobalSources.com, ThomasNet.com, IndiaMART.com, Amazon Business	Improved coordination, better relationship management
Analytics and reporting	Tools to track and analyze purchasing and sales data, providing insights	Alibaba.com, GlobalSources.com, ThomasNet.com, IndiaMART.com, Amazon Business	Data-driven decision making, optimization of procurement strategies
Secure transactions	Security features like encryption, secure payment gateways, and industry compliance	Alibaba.com, GlobalSources.com, ThomasNet.com, IndiaMART.com, Amazon Business	Protection of sensitive data, secure business transactions
Efficiency	Streamlines procurement processes, reducing time and effort	All examples	Time-saving, operational efficiency

(continued)

Table 33.8 (continued)

Variable	Description	Examples	Benefits
Cost savings	Competitive bidding and bulk purchasing leading to lower costs	All examples	Reduced procurement costs, better deals
Global reach	Connects businesses with global suppliers and buyers, expanding market opportunities	Alibaba.com, GlobalSources.com, ThomasNet.com, IndiaMART.com, Amazon Business	Expanded business opportunities, access to a larger market
Transparency	Detailed information on products, suppliers, and transactions	Alibaba.com, GlobalSources.com, ThomasNet.com, IndiaMART.com, Amazon Business	Enhanced trust, better decision making
Convenience	Centralizes various B2B transaction aspects in one platform	Alibaba.com, GlobalSources.com, ThomasNet.com, IndiaMART.com, Amazon Business	Simplifies operations, easy manage

8. *Ensure compliance:* Adhere to data protection regulations to maintain customer trust.
9. *Build strong B2B brands:* Develop strong brands through consistent, high-quality deliveries and valuable content.
10. *Embrace content marketing:* Focus on creating and distributing valuable content to build trust and establish thought leadership.

Many students think B2B marketing is boring—until they realize how much relationship-building happens outside the office, like playing golf with customers and engaging in other enjoyable activities. Understanding and implementing effective B2B digital marketing strategies is essential for staying competitive in today's market. By focusing on data-driven insights, automation, and content marketing, companies can enhance their marketing efforts and build strong, lasting relationships with their customers. In the world of B2B marketing, it's all about building trust and demonstrating value. Just like a good joke, timing and delivery are everything!

Reference

McNally, D., & Speak, K. D. (2002). Be your own brand: A breakthrough formula for standing out from the crowd. Berrett-Koehler.

Further Reading

Holliman, G., & Rowley, J. (2014). Business to business digital content marketing: Marketers' perceptions of best practice. *Journal of Research in Interactive Marketing, 8*(4), 269–293.

Järvinen, J., & Taiminen, H. (2016). Harnessing marketing automation for B2B content marketing. *Industrial Marketing Management, 54*, 164–175.

Lashgari, M., Sutton-Brady, C., Solberg Söilen, K., & Ulfvengren, P. (2018). Adoption strategies of social media in B2B firms: A multiple case study approach. *Journal of Business & Industrial Marketing, 33*(5), 730–743.

Pulizzi, J. (2012). The rise of storytelling as the new marketing. *Publishing Research Quarterly, 28*(2), 116–123.

Wang, A. (2006). Advertising engagement: A driver of message involvement on message effects. *Journal of Advertising Research, 46*(4), 355–368.

34 Impact on Employment

34.1 Definition and Importance

The Internet revolutionized society and the business landscape, with digital marketing becoming crucial part to modern strategies. Companies transitioned from traditional billboards to digital ads, leading to a need for new organizational structures.

The impact of AI on digital marketing jobs next year is expected to be significant, with a shift towards more specialized roles. AI will automate routine tasks, reducing the need for manual data entry and basic analysis roles. However, an increased demand for positions will involve managing and interpreting AI-generated data. Jobs related to AI strategy, implementation, and oversight will grow. Additionally, roles focusing on creative content and human-AI collaboration will become more important.

- Increased demand for AI strategists and implementers.
- Growth in data analysis and interpretation roles.
- Rise in creative content creation and human-AI collaboration positions.
- Reduction in routine task roles.

34.2 Digital Marketing Jobs in a Perspective

Digital marketing began in the early '90 s with search engines like Archie and Yahoo! and saw a significant impact with Google's launch in 1998. The rise of the Internet and social media platforms like Facebook and Twitter changed how companies approached marketing, necessitating new technical skills and roles. In 2000, Google launched AdWords, revolutionizing online advertising by allowing businesses to target specific keywords. AdWord, whereby customers bid for advertising based on keywords, is one of the best business models ever created. The mid-2000s saw the advent of social media marketing, with companies leveraging platforms like Facebook, YouTube, and later Instagram for brand promotion. The introduction of

K. Solberg Söilen, *Digital Marketing*, Springer Texts in Business and Economics, https://doi.org/10.1007/978-3-031-69518-6_34

smartphones in the late 2000s further transformed digital marketing, as mobile marketing became a key focus. By the 2010s, data analytics and SEO became crucial, enabling more precise targeting and performance measurement. Marketing automation tools like HubSpot and Marketo emerged, simplifying complex marketing tasks. Today, AI and machine learning are driving further innovation, personalizing customer experiences and optimizing campaign strategies.

- 2000: Google AdWords introduced targeted keyword advertising.
- Mid-2000s: Social media marketing on platforms like Facebook and YouTube.
- Late 2000s: Rise of mobile marketing with the advent of smartphones.
- 2010s: Importance of data analytics and SEO.
- Emergence of marketing automation tools like HubSpot and Marketo.
- Present: AI and machine learning driving innovation in personalized marketing strategies.

For a long time, AdWords, now simply Ads, represented the majority of Google's income. This reliance on a single revenue stream posed a risk, particularly with the potential changes AI could bring to the way we search for information in the future. Fortunately for Google, they now also derive substantial income from YouTube ads and cloud computing. In 2023, Google generated $307.39 billion in revenue, with $31.51 billion coming from YouTube ads and $33.09 billion from Google Cloud services. This diversification strategy is crucial for the company's long-term stability and growth, reducing its dependency on search advertising alone.

34.3 Traditional Versus Digital Marketing

Traditional marketing, which includes print and broadcast media, has been largely replaced by digital marketing methods such as social media, Google ads, and email. Digital marketing allows for precise tracking and targeting, making it more effective and accessible, especially for smaller companies. Table 34.1 shows what competences are required in traditional marketing jobs.

Now, let's do the same for digital marketing jobs, as illustrated in Table 34.2.

We see that the shift from traditional to digital marketing has transformed the landscape of marketing jobs. Traditional roles such as Print Media Specialists and Broadcast Media Planners have given way to new digital roles like Social Media Managers and SEO Specialists. Digital marketing offers precise tracking and targeting, making it more efficient and accessible, especially for smaller companies. This transition requires new competences, including data analysis, content creation, and platform-specific skills. While traditional marketing focuses on broad reach through print and broadcast media, digital marketing leverages technology to deliver personalized and measurable results.

Table 34.1 Traditional marketing jobs[a]

Type of job	Description	Competences required
Print media specialist	Creates and manages print advertisements, brochures, and flyers.	Graphic design, copywriting, knowledge of print processes.
Broadcast media planner	Plans and buys TV and radio ad spots, manages broadcast schedules.	Negotiation skills, media buying, understanding of audience demographics.
Direct mail coordinator	Designs and executes direct mail campaigns.	Copywriting, design, project management, data analysis.
Public relations specialist	Manages media relations and public image through press releases and events.	Communication, relationship building, media relations.
Market research analyst	Conducts surveys and focus groups to understand market trends.	Statistical analysis, data interpretation, qualitative research.

[a]Verified using ChatGPT 4 (June 2024)

34.4 The Job-Seeking Process in the Digital Era

Job searching has evolved with digital tools, with five main methods: job sites, direct contact, employers contacting candidates, networking, and social media. Recruitment processes have also been digitalized, utilizing online ads and electronic administrative systems. Digital platforms like LinkedIn have become crucial for job seekers, offering features for networking and job applications.

Companies now use applicant tracking systems (ATS) to streamline hiring, making it essential for applicants to optimize resumes for keywords. Online job fairs and virtual interviews have become standard, expanding opportunities beyond geographic limitations. Social media presence can significantly impact job prospects, with employers often researching candidates' online profiles. Moreover, personalized job recommendations and alerts from job sites have made the search process more efficient for candidates.

34.5 Impact on Employment: Job Creation Versus Job Counteracting

Digital marketing tools have created new jobs in tech and data analysis but have also replaced traditional roles. AI and chatbots represent significant advancements, potentially reshaping the labor market further by automating tasks previously performed by humans. This shift has led to the emergence of roles such as data scientists, SEO specialists, and digital strategists, focusing on leveraging technology for marketing efficiency. Conversely, jobs in print media and traditional advertising have seen a decline.

The rise of marketing automation tools allows for more precise targeting and personalization, requiring fewer human resources for repetitive tasks. Companies

Table 34.2 Digital marketing jobs[a]

Type of job	Description	Competences required
Social media manager	Manages social media accounts, plans content, and engages with the audience.	Content creation, social media analytics, community management.
SEO specialist	Optimizes website content for search engines to improve ranking.	Keyword research, on-page and off-page SEO, analytics.
Email marketing specialist	Designs and executes email marketing campaigns.	Email platform expertise, copywriting, segmentation.
Digital advertising specialist	Manages online ad campaigns across platforms like Google Ads and Facebook Ads.	PPC, ad targeting, budget management, analytics.
Content marketing strategist	Develops and manages content strategy to attract and engage customers.	Content creation, SEO, analytics, strategic planning.
Web analytics specialist	Analyzes website traffic data to improve performance and user experience.	Google Analytics, data analysis, reporting.
PPC specialist	Manages pay-per-click advertising campaigns, optimizing for clicks and conversions.	PPC management, keyword research, bid strategy.
Influencer marketing manager	Collaborates with influencers to promote products and services.	Relationship management, negotiation, social media.
Affiliate marketing manager	Oversees affiliate programs and partnerships to drive sales.	Affiliate networks, relationship management, analytics.
Marketing automation specialist	Implements and manages automated marketing campaigns.	Marketing automation platforms, data segmentation, workflow creation.

[a]Idem

now need employees with advanced technical skills, including data analytics, AI proficiency, and digital content creation. This evolution in the job market highlights the importance of continuous learning and adaptation to new technologies for career growth and stability.

34.6 Artificial Intelligence and Chatbots

AI's ability to analyze large data sets allows for highly personalized marketing. Chatbots enhance customer service, with a substantial percentage of businesses planning to implement them, significantly impacting job roles in customer service. AI-driven analytics enable companies to target their marketing strategies more precisely, optimizing customer engagement and satisfaction. As chatbots handle routine inquiries, customer service representatives can focus on more complex issues, enhancing service quality. This shift towards automation reduces labor costs while maintaining high service standards. Additionally, AI tools are evolving to provide deeper insights into consumer behavior, helping businesses tailor their offerings more effectively. The growing adoption of AI and chatbots signifies a transformative trend in digital marketing, reshaping how companies interact with customers and manage their workforce.

34.7 Types of Education Needed to Fill Jobs in Digital Marketing

One way to see how marketing has changed fundamentally since the introduction of the internet is to look at the kind of jobs needed to qualify for roles in digital marketing. For one thing, these jobs have become much more technical, so it is not enough for business students to remain within the social sciences. They must become interdisciplinary. Otherwise, future marketing jobs will not be filled by business students but by other students, like data scientists and computer scientists.

Another change is that the level of education required today is higher than it used to be. Before, it was enough to take one or two marketing courses, which could be covered in a year, like an introductory course in marketing, perhaps followed by a course on B2B marketing or some specialty in communications and brand management. Today, basic technical skills alone will require a year minimum. Another big difference is that hands-on experience has become much more important today than it used to be. That means students should sit in front of computers and actually do the work, like SEO, not only read about it.

All of this brings up an old idea that I find has become much more important now: business studies should have a parallel requirement for students to learn how to start up or work with a company. This way, whatever you learn in theory can be applied in practice simultaneously. We see in Table 34.3 that today's work in marketing requires a combination of business and computer science skills. That is, marketing as a relevant discipline has already become multidisciplinary.

The table lists various digital marketing job types, titles, required education, and the number of years needed to attain that education. Each job type corresponds to specific roles, from content creation to video production, with most requiring a bachelor's degree spanning 3–4 years in relevant fields such as Marketing, Computer Science, Communications, and more.

34.8 Key Takeaways for Managers

Here are the main takeaways from this chapter:

1. Digital marketing requires an interdisciplinary approach, combining business, technology, and data analysis skills.
2. The shift from traditional to digital marketing has created new, highly specialized job roles.

Table 34.3 Types of education needed in digital marketing[a]

Job type	Job titles	Education needed	Number of years of university education
Content creation	Content Writer, Copywriter, Blogger	Degree in English, Journalism, Marketing	3–4 years
SEO specialist	SEO Analyst, SEO Manager	Degree in Marketing, IT, Computer Science	3–4 years
Social media management	Social Media Manager, Social Media Specialist	Degree in Marketing, Communications, Public Relations	3–4 years
Data analysis	Data Analyst, Marketing Analyst	Degree in Statistics, Data Science, Computer Science	3–4 years
Email marketing	Email Marketing Specialist, CRM Manager	Degree in Marketing, Business Administration	3–4 years
Digital advertising	PPC Specialist, Digital Advertising Manager	Degree in Marketing, Business, Advertising	3–4 years
Content marketing	Content Marketing Manager, Brand Journalist	Degree in Marketing, Communications, Journalism	3–4 years
Web development	Front-End Developer, Web Designer	Degree in Computer Science, Web Development	3–4 years
Graphic design	Graphic Designer, Visual Designer	Degree in Graphic Design, Fine Arts, Visual Communication	3–4 years
Video production	Video Editor, Video Content Creator	Degree in Film Studies, Multimedia, Communications	3–4 years

[a]Verified using ChatGPT 4 (June 2024)

3. AI and automation are reshaping job requirements, focusing on technical skills and hands-on experience.
4. Job seekers must adapt to digital tools and platforms for job searching and networking.
5. Companies need to invest in continuous learning and upskilling to keep up with technological advancements.
6. Digital marketing roles demand higher education levels and specific technical competencies.
7. Hands-on experience and practical application of skills are crucial for success in digital marketing.
8. AI and chatbots are transforming customer service roles, requiring fewer human resources for routine tasks.
9. The digitalization of recruitment processes necessitates optimizing resumes for applicant tracking systems.
10. Future marketing jobs will increasingly focus on data-driven strategies and AI integration.

The digital era has fundamentally transformed marketing and its job market. As AI and automation continue to advance, the need for specialized, interdisciplinary skills grows. This shift requires both companies and job seekers to prioritize continuous learning and adaptability.

Further Reading

Autor, D. H. (2015). Why are there still so many jobs? The history and future of workplace automation. *Journal of Economic Perspectives, 29*(3), 3–30.

Brynjolfsson, E., & McAfee, A. (2014). *The second machine age: Work, progress, and prosperity in a time of brilliant technologies*. W.W. Norton & Company.

Chui, M., Manyika, J., & Miremadi, M. (2016). Where machines could replace humans—And where they can't (yet). *McKinsey Quarterly, 3*(1), 20–27.

Davenport, T. H., & Kirby, J. (2016). *Only humans need apply: Winners and losers in the age of smart machines*. Harper Business.

35 The Evolution of PR and Communications in the Digital Age

35.1 Background

The chapter explores the evolution of public relations (PR) and communications, highlighting significant changes over the years. In the past, PR focused on managing brand reputation through traditional media like newspapers and TV.

Today, PR is a critical component in a 24/7 online world, requiring new tools and techniques to engage with audiences. The impact of digitalization and social media has transformed PR into a dynamic and interactive field.

35.2 Definitions and Importance

Public relations (PR) is strategically focused on building mutually beneficial relationships between organizations and their publics. The field has evolved to include managing communication, building reputations, handling rumors and crises, and influencing media exposure. Understanding key terms and concepts in PR is essential for grasping its importance and current practices:

Key terms include[1]:

1. *Company spokesperson*: Represents the company or cause in the media, delivering key messages and managing public perception.
2. *Press kit*: A comprehensive information package that outlines a company's products, services, and key messages, often used for media relations.
3. *Press release*: An official statement issued to the media to inform the public about significant company developments, covering essential details like who, what, where, when, how, and why.

[1] Verified using ChatGPT 4 (June 2024).

K. Solberg Söilen, *Digital Marketing*, Springer Texts in Business and Economics, https://doi.org/10.1007/978-3-031-69518-6_35

4. *Online influencers*: Individuals with substantial online followings, such as journalists, bloggers, and celebrities, who can shape public opinion and brand perception.
5. *Social media governance*: Guidelines and policies that dictate how a company should respond to social media mentions and engage with the public online.
6. *Social media listening*: The use of monitoring tools to review and analyze mentions of a brand, relevant keywords, and public sentiment on social media platforms.

These definitions highlight the critical components of modern PR, emphasizing the strategic management of communication channels and the importance of engaging with both traditional media and new digital platforms. The evolution of PR from traditional methods to incorporating digital strategies underscores its vital role in shaping public perception and managing reputations in today's fast-paced, connected world.

35.3 Public Relations Versus Marketing

PR differs from advertising and marketing in several keyways: While advertising relies on paid media to persuade consumers, PR focuses on building positive relationships with various stakeholders, including consumers, investors, media, and government. The primary goal of PR is to manage the company's reputation and communicate effectively with the public, often through earned media coverage. Although PR and marketing overlap in areas like brand-building and content creation, PR places a greater emphasis on media relations and stakeholder engagement. Additionally, PR is more concerned with managing perceptions and handling crises, whereas marketing is primarily focused on promoting products and driving sales. Effective PR strategies enhance credibility and trust, while marketing aims to generate immediate consumer actions.

35.4 Online Public Relations

The digital age has significantly influenced PR practices by shifting much of the work online. Online PR encompasses corporate and social blogs, influencer outreach, and reputation management through monitoring and controlling online messages. It has become a cost-effective strategy crucial for businesses of all sizes. Online PR enables companies to engage with a broader audience through social media platforms and digital content. It allows for real-time interaction, feedback, and crisis management. Additionally, online PR supports SEO efforts by generating valuable backlinks and increasing online visibility, further solidifying a company's reputation and reach.

35.5 Storytelling

Storytelling, which we have discussed at length earlier, is a vital skill for PR practitioners, enabling them to capture and retain the audience's attention. Effective storytelling follows a narrative structure that engages audiences from beginning to end, much like traditional epic tales.

Today, storytelling often occurs on social media platforms, where compelling and relatable content can significantly draw and maintain audience interest. This modern approach to storytelling allows for interactive and dynamic engagement. By sharing authentic and emotionally resonant stories, PR professionals can build stronger connections with their audience, fostering trust and loyalty.

35.6 Functions of a Traditional PR Specialist

The functions of traditional PR specialists differ significantly from those of online PR specialists, reflecting the evolution of public relations in the digital age. Traditional PR focuses on established media channels such as press releases, media events, and direct community engagement. In contrast, online PR leverages digital platforms, social media, and influencer partnerships to reach and engage audiences.

Table 35.1 below compares these functions, highlighting how traditional and online PR specialists manage similar roles using different methods and tools.

This table highlights the different approaches and tools used by traditional and online PR specialists in their respective roles.[2]

Table 35.1 Comparing traditional PR specialists with online PR specialists

Function	Traditional PR specialists	Online PR specialists
Press relations or press agency	Creating and placing newsworthy information in traditional media	Creating and placing content on digital platforms, blogs, and websites
Product publicity	Promoting specific products through press releases and media events	Promoting products through social media posts, influencer partnerships
Public affairs	Building relationships with local and national communities	Engaging with online communities and managing social media presence
Lobbying	Building relationships with lawmakers to influence legislation	Utilizing online petitions and social media campaigns to influence policymakers
Investor relations	Maintaining relationships with financial stakeholders	Managing digital communications with investors through email newsletters and online updates
Development	Gaining financial or volunteer support for nonprofits through events and direct mail	Raising support through crowdfunding platforms and online campaigns

[2] Gedda et al. (2016).

35.7 PR Tools

PR tools have significantly evolved with the advent of the Internet and social media. Traditional tools such as press releases, speeches, special events, written materials, audiovisual materials, corporate identity materials, and public service activities remain fundamental. However, the inclusion of digital tools has transformed the PR landscape.

35.7.1 Traditional PR Tools

Traditional PR channels focus on the general press, niche publications, TV, and radio. These methods involve media tactics such as event coordination, crisis communications, reputation management, trade shows, sponsorship opportunities, and press release distribution. PR specialists create or leverage favorable news stories, speeches, special events, written materials, audiovisual materials, and corporate identity materials to build a reputation or create buzz. Table 35.2 lists a number of traditional PR tools and how to use them.

35.7.2 Digital PR Tools

We can now compare the traditional PR tools with the new digital tools. Digital PR tools focus on engaging with audiences through various online platforms, making use of the interactive and instantaneous nature of the internet, as seen in Table 35.3.

Table 35.2 Traditional PR tools

Tool	Description	Application for HeritageStride
Press releases	*Announcements sent to media to inform about new products or updates*	*Announce new sports shoe launches, company milestones, and event participation*
Speeches	*Public addresses to communicate important messages*	*CEO or executives presenting at industry events or conferences*
Special events	*Organized events to promote products or causes*	*Launch events for new sports shoe lines or community engagement activities*
Written materials	*Brochures, pamphlets, and other written documents*	*Distribute at trade shows or include in press kits*
Audiovisual materials	*Videos and multimedia presentations*	*Product demonstration videos and promotional content for social media and website*
Corporate identity materials	*Items that establish brand identity such as logos and business cards*	*Branded merchandise, packaging, and company uniforms*
Public service activities	*Community-oriented initiatives*	*Organize or sponsor sports events and community fitness programs*

Table 35.3 Digital Marketing Tools[a]

Tool	Description	Application for HeritageStride
Social media posts	Updates shared on platforms like Facebook, Instagram, and twitter.	Engage with customers, share behind-the-scenes content, and promote sales.
Influencer partnerships	Collaborations with individuals who have large online followings.	Partner with fitness influencers to review and promote HeritageStride's shoes.
Blogs and online articles	In-depth articles about industry trends and company insights.	Publish articles on HeritageStride's website about the benefits of their sports shoes.
Webinars and live streaming	Live online sessions to engage directly with the audience.	Host webinars on the best shoes for different sports, live Q&A sessions.
E-newsletters and X	Regular emails to subscribers with updates and promotions.	Send newsletters featuring new products, upcoming sales, and exclusive offers.
Podcasts and video content	Audio and video content shared on platforms like YouTube and Spotify.	Create podcast episodes about sports trends, upload videos of product reviews.
SEO and online reputation management	Techniques to improve online visibility and manage brand image.	Optimize website content for search engines, monitor and respond to online reviews.

[a]Verified using ChatGPT 4 (June 2024)

PR tools have diversified from traditional methods to incorporate a variety of digital strategies.

Our Sports Shoe Company, HeritageStride, can leverage these tools to enhance its brand presence, engage with its audience, and create impactful campaigns. Traditional tools like press releases and special events remain relevant, while digital tools such as social media and influencer partnerships offer new opportunities for interaction and engagement. By combining these approaches, HeritageStride can build a comprehensive PR strategy that effectively reaches and resonates with its target market.

Digital PR offers several advantages over traditional PR methods. Firstly, digital media allows for direct dialog with the public, enabling organizations to engage in real-time conversations and build stronger relationships. Secondly, audience members are connected to each other through social networks, amplifying the reach of PR messages as they share content within their circles. Thirdly, the audience has access to a wide range of information sources, making transparency and authenticity crucial for PR efforts. Lastly, digital PR operates on an inbound marketing model, where audiences actively seek out information, making content creation and SEO vital components of a successful PR strategy.

In Table 35.4, we compare the two different types of PR tools with each other.

Table 35.4 Traditional versus digital PR

Aspect	Traditional PR	Digital PR
Communication channel	One-way (press releases, TV, radio)	Two-way (social media, blogs, forums)
Audience engagement	Limited interaction	High interaction and engagement
Response time	Slower, pre-planned	Real-time, agile
Control over message	High control, few media outlets	Less control, many online platforms
Measurement	Difficult to measure	Easier with analytics tools
Cost	High (media placements)	Cost-effective (social media, influencer partnerships)
Example tools	Press releases, press kits, speeches	Social media listening tools, influencer outreach

Digital media has revolutionized PR by enabling real-time interaction, peer-to-peer connectivity, broad access to information, and an inbound approach where audiences actively seek out content. These advancements require PR professionals to be more agile, transparent, and strategic in their communication efforts, utilizing tools that measure impact and engagement effectively.

35.7.3 Negative Word-of-Mouth (WOM)

Word-of-mouth marketing leverages customer recommendations and organic discussions to promote products. This relies on satisfied customers sharing positive experiences, leading to increased trust and credibility. Social media and online reviews have amplified WOM marketing's reach and impact, making it highly effective as people trust personal recommendations more than traditional advertising. However, negative WOM, as exemplified in Table 35.5, can significantly impact a brand, as consumers often weigh negative comments more heavily than positive ones, making it crucial to maintain good relationships with the audience.

Negative word-of-mouth can be a significant challenge for any brand, including our HeritageStride example. By actively monitoring social media and online reviews, promptly addressing complaints, and maintaining transparency, HeritageStride can mitigate the effects of negative WOM. Engaging directly with customers and influencers and showcasing improvements and resolutions will help rebuild trust and maintain a positive brand reputation.

35.8 Key Takeaways from the Chapter

The chapter explores how the PR and communications profession has evolved, driven by digitalization and the rise of social media. Here are the key takeaways:

Table 35.5 Negative WOM—problem and solution for HeritageStride

Problem	Example for HeritageStride	Solution
Negative customer reviews	A customer posts a negative review about the durability of HeritageStride sports shoes on social media.	Monitor social media and promptly respond to negative reviews with apologies and offers to replace defective products. Ensure the customer feels heard and valued.
Viral negative posts	A viral post criticizes the quality of materials used in HeritageStride shoes.	Address the concerns publicly, provide transparency about material sourcing, and highlight quality control measures. Offer to resolve individual issues through customer service.
Influencer backlash	An influencer negatively reviews HeritageStride shoes, impacting their followers' perceptions.	Engage with the influencer directly, offering to address their concerns and potentially sending improved products for re-evaluation.
Customer service complaints	Complaints about poor customer service are shared widely online.	Improve customer service training and response times, and publicly share improvements and customer service success stories to rebuild trust.
Product recall issues	A recall of a defective shoe model is mishandled, leading to negative publicity.	Communicate the recall clearly and proactively, offering compensation and ensuring all affected customers are promptly addressed and assisted.

1. *Transformation of PR*: The shift from traditional media relations to digital engagement has broadened the scope of PR.
2. *Role of digital tools*: Tools such as social media, blogs, and influencer partnerships have become crucial in modern PR strategies.
3. *Importance of storytelling*: Effective storytelling remains central, now adapted to digital platforms to engage audiences.
4. *Functions of PR*: Traditional functions like press relations, product publicity, and public affairs have adapted to include digital methods.
5. *Online PR benefits*: Cost-effectiveness, real-time interaction, and broader audience reach are significant advantages of online PR.
6. *Managing negative WOM*: Strategies for addressing negative word-of-mouth are crucial for maintaining a positive brand reputation.
7. *PR versus marketing*: PR focuses on relationship building and reputation management, whereas marketing aims at product promotion and sales.
8. *Measuring success*: Digital PR offers better tools for measuring impact and engagement compared to traditional PR.
9. *Crisis management*: Faster response times and real-time crisis management are essential in the digital age.
10. *Integration of traditional and digital*: A comprehensive PR strategy now integrates both traditional and digital tools to maximize reach and effectiveness.

PR has garnered a poor reputation in digital marketing due to the rise of "fake news" and misinformation, which have led to public skepticism about the authenticity of online content. Additionally, the practice of paying influencers and bloggers to promote products without transparent disclosure has eroded trust. Lastly, the relentless focus on viral content and sensationalism often overshadows genuine relationship-building and value-based communication, further diminishing the credibility of PR efforts. This is something that the PR function needs to rectify.

References

Gedda, D., Nilsson, B., Såthén, Z., & Söilen, K. S. (2016). Crowdfunding: Finding the optimal platform for funders and entrepreneurs. *Technology Innovation Management Review, 6*(3), 31–40.

Further Reading

Arthur W. Page Society. (2007). *The authentic enterprise: Relationships, values and the evolution of corporate communications*. Retrieved from https://page.org/

Gregory, A. (2010). *Planning and managing public relations campaigns*. Kogan Page Publishers.

Grunig, J. E., & Hunt, T. (1984). *Managing public relations*. Holt, Rinehart and Winston.

Hutton, J. G. (1999). The definition, dimensions, and domain of public relations. *Public Relations Review, 25*(2), 199–214.

Macnamara, J. (2014). *The 21st century media (R)evolution: Emergent communication practices*. Peter Lang.

Phillips, D., & Young, P. (2009). *Online public relations: A practical guide to developing an online strategy in the world of social media*. Kogan Page Publishers.

Smith, R. D. (2013). *Strategic planning for public relations*. Routledge.

The Art and Science of Copywriting 36

36.1 Evolution of Copywriting

We all use words every day to communicate, so what's the problem? Why do we need a chapter about copywriting? Copywriting is about telling a story that convinces the audience and gets people involved and interested by choosing the right words.

Before we start discussing how to write a copy, we need to understand what an ad is. Advertising is placing a message about an idea, product, or service in one or more media (newspapers, television, magazines, radio, outdoors, point of purchase, and direct mail), for which the advertiser pays a fee. Modern advertising developed around the 1880s and became an important object of knowledge and an economic resource. Modern advertising has become essential to manage to create competitive advantages.

Advertising has become the most extensive form of modern rhetoric. The discipline in how the advertising should be structured can differ but is of great importance for the end result. Copywriters help advertisers strengthen a crucial element of the invention phase. The copywriter is a profession in the advertising and PR industry. It is a creator who has the main responsibility for text in advertising. Copywriters are employed to deliver the text to the advertisement. To be a copywriter, it's more than that; they have to supply an essential element in the process. There will be no effective advertising without the copywriter's clever way with words and their power to originate ideas with maximum impact. The most successful copywriters are as good with the visual as they are with the verbal. That is important because in creating advertisements, the company is trying to define a connection with the audience through an association of pictures and words.

To start working as a copywriter at the basic level, some formal training is required. If you want to focus on advertising, you will need a bachelor's degree in marketing, communication, journalism, English, or a similar subject. There are also copywriting courses on internet platforms and social networks. Distance education courses and online courses on copywriting are available every 2 to 3 months. There

K. Solberg Söilen, *Digital Marketing*, Springer Texts in Business and Economics, https://doi.org/10.1007/978-3-031-69518-6_36

are also websites that are platforms for the exchange of information between the customer and the publisher. These are so-called self-websites.

Thus, it is not enough with traditional teaching and training forms to become a copywriter. But even if you have a bachelor's degree, it can help with writing certifications to develop as a copywriter and get a higher income. The certifications that are applied are in communication, technical writing, and creative writing. It is important that copywriters have a strong understanding of communication and computer systems with word processors and even mobile media.

As Jerry Della Femina said in his autobiographical book, "From Those Wonderful Folks Who Gave You Pearl Harbor: Front-Line Dispatches from the Advertising War," published in 1970, "Advertising is the most fun you can have with your clothes on." Copywriting is the most fun you can have with a pencil and paper, we might say, if you want a steady income.

36.2 Understanding Copywriting

A copywriter is a writer of advertising or publicity copy. Or, as is often quoted, "Copywriting is the job of using the right words, to say the right thing, to the right people, to get the right response." Copywriting is the business of selling content. It is about persuading the public with a certain product, service, argument, or something else. When you persuade your public, you should get them to act accordingly.

36.3 The Role of Copywriting in Marketing

Marketing and advertising are about engaging people and building relationships between customers and companies. Therefore, it becomes more important for companies to be able to formulate their message right to get customers more engaged and interested in what they sell or offer. There are many different ways to formulate their message, and it can be difficult for brands to know where and how to make their message correctly perceived by customers. This is where the copywriter's task plays a major role; it is their job to capture the public in a convincing way that strengthens the customer and the company's relationship. You can convey all information or any message, but only if it is done correctly.

The approaches are infinitely many, and it is necessary to have enough knowledge to put the right words into the right picture, etc. The most important thing is that the message you want to convey appears in a text. The text does not have to be long and eventful for it to be interesting; sometimes, it is enough with just a few words, or maybe not a few words at all. A picture can say more than a thousand words. The most important thing is that the copy or message is appealing and creates consumer engagement.

36.4 Crafting the Copy: The Brief

As a copywriter, it is your job to learn as much as you can about the product or service you are going to work with. It starts with a briefing meeting; sometimes, it is the only opportunity for the copywriter to understand the product. The brief helps you to sort out facts from personal opinions. Therefore, it is very important to ask questions to the team or the client you work for so you can clarify all details you are not sure about.

Many people do not dare to ask questions; they are afraid that they look foolish. But to be a good copywriter, you need to learn quickly, so you must get the answers before you can begin to consider creative ideas. It is important that you agree on the brief, like signing off a sort of written contract.

A straightforward copy brief contains[1]:

- Describe your target group (demographic).
- What is the Unique Selling Point?
- Has the audience heard from you before?
- What is the offer, and what are the benefits?
- What is your product's or service's SWOT? (Strengths, Weaknesses, Opportunities, Threats).
- How should the feeling be for the brand?
- Name the three most common customers.
- Is your product or service used daily, or does it need a detailed description?
- What are your product or service benefits?
- List your top three competitors.
- Look at old works.
- Do you want the customers to take any action?
- Are there any limitations that must be considered?
- Deadlines.

We can turn this into a working process, as shown in Fig. 36.1.

This diagram breaks down the essential steps and components of a copywriter's job, from initial briefing to agreeing on a detailed copy brief.

36.5 The Importance of Research in Copywriting

Research is important in copywriting and can take many forms. It is good to look at what others have made before. Sometimes, you do not have to reinvent the wheel but just develop the next step on the same theme, or it is time to look for an entirely fresh approach. Either way, it is important to understand what's gone before to be sure that your ideas are sufficiently good for the new campaign.

[1] Verified using ChatGPT 4 (June 2024).

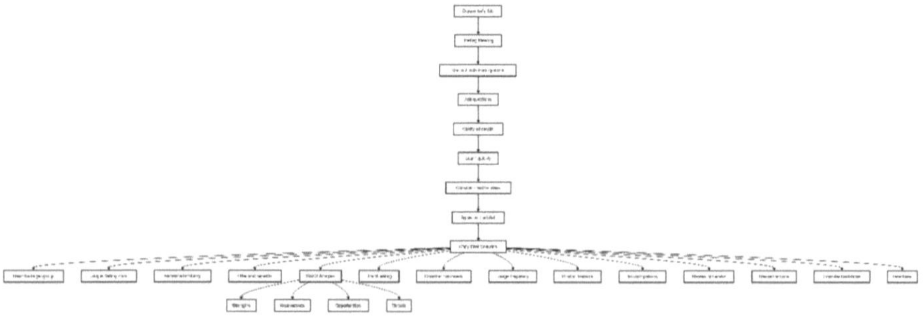

Fig. 36.1 The copywriter's working process

As a copywriter, you must have an open mind to concentrate all your attention on the specific product and its benefits. You must show the same level of enthusiasm for every brief you get. Sometimes, it is easier to come up with good ideas for unusual products than very well-known products.

When you do consumer research, you will find out what's going on in the market's messy world. Too often, one fails to achieve the goals of consumer research. It replaces the important search with simplicity and relies on past research instead of looking outside the box. Therefore, there is a difference between research and what really happens in reality, which results in a challenge for marketers and copywriters. It is important for the research to show how people actually behave to get something out of it and reach the people that the advertising should target. Copywriters handle the messy world every day and try to communicate with customers in a way that makes them break through with their ideas, which will lead to the purchase of a brand and/or product/service. This in a way that evokes emotions in advertising. Copywriters' most common failure is to (1) present the advertisement, (2) to a potential customer, (3) in an environment that reflects the real-life situation, and (4) measure the result in a meaningful way.

Much academic research on advertising influences consists of being able to make a statement (written or oral) that conveys the message in advertising. This is also called the concept statement and is used to see if the rational core message can be communicated. If you use concise statements, it can be difficult to convey emotions, actions, or interactions.

A lot of research is needed on what your potential customer's reaction will be to the ad. Is it the same reaction for a student as it is for an adult? This is what copywriters need to find out. For the ad to produce the best possible results, it is important to ensure customer reactions before it is too late.

There is a difference between a research environment and a fast-paced viewing environment. The participants in a research environment know they are there to do something and contribute to some form of research. In the real environment, there are no such formal constraints for the customers, and it, therefore, becomes a challenge for copywriters to capture these customers in the actual environment. In an environment that is controlled, one does not allow any freedom, but it is controllable; therefore, the result will differ from what the research shows and what is actually true. This is what many researchers think is a waste of money and time when it does not reflect the real environment. It is required that copywriters' research provides the participants with stimulus and freedom to reflect the real world and produce a fair result.

36.6 Crafting Headlines and Slogans

A great headline makes all the difference. A powerful headline is the most important factor for putting more money in your pocket. If it is for a website, marketing brochures, newspaper, or magazine ad, the right advertising headline will attract, persuade, and retain your most loyal, valuable customers. Scientific tests have proven it over and over: Just by changing a headline, you can increase an ad's profitability by two, three, or even five times.

In a print ad, 75% of the buying decisions are made at the headline. The writer who creates the headline must create enough interest and desire so that passers-by pick up a magazine and buy it. When you are writing a headline, your biggest effort is to make your customers read more and get them interested, so you force them to read the first sentence. After that, you have caught them, so there is an interest in reading more. To help you catch the customers, there are four rules to assist us, as described in Table 36.1.

This table outlines the four essential principles of creating effective headlines for advertising and copywriting. Each principle ensures the headline captures the reader's attention, provides valuable information, and motivates action. By following

Table 36.1 The four u's

Principle	Description
Unique	To make your title unique, your business needs to stand out from the crowd. Create an image that differentiates your company from competitors. A unique headline attracts customers to your product or service, offering a competitive advantage. Without uniqueness, customers may not find a compelling reason to choose your product over others.
Ultra-specific	The headline should be ultra-specific, providing clear and detailed information to make the offer interesting. Specificity helps capture the attention of the target group, making customers genuinely interested in what you are offering.
Urgency	Whenever possible, the headline should convey a sense of urgency, compelling the reader to act immediately. This urgency can prioritize the text for the reader, making them feel they must continue reading or risk missing out. Although this rule cannot be applied every time, it is highly effective when used appropriately.
Useful	The headline must be useful, offering some kind of benefit to the customer. If it fails to communicate an advantage, there is little reason for customers to keep reading. It is crucial to present the headline in a way that clearly states the benefit, ensuring it is both attractive and valuable to the reader. Companies often neglect this, leading to a loss of reader engagement.

these guidelines, companies can create compelling and engaging headlines that effectively communicate their message and attract their target audience.

36.7 Digital Copywriting

The digital world is only getting bigger and bigger, so it is becoming increasingly important for copywriters to be able to write a copy that works in this particular digital world. There are three keys to consider when writing a text, as seen in Table 36.2: Human emotion, data, and compliance. These three have influenced how a copy is written, evaluated, and tested today.

The table highlights the three essential keys to writing effective digital copy: human emotion, data analytics, and digital compliance. By understanding and leveraging these elements, copywriters can create engaging, data-driven, and compliant content that resonates with their audience and performs well across digital platforms. Implementing these practices involves a blend of emotional intelligence, analytical skills, and adherence to platform guidelines, ensuring that the copy is both impactful and compliant.

36.8 The AIDA Model

A well-known and much-used promotional theory in marketing is the Attention-Interest-Desire-Action (AIDA) model, initially introduced as a sales strategy and now a communication technique. Copywriting should be viewed as a selling skill, not just creative writing. The AIDA model helps in crafting effective copy,

Table 36.2 Keys to writing effective digital copy

Key	Description	Implementation
Human emotion	*Understanding human emotions is crucial for creating compelling copy. Despite the digital world's growth, human nature and motivations remain unchanged. Effective copywriting requires knowing the audience's thoughts, motivations, and reasons for purchasing.*	*Create personas to represent target audiences, use storytelling techniques, and address emotional triggers.*
Data analytics	*Analyzing data is essential to understand the real-world context. Copywriters need to collect and analyze data to ensure their copy is based on facts and current market conditions. Data-driven insights help refine and optimize copy for better engagement.*	*Use tools like Google analytics, A/B testing, and market research to gather and interpret relevant data.*
Digital compliance	*Compliance with digital platform guidelines and rules is necessary to ensure ad approval and visibility. Copywriters must be aware of each platform's requirements to avoid disapproval and ensure their ads reach the intended audience.*	*Stay updated on platform policies, use SEO best practices, and review compliance checklists before publishing.*

encouraging audiences to take the next step, whether buying a product or donating to a cause.

AIDA explained:

1. Attention: Capture the reader's attention with a compelling opening, considering they are exposed to numerous messages daily.
2. Interest: Transition seamlessly from capturing attention to sparking interest by highlighting the product or service benefits.
3. Desire: Build on the interest to create an emotional connection, focusing on the customer's wishes and needs.
4. Action: Encourage the customer to take a specific action, ensuring not to falter at the final step.

Additionally, the suggestion of adding "C" for Convincing (AIDCA) emphasizes the importance of reasoning and substantiation to drive action. Each step in the AIDA model is crucial for effective copywriting and achieving desired outcomes.

36.9 SEO Copywriting

Copywriting is an essential component of integrated communication strategies across traditional and modern media. Despite the rapid development of digital technology, the core of communication strategies remains the written word and how it is used to create a company's image and foster long-term customer relationships. The evolution of copywriting has expanded from merely designing advertising text to creating various types of text for different purposes.

Effective copywriting is vital for building and maintaining a company's image and establishing long-term customer relationships. Despite advances in digital technology, the essence of communication remains rooted in the strategic use of words. The ability to craft compelling text is crucial for efficient communication and fostering audience trust. Table 36.3 describes the different types of copywriting common in digital marketing.

SEO copywriting is particularly significant today, combining technical and linguistic skills to enhance website visibility. It involves creating clear, simple texts that incorporate keywords strategically to improve search engine rankings. SEO copywriters also focus on tagging keywords with hyperlinks, managing colors and

Table 36.3 Types of copywriting[a]

Type of copywriting	Description
Literary copywriting	Crafting creative and artistic texts
Media copywriting	Writing for various media platforms
Advertising copywriting	Creating persuasive advertising content
PR copywriting	Managing public relations through strategic text
SEO copywriting	Optimizing online content for search engines

[a]Verified using ChatGPT 4 (June 2024)

fonts, and maintaining originality to ensure the content stands out and reaches the desired audience.

Table 36.4 gives some advice on how to succeed with copywriting.

The table highlights the various types of copywriting and the specific considerations for SEO copywriting. Effective SEO copywriting requires balancing clarity, keyword placement, and technical optimization to enhance website visibility and user engagement. Copywriters must be versatile, continually adapting to new skills and trends to create relevant and impactful content.

Mastering the art of copywriting is about more than just writing; it involves understanding human emotions, data analytics, and digital compliance. The best copywriters are curious, well-read, and eager to learn and adapt. By focusing on these aspects, copywriters can create compelling texts that resonate with audiences and achieve business objectives.

36.10 Key Takeaways

In this chapter, we explored the multifaceted role of copywriting in modern advertising and marketing. Here are the key takeaways:

- *Importance of copywriting:* Copywriting is about crafting persuasive text that engages and convinces the audience, making it a critical component of effective advertising.
- *Role evolution:* The role of a copywriter has evolved to require both creative and technical skills, including an understanding of human emotions and data analytics.
- *SEO copywriting:* SEO copywriting is essential in the digital age, involving the creation of keyword-rich content optimized for search engines to improve site rankings.

Table 36.4 Key aspects of SEO copywriting[a]

Aspect	Description
Clear and simple text	Ensuring readability and understanding for the audience
Keyword placement	Using keywords in the right places to create meaningful content
Content optimization	Increasing the quality and relevance of website content through analysis
HTML tags	Utilizing title and description tags to inform search engines about page content
Technical SEO	Optimizing the HTML code and other technical aspects to improve search engine rankings

[a]Idem

- *AIDA model:* The AIDA (Attention, Interest, Desire, Action) model is a valuable framework for creating compelling copy that drives audience engagement and actions.
- *Research and targeting:* Thorough research and a deep understanding of the target audience are crucial for crafting messages that resonate and drive consumer behavior.
- *Headlines and slogans:* Effective headlines and slogans are key to capturing attention and making a lasting impression on the audience.
- *Digital compliance:* Adherence to digital platform guidelines and compliance rules is necessary for the approval and visibility of online ads.
- *Product knowledge:* Knowledge of the product's features and benefits, along with a clear articulation of the unique selling points (USPs), is vital for successful copywriting.
- *Technical and creative balance:* Balancing technical SEO requirements with creative and engaging content is crucial for effective online copy.
- *Continuous learning:* Continuous learning and adaptation to new technologies, consumer behaviors, and market trends are essential for staying relevant as a copywriter.

Copywriting is both fun and essential, and digital marketing has only heightened its importance. Mastering the art of engaging language, capturing attention with words, and crafting compelling headlines requires significant practice and extensive reading. Effective copywriting remains an art form, crucial for attracting and retaining an audience in the digital age.

Further Reading

Bly, R. W. (2006). *The Copywriter's handbook: A step-by-step guide to writing copy that sells.* Henry Holt and Company.

Carroll, B. (2014). *SEO copywriting: The complete guide to writing search engine optimized copy.* CreateSpace Independent Publishing Platform.

Collier, C. (1985). *Tested advertising methods.* Prentice-Hall.

Godin, S. (2005). All marketers are liars: The power of telling authentic stories in a low-trust world. *Portfolio.*

Halvorson, K., & Rach, M. (2012). *Content strategy for the web.* New Riders.

Handley, A., & Chapman, C. C. (2011). *Content rules: How to create killer blogs, podcasts, videos, Ebooks, webinars (and more) that engage customers and ignite your business.* Wiley.

Ogilvy, D. (1985). *Ogilvy on advertising.* Vintage.

Ethics in Digital Marketing 37

37.1 Background

Digital marketing is full of ethical dilemmas. For example, dark patterns in e-commerce are deceptive design practices that manipulate users for profit. These patterns include tactics like trick questions, sneaking into the baskets, roach motel, and privacy zuckering. These practices can mislead users into actions they did not intend, such as signing up for unwanted services or sharing personal information. Companies use these patterns to increase conversions, but they erode trust and damage reputations. Ethical design prioritizes user consent and transparency, ensuring users are fully aware of their actions and the implications. Social media amplifies the impact of these missteps, quickly spreading awareness and potentially causing a backlash against the offending company. Here are some of the major ethical dilemmas[1]:

Trick questions: While filling in a form, you respond to a question that tricks you into giving an answer you did not intend. When glanced at quickly, the question appears to ask one thing, but when read carefully, it asks another thing entirely.

Sneak-into-basket: You attempt to purchase something, but somewhere in the purchasing journey, the site sneaks an additional item into your basket, often through the use of an opt-out radio button or checkbox on a prior page.

Roach motel: You get into a situation very easily, but then you find it hard to get out of it (e.g., a premium subscription).

Privacy zuckering: You are tricked into publicly sharing more information about yourself than you really intended to. Named after Facebook CEO Mark Zuckerberg.

Price comparison prevention: The retailer makes it hard for you to compare the price of an item with another item, so you cannot make an informed decision.

[1] Verified using ChatGPT 4 (June 2024).

K. Solberg Söilen, *Digital Marketing*, Springer Texts in Business and Economics, https://doi.org/10.1007/978-3-031-69518-6_37

Misdirection: The design purposefully focuses your attention on one thing to distract you from another.

Hidden costs: You get to the last step of the checkout process, only to discover some unexpected charges have appeared, e.g., delivery charges, tax, etc.

Bait and switch: You set out to do one thing, but a different, undesirable thing happens instead.

Confirmshaming: The act of guilting the user for opting into something. The option to decline is worded in such a way as to shame the user into compliance.

Disguised ads: Adverts that are disguised as other kinds of content or navigation to get you to click on them.

Forced continuity: When your free trial with a service comes to an end, and your credit card silently starts getting charged without any warning. In some cases, this is made even worse by making it difficult to cancel the membership.

Friend spam: The product asks for your email or social media permissions under the pretense it will be used for a desirable outcome (e.g., finding friends) but then spams all your contacts in a message that claims to be from you.

37.1.1 Mason's Ethical Issues

Mason[2] presents four main ethical issues: privacy, accuracy, property, and accessibility.

Privacy: What kind of information can people keep to themselves and not share with others? There are two main topics that threaten our integrity. The first is technology that improves the information systems to monitor, communicate, store, and retrieve information. The second threat is the increasing value of information regarding decision-making. Information is valuable for decision-makers. An example of this was when the Tallahassee Community College used monitors in public bathrooms to gather information regarding the usage of the bathrooms. Students and staff felt that this was an invasion of their integrity and a violation of their rights.

Accuracy: Who is responsible for the authenticity and trustworthiness of the information? Who will be in charge of the wrong information and its damage? When people trust the information's accuracy as if it were a life-or-death situation, there is a burden on the information itself. It is a risk when we create information systems and place the information in our databases that we can use in decision-making. It is a responsibility that the information is accurate. Today, we are producing a lot of information about people and their activities, and a lot of the information is not correct. The question is, who owns the information?

Property: "Who owns information?" There are ethical and economic issues about the question of immaterial rights, and it is the most convoluted question. Information costs money to create from the beginning, and the information can further be easy to reproduce and share with others. If the information is reproduced, it can damage the original, and it is hard to secure the original information from

[2] Mason (1986).

being damaged. It is also hard to protect the original, and it is hard to get a replacement for information being used by another. Institutions protect immaterial rights, such as copyrights and patents, yet there is a problem securing information. Organizations and individuals are using communication more frequently because it is profitable for them to do so. The use of bandwidth is inadequate, and noise can destroy the clear pattern of information. The questions remain: how will the use of bandwidth be distributed, and who has access to it?

Accessibility: What kind of rights to information does an organization or a person have, under which circumstances, and what kind of protection? Our most important way to information is through literacy. In an information society, people must have three things to be literate:

1. One must have the skill to access information such as reading and writing.
2. One must have access to where the information is gathered, such as libraries, radio, and televisions.
3. One must have access to the information itself.

The last two are a problem in social economics. It is also important to know what's correct and not while marketing your products.

Ethics is much up to us, but the laws are strict and must be followed.

37.2 Data Protection and Privacy Law

Laws help individuals and companies follow a framework and behave ethically. There are laws that companies need to consider while marketing themselves online, and they help to prevent unethical behaviors. Companies need to be careful not to be unethical as this can damage the reputation of the company.

Today, identity theft is very common. Companies need to avoid this as individuals are more concerned about their personal affairs with a third party. The European Union has a directive about data protection (95/46/EC), giving individuals rights, and it applies to those who collect data. They have to be open about their usage and consider the principles of the regulation. This law has been replaced with another directive from the European Union, 2016/679. This law is a protection for individuals about their data and protects individuals' fundamental rights and obligations.

Personal data is any information associated with an individual that can be identified. An identified individual is any individual that, for example, can identify themselves with an identification number or location data. Any information that relates to a living human and any information that can identify a person is considered personal data. Information about a customer or an employee that is stored by a company is also considered personal data. It is important for organizations to know how information is collected and used. Information about an individual that is most common for online brands is online identification.

37.2.1 General Data Protection Regulation

GDPR stands for General Data Protection Regulation. GDPR is a regulation from the European Union, and the regulation is used to protect the EU resident's personal information. It was enforced on May 25, 2018. The GDPR law applies to all the members of the European Union and also to other countries that provide services for the European Union.

The law has two main purposes:

- Protecting the rights, privacy, and freedoms of natural persons in the EU.
- Reducing barriers to business by facilitating the free movement of data throughout the EU.

Because every member state of the EU has accepted this regulation, they cannot modify or change the regulation.

According to GDPR, personal data should be processed according to the law and regulations and be justly and openly communicated to the individual. The information that is processed should have a purpose and not be used further and be limited to that purpose. Any data stored that is no longer necessary and does not fulfill the purpose should be erased immediately. The information can be stored longer exclusively if there is a public interest or statistical purpose, in which case they need to protect the information in a way that GDPR provides for an individual's safety and freedom. Stored information about an individual has to be securely stored so that unauthorized individuals do not have access to the information, and systems need to be in place to secure personal information. Companies need to destroy personal data in a safe way.

Every business that collects and stores personal data has an obligation to handle this information securely. A person's right to privacy is an essential part of human rights and refers to all of us. Companies have to consider if they are in possession of personal information and if it is appropriate for the company to have this kind of information. The information can only be used if the consumer gives the company the right to use it. The customer has the right to revoke any kind of information whenever they want.

37.2.2 PECR (Privacy and Electronic Communications Regulations)

PECR stands for The Privacy and Electronic Communications (EC Directive) Regulations and is a regulation from 2003. This law is a European law and is also known as the e-privacy directive. This law is also known as the "cookie law." This law applies alongside GDPR.

In the future, this law will be included in GDPR. This law protects marketing through email, telephone marketing, and the usage of cookies on websites that track information about individuals. The law also protects public electronic communications services and the privacy of individuals using communication networks regarding location data.

37.2.3 Cookies

Cookies are another aspect controlled by law. These are used to identify the user through small text files on a user's computer. Cookies store information about a visitor until the next time the visitor comes back. The website uses the previous information from these cookies about the user when they return. The purpose of the cookies is to get information for following server–browser communication without asking for the same information again. Cookies can, for example, store information about a credit card, the number, and the user's name. This involves a risk for the user. Some secure cookies provide three types of security services: authentication, integrity, and confidentiality. Authentication verifies the cookie's owner. Integrity protects against unauthorized modification of cookies. Finally, confidentiality protects against the cookie's values being revealed to an unauthorized entity.

"Users can change their settings to stop this tracking by turning on 'Don't Track.' Once that functionality is turned on, then the user is not identifiable."

To better understand the customer, be clear with what kind of information you collect. You can provide information about how cookies are used in the privacy policy. Explain to the customer why cookies are used on the webpage and why it is relevant. Let the customer agree to cookies and tracking, and let them know that they can decline it at any time.

37.2.4 Brand and Trademark Protection

Online brand and trademark protection is also a major area regulated by laws and cover several areas, including the use of a brand name within domain names and the use of trademarks within other websites and online adverts. If a company registers a domain, it refers to the company's website and cannot be used by another company. The domain ".co.uk" has to be renewed every 2 years. It is important to check up on the domain name; otherwise, the company can lose their domain name. The brand could be damaged if the ads are placed on a website that the company does not want to be associated with.

Being sued for any unlawful behavior can easily bring a company to bankruptcy. For example, the luxury fashion brand Burberry faced a significant legal battle when it sued Target for trademark infringement in 2018. Burberry claimed that Target was selling products with a pattern that closely resembled its iconic check design without permission. The case highlighted the importance of brand and trademark protection, as Burberry sought to protect its brand identity and market position. While Burberry did not go bankrupt, the case underscored the potential financial and reputational risks associated with trademark infringement litigation.

37.2.5 Intellectual Property Rights (IPRs)

This law protects designs, inventions, and ideas. The law also protects content developed for e-commerce. It is divided into two areas: one part related to copyright and the other to industrial properties. Industrial properties protect signs related to trademarks. The other part of industrial properties is designs and creations related to patents.

Copyright protects producers, authors, and performers. Copyright is a law from the European Union, and it applies to all countries in the European Union. It helps ensure that competition online is not distorted. Copyright protects the authors and gives them the right to allow or prohibit any transmission to the public of their work.

For example, the case of "Happy Birthday to You" is a notable instance of copyright protection. Originally composed in the late nineteenth century, the song's lyrics were copyrighted, and Warner/Chappell Music held the rights for many years, collecting royalties whenever the song was used in films, television, or public performances. It was not until 2016 that a court ruled the copyright claim invalid, placing the song in the public domain. This case illustrates how copyright laws can protect authors' works and also how legal challenges can redefine the scope of these protections.

37.2.6 Online Advertising Law

When companies are using online advertising, the advertising needs to be clear, and the consumer has to know that it is an ad. In Sweden, there is a law called "the marketing law," which protects the consumer from undue marketing. This law refers to all members of the European Union to provide security for consumer rights. The marketing must be clear, right, and understood; the customer has to know that it is advertising. The company that markets must clarify who is responsible for the marketing.

An example of deceptive marketing was when Toyota sued Volvo for advertising that their car was "Volvo XC60—the world's safest car." Toyota assumed that the information was wrong, but Volvo said it was right and continued with the marketing. In Toyota's lawsuit, they said that Volvo's marketing was a deception for the customer and pointed out that there was no evidence or proof that it was the case. Toyota demanded that Volvo be banned from using that phrase in their marketing. This lawsuit ended with a fine for Volvo of one million SEK for using "the world's safest car" when this was not the case. They were prohibited from using this phrase further in their marketing and had to compensate Toyota for the trial costs.

37.3 Types of Information Collected from Customers

Chaffey and Ellis-Chadwick (2019) identify five key types of information that companies collect from customers, each controlled by ethics and legislation. These categories are essential for understanding customer behavior and personalizing marketing strategies while adhering to legal standards. They are:

1. *Contact information*
   - Includes customer's address, name, and email.
   - Collected via cookies on websites, helping to remember a customer's visits.
2. *Profile information*
   - Helps segment the customer by age, gender, etc.
   - Useful for creating targeted marketing strategies.
3. *Platform usage information*
   - Collected through web analytics systems.
   - Identifies which computer and database a visitor uses on the website.
4. *Behavioral information on a single site*
   - Information about purchases stored in company databases.
   - Cookies track visitor behavior on the website.
5. *Behavioral information on multiple sites*
   - Tracks how an individual uses different platforms simultaneously.
   - Examples include Google's use of cookies for its ads pay-per-click program.

Additionally, companies use other methods to engage with customers:

37.4 Text Message Marketing

Text message marketing involves sending promotional offers via text messages to customers. This method of communication requires careful consideration to avoid negative feelings towards the brand. Text messages are often seen as more intimate than other forms of communication, making it essential for companies to ensure their messages are welcome.

To comply with data protection legislation, companies must get explicit consent from customers before sending messages. Additionally, the content of the messages should be relevant and valuable to the recipient. Overuse or misuse of text messaging can lead to customer annoyance and damage the brand's reputation. Therefore, it is crucial to strike a balance between effective marketing and respecting customer boundaries.

37.5 Email Marketing

Email marketing remains a powerful tool for building and maintaining customer relationships. However, to avoid being perceived as spam, companies must ensure their emails are relevant and valuable to the recipient. The design of the emails should be engaging and capture the consumer's interest to increase open and click-through rates. Collecting email addresses must be done in compliance with data protection laws, ensuring customers have given their consent. Effective email marketing campaigns often segment their audience to tailor messages to specific customer groups. Regularly analyzing the performance of email campaigns can help refine strategies and improve results. Overall, email marketing, when done correctly, can significantly enhance customer engagement and loyalty.

37.6 Online Reviews and Fake Reviews

Online reviews play a critical role in helping customers make informed decisions about products and services. Positive reviews can boost a company's reputation, while negative reviews can provide valuable feedback for improvement. However, the prevalence of fake reviews poses a significant ethical challenge. Companies may create fake positive reviews to enhance their image or fake negative reviews to undermine competitors.

Spotting fake reviews often involves identifying unverified sources and unusually high ratings in a short period. Ethical companies should focus on encouraging genuine customer feedback and addressing legitimate concerns. By maintaining transparency and integrity in their review practices, companies can build trust and credibility with their customers.

37.7 Key Takeaways on Ethical Considerations in Digital Marketing

Understanding ethical issues in digital marketing is crucial for managers to build trust and maintain a positive reputation. Here are some key takeaways from the chapter:

1. *Transparency*: Ensure all marketing practices, such as cookie usage and data collection, are clearly communicated to customers.
2. *Consent*: Get explicit consent from customers before collecting their data or sending promotional messages.
3. *Privacy*: Safeguard customer information and comply with regulations like GDPR to protect personal data.
4. *Accuracy*: Ensure all marketing content is truthful and avoid misleading information that could harm customer trust.

5. *Property*: Respect intellectual property rights and avoid using unauthorized content.
6. *Accessibility*: Make sure information is accessible to all customers, including those with disabilities.
7. *Authenticity*: Focus on genuine customer reviews and feedback rather than relying on fake reviews to manipulate perceptions.
8. *Avoid dark patterns*: Refrain from using deceptive design tactics like hidden costs, bait and switch, or forced continuity.
9. *Reputation management*: Monitor social media and online reviews to quickly address any negative feedback.
10. *Ethical communication*: Maintain ethical standards in all forms of digital communication, including email marketing and text messaging.

As companies, we need to make a clear distinction between genuine ethics and mere window dressing, often seen in practices like greenwashing or exaggerated self-promotion. Much of this happens because we succumb to external pressures, only to realize later that we cannot uphold our promises. This erosion of trust is widespread and detrimental, damaging the public's confidence in our organizations and products. Therefore, it is better to speak less about ethics, but when we do, ensure we back our words with real actions.

References

Chaffey, D., & Ellis-Chadwick, F. (2019). *Digital marketing*. Pearson uk.

Mason, R. O. (1986). Four ethical issues of the information age. *Management Information Systems Quarterly, 10*(1), 5–12.

Further Reading

Caroll, A. B., & Buchholtz, A. K. (2008). *Business & society: Ethics and stakeholder management*. Cengage Learning.

Cranor, L. F. (2002). *Web privacy with P3P*. O'Reilly Media, Inc.

Mason, R. O., Mason, F. M., & Culnan, M. J. (1995). *Ethics of information management*. SAGE Publications.

Spinello, R. A. (2014). *Cyberethics: Morality and law in cyberspace*. Jones & Bartlett Learning.

Tavani, H. T. (2013). *Ethics and technology: Controversies, questions, and strategies for ethical computing*. John Wiley & Sons.

Banner and Native Advertising, Display Campaigns 38

38.1 Introduction

Banner ads remain relevant today, but their effectiveness has evolved with digital advancements and changes in user behavior. While banner ads were once dominant, the rise of ad blockers and banner blindness—where users ignore banner-like information—has impacted their visibility and click-through rates. However, when used strategically, banner ads can still drive traffic and increase brand awareness, especially when targeted accurately. Innovations like dynamic and interactive banners, coupled with precise targeting and retargeting strategies, have helped maintain their relevance in a comprehensive digital marketing mix.

Unlike banner ads, native ads are highly relevant today because of their ability to blend seamlessly with the content that surrounds them, providing a nondisruptive user experience. Unlike traditional banner ads, native ads match the form and function of the platform on which they appear, making them less likely to be ignored. They offer better engagement rates and higher credibility and can effectively bypass ad blockers. Native advertising is especially valuable in mobile environments and social media platforms, where user attention is more fragmented and traditional ads are often overlooked. Their contextual relevance and targeted approach contribute significantly to their effectiveness in modern digital marketing strategies.

Display campaigns remain highly relevant in today's digital marketing landscape because of their versatility and reach. They allow advertisers to deliver visually engaging ads to targeted audiences across a vast network of websites, social media platforms, and mobile apps. Display ads are particularly effective for brand awareness, retargeting, and driving traffic to websites. With advancements in targeting options and real-time bidding, display campaigns can be finely tuned to reach specific demographics, behaviors, and interests, making them a crucial component of integrated marketing strategies. They also benefit from improved measurement and analytics, helping marketers optimize performance and ROI.

The first clickable banner ad, introduced in 1993, marked the inception of digital marketing. Since then, online ads have evolved from simple newspaper-like formats

K. Solberg Söilen, *Digital Marketing*, Springer Texts in Business and Economics, https://doi.org/10.1007/978-3-031-69518-6_38

to becoming a primary revenue source for websites. The rise in social media usage has driven companies to develop relevant and effective advertisements. For an ad to be effective, it must capture the consumer's attention, be understood, and prompt the desired action, ultimately fostering a positive attitude towards the product and the company. Display advertising has thus remained a critical aspect of marketing strategies.

Figure 38.1 shows a diagram that summarizes the relationship between the relevance of banner ads, native ads, and display campaigns in today's digital marketing landscape:

38.2 Practicalities of Banner Ads

Banner advertisements were among the first to appear on the Internet, typically consisting of a static or animated image and a small amount of text. They can be positioned at the top, bottom, or sides of a webpage. The main purposes of banners are to inform about new products, grab attention, and drive users towards a company's website, often aiming to increase brand awareness.

Ad servers determine which ads to display on a website, utilizing targeting parameters and data collection. They manage online ad campaigns by collecting data such as impressions and clicks, providing insights and results for advertisers.

38.3 Definition of Native Ads

Native advertising is a relatively new digital marketing method that is constantly growing. Unlike display ads or banner ads, native ads do not look like ads. They blend into the editorial flow of the page. The word "native" means to blend in, which describes the ad's primary goal. This can be a balancing act as the ad must be recognized as an ad by the reader and should not be confused with the editorial content. Thus, all native ads must be labeled as ads.

Native ads can be anything from a sponsored tweet to a Facebook post or an advertised article. It is about creating editorial content that catches the consumer's attention.

Native advertising is the fastest-growing form of advertising globally. Budgets for native advertising are expected to grow significantly, with thousands of trademarks using this method.

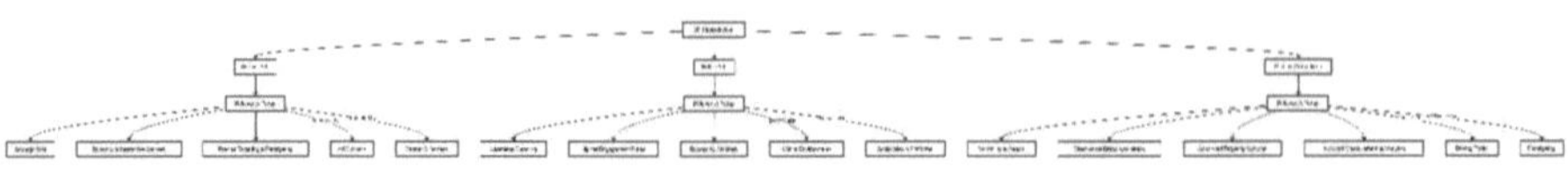

Fig. 38.1 Relevance of banner ads, native ads, and display campaigns

38.4 Difference between Banner and Native Advertising

Banner advertising has evolved from newspapers to the web. Banners aim to disrupt the consumer's online experience and direct them to the company's website. This often results in "banner blindness," where consumers do not notice the ad at all.

Native advertising, on the other hand, aims to blend in and not interfere with the consumer's online experience. Native ads must be labeled as ads and have a clear sender. They can open directly to the company's website or expand into a "lightbox" when clicked. Unlike banners, native ads cannot be blocked by ad blockers.

38.5 How to Create a Good Native Advertisement

The rise in Internet users has led to market fragmentation, necessitating advertisers to tailor content across various platforms to meet diverse consumer preferences. Online advertising should aim to minimize disruptions in the consumer's online experience. By optimizing ad placement and enhancing relevance, ads can blend seamlessly into the environment, thereby reducing interruptions. Social media offers companies the opportunity to reach large audiences at a low cost, emphasizing the importance of engaging, nonirritating posts.

Many companies attempt to stand out aggressively, which can be counterproductive. Ads that disrupt the consumer's experience are often seen as intrusive and undesirable. Effective native ads integrate smoothly with the user's experience, providing value and fitting contextually. Misleading ads may boost short-term impressions but ultimately erode brand trust. Table 38.1 shows ways to succeed with native advertising.

Table 38.1 Key aspects of effective native advertising[a]

Aspect	Description	Example/application
Market fragmentation	Dividing consumers into segments with different preferences and needs.	Creating targeted content for specific social media platforms.
Minimizing disruptions	Reducing interruptions in the user's online experience.	Placing ads that blend with content seamlessly.
Social media engagement	Leveraging social media to build large audiences at low cost.	Crafting engaging posts that resonate with followers
Nondisruptive ads	Ads that fit the user's experience and are sometimes desirable.	Sponsored content that matches the tone and style of the platform.
Clear source and value	Native ads should clearly indicate the source and provide value.	Articles or videos that offer useful information while subtly promoting a product.
Avoiding misleading ads	Ensuring ads are honest to maintain brand trust.	Transparent sponsored posts that inform and engage without deceiving.
Following trends	Staying updated with advertising trends and audience preferences.	Using popular formats and platforms preferred by the target audience.

[a]Verified using ChatGPT 4 (June 2024)

Native advertising should seamlessly integrate into the consumer's online experience, providing value without being intrusive. Effective native ads are transparent, relevant, and engaging, fostering long-term loyalty by meeting consumer needs without deception. Understanding the target audience and staying updated with advertising trends are crucial for creating successful native ads that enhance brand engagement.

38.6 Building Brand Awareness through Banner Advertising

Web advertising revenues in the United States reached approximately $246 billion in 2023, surpassing TV advertising. Social media advertising spending is projected to exceed $76.4 billion in 2024, accounting for a significant portion of total online advertising expenditure. This trend underscores the importance and growth of digital advertising channels in the modern marketing landscape.

Consumers' increased use of social media has elevated the importance of online advertising in marketing strategies. Studies reveal that exposure to web ads significantly boosts brand awareness, which is crucial for fostering a positive attitude towards a company. Effective ads must capture attention, be understood, and prompt the desired consumer action. Repeated exposure to ads generally enhances responses until saturation occurs, leading to consumer fatigue. Table 38.2 gives some advice on how to succeed with banner advertising.

Banner advertising remains an essential tool in digital marketing. While the landscape has evolved with the advent of ad blockers and changing user behavior, strategically implemented banner ads continue to drive traffic and enhance brand awareness. Leveraging dynamic and interactive elements, along with precise targeting, can optimize the effectiveness of banner ads in today's competitive digital environment. Integrating native and display ads within a cohesive marketing strategy ensures a comprehensive approach to engaging diverse audiences.

38.7 Display Ads and Third-Party Cookies

Third-party cookies play a crucial role in collecting data from website visitors to personalize ads. The data collected, which includes location, age, interests, and search trends, is used to tailor advertisements to specific user profiles. Advertisers purchase or receive this information to enhance the relevance of their ad campaigns. Cookies also help improve website functionality by analyzing user behavior, allowing for a more seamless and engaging user experience.

By understanding user preferences, websites can present relevant content and ads, increasing the likelihood of user interaction and conversion. This practice not only benefits advertisers but also aims to provide users with a more personalized browsing experience. However, it is important to note the growing concerns over privacy and the use of cookies in online advertising.

Table 38.2 Key Points on Banner Advertising[a]

Aspect	Description	Example/application
Web advertising revenue	In 2023, web advertising revenues in the US hit $246 billion, highlighting its dominance over traditional TV advertising.	Major platforms like Google and Facebook contribute significantly to this revenue through ads.
Social media spending	Projected to surpass $76.4 billion in 2024, showing a substantial share of online advertising.	Companies like Coca-Cola and Nike invest heavily in social media campaigns to reach targeted demographics.
Consumer behavior	Increased social media use drives higher online ad integration, with studies indicating web ads significantly boost brand awareness.	Brands use Instagram and TikTok to engage users with interactive and visually appealing content.
Ad effectiveness	Effective ads must be seen, paid attention to, understood, and acted upon. Repetition increases response until consumer fatigue sets in.	Repeated ads for products like the apple iPhone maintain consumer interest until purchase intent is achieved.
Banner advertising	Banner ads are effective for marketing products, generating traffic, fostering positive brand attitudes, and increasing sales.	Retailers like Amazon use banner ads to promote deals and new products.
Ad types and attributes	Static banners are passive and require more exposure; pop-ups gain immediate attention but can cause irritation. Rational ads focus on functionality, while emotional ads drive imagery.	Static banners: Product launches; pop-ups: Flash sales; rational: Tech specs; emotional: Luxury brands.
Product involvement	High-involvement product ads are clicked more frequently than low-involvement product ads. Static and emotional ads benefit from frequency, while pop-up and rational ads benefit from reach.	High-involvement: Tech products like laptops; low-involvement: Consumables like snack.

[a]Verified using ChatGPT 4 (June 2024)

38.8 Challenges with Banner and Native Advertising

Advertising is a crucial tool for businesses to succeed. It builds a relationship between consumers and the brand, explaining what the brand stands for and why the consumer should buy the product. Market communication is essential for creating a unique image and differentiating in the market.

The increase in online ads has led to ad avoidance by consumers. Every time a consumer is exposed to advertising, there is a selection and treatment process required for the advertisement to be recognized. Ads should be in the right place and context to avoid being scrolled past unnoticed.

Banner blindness occurs when consumers ignore ads they perceive as irrelevant. Although native ads aim to blend in, they must be clearly branded as ads to avoid violating advertising regulations. Many people find it challenging to recognize native advertising. This challenge is compounded by the rise of ad blockers, which allow users to prevent ads from appearing altogether.

Moreover, the over-saturation of ads in the digital space can lead to consumer fatigue, where users become overwhelmed by the sheer volume of advertisements they encounter daily. This fatigue can result in a negative perception of brands that heavily rely on intrusive ad formats. As banner ads become less effective, marketers must innovate to capture and retain consumer attention.

In addition to these challenges, there is a growing emphasis on data privacy and user consent. Regulations like the GDPR and CCPA require advertisers to be transparent about data collection and use, adding complexity to targeting strategies. Ensuring compliance with these regulations while delivering personalized ads is a delicate balance that marketers must achieve to maintain consumer trust and avoid legal repercussions.

38.9 Ad Blockers

The number of Internet users employing ad blockers is rapidly increasing worldwide, posing a significant challenge to digital advertisers. New forms of online advertising are continually developed to capture consumers' attention. However, when ads are too intrusive or overly targeted, they often drive users to seek ways to block them. Ad blocking is a significant problem in the digital world, affecting both advertisers and publishers.

Ad blockers not only eliminate ads but also prevent tracking, which has privacy implications for consumers. For instance, ad blockers can prevent cookies from tracking user behavior across websites, thereby enhancing user privacy. Consumer privacy involves controlling when, how, and to what extent personal information is shared with others. By blocking ads and trackers, consumers can navigate the web without constant surveillance.

Since ad blockers can hide native ads, advertisers have had to become more creative and less intrusive in their approach. Native ads, which blend seamlessly with the surrounding content, are less likely to be blocked and can be more effective in engaging users. For example, a travel blog featuring native ads for travel gear or booking services can provide value to readers without disrupting their experience.

Native ads allow companies to market their brand and products in an entertaining and value-adding way. By providing relevant information, native ads reduce the sense of intrusion. For instance, an article about healthy living that includes a native ad for a fitness app integrates the ad into useful content, making it more acceptable to the reader.

Ad blockers push advertisers to adapt to the changing market by focusing on nonintrusive, high-quality content. Companies should create ads that are relevant and engaging, such as video tutorials, informative articles, or interactive content that users find genuinely useful. This approach not only bypasses ad blockers but also builds a positive relationship with consumers.

Moreover, advertisers are exploring alternative methods to reach audiences, such as influencer marketing and sponsorships, which are less likely to be affected by ad blockers. For instance, a beauty brand might partner with a popular YouTuber to showcase its products, reaching the audience through content they actively seek out and enjoy.

In conclusion, while ad blockers pose a significant challenge, they also encourage innovation and better practices in digital advertising. By focusing on relevance, value, and user experience, advertisers can create more effective and acceptable ads, ultimately benefiting both consumers and brands.

38.10 Key Takeaways for Managers

This chapter covers the evolution and current relevance of various digital advertising methods. Here's a summary of key takeaways for managers, focusing on strategies, challenges, and compliance issues in the digital marketing landscape:

- *Banner ads relevance*:
  - Banner ads still drive traffic and brand awareness with strategic targeting and innovations like dynamic and interactive banners.
  - *Example*: Using retargeting strategies to show ads to users who previously visited the site.
- *Native ads efficiency*:
  - Native ads blend seamlessly with content, leading to higher engagement and bypassing ad blockers.
  - *Example*: Sponsored articles that match the tone and style of the platform they appear on.
- *Display campaigns versatility*:
  - Display campaigns offer broad reach across websites, social media, and apps, making them effective for brand awareness and retargeting.
  - *Example*: Utilizing real-time bidding to target specific demographics and interests.
- *Ad blockers impact*:
  - The rise of ad blockers challenges traditional advertising, pushing marketers to adopt nonintrusive, high-quality content strategies.
  - *Example*: Creating valuable content that users seek out, like informative articles or video tutorials.
- *Data privacy compliance*:
  - Adherence to GDPR and other regulations is essential, ensuring transparency and user consent in data collection and ad targeting.
  - *Example*: Informing users about data collection practices and offering opt-out options.
- *Challenges with banner and native ads*:
  - Ad fatigue and banner blindness necessitate innovative and contextually relevant ad placements to maintain effectiveness.

  - *Example*: Rotating ad creatives frequently to avoid user fatigue and maintain user interest.
- *Leveraging social media*:
  - Effective use of social media advertising can build large audiences at a low cost, emphasizing the importance of engaging, nonirritating posts.
  - *Example*: Interactive social media campaigns that encourage user participation and sharing.

A good banner ad can still be effective. To navigate the complexities of digital advertising, managers must stay informed about the evolving landscape and adapt strategies to maintain relevance and effectiveness. Emphasizing high-quality, nonintrusive content, adhering to privacy regulations, and leveraging innovative ad formats will help build strong, positive relationships with consumers.

Further Reading

Google. (n.d.). *Ad blockers: Block or allow pop-ups in Chrome*. Retrieved from https://support.google.com/chrome/answer/95472?hl=en

Interactive Advertising Bureau. (2020). *IAB internet advertising revenue report*. Retrieved from https://www.iab.com/insights/iab-internet-advertising-revenue-report/

Native Advertising Institute. (n.d.). *What is native advertising?* Retrieved from https://nativeadvertisinginstitute.com/what-is-native-advertising/

Trustworthy Accountability Group. (2019). *The economic impact of ad blockers*. Retrieved from https://www.tagtoday.net/economic-impact-of-ad-blockers/

Digital Cultures

39

39.1 Digital Marketing Strategy: Business Models

Digital culture is a broad area that refers to the behaviors, practices, and norms shaped by the use of digital technologies and online platforms. It encompasses the ways in which digital interactions influence social structures, communication, and cultural identities. These cultures will be different depending on where digital marketing is done, divided by countries, and also by sectors and industries.

This chapter could have been much larger but expanding it further would delve into other disciplines, particularly sociology, where the author has limited knowledge. Still, we should at least be aware of this larger perspective.

Understanding digital cultures is crucial for several reasons[1]:

1. Consumer behavior: Digital cultures influence how consumers interact with brands and make purchasing decisions.
2. Marketing strategies: Effective digital marketing requires adapting to the cultural contexts of various online communities.
3. Global reach: Digital cultures transcend geographical boundaries, enabling businesses to connect with a global audience.
4. Innovation: Staying updated with digital cultural trends fosters innovation and competitiveness.
5. Brand reputation: Awareness of digital cultures helps avoid cultural missteps that can harm a brand's reputation.
6. Engagement: Engaging with digital cultures fosters deeper connections with consumers and enhances brand loyalty.

[1] Verified using ChatGPT 4 (June 2024).

K. Solberg Söilen, *Digital Marketing*, Springer Texts in Business and Economics, https://doi.org/10.1007/978-3-031-69518-6_39

39.2 Understanding Digital Cultures

39.2.1 Cultural Awareness in Marketing

Cultural awareness is essential for effective marketing. It allows brands to translate their symbols and features while maintaining integrity. For example, cultural diversity within and across countries complicates marketing campaigns, requiring a deep understanding of cultural nuances to avoid mismatches that could lead to failures. In general, we may say that digital cultures, influenced by social movements and technological advancements, shape consumer behavior and expectations.

39.2.2 Digital Cultures and Social Movements

Digital platforms empower citizens to voice opinions and challenge higher powers, as seen in the 2014 Umbrella Movement in Hong Kong. Similarly, during the Arab Spring, digital platforms played a crucial role, particularly in Egypt, where protesters organized and gathered in Tahrir Square, leading to significant political change. Another example is the 2014 revolution in Kyiv, Ukraine, where social media and digital communication were instrumental in mobilizing and coordinating protests. These movements highlight the profound influence of digital culture on political and societal changes. Companies must understand these cultural shifts to align their marketing strategies with current societal values and avoid backlash.

39.2.3 Creating Digital Cultures

Digital cultures are created through information technology, breaking down spatial and physical boundaries and fostering new socialization. These cultures address issues like gender and sexuality, providing platforms for support and community formation. However, they can also perpetuate negative practices, such as online harassment. Companies create digital cultures to better understand and market to their target audiences, tailoring strategies to fit specific digital environments.

39.2.4 Boundaries of Digital Cultures

Digital media and cultures have boundaries shaped by social structures and access to technology. These boundaries are becoming increasingly blurred as digital technologies become integral to daily life. Marketers must navigate these boundaries to reach diverse audiences effectively, understanding different cultural perspectives to avoid offending potential customers.

39.2.5 Global Digital Cultures

The global economy is influenced by digital cultures driven by information exchange. Globalization blurs social class boundaries, fostering a more inclusive digital culture. The Internet offers new ways of communication and political participation, although it often limits interactions to like-minded individuals. Governments and organizations use digital platforms for transparency and public engagement, but achieving global democracy through digital culture remains a challenge.

39.2.6 Opportunities for Digital Culture

Digital cultures offer opportunities for growth and development by leveraging various digital tools to meet consumer needs. Younger generations drive digital culture, making it adaptable and responsive to trends. They also have more time for this. While the rapid expansion of the Internet presents challenges, it also provides opportunities for innovation and engagement. Marketers can use influencer marketing to connect authentically with audiences, leveraging influencers' understanding of digital cultures.

39.3 Key Takeaways for Managers

Here are the key takeaways from this short chapter:

- *Understand cultural differences*:
  - Cultural awareness is crucial for effective marketing, allowing brands to maintain integrity while appealing to diverse audiences.
- *Leverage digital platforms*:
  - Digital platforms empower consumers and influence societal changes. Align marketing strategies with current societal values to avoid backlash.
- *Use customer insights*:
  - Research consumer motivations and behaviors to create appealing and relevant online content.
- *Adapt to digital boundaries*:
  - Navigate social and technological boundaries to reach diverse audiences effectively without offending them.
- *Globalize digital strategies*:
  - Embrace globalization to create a more inclusive digital culture and leverage global communication opportunities.
- *Drive innovation with digital tools*:
  - Use digital tools to meet consumer needs, leveraging influencer marketing to connect authentically with audiences.
- *Stay adaptable*:

– Keep up with technological advancements and understand diverse digital cultures to innovate and engage effectively.

Just like there are cultures in the offline world, there are digital cultures online. In the end, these are only different groups who portray different behaviors, often forming what we understand by subcultures. By integrating these insights, managers can navigate the complexities of digital cultures, fostering effective marketing strategies that resonate with diverse audiences and drive brand success. Understanding and leveraging digital cultures is essential for staying relevant and competitive in today's dynamic digital landscape. Companies catch these trends and changes through environmental scanning and different forms of business intelligence analysis focusing on their external environment.

Further Reading

Global Web Index. (2020). *Social media trends 2020.* Retrieved from https://www.globalwebindex.com/reports/social

Kietzmann, J. H., Hermkens, K., McCarthy, I. P., & Silvestre, B. S. (2011). Social media? Get serious! Understanding the functional building blocks of social media. *Business Horizons, 54*(3), 241–251.

Statista. (2021). *Number of social media users worldwide from 2010 to 2021.* Retrieved from https://www.statista.com/statistics/278414/number-of-worldwide-social-network-users/

We Are Social. (2020). *Digital 2020: Global digital overview.* Retrieved from https://wearesocial.com/digital-2020

Strategies and Business Models in Digital Marketing 40

40.1 Background, Definitions, and Examples

Digital marketing strategies are structured plans that use various online channels to achieve marketing goals. They involve the deployment of specific tactics to engage target audiences, increase brand awareness, drive traffic, and convert leads into customers. These strategies typically include:

- *Search engine optimization (SEO)*: Enhancing a website's visibility in search engine results through keyword optimization, quality content, and backlinks.
- *Content marketing*: Creating and sharing valuable content to attract and engage a target audience, ultimately driving profitable customer actions.
- *Social media marketing*: Using social media platforms to promote products/services, engage with audiences, and build brand loyalty.
- *Email marketing*: Sending targeted emails to a subscriber list to nurture relationships, inform about products/services, and drive sales.
- *Pay-per-click (PPC) advertising*: Paying for ads that appear on search engines or other websites where advertisers are only charged when users click on the ads.
- *Affiliate marketing*: Partnering with affiliates who promote products and earn commissions on sales generated through their links.
- *Influencer marketing*: Collaborating with influencers who have a large following to promote products/services to their audience.
- *Video marketing*: Using videos to promote products/services, explain concepts, and engage with customers.

Digital business models describe the various ways companies create, deliver, and capture value using digital technologies. These models often leverage the Internet and digital tools to facilitate business operations and interactions with customers.

A list of digital business models with examples is provided below[1]:

[1] Verified using ChatGPT 4 (June 2024).

K. Solberg Söilen, *Digital Marketing*, Springer Texts in Business and Economics, https://doi.org/10.1007/978-3-031-69518-6_40

1. *E-commerce Model*
   - *Amazon and eBay*: These platforms facilitate the buying and selling of goods and services online. Amazon offers a vast marketplace for various products, from books to electronics, while eBay allows users to auction items or sell them at fixed prices, providing a space for both new and used goods.
2. *Subscription model*
   - *Netflix and Spotify*: Netflix charges a monthly fee for access to its extensive library of movies and TV shows. Spotify offers a free version with ads and a premium version with additional features like offline listening and ad-free music for a monthly fee.
3. *Freemium model*
   - *LinkedIn and Dropbox*: LinkedIn provides basic networking features for free but charges for premium services like advanced search and professional training. Dropbox offers a free tier with limited storage and charges for additional space and advanced features.
4. *Advertising model*
   - *Google and Facebook*: Google generates revenue by displaying targeted ads based on users' search queries and online behavior. Facebook uses user data to show personalized ads in user's feeds, stories, and videos, making significant revenue from advertisers.
5. *Affiliate marketing model*
   - *Skimlinks and Amazon Associates*: Skimlinks convert regular product links into affiliate links, allowing publishers to earn commissions on sales. Amazon Associates enables website owners to earn advertising fees by linking to Amazon products.
6. *On-demand model*
   - *Uber and DoorDash*: Uber provides ride-sharing services, where users can book rides via an app, with drivers responding in real-time. DoorDash offers food delivery services, where customers can order from local restaurants and get their food delivered quickly.
7. *Crowdsourcing model*
   - *Kickstarter and Threadless*: Kickstarter allows creators to fund their projects by soliciting small contributions from a large number of people. Threadless crowdsources designs from artists and prints the most popular ones on apparel, which are then sold online.
8. *Peer-to-Peer (P2P) model*
   - *Airbnb and LendingClub*: Airbnb connects property owners with people looking for short-term rentals. LendingClub facilitates personal loans between peers, bypassing traditional banks.
9. *Open-Source model*
   - *Linux*: Linux offers free access to its operating system, with revenue generated from support, customization, and premium services. Companies can use and modify Linux for their own needs, often contributing improvements back to the community.
10. *Experience-based model*

- *IKEA*: IKEA offers a unique shopping experience with showrooms where customers can see and interact with products before purchasing. This model focuses on creating a memorable in-store experience that encourages customers to explore and buy.

11. *Mass market business-to-consumer (B2C) model*
    - *Walmart*: Walmart targets a broad audience by offering a wide range of affordable products. It uses mainstream media advertising, and an extensive network of physical stores, and an online platform to reach a vast customer base.

By understanding and leveraging these strategies and business models, companies can effectively navigate the digital landscape, reach wider audiences, and achieve their marketing objectives. Table 40.1 gives an overview of what business models some of the larger and more famous Internet companies have used to succeed.

40.2 The Process of Selecting a Business Model

Selecting the appropriate business model(s) is crucial for a company's success. Start by understanding your market and audience. Research market needs and analyze the demands and preferences of your target market. Gain customer insights to

Table 40.1 Business models for digital marketing

Business model	Description	Example/application
E-commerce model	Facilitates online buying and selling of goods and services	Amazon, eBay
Subscription model	Charges users a recurring fee for continuous access to a service	Netflix, Spotify
Freemium model	Offers basic services for free, with the option to upgrade to premium features	LinkedIn, Dropbox
Advertising model	Generates revenue by attracting users to a free service and monetizing ads	Google, Facebook
Affiliate marketing model	Partners with affiliates who promote products and earn commissions	Skimlinks, Amazon associates
On-demand model	Provides immediate access to services or products as needed	Uber, DoorDash
Crowdsourcing model	Leverages the public to solve problems, gather information, or fund projects	Kickstarter, Threadless
Peer-to-peer (P2P) model	Involves direct transactions between individuals without intermediaries	Airbnb, LendingClub
Open-source model	Provides freely distributed software without fees, with paid customization	Linux
Experience-based model	Offers customer engagement and interaction with a brand	IKEA
Mass market B2C model	Targets a broad audience with affordable products	Walmart

understand their behaviors, preferences, and pain points. Next, assess your value proposition by identifying what makes your product or service unique and clearly defining its benefits.

Evaluate each business model to see which aligns best with your goals. The e-commerce model is suitable for companies with physical products aiming for a broad reach, as exemplified by Amazon and eBay, which facilitate online buying and selling. The subscription model works well for services or content that can be provided on an ongoing basis, like Netflix and Spotify, which charge users a regular fee for continuous access to their content. The freemium model is effective for digital products with premium features, such as LinkedIn and Dropbox, which offer basic services for free while charging for premium features.

For platforms with high traffic where user data can be monetized through ads, consider the advertising model. Google and Facebook attract users to free services and monetize through advertisements. The affiliate marketing model is useful for businesses looking to earn commissions by promoting other companies' products or services. Websites like Skimlinks and Amazon Associates operate on this model.

The on-demand model suits companies providing immediate access to services or products as needed, like Uber and DoorDash. The crowdsourcing model leverages the public to gather ideas, solve problems, or fund projects, as seen with Kickstarter and Threadless. The peer-to-peer model allows direct transactions between individuals without intermediaries, exemplified by platforms like Airbnb and LendingClub.

Finally, consider the open-source model for software distribution, offering free access while generating revenue through support and customization services, as Linux does. The experience-based model engages customers through brand interactions, such as IKEA's showroom experience. The mass market B2C model targets a broad audience with affordable products, utilizing mainstream media advertising to reach a wide customer base.

By thoroughly evaluating these models and aligning them with your market understanding and value proposition, you can select the most effective business model(s) for your company's growth and success.

We may express this process in a diagram as in Fig. 40.1:

This diagram illustrates the process of choosing the right business model for a company, starting with understanding the market and audience, followed by

Fig. 40.1 The process of choosing the right business model for digital marketing

evaluating various business models and their suitability based on company goals and market demands.

40.3 Key Takeaways

Here are a few general takeaways from this chapter:

- The shift from offline to online markets necessitates new digital marketing strategies and business models to stay competitive.
- Understanding market needs and customer insights is crucial for developing effective digital marketing strategies.
- Various digital business models, such as e-commerce, subscription, freemium, and advertising, offer different ways to create, deliver, and capture value.
- Selecting the right business model involves evaluating market demands, customer behaviors, and the unique value proposition of the product or service.
- Digital marketing strategies should align with business goals to drive engagement, brand awareness, and customer loyalty.

There is a lot of hype around business models. Essentially, a business model describes how a company creates, delivers, and captures value—in other words, how it makes money. Every business operates under some form of business model, but the Internet has revolutionized this concept by enabling entirely new ways of generating revenue. With the advent of digital technology, businesses can now utilize innovative models such as subscription services, freemium models, and platform-based ecosystems that connect buyers and sellers globally. This technological shift allows for scalability, reduced operational costs, and value creation in previously unimaginable ways.

By leveraging the appropriate digital marketing strategies and business models, companies can effectively navigate the digital landscape, reach wider audiences, and achieve their marketing objectives. Understanding customer insights and market needs and aligning strategies with business goals are key to sustainable growth and success in the digital era. Not all business models can be as successful as Google's AdWords/Ads, but at least one advantage with digital marketing is that whatever business model you choose, you quickly get good data to see if it was successful.

Further Reading

Deloitte. (2019). *2019 global marketing trends: Future of marketing*. Retrieved from https://www2.deloitte.com/global/en/insights/topics/marketing-and-sales-operations/global-marketing-trends.html

HubSpot. (2020). *The ultimate guide to digital marketing in 2020*. Retrieved from https://blog.hubspot.com/marketing/digital-marketing

McKinsey & Company. (2020). *The new digital edge: Rethinking strategy for the post-pandemic era*. Retrieved from https://www.mckinsey.com/business-functions/mckinsey-digital/our-insights/the-new-digital-edge-rethinking-strategy-for-the-post-pandemic-era
Smart Insights. (2021). *2021 marketing trends: The latest innovations in marketing strategies*. Retrieved from https://www.smartinsights.com/digital-marketing-strategy/2021-marketing-trends/

Cookies and Privacy Concerns 41

41.1 Background and Definitions

We mentioned cookies earlier, but as they are such a large topic and consist of many different types, they deserve their own chapter in this book. Cookies are small text files stored on a user's device by a web browser. They play a crucial role in digital marketing by tracking user behavior, personalizing ads, and enhancing user experience. The different types and their functions are listed in Table 41.74 below:

Cookies are vital in digital marketing for tracking user behavior, targeting ads, and improving website functionality. There are several types of cookies, each serving different purposes, from session management to persistent tracking. Users can manage or prevent cookies through browser settings, privacy-focused extensions, or specialized anti-tracking software. Understanding and controlling cookies can help balance the benefits of personalized web experiences with privacy concerns.

41.2 Evolution of Cookies

Cookies were invented by Lou Montulli in 1994 as a means to enhance user interaction with websites by remembering previous interactions, such as items in an e-commerce shopping cart. Initially, cookies were intended to improve browsing speed and user experience. However, their ability to track online behavior quickly led to their widespread use in monitoring user activities across the web. This tracking raised privacy concerns as users realized that websites were storing information on their computers without explicit consent. Despite these concerns, cookies became an integral part of online advertising and personalization. They allowed advertisers to deliver targeted ads based on users' browsing habits.

Over time, the use of cookies expanded to include session management, personalization, and analytics. The introduction of third-party cookies further complicated privacy issues, as they enabled tracking across multiple sites. In response to growing privacy concerns, regulations like the GDPR and CCPA were introduced to give

K. Solberg Söilen, *Digital Marketing*, Springer Texts in Business and Economics, https://doi.org/10.1007/978-3-031-69518-6_41

Table 41.74 Types of cookies and their functions[a]

Type of cookie	Function	How to prevent
Session cookies	Store temporary data during a browsing session; deleted once the browser is closed.	These are automatically deleted when you close your browser.
Persistent cookies	Remain on a user's device for a set period; used for remembering login details and preferences.	Clear cookies through browser settings; set browser to clear cookies upon exit.
First-party cookies	Created by the website a user is visiting directly; used for improving user experience.	Block cookies via browser settings or use privacy-focused browsers.
Third-party cookies	Created by domains other than the one a user is visiting; commonly used for tracking and advertising.	Use browser settings to block third-party cookies; use ad-blockers or privacy-focused extensions.
Secure cookies	Only transmitted over secure (HTTPS) connections; used to enhance security.	Not generally blocked unless all cookies are disabled.
HttpOnly cookies	Accessible only by the server, not by JavaScript; used to enhance security against XSS attacks.	Not generally blocked unless all cookies are disabled.
Zombie cookies	Recreated after deletion from backups stored outside the typical cookie storage locations.	Use specialized anti-tracking software and clear flash cookies as well.

[a]Verified using ChatGPT 4 (June 2024)

users more control over their data. Browsers also began implementing features to block or limit cookies. Despite these measures, cookies remain a fundamental technology in the digital marketing ecosystem, balancing functionality with ongoing privacy debates.

41.3 Pros and Cons of Cookies

41.3.1 Advantages of Cookies

Despite privacy concerns, cookies offer significant advantages for both users and website owners. They enable personalized user experiences, such as remembering login details and preferences, facilitating online shopping, and providing relevant content and advertisements. Cookies also help website owners track and analyze user behavior, improving site functionality and user satisfaction.

41.3.2 Drawbacks of Cookies

The primary drawback of cookies is their potential to invade user privacy. They can track users across different websites, gathering extensive data on their online activities. This information can be used for targeted advertising, sometimes without the user's knowledge or consent. Additionally, cookies can be vulnerable to security risks, such as unauthorized access and data breaches.

41.4 Technical Alternatives to Cookies and Reasons they Were Not Chosen

Despite being essential tools for companies to enhance user experience and collect valuable data, cookies are generally disliked by customers. Many users perceive cookies as intrusive because they track online behavior and collect personal information without explicit consent. This tracking often leads to targeted ads, which can feel invasive. Companies, however, rely on cookies to personalize content, improve website functionality, and analyze user behavior for better marketing strategies. The balance between leveraging cookies for business benefits and respecting user privacy remains a significant challenge. Table 41.75 lists some of the major limitations with alternatives to cookies:

Despite the availability of these alternatives, cookies remain the most widely used method for tracking and personalization because of their simplicity and effectiveness. Local storage and session storage are often limited by their lack of persistence and domain restrictions. More advanced options like IndexedDB and server-side storage increase complexity and are not uniformly supported. Privacy concerns and regulatory compliance issues often restrict the use of fingerprinting and device identifiers. Web beacons and URL parameters are easily blocked or manipulated, making them less reliable for comprehensive tracking.

41.5 Opt-in or Opt-out?

There are two primary models for obtaining user consent for cookies: opt-in and opt-out. The *opt-in model* needs users to actively consent to the use of cookies, providing greater privacy protection. The *opt-out model* allows cookies to be set by default, with users needing to take action to disable them. The opt-in model is more privacy-friendly, as it ensures that users are aware of and agree to the collection of their data.

41.6 Privacy Concerns with Cookies

Cookies have become a significant privacy issue primarily due to the use of third-party cookies, which track user behavior without explicit consent. These cookies can compile detailed behavioral profiles, posing substantial privacy and security risks. Users are concerned that their personal information could be accessed and misused, resulting in a loss of control over their data. Privacy concerns are heightened by the unauthorized collection and use of personal data through cookies, leading to increased use of adblockers and privacy tools. To address these concerns,

Table 41.75 Technical alternatives to cookies[a]

Alternative	Description	Limitations
Local storage	Stores data locally within a user's browser.	Limited to the same domain, lacks expiration functionality, not suitable for cross-site tracking.
Session storage	Similar to local storage but only available for the duration of the page session.	Data is cleared when the session ends, not persistent between sessions.
IndexedDB	A low-level API for storing large amounts of structured data.	More complex implementation, not designed for simple tracking, not uniformly supported across all browsers.
Web SQL database	Deprecated API for storing data in databases with SQL.	Deprecated by W3C, lacks support, and better alternatives like IndexedDB.
Server-side storage	Stores session data on the server side.	Increases server load and complexity, does not facilitate client-side personalization without frequent calls.
Fingerprinting	Collects various device attributes to create a unique identifier.	Highly invasive, significant privacy concerns, often blocked by browsers and regulations.
ETags (entity tags)	HTTP headers used for web cache validation repurposed for tracking.	Easily detected and blocked by browser settings, ethical and legal issues.
URL parameters	Appends tracking information to URLs.	Visible to users, easily removed or manipulated, not suitable for cross-session or cross-site tracking.
Device and OS identifiers	Uses unique device or OS identifiers for tracking.	Not universally available, significant privacy concerns, often restricted by device manufacturers and OS providers.
Web beacons	Small image files included in web pages or emails that report when viewed.	Limited to page views, can be blocked by users or email clients.

Verified using ChatGPT 4 (June 2024)

regulations like the GDPR have been introduced, requiring websites to obtain explicit user consent before storing cookies on their devices. This regulation aims to protect user privacy and give users more control over their personal information online.

41.7 Key Takeaways for Managers

Understanding the significance of cookies and privacy concerns in digital marketing is essential for managers. Here are some key points from the chapter:

- *Cookies are vital tools* in digital marketing, aiding in tracking user behavior, personalizing ads, and improving website functionality.
- *Types of cookies* include session, persistent, first-party, third-party, secure, HttpOnly, and zombie cookies, each serving different purposes.

- *Privacy concerns* mainly arise from third-party cookies, which track user behavior without explicit consent, leading to detailed behavioral profiles and significant privacy risks.
- *GDPR and similar regulations* require websites to obtain explicit user consent before storing cookies, aiming to protect user privacy and give users control over their data.
- *Users can manage cookies* through browser settings, privacy-focused extensions, or specialized anti-tracking software, balancing personalized web experiences with privacy concerns.
- *Historical context*: Cookies were invented in 1994 by Lou Montulli to enhance user interaction with websites, but their tracking capabilities quickly led to privacy concerns.
- *Technical alternatives* to cookies include local storage, session storage, IndexedDB, server-side storage, fingerprinting, ETags, URL parameters, device identifiers, and web beacons. However, these alternatives often have limitations that make cookies more effective and widely used.
- *Users generally dislike cookies* because of their intrusive nature, while companies rely on them for data collection and personalized marketing strategies.
- *Opt-in versus opt-out models*: The opt-in model requires user consent for cookies, providing better privacy protection, while the opt-out model sets cookies by default, with users needing to disable them.
- *Adapting to privacy concerns* is crucial for maintaining user trust and complying with regulations, balancing the benefits of cookies for companies with the need to respect user privacy.

In conclusion, while cookies are essential tools in digital marketing, their usage raises significant privacy concerns. Managers must understand these concerns and implement strategies to ensure compliance with regulations while respecting user privacy. This balance is critical for maintaining user trust and effectively leveraging cookies for marketing benefits.

Further Reading

Ayanso, A., & Mokaya, B. O. (2014). Internet users' information privacy concerns (IUIPC) and the perceived impact of internet security on e-commerce success. *International Journal of Business and Social Science, 5*(6), 10–22.

Brill, J. (2010). The impact of privacy laws on marketing: An analysis of the general data protection regulation (GDPR) and the California consumer privacy act (CCPA). *Journal of Marketing Research, 47*(2), 120–135.

Krishnamurthy, B., & Wills, C. E. (2006). Generating a privacy footprint on the internet. *ACM SIGCOMM Computer Communication Review, 36*(4), 95–100.

Lwin, M. O., Wirtz, J., & Williams, J. D. (2007). Consumer online privacy concerns and responses: A power-responsibility equilibrium perspective. *Journal of the Academy of Marketing Science, 35*(4), 572–585.

Montulli, L. (1994). *How I invented the web cookie*. Retrieved from. https://internethistorypodcast.com

Solove, D. J. (2006). A taxonomy of privacy. *University of Pennsylvania Law Review, 154*(3), 477–560.

Turow, J., Hennessy, M., & Draper, N. (2015). The tradeoff fallacy: How marketers are misrepresenting American consumers and opening them up to exploitation. *SSRN Electronic Journal.* https://doi.org/10.2139/ssrn.2820060

Warren, S. D., & Brandeis, L. D. (1890). The right to privacy. *Harvard Law Review, 4*(5), 193–220.

Zuboff, S. (2015). Big other: Surveillance capitalism and the prospects of an information civilization. *Journal of Information Technology, 30*(1), 75–89.

42 Using Google Ads in Digital Marketing

42.1 The Competitors of Google Ads

Google Ads may be the biggest game in town, but it is not the only one.

The main global competitors of Google Ads include several major platforms. Facebook Ads, along with Instagram Ads, offers targeted advertising based on user demographics, interests, and behaviors, with various ad formats like image, video, carousel, and story ads. Amazon advertising allows brands to reach consumers directly on Amazon's platform through sponsored products, sponsored brands, and display ads, leveraging Amazon's e-commerce dominance. Microsoft advertising, formerly known as Bing Ads, enables ads on the Bing search engine and its partner networks, offering competitive targeting options.

Apple Search Ads provide opportunities for app developers to promote their apps at the top of App Store search results, which is particularly significant for mobile app-focused businesses. LinkedIn Ads are tailored for B2B marketing, offering targeting based on professional criteria like job title, industry, and company size, making it valuable for reaching professionals and decision-makers. Twitter Ads offer promoted tweets, accounts, and trends to engage users in real-time conversations, ideal for reaching audiences interested in current events.

Snapchat Ads provides interactive ad formats such as Snap Ads, Story Ads, and Sponsored Lenses, targeting younger audiences effectively. TikTok Ads leverage the platform's popularity among younger demographics with engaging video ad formats. Pinterest Ads are visually driven and cater to users seeking inspiration and ideas, which is valuable for businesses in the fashion, home decor, and lifestyle industries. AdRoll focuses on retargeting and prospecting through programmatic advertising, helping businesses reengage visitors who have shown interest in their products but have not converted. These platforms offer diverse advertising solutions and targeting options, making them significant competitors to Google Ads in the digital advertising space.

In China, the main competitors to Google Ads are several prominent local platforms. Baidu advertising leads the market as the largest search engine in the

K. Solberg Söilen, *Digital Marketing*, Springer Texts in Business and Economics, https://doi.org/10.1007/978-3-031-69518-6_42

country, offering various advertising solutions. Alibaba's Alimama allows businesses to advertise across its extensive ecosystem, including Taobao and Tmall. Tencent advertising leverages its popular services like WeChat and QQ for targeted ads. ByteDance, known for Toutiao and Douyin (TikTok), provides powerful advertising opportunities using sophisticated algorithms.

Sina Weibo advertising, comparable to Twitter, offers promoted posts and display ads. Qihoo 360's 360 Search and Sogou provide competitive search engine marketing options. JD.com utilizes its vast consumer data for effective advertising on its e-commerce platform. Kuaishou, another major short video platform, is especially popular in smaller cities. Xiaohongshu (Little Red Book) focuses on lifestyle and fashion, offering influencer marketing and native ads. These platforms are essential for businesses aiming to reach the Chinese market with targeted and extensive advertising opportunities.

42.2 Background to Google Ads

Google Ads and AdWords are essentially the same platform but with a different name. Google AdWords was the original name of Google's online advertising platform, launched in 2000. In 2018, Google rebranded AdWords to Google Ads to better reflect the platform's full suite of advertising capabilities across different types of campaigns and placements, including search, display, video, and app ads.

Google Ads is an online advertising platform where businesses can create and run ads to reach potential customers through Google's vast network, including search results, websites, YouTube, and apps. It is crucial for businesses as it allows precise targeting based on keywords, demographics, and user behavior, maximizing the chances of reaching interested audiences. Users bid on keywords, and when someone searches using those terms, relevant ads are displayed, leading to potential clicks and conversions. Google Ads also provides analytics to track performance, optimize campaigns, and adjust strategies to improve ROI. Overall, it is a powerful tool for businesses aiming to increase visibility and drive sales online.

The service looks something like in Fig. 42.1 when you log on, depending on what language you have set for your account.

Google Ads is a versatile platform used by marketers to promote their products, services, or brands through various advertising methods, including Search, Display, Video, Gmail, and Shopping Ads.

In 2023, Google's advertising revenue reached approximately $200.34 billion, accounting for 73.5% of the company's total revenue of $272.14 billion. This platform enables advertisers to showcase ads, products, and service offerings across the Google advertising network to potential consumers.

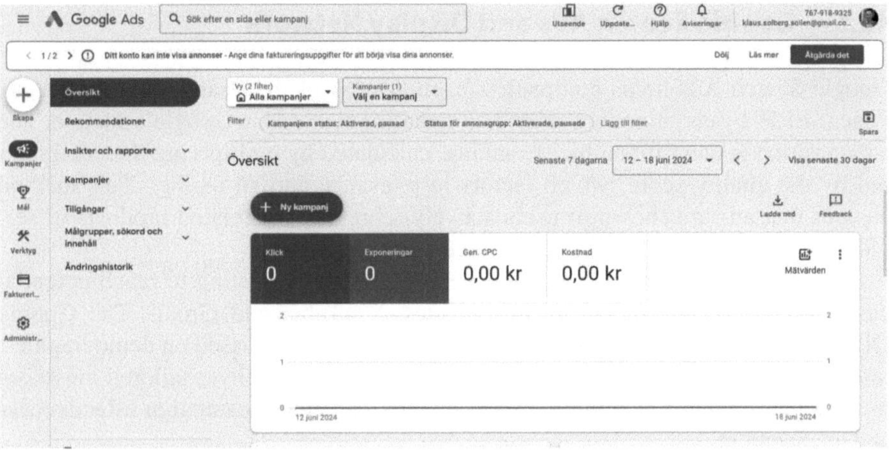

Fig. 42.1 Google Ads desktop or dashboard screenshot

42.3 Search Engine Optimization and Google Organic Search

Search engine optimization (SEO) is a strategy designed to enhance the visibility of a website for both search engines and users. The primary objective of SEO is to deliver relevant information to users by improving a website's technical structure, content quality, and authority.

Google, which held an 88.13% market share of all online search engines as of January 2024, employs intricate algorithms to rank websites based on a multitude of criteria, ensuring the most pertinent results are displayed to users. Unlike paid advertising, organic search results on Google cannot be directly influenced by monetary means and are ranked purely on relevance to the search term, emphasizing the importance of SEO in achieving long-term visibility and traffic growth.

42.4 Search Visibility and Search Console

Search visibility pertains to the prominence of content in search engine results, with highly visible content appearing at the top of organic search results, attracting more clicks and traffic. This visibility is crucial for increasing brand awareness, driving conversions, and establishing authority within a particular niche.

Google Search Console plays a pivotal role in this process by providing webmasters and marketers with a suite of tools to measure, review, and analyze data related to their website's performance in Google search. It helps in monitoring traffic trends, click-through rates, and the effectiveness of SEO efforts. Additionally, Search Console offers detailed insights into search queries that lead users to the website, enabling informed decisions on optimizing content and improving overall search visibility. By leveraging these tools and insights, businesses can enhance their online presence and maximize the impact of their SEO strategies over time.

42.5 Google Search Ads and Display Network

Google Search Ads helps companies reach the top of the Search Engine Results Page (SERP) by enabling them to bid on specific keywords in Google's auction. The ad's position is determined by its ranking, calculated by multiplying the maximum bid by the quality score, which factors in relevance and ad quality. This method ensures that ads are shown to users actively searching for related products or services, maximizing the likelihood of clicks and conversions.

Conversely, Google Display Ads leverage audience targeting to reach potential customers across a wide array of websites, YouTube, and Gmail. The Google Display Network facilitates precise audience segmentation based on demographics, interests, and browsing behavior, enabling advertisers to deliver tailored messages to the right audience at optimal times, thereby enhancing campaign effectiveness and engagement.

42.6 Google Video Ads

Google Ads also offers powerful video advertising opportunities on YouTube, the world's largest video platform. Advertisers can create video campaigns using various formats to suit different marketing objectives. For instance, skippable in-stream ads allow viewers to skip after a few seconds, ensuring that engaged users watch longer if the content is compelling. Video discovery ads appear alongside related YouTube videos, enticing users to click and watch based on their interests. Nonskippable in-stream ads play before, during, or after a YouTube video, capturing viewers' full attention for the duration of the ad. Outstream ads, on the other hand, are designed for mobile devices and appear on partner sites and apps within the Google Display Network, expanding their reach beyond YouTube.

These video ad formats are effective in engaging audiences and conveying messages through compelling visual content. For example, a fashion retailer might use skippable in-stream ads to showcase a new clothing line, allowing viewers to engage with the ad based on their interest in fashion. A technology company might opt for video discovery ads to promote a new product demonstration, reaching users actively searching for tech reviews and tutorials. Nonskippable in-stream ads could be used by a travel agency to captivate potential customers with scenic vacation destinations, ensuring the message is delivered uninterrupted. Meanwhile, outstream ads could help a fitness brand target mobile users on health and wellness websites, showcasing workout routines or new fitness gear.

By leveraging these diverse video ad formats, advertisers can effectively capture attention, drive engagement, and achieve their marketing goals on YouTube and across the Google Display Network, leveraging the platform's extensive reach and targeting capabilities to maximize campaign effectiveness and audience impact.

42.7 Ad Groups

Ad groups serve as a vital organizational tool within Google Ads, facilitating the structured management of campaigns targeting specific audiences or themes. By grouping related ads and keywords together, advertisers can ensure relevance and coherence in their advertising strategies. This structure also enables marketers to optimize bidding strategies and ad messaging based on the distinct characteristics of each group.

Google Ads offers significant scalability, allowing up to 25 campaigns and 2000 ad groups per campaign. This flexibility empowers advertisers to meticulously segment their target audiences and tailor their messages accordingly, whether by geographic location, demographics, or behavioral patterns. Effective use of ad groups not only enhances campaign performance but also simplifies the monitoring and adjustment of ad budgets and targeting criteria. Overall, leveraging ad groups effectively in Google Ads can lead to more efficient advertising campaigns and improved ROI by aligning marketing efforts with specific business objectives and audience preferences.

42.8 PPC (Pay-Per-Click)

Pay-Per-Click (PPC) is a pivotal component of Search Engine Marketing (SEM) that drives revenue for search engines by allowing advertisers to bid on keywords relevant to their products or services. When users conduct searches using these keywords, relevant ads are displayed, and advertisers pay a fee each time someone clicks on their ad.

Google Ads (formerly Google AdWords) and Yahoo! Search Marketing exemplify prominent PPC platforms, offering advertisers precise targeting capabilities and measurable results. Unlike traditional advertising models, PPC ensures that advertisers only incur costs when their ads attract user engagement, whether through clicks, calls, or website visits. This performance-based model encourages efficient budget allocation and allows for real-time optimization of ad campaigns based on immediate feedback and analytics. By leveraging PPC, businesses can enhance visibility, attract qualified traffic, and achieve specific marketing objectives, such as lead generation or sales conversions, effectively aligning advertising expenditures with tangible business outcomes.

42.9 Conversion Tracking and ROI

Conversion tracking is a fundamental tool within digital advertising that enables advertisers to gauge the impact of their paid campaigns accurately. By tracking user actions post-click, such as purchases, sign-ups, or downloads, conversion tracking provides invaluable insights into ad performance and campaign effectiveness. These insights are crucial for optimizing ad strategies, identifying high-performing ads, and refining targeting to maximize ROI.

ROI calculation in conversion tracking measures the profitability of advertising expenditures by comparing the revenue generated from conversions to the total advertising costs. This metric plays a pivotal role in evaluating campaign success and guiding strategic decisions regarding budget allocation and resource deployment. Ultimately, conversion tracking empowers advertisers to make data-driven adjustments, enhance campaign efficiency, and achieve meaningful business outcomes, ensuring that marketing efforts align closely with organizational goals and objectives.

42.10 Choosing Keywords

Selecting the right keywords is a pivotal aspect of optimizing the relevance and cost-effectiveness of ads in digital advertising campaigns. Keywords directly influence where and when ads appear in search engine results, shaping their visibility and potential impact on target audiences. It is essential for advertisers to strike a balance between choosing popular keywords that attract significant search volume and selecting less competitive keywords to optimize ad spend and enhance ad performance.

By conducting thorough keyword research and analysis, advertisers can identify strategic keywords that align closely with their target audience's search intent and behavior. This approach not only improves ad relevance but also enhances the likelihood of attracting qualified leads and driving conversions. Additionally, ongoing keyword optimization and refinement based on performance data allow advertisers to continuously fine-tune their campaigns, ensuring sustained effectiveness and maximizing return on advertising investment (ROI). In essence, strategic keyword selection is integral to achieving campaign objectives and achieving optimal outcomes in digital advertising efforts.

42.10.1 Types of Keywords

Understanding different types of keywords is crucial for optimizing ad campaigns, minimizing unnecessary costs, and effectively targeting the right audience:

- Commercial keywords: These keywords indicate strong buying intent, such as "buying a travel guide" or "best price on laptops." Users using these keywords are often close to making a purchase decision, making them highly valuable for conversion-focused campaigns.
- Informational keywords: While these keywords generate high search volume, they are primarily used for gathering information rather than making immediate purchases. Examples include "traveling tips," "how to fix a leaking faucet," or "history of Ancient Rome." Advertisers can use informational keywords to attract

users early in the buying cycle and nurture them towards a purchase decision through content marketing or educational campaigns.

- Navigational keywords: These keywords direct users to specific brand websites or pages. Examples include “Amazon books,” “Nike official site,” or “Microsoft support.” Advertisers bidding on navigational keywords aim to capture users already familiar with their brand or products, ensuring direct traffic and reinforcing brand authority.
- Transactional keywords: These keywords indicate the user’s readiness to complete a transaction, such as “discounted flights to New York,” “coupon code for shoes,” or “order pizza online.” Transactional keywords are highly valuable for campaigns focused on immediate conversions and sales.
- Long-tail keywords: These are specific, often longer phrases that capture niche or detailed search queries. Examples include “best laptop for graphic design under $1000,” “organic dog food delivery service in Chicago,” or “affordable wedding venues near me.” Long-tail keywords typically have lower competition and higher conversion rates because of their specificity and relevance to user needs.

Understanding and categorizing keywords into these types enables advertisers to tailor their ad campaigns more precisely. By matching the right keywords to specific campaign objectives and user intents, advertisers can optimize ad spend, improve ad relevance, and enhance overall campaign performance effectively.

42.10.2 Google Keyword Planner

The Google Keyword Planner is an indispensable tool for advertisers seeking comprehensive insights into keyword dynamics. Beyond suggesting relevant keywords for campaigns, it offers critical data such as search volume trends and cost-per-click estimates. This information empowers advertisers to make informed decisions about which keywords to target based on their budget and marketing goals.

Moreover, the Keyword Planner provides performance predictions, helping advertisers forecast the potential impact of their chosen keywords on ad visibility and engagement. By leveraging these insights, advertisers can optimize their keyword strategies to maximize traffic, improve ad targeting precision, and achieve better overall campaign outcomes in Google Ads.

42.10.3 Negative Keywords

Negative keywords play a crucial role in refining ad targeting and optimizing ad spend within Google Ads campaigns.

By specifying terms like "free" or "cheap," HeritageStride Shoes can prevent their ads from appearing in searches unrelated to their premium footwear offerings. This strategic use of negative keywords ensures that their ad budget is allocated efficiently, focusing on users searching for quality shoes rather than those seeking discounts or freebies.

By excluding irrelevant searches, HeritageStride Shoes can increase the relevance of their ads to potential customers, enhance click-through rates, and ultimately improve the ROI of their advertising efforts. Negative keywords thus serve as a proactive tool for enhancing campaign effectiveness and driving qualified traffic to their online store.

42.11 Quality and Relevance

Selecting high-quality and relevant keywords is paramount for ensuring the effectiveness of advertising campaigns. Google provides several tools, such as the Keyword Planner and Keyword Quality Score, which enable advertisers to meticulously plan and optimize their keyword selections. These tools analyze factors like search volume, competition, and user intent, helping advertisers align their ads with the most promising opportunities.

By prioritizing quality and relevance in their keyword strategy, advertisers can enhance ad performance, attract more qualified leads, and optimize their ad spending effectively. This approach not only improves the visibility and click-through rates of ads but also contributes to achieving a higher ROI by targeting audiences more likely to convert. Ultimately, leveraging Google's tools to refine keyword choices ensures that advertising efforts are both efficient and impactful in reaching and engaging the desired audience.

42.12 Key Takeaways

Google Ads is an essential online advertising platform that allows businesses to reach potential customers across Google's extensive network, including search results, websites, YouTube, and apps. By leveraging precise targeting based on keywords, demographics, and user behavior, businesses can maximize their visibility and drive online sales effectively. This chapter explores key aspects of Google Ads and its impact on digital marketing strategies.

Key takeaways from this chapter:

1. Google Ads offers diverse advertising methods such as Search, Display, Video, Gmail, and Shopping Ads, enabling marketers to showcase products and services across multiple platforms.
2. In 2023, Google's advertising revenue reached approximately $200.34 billion, highlighting its dominance in the digital advertising space and its significance for businesses globally.
3. Search engine optimization (SEO) plays a critical role in enhancing website visibility on Google's organic search results, emphasizing the importance of optimizing content for search engines.
4. Google Search Ads enable businesses to bid on keywords and display ads prominently on the Search Engine Results Page (SERP), driving targeted traffic and conversions.
5. Video advertising through Google Ads, particularly on YouTube, offers various formats like in-stream, discovery, nonskippable, and outstream ads, catering to different marketing objectives and audience preferences.
6. Ad groups in Google Ads facilitate organized campaign management by grouping related ads and keywords and optimizing ad relevance and performance.
7. PPC advertising allows advertisers to bid on keywords and pay only when users click on their ads, ensuring cost-effective and measurable results.
8. Conversion tracking in Google Ads provides insights into ad performance and ROI by tracking user actions post-click, such as purchases and sign-ups.
9. Strategic keyword selection is crucial for targeting the right audience and optimizing ad spend in digital advertising campaigns.
10. Utilizing tools like the Google Keyword Planner and negative keywords help advertisers refine their keyword strategies, enhance ad targeting precision, and improve overall campaign effectiveness.

These key takeaways underscore the importance of leveraging Google Ads as a powerful tool for businesses to enhance visibility, drive engagement, and achieve their marketing objectives effectively in the digital landscape. If Google Ads will also be the go-to place for advertising in a decade, we do not know.

Further Reading

Abou Nabout, N., & Skiera, B. (2012). Return on quality improvements in search engine marketing. *Journal of Interactive Marketing, 26*(3), 141–154.

Armstrong, G., Kotler, P., Harker, M., & Brennan, R. (2015). *Marketing: An introduction*. Pearson Education.

Edelman, B. (2010). Advertising arbitrage. *Harvard Business Review, 88*(7/8), 19–21.

Ghose, A., & Yang, S. (2009). An empirical analysis of search engine advertising: Sponsored search in electronic markets. *Management Science, 55*(10), 1605–1622.

Jansen, B. J., & Schuster, S. (2011). Bidding on the buying funnel for sponsored search and keyword advertising. *Journal of Electronic Commerce Research, 12*(1), 1–18.

Varian, H. R. (2007). Position auctions. *International Journal of Industrial Organization, 25*(6), 1163–1178.

Wilbur, K. C., & Zhu, Y. (2009). Click fraud. *Marketing Science, 28*(2), 293–308.

Zhang, K. Z., & Benyoucef, M. (2016). Consumer behavior in social commerce: A literature review. *Decision Support Systems, 86*, 95–108.

E-governance 43

43.1 Background

The public sector increasingly uses the internet to enhance transparency and accessibility in governance, allowing citizens to access information and services more conveniently. In elections, digital platforms facilitate voter registration, provide election information, and enable candidates to engage directly with voters through social media and online campaigns, fostering broader participation and democratic engagement. This shift reflects a growing reliance on digital technologies to improve civic processes and communication between governments and citizens.

e-governance, also known as electronic governance, refers to the application of information and communication technology (ICT) to deliver government services, exchange information, communicate transactions, and integrate various standalone systems and services between government-to-citizen (G2C), government-to-business (G2B), government-to-government (G2G), and government-to-employees (G2E). The aim of e-governance is to enhance the efficiency, effectiveness, transparency, and accountability of government processes and operations. Table 43.1 lists the different dimensions of e-governance, their services provided, benefits, and challenges.

In conclusion, the adoption of digital technologies in government operations across government-to-citizen (G2C), government-to-business (G2B), government-to-government (G2G), and government-to-employees (G2E) sectors promises significant benefits, including enhanced efficiency, transparency, and accessibility. These advancements facilitate improved service delivery and citizen participation while addressing challenges such as the digital divide, security concerns, interoperability issues, and the need for effective change management strategies in implementing digital transformation initiatives.

K. Solberg Söilen, *Digital Marketing*, Springer Texts in Business and Economics, https://doi.org/10.1007/978-3-031-69518-6_43

Table 43.1 E-governance[a]

Dimension	Services provided	Examples	Benefits	Challenges
Government-to-citizen (G2C)	Online tax filing, voting registration, issuing permits and licenses, social welfare programs, public information dissemination	Online tax filing portals, e-passport services, digital identity systems (e.g., Aadhaar in India)	– Efficiency and cost savings – Transparency and accountability – Accessibility – Improved service delivery – Citizen participation	– Digital divide – Security and privacy – Interoperability – Change management
Government-to-business (G2B)	Business registration, procurement processes, licenses and permits, compliance reporting	e-Procurement systems, business registration portals, electronic tendering platforms	– Efficiency and cost savings – Transparency and accountability – Accessibility – Improved service delivery – Citizen participation	– Digital divide – Security and privacy – Interoperability – Change management

(continued)

Table 43.1 (continued)

Dimension	Services provided	Examples	Benefits	Challenges
Government-to-government (G2G)	Interdepartmental data sharing, national digital databases, shared services platforms	Interdepartmental data sharing systems, national digital databases, shared services platforms	– Efficiency and cost savings – Transparency and accountability – Accessibility – Improved service delivery – Citizen participation	– Digital divide – Security and privacy – Interoperability – Change management
Government-to-employees (G2E)	Human resource management, payroll systems, training programs, internal communication platforms	Employee self-service portals, e-learning platforms for government staff, digital payslip systems	– Efficiency and cost savings – Transparency and accountability – Accessibility – Improved service delivery – Citizen participation	– Digital divide – Security and privacy – Interoperability – Change Mana

[a]Verified using ChatGPT 4 (June 2024)

43.2 Key Takeaways from Selected Programs

Governance is a global phenomenon characterized by diverse approaches and systems across nations, shaped by cultural, political, and economic contexts. It encompasses the structures and processes through which decisions are made and implemented, influencing the stability, and development of societies worldwide. As globalization continues to deepen interconnectedness, the evolution and adaptation of governance frameworks play a crucial role in addressing contemporary challenges and fostering sustainable development on a global scale.

43.2.1 India

India has launched the *Digital India Mission* in 2015, which aims to digitally empower the nation. This initiative focuses on creating secure digital infrastructure, delivering government services digitally, and achieving universal digital literacy. Notable projects under this mission include *Digi-Locker*, a platform for storing important documents; *Mobile Seva*, which allows access to government services via mobile apps; and *myGov.in*, a platform for citizen engagement in policy-making.

Despite these advancements, India faces several challenges in its e-governance initiatives. These include a significant digital divide, high costs associated with infrastructure development, and resistance to change among some segments of the population. Future directions for India's e-governance efforts include enhancing digital inclusion, strengthening data protection laws, and ensuring interoperability of various e-governance systems.

43.2.2 European Union

The *Digital Europe Program* is a significant initiative in the European Union, aiming to boost digital capabilities by investing in supercomputing, artificial intelligence, cybersecurity, and advanced digital skills. The European Commission is particularly focused on integrating AI to enhance e-governance services and ensuring that communication systems are secure and capable of withstanding future cyber threats.

43.2.3 United States

In the United States, the *Digital Government Strategy* has been implemented to make federal government services more efficient and accessible. This strategy involves modernizing IT infrastructure, adopting cloud services, and enhancing cybersecurity measures. Additionally, the US government is leveraging AI to improve public service efficiency, such as using predictive analytics for better decision-making and deploying chatbots for citizen services.

43.2.4 Caribbean

Caribbean countries are collaborating regionally to enhance their e-governance frameworks. These collaborations aim to improve access to information, promote open data initiatives, and leverage ICT for social and economic development. The key focus areas for e-governance in the Caribbean include energy management, disaster preparedness, and climate change resilience, supported by various e-governance tools.

In summary, while the specific initiatives and challenges vary, the common goal across these regions is to improve the efficiency, transparency, and accessibility of government services through digital technologies. Each region faces unique challenges but shares the overarching objective of enhancing governance and service delivery through digital means.

43.3 Downsides to e-Governance

Despite its benefits, e-governance faces several downsides globally:

1. Digital divide: Access to technology and internet connectivity varies widely across regions and demographics, exacerbating inequalities and limiting access to e-governance services for marginalized communities.
2. Security concerns: e-governance systems are vulnerable to cyber threats such as hacking, data breaches, and malware attacks, posing risks to sensitive government information and citizen data.
3. Privacy issues: The collection and storage of personal data through e-governance platforms raise concerns about privacy violations and unauthorized access, requiring robust data protection measures.
4. Interoperability challenges: Integration and compatibility issues between different e-governance systems within and across government agencies can hinder seamless service delivery and data sharing.
5. Resistance to change: Bureaucratic inertia and resistance to digital transformation among government officials may impede the adoption and effective implementation of e-governance initiatives.
6. Technological dependence: Reliance on technology for governance processes may lead to disruptions in service delivery during technological failures or outages, affecting citizen access to essential services.
7. Legal and regulatory frameworks: Developing and enforcing comprehensive legal frameworks and regulations for e-governance to address issues such as data protection, cybersecurity, and digital rights poses significant challenges globally.

Addressing these downsides needs careful planning, investment in infrastructure and cybersecurity, inclusive policies to bridge the digital divide, and continuous adaptation to technological advancements while safeguarding citizen rights and privacy.

43.4 Takeaways on e-Governance

e-governance represents a transformative approach that offers significant opportunities for enhancing government efficiency, transparency, and citizen engagement globally. Alongside these benefits, it also faces several challenges:

1. *Efficiency and accessibility*: e-governance streamlines administrative processes, reducing bureaucratic delays and improving service delivery efficiency. Citizens can access government services conveniently from anywhere, reducing time and effort.
2. *Transparency and accountability*: Digital platforms enable governments to provide transparent information on policies, expenditures, and decision-making processes, fostering trust and accountability among citizens.

3. *Enhanced citizen participation*: e-governance facilitates direct citizen engagement through digital platforms, enabling feedback, consultations, and participatory decision-making in policy formulation and governance.
4. *Digital inclusion*: While e-governance can bridge gaps in service delivery, disparities in technology access and digital literacy persist, requiring targeted efforts to ensure inclusivity and equal access for all segments of society.
5. *Security and privacy*: Protecting citizen data and government systems from cyber threats is critical. Strong cybersecurity measures and robust data protection policies are essential to safeguard sensitive information and maintain public trust.
6. *Interoperability and integration*: Ensuring seamless integration and interoperability of e-governance systems across different government departments and agencies enhances coordination and efficiency in service delivery.
7. *Resilience and adaptability*: e-governance systems must be resilient to technological failures and adaptive to evolving digital threats, ensuring uninterrupted access to essential services and information.
8. *Legal and regulatory frameworks*: Developing and enforcing comprehensive legal frameworks and regulations is essential to mitigate risks associated with e-governance, addressing issues such as data privacy, cybersecurity, and digital rights.

e-governance, when implemented effectively, empowers governments to deliver better services, engage citizens more meaningfully, and foster inclusive and sustainable development. By addressing challenges proactively and leveraging their transformative potential, governments can harness the benefits of digital technologies to build more responsive, accountable, and citizen-centric governance systems worldwide. This promises to be the future of democratic rule. Combine this with Central Bank Digital Currencies (CBDCs) and many think that a bright future for greater transparency and fairness can be achieved.

References

Bertot, J. C., Jaeger, P. T., & Hansen, D. (2012). The impact of policies on government social media usage: Issues, challenges, and recommendations. *Government Information Quarterly, 29*(1), 30–40.

Dawes, S. S. (2008). The evolution and continuing challenges of e-governance. *Public Administration Review, 68*, S86–S102.

Heeks, R. (2006). *Implementing and managing eGovernment: An international text*. SAGE Publications.

Janssen, M., & Estevez, E. (2013). Lean government and platform-based governance—Doing more with less. *Government Information Quarterly, 30*, S1–S8.

Luna-Reyes, L. F., Gil-Garcia, J. R., & Cresswell, A. M. (2007). Knowledge and information sharing in collaborative electronic government programs: Lessons from the GT2 project. *International Journal of Electronic Government Research, 3*(1), 27–42.

Norris, D. F., & Reddick, C. G. (2013). Local e-government in the United States: Transformation or incremental change? *Public Administration Review, 73*(1), 165–175.

Sang, S., Lee, J. D., & Lee, J. (2009). E-government adoption in ASEAN: The case of Cambodia. *Internet Research, 19*(5), 517–534.

Scholl, H. J. (2005). *Interoperability in e-government: More than just smart middleware*. In Proceedings of the 38th Annual Hawaii International Conference on System Sciences. https://doi.org/10.1109/HICSS.2005.60.

Social Networks and E-learning 44

44.1 Background of Social Networks

Social networks are online platforms that facilitate the creation and sharing of information, ideas, interests, and other forms of expression through virtual communities and networks. So, what is the difference with social media? Social networks are platforms primarily designed for people to connect with each other, build relationships, and interact on a personal level, like Facebook or LinkedIn. Social media encompasses a broader range of online tools and platforms that allow users to create, share, and consume content, such as blogs, forums, and multimedia-sharing sites like YouTube and Instagram.

These platforms help users to connect with friends, family, colleagues, and others with shared interests. Some key features and aspects of social networks include:

- *User profiles*: Each user has a personal profile where they can share information about themselves, such as their interests, work history, and contact information.
- *Friendship connections*: Users can connect with others by sending friend requests, following, or joining groups and communities.
- *Content sharing*: Users can post text updates, photos, videos, and links to other content, which can be shared and commented on by their connections.
- *Messaging*: Many social networks offer private messaging services, allowing users to communicate directly with one another.
- *News feeds*: Social networks typically have a news feed feature that displays updates and content from a user's connections.

Popular examples of social networks include Facebook, X (former Twitter), LinkedIn, and Instagram. These platforms have revolutionized communication, allowing instant information sharing, and fostering communities of like-minded individuals.

K. Solberg Söilen, *Digital Marketing*, Springer Texts in Business and Economics, https://doi.org/10.1007/978-3-031-69518-6_44

44.2 E-learning

Social networks facilitate e-learning by providing platforms for students and educators to connect, collaborate, and share resources, enhancing the learning experience. They enable the creation of online communities where users can discuss course material, exchange ideas, and support each other's academic progress.

E-learning, or electronic learning, refers to the use of digital technologies and the Internet to deliver educational content outside of traditional classroom settings. It encompasses a wide range of formats, including online courses, virtual classrooms, and digital learning resources. Key components of e-learning include:

1. *Learning management systems (LMS)*: Platforms like Moodle, Blackboard, and Canvas that facilitate the administration, documentation, tracking, and delivery of educational courses.
2. *Online courses*: Structured courses offered by educational institutions or platforms like Coursera, edX, and Udacity, often leading to certifications or degrees.
3. *Webinars and video lectures*: Live or recorded video sessions that provide instruction on various topics.
4. *Interactive learning*: Tools and resources that encourage interactive engagement, such as quizzes, discussion forums, and simulations.
5. *Self-paced learning*: Courses and resources that allow learners to study at their own pace, making education more flexible and accessible.

e-learning has become increasingly popular due to its flexibility, accessibility, and ability to cater to different learning styles. It is used in various contexts, including higher education, professional development, and corporate training.

Some well-known e-learning platforms include, as depicted in Table 44.1.

Some places where you can learn digital marketing not on the list include YouTube and Google's Digital Garage, which offers free courses on various digital marketing topics. HubSpot Academy provides comprehensive free and paid courses with certifications in inbound marketing, content marketing, and more. Another option is Moz Academy, which focuses on SEO and offers both free and paid

Table 44.1 E-learning companies[a]

Company	Type of learning	Number of users (millions)	HQ location
Coursera	Online courses	82	Mountain view, CA
Udemy	Online courses	40	San Francisco, CA
edX	Online courses	35	Cambridge, MA
LinkedIn learning	Professional development	27	Sunnyvale, CA
Khan academy	Free educational content	18	Mountain view, CA

[a]Verified using ChatGPT 4 (June 2024)

courses. Additionally, Skillshare offers a wide range of digital marketing classes taught by industry professionals. Lastly, Facebook Blueprint provides free courses and certifications to help you master Facebook and Instagram marketing.

44.3 Integration of Social Networks and E-learning

The integration of social networks and e-learning has led to the development of social learning platforms. These platforms leverage the collaborative and interactive nature of social networks to enhance the learning experience.

Features of social learning platforms include:

- *Collaborative learning*: Tools that allow students to work together on projects, share resources, and provide peer feedback.
- *Discussion forums*: Online spaces where learners can discuss course content, ask questions, and interact with instructors and peers.
- *Content sharing*: Platforms that enable learners to share educational resources, such as articles, videos, and links.
- *Live interaction*: Features that support live communication, such as video conferencing and real-time messaging, to foster a more interactive learning environment.
- *Gamification*: The use of game-like elements, such as points, badges, and leaderboards, to motivate and engage learners.

Table 44.2 shows some of the differences between social networks, e-learning platforms, and social learning platforms.

In recent years, e-learning and social networks have undergone significant transformations driven by technological advancements and changing user behaviors. Here are the key trends and takeaways:

> E-learning has increasingly integrated artificial intelligence (AI) to personalize learning experiences. AI-driven analytics help track learners' progress and provide tailored recommendations to improve engagement and outcomes.
>
> Gamification is another major trend, making learning more interactive and enjoyable by incorporating game elements like points, badges, and leaderboards. The use of immersive technologies such as virtual reality (VR) and augmented reality (AR) has enhanced experiential learning, allowing students to engage in simulations and practical exercises in a virtual environment.
>
> Mobile learning continues to rise in popularity, with more educational content optimized for smartphones and tablets, enabling learning on the go.

Social networks are playing a pivotal role in e-learning by fostering collaborative learning environments. Platforms like LinkedIn Learning and Facebook Groups facilitate peer-to-peer learning and professional development. These networks also support microlearning, where learners consume small, bite-sized pieces of content

Table 44.2 Comparison of social networks with e-learning and social learning platforms

Feature	Social networks	E-learning	Social learning platforms
Definition	Online platforms for creating and sharing information, ideas, and interests through virtual communities.	The use of digital technologies and the internet to deliver educational content outside traditional classrooms.	Platforms that integrate social networking and e-learning features.
User profiles	Personal profiles with information about interests, work history, and contact details.	User accounts with course history, progress tracking, and learning preferences.	Profiles that combine personal information with educational history and progress.
Friendship connections	Connections with friends, family, colleagues, and others.	Connections with instructors, peers, and educational communities.	Connections with both social and educational contacts.
Content sharing	Posting text updates, photos, videos, and links.	Sharing educational resources, course materials, and assignments.	Sharing educational content, updates, and multimedia resources.
Messaging	Private messaging services for direct communication.	Communication tools such as emails, chat rooms, and discussion forums.	Messaging services for both social and educational interactions.
News feeds	Feeds displaying updates from user connections.	Announcements and updates from courses and instructors.	Combined news feeds from social and educational sources.
Learning management systems (LMS)	N/A	Platforms like Moodle, blackboard, and canvas for course administration.	LMS features integrated with social networking capabilities.
Online courses	N/A	Structured courses offered online, often leading to certifications or degrees.	Courses offered within a social learning environment.
Webinars and video lectures	N/A	Live or recorded video sessions for instructional purposes.	Webinars and video lectures with interactive and social features.
Interactive learning	Interactive engagement through comments and likes.	Interactive tools such as quizzes, simulations, and interactive modules.	Interactive learning with social engagement tools.

(continued)

Table 44.2 (continued)

Feature	Social networks	E-learning	Social learning platforms
Self-paced learning	N/A	Courses that allow learners to study at their own pace.	Self-paced learning with social support and interaction.
Collaborative learning	N/A	Tools for group projects and peer feedback.	Enhanced collaborative tools for group learning and projects.
Discussion forums	Groups and forums for discussions on various topics.	Online forums for course discussions and Q&A sessions.	Integrated forums for both social and educational discussions.
Content sharing (educational)	N/A	Sharing of articles, videos, and other educational content.	Facilitated sharing of educational content with social features.
Live interaction	Real-time communication through chats and video calls.	Features for live communication such as video conferencing.	Real-time interactions combining social and educational contexts.
Gamification	N/A	Game-like elements like points, badges, and leaderboards.	Gamified elements to enhance both social and educational engagement.

that are easy to digest and integrate into their daily routines. The trend towards video-based learning has been bolstered by social media, with platforms like YouTube and TikTok becoming valuable resources for educational content. Live streaming and webinars are increasingly used for real-time interaction and engagement, providing immediate feedback and fostering community.

The intersection of e-learning and social networks has led to the development of social learning platforms, which combine the structured courses of traditional e-learning with the interactive and community-driven elements of social media. These platforms leverage social features such as discussion forums, peer reviews, and collaborative projects to enhance the learning experience.

In summary, the key trends in e-learning and social networks today include the integration of AI, gamification, immersive technologies, mobile learning, collaborative environments, microlearning, video-based learning, and live streaming. These trends are reshaping the way people learn and interact, making education more accessible, engaging, and effective.

44.4 Takeaways

Chapter 44 of the book on Social Networks and E-learning highlights the relationship between these two domains and their evolution. Here are a selection of ten key takeaways from the chapter:

1. Definition and differentiation: Social networks are platforms primarily designed for building connections and interactions on a personal level, while social media encompasses a broader range of tools for creating, sharing, and consuming content.
2. Key features of social networks: Social networks include user profiles, friendship connections, content sharing, messaging services, and news feeds, which facilitate interaction and community building.
3. Popular social networks: Platforms such as Facebook, X (formerly Twitter), LinkedIn, and Instagram have revolutionized communication by enabling instant information sharing and fostering communities of like-minded individuals.
4. Role in E-learning: Social networks enhance e-learning by providing platforms for students and educators to connect, collaborate, and share resources, thus improving the learning experience.
5. Components of E-learning: E-learning includes learning management systems (LMS), online courses, webinars, video lectures, interactive learning tools, and self-paced learning, making education more flexible and accessible.
6. Integration of social networks and E-learning: Social learning platforms combine the collaborative and interactive nature of social networks with e-learning, featuring collaborative learning tools, discussion forums, content sharing, live interaction, and gamification.
7. Technological advancements: The integration of AI in e-learning personalizes learning experiences by providing tailored recommendations and tracking learner progress through AI-driven analytics.
8. Gamification: Incorporating game elements like points, badges, and leaderboards in e-learning makes learning more interactive and enjoyable, enhancing engagement and motivation.
9. Immersive technologies: The use of virtual reality (VR) and augmented reality (AR) in e-learning provides experiential learning opportunities, allowing students to engage in simulations and practical exercises in virtual environments.
10. Mobile and video-based learning: The rise of mobile learning and video-based learning, supported by platforms like YouTube and TikTok, enables learners to access educational content on-the-go and through engaging formats like live streaming and webinars.

These points illustrate the dynamic relationship between social networks and e-learning, emphasizing how technological advancements and interactive features are reshaping the educational landscape.

Further Reading

Aragon, S. R. (2003). Creating social presence in online environments. *New Directions for Adult and Continuing Education, 100*, 57–68.

Greenhow, C., & Robelia, B. (2009). Informal learning and identity formation in online social networks. *Learning, Media and Technology, 34*(2), 119–140.

Hrastinski, S. (2008). Asynchronous and synchronous e-learning. *Educause Quarterly, 31*(4), 51–55.

Kane, G. C., Alavi, M., Labianca, G. J., & Borgatti, S. P. (2014). What's different about social media networks? A framework and research agenda. *MIS Quarterly, 38*(1), 275–304.

Manca, S., & Ranieri, M. (2016). Facebook and the others. Potentials and obstacles of social media for teaching in higher education. *Computers & Education, 95*, 216–230.

Digital Healthcare 45

45.1 Background

Digital healthcare refers to the integration of digital technologies into health and medical care to improve the efficiency, accessibility, and quality of health services. It encompasses a wide range of applications, including telemedicine, mobile health apps, electronic health records, and wearable devices.

Health innovation refers to the development and implementation of new ideas, technologies, processes, and services aimed at improving health outcomes, enhancing the efficiency of healthcare delivery, and advancing the overall health and well-being of individuals and populations. Health innovations can occur in various forms, including medical technologies, digital health tools, healthcare delivery models, and public health initiatives. Table 45.1 gives a description of different aspects of health innovations with examples and critical takeaways.

45.2 The Intersection of Digital Healthcare and Marketing

Digital healthcare and marketing intersect in several significant ways, impacting both the promotion of health services and the engagement of patients and consumers. Digital healthcare tools and platforms, such as mobile health apps, telemedicine services, and wearable devices, provide opportunities for healthcare providers and companies to engage and educate patients. Marketing strategies can be used to promote these tools, encouraging patients to take an active role in managing their health. With the data collected from digital health tools, companies can develop personalized marketing campaigns tailored to individual patient's needs and preferences. This can include personalized health recommendations, reminders for appointments, or targeted promotions for health-related products and services.

Digital healthcare companies can use various digital marketing strategies, such as social media marketing, content marketing, and search engine optimization, to build brand awareness and trust among consumers. Providing valuable content,

K. Solberg Söilen, *Digital Marketing*, Springer Texts in Business and Economics, https://doi.org/10.1007/978-3-031-69518-6_45

Table 45.1 Aspects of health innovation in digital healthcare

Aspect	Definition	Examples	Critical takeaways
Health innovation	Development and implementation of new ideas, technologies, processes, and services in healthcare	– Telemedicine: Remote clinical services via telecommunications – Wearable health devices: Real-time health monitoring (e.g., fitness trackers and ECG monitors) – Electronic health records (EHRs): Digital patient records	– Continued investment in R&D – Regulatory compliance and data privacy – Reducing healthcare disparities through technology – Collaboration among healthcare providers, tech companies, policymakers, and patients
Examples	Specific instances of health innovation	– AI in healthcare: Algorithms for data analysis and decision-making – 3D printing in medicine: Customized medical devices and implants – Precision medicine: Tailored treatments based on genetics, environments, and lifestyles	– Proactive health management – Improved patient outcomes – Effective and targeted therapies – Reduced errors and enhanced care coordination
		– Mobile health apps: Health-related services and information on smartphones – Robotic surgery: Robotic systems assisting in surgery -Genomic medicine: Healthcare decisions based on genetic information	
		– Health information exchanges (HIEs): Secure sharing of health information across organizations	

such as informative articles, videos, and patient testimonials, helps establish credibility and attract potential users. Digital healthcare platforms can integrate customer relationship management (CRM) systems to manage patient relationships effectively. By tracking patient interactions and feedback, healthcare providers can improve service delivery and patient satisfaction. Marketing efforts can be aligned with CRM insights to nurture long-term patient relationships.

Healthcare apps are becoming ever more popular. Table 45.2 lists some of the healthcare apps, their functions, company owners, HQ locations, number of employees, and number of customers.

Not all apps are useful, and many flops as they do not deliver enough value, but healthcare and training apps are here to stay. The 1177 Vårdguiden app in Sweden

Table 45.2 Example of healthcare apps[a]

App Name	Function	Company owner	HQ location	Number of employees	Number of customers (millions)
MyFitnessPal	Calorie counting and fitness tracking	Under Armour	Baltimore, MD	2700	200
Headspace	Meditation and mindfulness	Headspace Inc.	Santa Monica, CA	400	30
GoodRx	Prescription drug price comparison	GoodRx Holdings Inc.	Santa Monica, CA	600	15
Zocdoc	Doctor appointment scheduling	Zocdoc Inc.	New York, NY	500	6
Teladoc	Telehealth services	Teladoc Health Inc.	Purchase, NY	4300	51

Verified using ChatGPT 4 (June 2024)

is a prime example of a successful healthcare app. This app allows Swedish residents to access healthcare advice, book appointments, and manage their health records efficiently. It has proven to be an invaluable tool, especially during the COVID-19 pandemic, when the need for remote healthcare services surged. The app's success lies in its ability to provide essential, convenient services that meet the users' needs. This contrasts with many other apps that fail because they do not offer significant value or solve real problems for users. The 1177 app demonstrates how well-designed healthcare apps can become essential parts of everyday life, ensuring their longevity in the market.

The rise of telemedicine and online consultations has created new marketing opportunities for healthcare providers. Promoting these services through digital channels can attract patients seeking convenient and accessible healthcare options. Digital marketing campaigns can highlight the benefits of telemedicine, such as reduced wait times and access to specialist care. Digital healthcare platforms can also be used to launch and manage health campaigns aimed at promoting public health initiatives.

45.3 Example of Major Players in Digital Healthcare

Examples of major products and uses in digital healthcare include telemedicine platforms like Teladoc Health and Amwell, which provide remote consultations between patients and healthcare providers, enabling access to medical care from anywhere. Mobile health apps, such as MyFitnessPal and Fitbit, help individuals track their fitness, diet, and overall health metrics. Electronic health records systems, provided by companies like Cerner Corporation and Epic Systems, store patients' medical histories digitally, allowing for easy access and sharing among healthcare providers. Wearable devices, such as the Apple Watch and Garmin wearables, monitor vital signs, physical activity, and sleep patterns, providing real-time health data to users and healthcare professionals. Remote monitoring solutions, like those from Philips Healthcare, offer continuous observation and management of patient health outside traditional healthcare settings. Additionally, artificial intelligence and machine learning tools analyze large datasets to help in diagnostics, personalized medicine, and predicting health outcomes.

Table 45.3 shows some of the major companies involved in digital healthcare and their relative size.

The critical takeaways for the digital healthcare industry today include several key points: Accessibility and convenience are significantly enhanced by digital healthcare solutions, which provide on-demand healthcare options, especially in remote and underserved areas. However, the increasing use of digital health technologies raises concerns about data privacy and security, making the protection of sensitive health information paramount. Effective digital healthcare also needs seamless integration and interoperability among different systems and devices to ensure comprehensive and coordinated care. Digital health tools empower patients to take a more active role in managing their health through access to information, self-monitoring, and personalized care. The rapid advancement of digital health technologies necessitates evolving regulatory frameworks to ensure safety, efficacy, and compliance with health standards. Addressing disparities in access to digital health tools and ensuring equitable healthcare for all populations is a critical challenge. Lastly, developing sustainable and scalable digital health solutions that can adapt to varying healthcare systems and demands is essential for long-term success.

Overall, digital healthcare holds the promise of transforming the healthcare landscape by making medical services more accessible, efficient, and patient-centered.

Table 45.3 Major digital healthcare companies

Aspect	Description/examples	Major companies	Headquarters	Number of employees
Digital healthcare	Uses digital technologies to improve health outcomes	Teladoc Health	Purchase, New York, USA	4000+
		Amwell	Boston, Massachusetts, USA	1000+
		Babylon Health	London, UK	2000+
Services	Telemedicine, remote monitoring, mobile health apps, and electronic health records	Doctor on Demand	San Francisco, California, USA	500+
		Philips Healthcare	Amsterdam, Netherlands	80,000+
		Cerner Corporation	North Kansas City, Missouri, USA	26

However, addressing the associated challenges is crucial to realizing its full potential.

45.4 Key takeaways

This last chapter of the book covers the comprehensive landscape of digital healthcare, highlighting its significant impact on health services and innovation. Here are ten key takeaways from this chapter:

1. Integration of digital technologies: Digital healthcare integrates technologies like telemedicine, mobile health apps, electronic health records (EHRs), and wearable devices to enhance health services' efficiency, accessibility, and quality.
2. Health innovation: Innovations in digital healthcare include telemedicine for remote consultations, wearable devices for real-time health monitoring, and AI algorithms for data analysis and decision-making in medical care.
3. Benefits of digital healthcare: Digital healthcare improves accessibility and convenience, especially in remote and underserved areas, by providing on-demand healthcare options and reducing wait times.
4. Data privacy and security: With the increasing use of digital health technologies, protecting sensitive health information is crucial, necessitating stringent data privacy and security measures.
5. Patient empowerment: Digital health tools empower patients by providing access to information, self-monitoring capabilities, and personalized care plans, promoting proactive health management.
6. Regulatory frameworks: The rapid advancement of digital health technologies requires evolving regulatory frameworks to ensure safety, efficacy, and compliance with health standards.
7. Equitable access: Addressing disparities in access to digital health tools is essential to ensure equitable healthcare for all populations, bridging the gap between different demographic groups.
8. Sustainable solutions: Developing sustainable and scalable digital health solutions that can adapt to various healthcare systems and demands is critical for long-term success in the industry.
9. Major players: Major players in digital healthcare include Teladoc Health and Amwell for telemedicine, MyFitnessPal and Fitbit for mobile health apps, and Cerner Corporation and Epic Systems for electronic health records.
10. Marketing and engagement: Digital healthcare intersects with marketing by leveraging digital channels to promote health services, educate patients, and create personalized marketing campaigns based on data collected from digital health tools.

We all want to have our own family doctor available on the phone as soon as we need them. This dream is not that unrealistic today, and many companies already offer useful medical help over ome app. Combined with AI technology, this personal doctor could become affordable even for those with lower incomes. Achieving this would be a significant advancement in healthcare accessibility.

Further Reading

Bates, D. W., & Gawande, A. A. (2003). Improving safety with information technology. *New England Journal of Medicine, 348*(25), 2526–2534.

Buntin, M. B., Burke, M. F., Hoaglin, M. C., & Blumenthal, D. (2011). The benefits of health information technology: a review of the recent literature shows predominantly positive results. *Health Affairs, 30*(3), 464–471.

DesRoches, C. M., Campbell, E. G., Vogeli, C., Zheng, J., Rao, S. R., Shields, A. E., et al. (2010). Electronic health records' limited successes suggest more targeted uses. *Health Affairs, 29*(4), 639–646.

Goldzweig, C. L., Towfigh, A., Maglione, M., & Shekelle, P. G. (2009). Costs and benefits of health information technology: new trends from the literature. *Health Affairs, 28*(2), w282–w293.

Kruse, C. S., Stein, A., Thomas, H., & Kaur, H. (2018). The use of electronic health records to support population health: a systematic review of the literature. *Journal of Medical Systems, 42*(11), 214.

Index

K. Solberg Söilen, *Digital Marketing*, Springer Texts in Business and Economics,
https://doi.org/10.1007/978-3-031-69518-6